Spatial Patterns of
Office Growth
and Location

17/48

ES -
gen

R J Buswell
November 1979
NEWCASTLE

Spatial Patterns of Office Growth and Location

Editor:

P. W. DANIELS

Department of Geography
University of Liverpool

JOHN WILEY & SONS

CHICHESTER . NEW YORK . BRISBANE . TORONTO

Library of Congress Cataloging in Publication Data:

Main entry under title:

Spatial patterns of office growth and location.

  Includes index.
  1. Offices—Location—Addresses, essays, lectures.
I. Daniels, P. W.

HF5547.S649   658.2′1   78–8386

ISBN 0 471 99675 0

Photosetting by Thomson Press (India) Limited, New Delhi,
and printed in Great Britain at The Pitman Press, Bath.

For
Paul and Charlotte

Contents

Preface

The principal rationale for this book is the growing volume of contemporary research and increasing academic and public interest in the growth, location and changing distribution of office activities in advanced economic systems. It has only been realized during the last 10–15 years that most advanced economies, such as those of western Europe, Scandinavia or North America, have entered a post-industrial stage in their evolution. This entails a reduced growth, even decline, in manufacturing or blue-collar activities at the expense of a relatively rapid expansion of white-collar or service occupations. Administration and bureaucracy have permeated most corners of modern society and the associated office occupations continue to expand at the rate of more than one white-collar job for each additional blue-collar job. There are signs that the pace of change during recent years is beginning to slow down as machine and communications technology is increasingly used as a substitute for labour. The crux, however, is that the location patterns of office activities are very different from those of manufacturing activities and traditional industrial location theory is therefore rather more difficult to utilize in our attempts to explain and understand these patterns. Hence, a new area of interest has emerged which is devoted to a better understanding of the factors which determine office location behaviour and of the relationship between office activities and the more general processes of change within urban and regional systems. The latter has provided the basis for work concerned with an assessment of the effects of growing public intervention in office location in the interests of more balanced regional development or of ways of responding to the more dispersed structure of urban areas. It is hoped that the contents of this book reflect the diverse but not mutually exclusive dimensions of current research on office location and related matters by geographers, economists and planners. Some might argue that we already understand most aspects of the existing patterns of office location since the concentration of these activities in the central areas of cities is adequate testimony to their location requirements. But it remains far from clear how

ix

location decisions are made by organizations requiring office space; why office development takes place at some places more often and in larger quantities than at others; what the role is of the development and construction industries in determining the location of office activities; or the most effective way to redistribute these activities in order to redress some of the more marked imbalances in their distribution as well as to help to resolve some fundamental strategic, as well as local, urban and regional planning problems.

It remains surprising therefore that studies of office location have only stimulated the interest of a relatively small number of academic and other researchers. But there have already been a number of publications which cover this field of study, and these include the important early work of Cowan *et al.* in *The Office: A Facet of Urban Growth* (1969); the detailed empirical study of changing office location patterns and their causes in the United States by Armstrong in *The Office Industry: Patterns of Growth and Location* (1972); the work of Goddard which has consistently provided a firm and ongoing base for office location studies in Britain and is exemplified in *Office Location in Urban and Regional Development* (1975); and my own attempt to synthesize various aspects of the work on office location undertaken mainly during the last 20 years in *Office Location: An Urban and Regional Study* (1975).

The contents of this volume build upon the work reported in these and other studies and the contributors have been encouraged to write about their ideas and the results of research which, by and large, has not yet been reported elsewhere. The chapters have been written by some of the principal practitioners in office location studies from those countries where they have received most attention: from Sweden where some of the most important advances in methodology have been consistently forthcoming and have influenced studies undertaken elsewhere; from Britain and Ireland where a substantial volume of research has been completed, especially in the fields of communication studies and the assessment of the impact of office relocation on office workers and the urban and regional reception areas; and from the United States and Canada where interest in office location studies has tended to flicker on and off until recent years since when it seems to be gaining a more permanent momentum. This coverage is certainly not comprehensive, but it is hoped that the chapters which have been brought together will give a useful indication of the breadth of current research and will provide readers with insights into the way in which the results may be used to analyse and interpret the significance of office activities for urban and regional development in their own cities and countries.

While preparing their contributions, authors were asked to consider the ways in which their work might help to create a more rigorous conceptual framework for office location studies. Such a framework would loosen the bonds with industrial location theory, which has often provided some of the initial working hypotheses. It must be left to readers to decide whether such a search for separate identity is either desirable or possible, but there seems little doubt that new methods and techniques for analysing intra-urban office location as well as constructing explanatory models of location behaviour are still required, especially at the metropolitan scale where the needs of the inner cities have added a new dimension. In addition, there is scope for further empirical work which will lead to the development of predictive models of the socio-economic, communications, local multiplier and other effects of redistributing office activities more widely through urban and regional systems. Some research along these lines has already been undertaken but the results of spatially limited studies require confirmation in different social and economic circumstances. Brought together, this work will also help to make public intervention in the location behaviour of office activities more effective or, in countries where such intervention is considered unacceptable, it will help to rationalize the case for greater involvement in the forces which generate contemporary office location patterns.

The preparation of a book of this kind depends a great deal on the cooperation and patience of the contributors. I would like to thank them all for tolerating the quirks of my editorial hand and their willingness to amend their manuscripts in the interests of consistent presentation and a Welshman's interpretation of the English language. I am grateful to John Goddard for evaluating the idea for this book with me during its early days and for his subsequent assistance with contacting some of the contributors. Mrs Lynne Edwards, a graduate student undertaking research on office location in the Department of Geography at Liverpool, provided some constructive observations on the content and structure of the introductory chapter although I accept full responsibility for its final form. The maps and diagrams were redrawn or standardized by Miss Joan Treasure of the Drawing Office in the Department of Geography, University of Liverpool. I must also thank Mrs Joan Stevenson for her cheerful but careful approach to amending various manuscripts and retyping tables and her remarkable ability to interpret my own hieroglyphics; I invariably seemed to require manuscripts in a hurry. Finally, I owe a debt of gratitude to my wife for her invaluable encouragement and her unfailing ability to divert our young family from my study when editorial tasks beckoned. She has also provided assistance with proof-reading and the preparation of an index.

P. W. D.
University of Liverpool, March 1978

The Contributors

REGINA BELZ ARMSTRONG, M.A. (Univ. of Pittsburgh), is Chief Economist of the Regional Plan Association, New York. She is the author of *The Office Industry: Patterns of Growth and Location* (1972) and *Growth and Settlement in the U.S.: Past Trends and Future Issues* (1975). She has co-authored *Regional Energy Consumption* (1974) and is currently publishing *The Region's Money Flows II: The Business Accounts* and *III: The Household Accounts*, two reports which document the results of a system of income and product accounts constructed for the New York Region.

SUSAN BAILEY, B.A. (East Anglia), graduated in 1971 and was employed as a research assistant for two and a half years on the DI/EEC project. She is now a Research Assistant in the School of Economic and Social Studies at the University of East Anglia.

MICHAEL J. BANNON, B.A. (N.U.I.), M.A. (Alberta), Ph.D. (Dublin), is Lecturer in Town Planning, University College, Dublin. He is author of *Office Location in Ireland: The Role of Central Dublin* (1973) and co-author of *The Role of Service-Type Employment in Regional Development* (1977). He has edited a report on *Office Location and Regional Development* (1973) and is currently a member of an international team of researchers investigating *The Role of the Tertiary Sector in Regional Development in E.E.C. Countries* (1978). His field of interest relates to the role of communications in both urban and regional development, including the impact of white-collar employment growth in the labour force.

MICHAEL BATEMAN, B.A., Ph.D. (Leeds), is Senior Lecturer in Geography at Portsmouth Polytechnic. He is co-author of LOB Research Report No. 6 (1971). He is currently concerned with aspects of urban planning, with particular reference to France.

DAVID BURTENSHAW, M.A. (London), is Principal Lecturer in Geography at

xiii

Portsmouth Polytechnic. He is the author of *An Economic Geography of West Germany* (1974) and *Saar-Lorraine* (1976) and co-author of LOB Research Report No. 6 (1971). His current research concerns aspects of office location policies and city planning policies in western Europe.

RICHARD CRUM, B.A. (Cambridge), is a Lecturer in Economics at the University of East Anglia, having previously been a research officer at the National Institute of Economic and Social Research. During 1971–73 he was an economic adviser in the Central Policy Review Staff in the Cabinet Office. His main interests are industrial economics and regional economics.

P. W. DANIELS, B.Sc., Ph.D. (London), is Lecturer in Geography at the University of Liverpool. He is the author of *Office Location: An Urban and Regional Study* (1975) and co-author of *Movement in Cities* (1979). His field of interest concerns urban and regional aspects of service industry and office location, including the journey to work consequences of office relocation policies in Britain. He is currently directing a research project for the Department of the Environment which is a follow-up study on the journey to work impact of office dispersal to locations throughout Britain and at five major centres: Liverpool, Reading, Swindon, Southampton and Watford.

GUNTER H. K. GAD, Dr. Phil. (Erlangen-Nuremberg), Ph.D. (Toronto), is Assistant Professor in Geography at Erindale College, University of Toronto, Canada. Among his publications are *Büros im Stadtzentrum von Nürnberg, Ein Beitrag zur City-Forschung (Offices in the Centre of Nuremberg, A Contribution to CBD Research)* (1968) and *Central Toronto Offices: Observations on Location Patterns and Linkages* (1975). He has advised the City of Toronto Planning Board on office decentralization potentials and cooperated with other government agencies and consulting firms in studies on offices. His interests in offices cover a wide range from historical origin to architecture, communication linkages and location policies.

J. B. GODDARD is Professor of Regional Development Studies and Director of the Centre for Urban and Regional Development Studies, University of Newcastle-upon-Tyne. He is currently a member of the Human Geography Committee of the Social Science Research Council, of the Northern Economic Planning Council, and of the Organizing Committee of the Regional Studies Association. He is author of *Office Location in Urban and Regional Development* (1975), *Office Linkages and Location* (1973) and with Diana Morris of *The Communications Factor in Office Decentralization* (1976). He has acted as Consultant on office location matters to national and international agencies. Having examined the communication constraints on office dispersal from London whilst working at the London School of Economics, he is now directing a research project for the Department of the Environment on the likely impact of developments in telecommunications technology on the location of office work with particular reference to the possibilities of meeting the needs of office activities in peripheral regions of Britain.

GRAHAM GUDGIN, B.A. (Lond., Geog.), B.A. (O.U., Maths), Ph.D. (Leicester), is a researcher at the Centre for Environmental Studies in London. He is the author of *Industrial Location Processes and Regional Employment Growth* (1978) and co-author of *Seats, Votes and the Spatial Organization of Elections* (1978) and also of *Non-Production Employment in U.K. Manufacturing Industry* (1978). His main interest is in regional employment growth.

NIGEL MOOR, B.A., MCD (Liverpool), FRTPI. Before setting up his own town planning practice in 1972, he worked on the Covent Garden, Greenwich and Docklands projects in London. He is the author of *Planning Brief South East England* (1974) and has contributed articles on planning and development subjects to the *Planner, Built Environment, Building, Property Investment Review, Investors Chronicle* and *Estates Gazette*. His field of interest concerns central area redevelopment and large housing projects, and he has worked in Africa and the Middle East.

LARS-OLOF OLANDER, B.Sc. (Lund), is Research Assistant in Economic Geography at the University of Lund. He is the author of *Service and Work: Geographical Studies of the Use of Time with Reference to Transportation and Accessibility in South-West Skane* (1976) and is co-author of *People and Economic Activity Around the Öresund: Interaction in a Border-line Area* (1978 prel. title). His field of interest concerns the impact of mental, organizational and physical restrictions on human activity systems.

CHRISTER H. T. PERSSON, B.A., Ph.D. (Lund), is Research Assistant in Geography at the University of Lund. He is the author of *Kontaktarbete och framtida Lokaliseringsförändringar (Contact Work and Future Changes of Location Patterns within the Public Sector)* (1974) and *Some Geographers' Perception of Europe: Environmental Images and Personal Construct Theory* (1977). His field of interest concerns different aspects of information processing and exchange within and between administrative units. These aspects could be location problems in connection with regional policies and structures of information as a critical factor in decision-making.

ROGER PYE, B.A. (Oxford, Maths), M.Sc. (Sussex, Operational Research), is a director of Communications Studies and Planning Ltd. (CS&P), an international consultancy specializing in communications and information technology. CS&P carries out basic research, notably into human and organizational communications and into the effectiveness and acceptability of new technologies, and provides a wide range of related consultancy services. Before the formation of CS&P, Roger Pye was a member of the Communications Studies Group at University College London. The Group was established to research the effectiveness and potential impact of teleconferencing. He was particularly concerned with the impact on office location; much of the Group's early funding was provided by the Relocation of Government Review, which recommended the dispersal of thirty thousand civil service jobs from London and increased use of telecommunications to repair 'communications damage'. Work was sponsored by a wide range of UK and international organizations. One of several overseas assignments involved his participation in Stanford Research Institute's 'Technology Assessment of the Interaction Between Telecommunications and Travel', funded by the US National Science Foundation.

GAIL GARFIELD SCHWARTZ, B.A., M.A., Ph.D. (Columbia University, New York), is Visiting Senior Fellow, the Academy for Contemporary Problems, Columbus, Ohio and Washington, D.C. Until 1977 she was Director, Division of Economic Planning and Development, New York City Planning Commission. Dr Schwartz is the author of *The Economic Future of Cities* (1978) and numerous articles dealing with local economic development. She is presently engaged in policy analysis for several American governmental agencies, as well as a trinational comparison of strategies dealing with urban economic shifts in Great Britain, the Federal Republic of Germany and the United States.

ELIZABETH M. SIDWELL, B.Sc., Ph.D. (London), is at present studying for her Post Graduate Certificate of Eduction at the Department of Education, Cambridge University.

List of Tables

List of Figures

xxi

1

Perspectives on Office Location Research

P. W. DANIELS

Introduction

Office location research relies heavily upon an empirical rather than a theoretical base. Attention has largely been devoted to what actually happens (description) rather than to what ought to happen (normative), and although 'a body of literature on office location is developing this has mainly been concerned with intra-urban location of head office functions and of independent firms in the quaternary sector' (Goddard, 1975, p. 11). Office activities of one kind or another are found in every type of industry (Gudgin *et al.*, Ch. 5; Goddard, Ch. 2), and it has only recently been realized that research which ignores this will only partially assist with an understanding of the office location process. Progress in office relative to industrial location research has really only been taking place during the last 10 or 15 years; the latter has already advanced some way to maturity although the literature continues to be lively (Hamilton, 1974; Collins and Walker, 1975), while the former is, at best, at a rather youthful stage in its development.

An attempt to make a comparison of this kind may be unreasonable, however, since the origins of intellectual curiosity in office location, and in particular the problems which derive from it, are rather different. The neoclassical economic theories of industrial location have clearly dominated research in this field (Weber, 1909; Lösch, 1954; Isard, 1956; Greenhut, 1956). These are 'choice' theories in which the objective is an equilibrium condition which assumes that each company is optimally located with reference to markets, labour and raw materials and that there is perfect competition. Equilibrium is reached after a sequence of individual location changes which assume that each firm or individual behaves rationally in order to optimize its circumstances. Early interest in the location of individual manufacturing plants and the emergent industrial agglomerations of the nineteenth century was hardly surprising; the majority of the labour force was engaged in production, with administration and related tasks confined to a relatively small number of people who were often considered inferior to their blue-collar colleagues. Office work was subservient to the location requirements of production so long as the need did not arise for employees whose sole responsibility it was to arrange insurance cover for large quantities of raw cotton in a dockside warehouse; to organize the efficient and prompt delivery of manufactured products; to ensure that clients were satisfied with the service received and were aware of new and sometimes improved products; to negotiate for and to find new sources of business; or to keep accounts in order. As long as companies remained small many of these tasks could be performed by one individual, often the owner of the business, but diversification, competition and the need to grow to remain viable ensured that white-collar work would expand at an accelerating rate throughout this century (Fuchs, 1968; Bell, 1974).

It is probably true to say, however, that entrepreneurs remained suspicious of paperwork until the early years of this century; production staff were given responsibility for handling what paperwork there was so that opportunity costs were kept to a minimum. But developments in cost accounting methods, the emergence of the modern corporation with its almost mandatory headquarters (Schwartz, 1963), the development of more comprehensive and aggressive selling methods, including advertising, the introduction of various corporate taxes, all helped to provide 'the office' with a separate identity and a different labour force from the manufacturing plant. This was reinforced by the expansion of the banks, building societies, insurance and other financial offices which during the second half of the nineteenth century were already occupying distinctive premises of their own. Technological developments in communications, such as the telephone, the typewriter and the duplicator, or progress in office building construction, such as the introduction of elevators or steel frame structures (Daniels, 1975a), also abetted expansion and continued to promote separation of office from production functions. As the nineteenth century unfolded, there were more and more opportunities for individuals to provide a diverse range of specialist services which did not require attachment to points of production or distribution; indeed, there was unlikely to be enough work to sustain these specialist services (banking, accounting, property managing, industrial insurance, advertising) if they were solely responsible to a single organization. Put another way, the 'office and production functions physically separated when the economic benefits of obtaining and comparing information within the market became greater for the detached office than the cost savings of directing production from a plant-attached site' (Armstrong, 1972, p. 18). The CBD was the logical place for service and manufacturing industry offices to locate at the turn of the century, given the strong radial character of urban transport networks and the opportunities for office establishment interaction. It is interesting to note, however, that small manufacturers remained sceptical about locating separate offices in the CBD as late as the 1920s (Mason, 1928).

The opportunities which these changes presented for the analysis of office location were only slowly realized. The pace and scale of change, both in the number of office establishments and the levels of employment in office activities, remained small in comparison with employment in manual or 'productive' work. The consequences of these structural changes for location studies were not realized until the early 1920s when, during the preparation of background studies for the New York Regional Plan, Haig (1927) first drew attention, in a carefully researched report, to the location patterns of financial office activities in Manhattan. The significance of the quaternary sector for many aspects of urban form and development was fully illustrated but the message did not move far beyond New York. The empirical–inductive approach used by Haig relies on a description of the actual patterns of office activity in Manhattan and the derivation of an explanation for these patterns which stresses the role of accessibility and the premium attached by office organizations to rapid contact with each other. This contrasts markedly with progress in industrial location research, which began from a theoretical–deductive approach of the kind already outlined; perhaps one of the objectives of office location research should be to move towards a similar position. The route now being followed is tortuous since it is possible to identify particular strands of analysis, such as that based on office communications behaviour (Pye, Ch. 10), which dominate research activity at the expense of a better integrated approach in which the variables which determine office location are assessed together.

There is an assumption, of course, that an equilibrium approach to office location is the main requirement. Some might argue that a more fruitful alternative, tentatively developed in some of the contributions to this book, is to concentrate on the location behaviour of individual offices and the decision-makers within them (Olander, Ch. 6; Persson, Ch. 7) with a view to producing 'process' theories (Soederman, 1975). Simon's (1956) subjectively rational decision model which allows for uncertainty and suboptimal behaviour provides the platform for this approach to locational analysis, which has been largely used in industrial location theory (Townroe, 1969; Dicken, 1971; Lloyd and Dicken, 1972; Rees, 1974). Although the details of individual studies vary, the underlying objective is to establish the way in which organizations recognize a location problem, conduct a search, evaluate the alternatives, and make a final decision. The preliminary work reported by Persson (Ch. 7) and by Olander (Ch. 6) in this volume suggests that there is a growing recognition of the value of behavioural research for office location studies and that there is scope for much more work. In order to be successful this will depend on a thorough understanding of decision-making by individuals, by groups of individuals within an organization and by organizations themselves. The latter is a discipline in its own right while the first two kinds of decision-making have been mainly researched by psychologists. The environmental images of decision-makers are part of their psychological attributes and can be identified, but the link between these images and choice of location is not easy to measure and remains a matter for some speculation.

There must also be a suspicion, not yet completely verified, that it is not possible to analyse the location of office establishments within the context of industrial location theory. Symptomatic is a comment by Harkness (1973, p.63) that 'perhaps an office location model can be built and perhaps it will be sensitive to the cost of communicating just as existing industrial location models are sensitive to transport costs of raw materials and products'. An argument which can be applied in the case of manufacturing industry offices is that intermediate locations (between plants and concentrations of office activity) which balance off the attractions of plant interactions and interactions with other firms and access to a large clerical labour force are inappropriate (Malamud, 1971); offices spread over a wide area must either be located in distinctive agglomerations from which they can control other units or be attached to production units. Pred (1977) has clearly demonstrated the way in which over 717,000 jobs are controlled by multilocational business organizations with headquarters offices in just seven metropolitan complexes in the western United States. Nevertheless, most offices, in contrast to manufacturing plants, are suboptimally located since 'office location is perceived to be less sensitive to costs than are most economic activities' (Malamud, 1971, pp. 9–10) or there 'is no process of accounting that can weigh the enhancement in quality of executive decision-making in a given location against the costs of operating at that location' (Hoover and Vernon, 1959, p. 97). In other words, office location decisions lack the rigour imposed upon organizations when the location of manufacturing plants is being considered. The costs involved are relatively small and often intangible in relation to the turnover of many companies; tradition and the attitudes of those who control large enterprises are often the determining factors of location decision-making. In some ways this provides a ready justification for the reluctant appearance of a separate office location paradigm. In addition there is a very basic problem of how to identify office functions because the 'intangibility of office activity is a prime block to proper analysis' (Cowan *et al.*, 1969, p. 22).

Patterns of office location are a product of decisions which take into account the economic costs and benefits prevailing at alternative sites, access to markets, the ability to control other parts of the organization effectively, and all the other economic factors which influence location choice by any business activity. If offices do tend to locate at suboptimal sites this 'flexibility' is perpetuated by the ability of organizations to modify their operational practices in response to changing circumstances in a way which is much more difficult for manufacturing plants, since production lines and machinery are far more costly and time-consuming to modify or to replace than the introduction of word-processing typewriters, microcopiers, or computers. It has also been shown that the office or administrative overheads decline relative to the increasing size of enterprises, so that economies of scale also affect office activity. In his study of American manufacturing industry between 1899 and 1974, Melman (1951, p. 75) concludes that 'it seems reasonable to infer that size *per se* is, on average, a differentiating factor in administrative overhead', with the ratio of administrative to production personnel diminishing with increasing size of units. Changes in the office staff requirements of an organization can be initiated by a change in the volume of physical output, a change in the size of plant, an increase or decrease in the number of production personnel, a change in the locational concentration of the organization, a change in operating characteristics, or miscellaneous qualitative factors such as governement regulations, tax laws, government incentives or bureaucratic behaviour. Many of these causal factors apply equally to office activities in the primary, manufacturing and tertiary sectors but there does not appear to be a systematic relationship between these factors and the growth or decline of office functions in an organization (Melman, 1951). Some of the uncertainty emanates from the association between production plants and some kinds of office work, especially that concerned with the day-to-day control. At the same time, a large proportion of office establishments employ fewer than 25 persons, and the smaller the company the greater the probability that its administrative and production functions will occupy the same site. If this is correct then it is difficult for organizations to identify optimal office location strategies; it may always be preferable to adjust as far as possible at existing locations. It seems likely that the equilibrium and behavioural approaches to office location each contain elements relevant to the creation of a general model. A suboptimal location in economic terms may well possess non-economic attributes which counterbalance any economic disadvantages, while it is also equally likely that location decision-making incorporates social, psychological and environmental variables as well as more objective economic appraisal of alternatives.

A Locational Equilibrium Model

Malamud (1971) has attempted to construct a model of office location which is similar to some industrial location models. He assumes that production-linked office establishments are located on the basis of factors related to the production rather than administrative functions. A conventional gravity function is modified slightly so that masses of administrators interact on the basis of an agglomeration power less than 1.0; it is argued that the volume of interaction between two classes of executives increases less than proportionally with their numbers (in other words, most interactions are between a small number of high-level executives and managers). The expected interactions between masses of administrators are then linked to a normative model in which it is assumed that each firm seeks the administrative configuration which maximizes interaction values. The scale at which location analysis takes place is therefore crucial, since the initial problem is how to distribute administrative work *between* locations in different regions or cities and this is followed by the problem of how these offices are located *within* the cities selected. Two stages are involved in model solution: firstly, allocation of a firm's administrators between its plants and its headquarters office and, secondly, the choice of location for the headquarters within a particular city.

Malamud proceeds on the premise that the location of an office is influenced, at least as far as manufacturing is concerned, by the distribution of the establishments which are being administered; the latter are considered to be locationally fixed. This is endorsed by the observation that the office functions of small firms tend to be attached to the production activity itself, while the centralization of administration in larger organizations usually leads to a disproportionate distribution of office work at those locations where the activity is relatively greatest. A listing of the ratio of manufacturing administration to manufacturing employment in US cities shows that the ratios are highest for Pittsburgh (steel), Detroit (cars), Akron (tyres) and Stamford (electronics). These cities are therefore administrative as well as manufacturing centres, although Goodwin (1965) prefers to call them secondary centres since headquarters offices of banking or insurance activities are poorly represented (see also Semple, 1973). Over 60 per cent (56) of 92 US multiplant firms in 1970 (Malamud, 1971) had their headquarters in the same city as their largest plant; only 16 per cent had headquarters in New York (10) and Chicago (5) where they did not have plants. Ullman (1958, p. 194) also notes that 'home office and principal plants . . . may not be in the same place, but in a majority of cases they are, except for many New York City headquarters. Even in this case, if home office and principal plants are separated the principal plant is likely to be in the industrial belt'. Headquarters office will be established at the firm's largest plant and administrators associated with other plants will be drawn towards this location so that internal interactions, weighed by their importance, are maximized. But cities at the top of the urban hierarchy possess location attributes for manufacturing offices which exceed the costs of separation from the main production centre, so that distortion of the normative model is possible.

Once all firms have independently structured their plant offices, agglomeration of headquarters within a city then proceeds. As soon as headquarters are allowed to separate from production plants agglomeration is inevitable since external contacts increase greatly if the physical distance separating them is reduced, even though internal contacts will need to be stretched. At this point rents for office space enter Malamud's model and are used to locate office establishments within city centre agglomerations. This is conceptualized as an iterative process which eventually leads to an equilibrium state at which no firm wishes to change the location of its office. Such a clinical approach to office location model-building is justified in theoretical terms but more difficult to operationalize in the more applied context of real world decision-making.

Interaction potential is correctly identified by Malamud as a key location factor but in his model it is an inferred byproduct of the agglomeration of administrative workers rather than a measured variable. In this respect his model is rather abstract and he falls back on the standard measures of location costs such as employment data, rents, and accessibility. It is perhaps significant that he is sceptical about the value of his model for allocating administrators between plants and headquarters offices since he himself recognizes the insensitivity of office location decisions to economic factors and this 'is particularly true when the difficulty of measuring model parameters and translating interaction value limits into dollars is admitted. Vernon's (1960) observations that office location is more a matter of taste than calculation and the wide range of concentrations ovserved for firms . . . can be understood in this light' (Malamud, 1971, p. 182). The model is also partial in the sense that it excludes the offices in the tertiary sector which do not need to relate their location to points of production in a way which minimizes internal interactions costs and maximizes external interactions benefits.

The problem of how to balance the internal and external orientation of manufacturing company offices is likely to be less important for offices in the service sector. These offices exist primarily to export their control and expertise, and locations giving maximum market access may be the main consideration. Armstrong (1972) has suggested a classification based on the hierarchy of markets which such offices may serve: headquarters offices (national and international markets), middle market offices (regional markets) and local market offices. Rhodes and Kan (1971) have used a similar taxonomy. The 'range' of these offices depends on the size of the organization, its structure, the number of office establishments, the kinds of service provided and the degree of dependence on day-to-day customer contact. Armstrong observes that there is an inverse relationship between the level of centralization of offices and their position in the simple three-tier hierarchy; local market offices are essentially population oriented and as the distribution of population changes, so new local market offices are established or they migrate from areas of declining population. This descriptive model is intuitively acceptable at the local market scale, but the location of the headquarters and middle market offices of service sector industries is more difficult to relate to a schema which demands that headquarters offices will be found in the largest cities and that middle market offices will be found lower down the urban hierarchy (Pred, 1977). For insurance companies, building societies and banks there may also be an analogy with manufacturing industry offices in that they have a network of branches to monitor and control and the problem is where to locate the headquarters or regional (middle market) offices in relation to branches. Apart from a recent paper (Martz, 1976) on the location of Bank of America branch offices in California, there has been virtually no work on this aspect of the office location problem. To what extent, therefore, are the locational equilibrium problems for service sector offices similar to the kind experienced by manufacturing industry administrative offices?

The Role of Communications

A comprehensive office location model, whether based on equilibrium or behavioural principles, may not emerge until the role of communications interactions in office location is better understood. This is not to say that analyses of office communications behaviour have not occupied a significant part of the research literature on office activity since 1965 (Pye, Ch. 10), but only very recently have the results been used to construct models of office location based upon various communication variables (Pye, 1977; Goddard and Pye, 1977). In other words, the costs of maintaining contact between offices have not been examined; rather, the character and spatial characteristics of office communications have been the main object of analysis (Croft, 1969; Goddard, 1971; 1973; Bannon, 1973; Bannon et al., 1977; Gad, 1975; Goddard and Morris, 1976; Fernie, 1977; Gad, Ch. 11). Contacts between offices are of three kinds (Goddard, 1975), which represent, firstly, functional interdependencies (contacts between office sectors); secondly, spatial structure (contacts between office employees in a particular sector within the same or adjacent spatial units); and, thirdly, physical movements of individuals, documents and goods between areal units. The work of Rannells (1956) and Webber (1964) with reference to the relationship between urban structure and activity linkages provides the basis for this classification.

It has long been recognized that some urban activities, offices in particular, rely on rapid, efficient, and reliable interchange of information, ideas, knowledge or documentation. There is also an underlying demand for the sustenance of business confidence and prestige and these seem to be retained most easily where customers and competitors can 'see' each other. The growing number of office communication studies lend support to the hypothesis that contact patterns are a significant determinant of office location, but it remains to be shown whether the observed patterns of meeting frequency and spatial separation, telephone calls or business lunches are crucial prerequisites for efficient and effective operation of all city centre offices (Gad, Ch. 11) or simply reflect the location patterns which are following the trends established by firms in the last 20 years of the last century and which must impose limits on the range of contact opportunities. There are 750,000 office workers concentrated into the 11 square miles of central London and it is perhaps not surprising that communication surveys show that 33 per cent of the outside meetings at a sample of central London offices were reached on foot (Goddard, 1971) and 24 per cent via the underground; almost 80 per cent of the journeys took less than 30 minutes (almost half of these took less than 10 minutes). Of the 5266 telephone contacts recorded by Goddard, 46 per cent were concerned with the receipt or exchange of information while 28 per cent of the 1554 face-to-face meetings recorded involved exchange of information and only 9 per cent the receipt of information. Data of this kind can be cross-classified according to the status of the participants, the kinds of department involved or the business sectors concerned. Decision-makers usually have contacts, often in the form of meetings, which take more time, are arranged longer in advance and involve more complicated matters than meetings engaged in by executive or supervisory staff for example (Goddard, 1973).

While there are some imponderables about the precise weight attached by offices to communications in location decisions, there is no doubt that the studies which have been undertaken assist in the identification of those departments, divisions or individuals likely to suffer least from location decisions which may lead to greater separation from headquarters or clients (Pye, Ch. 10). If one-fifth of the telephone contacts of an individual or a department involve exchange of information or a quarter of the telephone contacts involve receipt of information, then whether the persons involved are 200 yards or 200 miles apart is almost immaterial. Differential telephone charges may cause problems but frequency of contact can be adjusted without necessarily leading to diminished efficiency. The problem is more difficult for face-to-face meetings because spatial separation involves participants in a trade-off between meeting frequency, length and travel time, especially the latter (Civil Service Department, 1973). If meetings form a major part of an individual's job profile (especially if held at other participants' offices), it makes sense to locate him where he can reach as many meetings as possible without extremely time-consuming or costly travelling. Alternatively, of course, it is possible that spatial proximity encourages more face-to-face contact than is really justified by the gravity of the matters to be discussed, or the real needs of the organizations involved.

Following Simon (1960), Thorngren (1970) has classified contacts into programmed, planning and orientation contacts. As its name implies, orientation contact involves several participants in exchanging ideas and techniques and recording progress in their particular business or service, which permits them to keep their organizations competitive and fully briefed about the needs of clients and the priorities and policies of competitors. Planning contacts are more likely to involve executives concerned with the implementation of actions necessitated by information obtained or requested as a result of orientation contacts. Even though the participants frequently know each other and are very often from the same organization, their specialist requirements for legal assistance, advertising agencies or investment advice will place some restraint on their locational alternatives. Programmed contacts are the most routine of the three kinds of contact classified by Thorngren and they are usually made by telephone between participants known to each other who deal on a regular basis with a set of standard tasks. This classification has proved very useful for the analysis of contact patterns and it is usually assumed that programmed contacts are least affected by increased separation. Yet it cannot be as straightforward as this, since both Törnqvist (1970) and Goddard (1973) have shown that the number of contacts per employee per week decreases rapidly with job level; in an eight-level classification a first-level administrator had three times as many contacts per week as a third-level administrator and nine times as many as a fifth-level administrator. The ratios are approximately the same if these contacts are related to time. Administrators at the sixth–seventh job levels have no significant contacts and, in theory, could be employed anywhere. This example has been cited because it illustrates a particular problem with using contact classifications to identify locationally 'tied' and 'footloose' office functions: some administrators, especially those at higher levels, are likely to be engaged in all three kinds of contact and rigorous job specification is unlikely to eliminate this. An individual's contact behaviour is therefore not mutually exclusive to one kind of contact and all three could occur during the same working day (see Goddard, 1973).

The implication of the work on office communications is that those firms with weak linkages such as head offices of manufacturing companies can be expected to leave the centre of London, New York or Toronto (see Gad, Ch. 11) with minimum difficulty, while those with strong and frequent linkages can stay and expand. Invariably, this is an oversimplification, since Rhodes and Kan (1971, p. 60) noted that some companies revealed a reluctance to move in a situation where their operating costs, even if not as low as they could be are small relative to that of the company as a whole. Manufacturing offices clearly fall into this category, while the headquarters offices of the financial sector represent a much larger proportion of total company operating costs and location costs are therefore more likely to merit regular assessment to see if they can be minimized.

Office Communications and Regional Development

One of the prime reasons for analysing office communication patterns is to identify those activities which can be removed from the large and disproportionate agglomerations of office employment in a limited number of major cities. Such research is to a degree rather less motivated by the search for a comprehensive office location model and more concerned with the practical problems which confront urban and regional development policies. Advocates of this approach are not numerous, but collectively the contributions of Törnqvist and Thorngren in Sweden, Goddard and Pye in Britain and Bannon (Ch. 4) in Ireland are substantial. Underlying their work is the view that it is not enough to study office location in its functional, spatial or communications dimension, but it must also be viewed within the context or organizational structure and the effect which this has on locational choice and decision-making. An organization is an open system which is comprised of interactions between its own components and between them and their social, economic and technological environment. The spatial attributes of these interactions are now fully recognized and govern the way in which organizations operate; hence the location patterns of the component parts or organizations, the ability to create interactions opportunities, and the structure of these interactions are of key importance for urban and regional development (Pred, 1973; 1977). In his hypothetical diagram of the linkages of three organizations with functions at different levels in the urban hierarchy, Wärneryd (1968) clearly shows how urban centres at the top of the hierarchy, where higher-level organizational decision-making is usually concentrated, reinforce their own growth through the control they exert on other interactions such as the purchase of goods and services generated by branches or regional headquarters in centres lower down the hierarchy. Multiplier leakage of service consumption by organizations back to the headquarters location has been well documented for a range of firms in Canada by Britton (1975), and this helps to explain the relatively weak and poorly diversified employment structures of developing areas within national economies. A continuing trend towards larger and more complex organizations through mergers and takeovers makes it possible to internalize more and more service needs and is likely to reinforce this problem, which in turns gives further weight to the disproportionate concentration of decision-making functions and their related multipliers in the largest cities (Parsons, 1972; Westaway, 1974; Pred, 1977). Therefore although intra-urban communications may dominate office interactions, there are also important inter-regional flows from lower-order centres to higher-order centres but few linkages between offices in centres lower down the urban hierarchy. The basic problem is how to stem these flows by diverting those parts of organizations which least need to be at centralized locations to those areas or regions where they are under-represented (but can still operate effectively), as well as how to achieve a more even distribution of the higher-order decision-making functions which are responsible for channelling so many communications flows towards the dominant metropolitan region (see Goddard, Ch. 2). Decentralization of this kind benefits both the exporting region, in terms of reduced congestion costs, and the importing region, in terms of increased demand for local goods and services, diversification of regional economic structure and improved employment opportunities. From the point of view of individual organizations there is the prospect of reduced accommodation and other operational costs as well as better living and travel-to-work conditions for personnel moved with their jobs.

It was argued earlier that some kinds of office contact can easily be 'stretched' without changing the significance of the information conveyed but Goddard and Morris (1976, p. 8) point out that it 'would be wrong to assume that the possibility of dispersal is solely a matter of the cost of stretching existing links'. Because of the office–environment relationship new patterns of communication emerge with the local area as the organization identifies new opportunities or, alternatively, it will adopt new procedures which match the attributes of the new environment. This again emphasizes the need to recognize organizations as open systems and the potential for flexibility in communications behaviour which follows from this. In a study of the communications patterns of offices which had moved from central London compared with offices which had remained there,

Goddard and Morris (1976) have shown that each had very different patterns of communication but are uncertain whether this is a product of differences in location or due to adjustments in the role which decentralized offices have within an organization when they are moved from one place to another. Decentralized offices have fewer external contacts and deal more with planning or programmed contacts than their central London counterparts, and such behaviour may well be an organizational objective since it seems certain that the distance moved from London does affect the nature of communications. Dispersal of routine functions has dominated the movement from London to places within 60 miles of the capital but 'such decentralization may be a poor alternative from a communications point of view' (Goddard and Morris, 1976, p. 75). London generates a shadow effect over the pattern of contact opportunities from locations within 60 miles, so that offices moving to these places must either retain central London links using the transportation and telecommunications systems which focus upon it or rescind those contacts altogether. This assumes that contacts with the local environment can be established, but the evidence suggests that substitution of this kind is limited with the result that there is a great deal of unnecessary travel. External contacts tend to be reduced with the result that time is therefore released for internal matters and the location of the office in a 'contact-poor' environment may, if this is the organization's objective, be perfectly reasonable. If administrative decentralization is an organizational objective there is therefore a good case for office dispersal over longer distances (over 60 miles from London) but this has always proved difficult to achieve. London's shadow effect on contact behaviour diminishes beyond 60 miles and offices can establish a larger proportion of their external contacts with the reception centre environment and so reduce the frequency and cost of travel to the capital. Such centres are likely to have the facilities which will permit telecommunications to replace some business journeys and their distance from London may also be an asset to organizations intent on setting up a regional network of offices.

The Impact of Telecommunications

Up to this point it has been assumed that the effects of locational change on the communications requirements of offices can only be mitigated by increased travelling or the development of external contacts at the new location. But there has been considerable speculation about the ability of telecommunications to substitute for travel ever since Meier (1962) queried the necessity for office buildings to be clustered in city centres if individuals could communicate adequately without leaving their desks. Advances in telecommunications technology have been many and varied and the Communications Study Group in London has devoted much energy to assessing the advantages and disadvantages of the teleconference, the video telephone, the remote meeting table, the various information and data transmission devices such as telex, facsimile, Viewdata, or remotely connected typewriters, as well as the social and psychological side-effects of using devices of this kind in place of the telephone or the face-to-face meeting (Pred, 1973; Christie and Elton, 1975). It has been shown, for example, that some 34 per cent of existing meetings consist of activities whose outcomes would not be significantly affected if audio teleconference devices and graphics displays were used. A further 10 per cent of existing meetings could be conducted without devaluing the result by using television-type visual teleconference devices, although the cost of holding such meetings is still high relative to the costs of travel (Cook, 1975). Probably the one major constraint in using these and other innovations is the cost of maintaining contact in this way. Few studies have included this in their overall assessment of office overheads and how they vary between locations or as a result of locational change. The most obvious place to begin to assess the likely impact of these costs on location decisions is in the context of office relocation policies and their cost effectiveness (Civil Service Department, 1973; Pye, 1977; Ch. 10). In a very detailed exercise undertaken during the early 1970s, the further possibilities for redistributing government office work from London were weighed up by identifying blocks of work (in which staff have an identifiable responsibility and are in day-to-day contract with each other) along with the strength of the links between them and then proceeding to measure the 'communication damage' incurred when separating these blocks (Daniels, 1975a). Only face-to-face meetings are considered since these are most likely to suffer from separation. Not surprisingly, the amount of damage and therefore the cost of separating linked blocks of works increases in direct proportion to the distance placed between them, but it is the character of the contacts between blocks and within them which determines the degree of dispersal which can be contemplated (Civil Service Department, 1973, Appendix 10). One crucial assumption used in these calculations, however, is that the meeting characteristics displayed by central London civil servants, such as one trip for one meeting, will continue after separation has occurred, but in practice this might overstate the degree of communication damage since more than one meeting can be held during one day and the length of meetings can be reduced (and probably made more effective as a result). Even if the initial costs of separation are high, there is no reason why the process of local contact substitution which would follow from a carefully devised location strategy, of the kind outlined earlier, should nor gradually reduce these costs and even lead to communications gain in the future.

More recently, Pye (1977) has a devised a model in which an attempt is made to compare the 1974–75 value of the financial benefits from changing location with the costs of maintaining contact. One of the most interesting points to emerge is that the average frequency of contact for which travel costs are equal to the financial savings of locating in a number of towns (assuming that the value of an employee's time is zero) decreases rapidly as distance from London increases, so that 'the increased economic benefits which are in general obtainable from longer distance moves (lower rents, cheaper rates, cheaper land costs, lower staff costs, government grants) do not offset the greater costs of communication' (Pye, 1977, p. 154). If the trade-off between communications costs and accommodation/staff costs is critical in office location decisions then this would appear to conflict with the observation by Goddard and Morris (1976) that offices should move further from London in the interests of escaping the shadow effect. The reasons for these contradictory findings are mainly related to the fact that Pye's model is exclusively cost-dependent while Goddard and Morris largely exclude this factor from their analysis. Pye (1977, p. 165) also concludes that 'the impact of telecommunications alone on the existing balance between communication costs and other benefits is small', and 'not only are the Assisted Areas unattractive to relocating offices, but also the development of new office employment . . . will be discouraged because of the lack of external economies. Policies aimed both at the development of teleconference systems and at increasing local contact autonomy have the advantage that they would also benefit locally originating office employment' (p. 167).

Other Location Variables

An extended review of research on office communications and their possible implications for location is clearly essential in view of the volume of work which has been published and the fact that most surveys of office location choice invariably show that communications are most important (Cowan *et al.*, 1969; Economist Intelligence Unit, 1964; Facey and Smith, 1968; Croft, 1969; Bannon, 1973; Martz, 1976). There are of course other factors such as staff availability, the supply of office floorspace, markets, tradition and prestige which influence location choice but which collectively have received much less attention from research workers. Specific reasons for this neglect are elusive but it can be suggested that the weak and intangible quality of some data sources and location variables present too many difficulties for objective analysis. There must be some doubt, for example, about the significance of tradition or prestige for location decision-making, since most studies permit these variables to emerge as *post-facto* rationalizations for location choice (Daniels, 1975a) which bear no relationship to actual reasons for discriminating between alternative sites or premises. Counteracting this essentially academic problem of objective measurement is the consensus among development companies and estate agents, for example, that the prestigious character of a building is always worth stressing, and it plays its part in influencing rental values. Indeed, development companies have an underestimated role in the office location process since the majority of office buildings are provided for occupation by organizations which are tenants rather than owners. Many buildings are constructed on a speculative basis which means that development companies need to anticipate the demand for office space and the locations where it will be required 3–10 years before it actually becomes available. Mismatch between supply and demand of the kind which has occurred in Manhattan frequently results (see Schwartz, Ch. 9), and while this causes problems for the developers it also introduces considerable inertia into the market for office space. When demand improves organizations will be required to take space where it is available rather than where they would like it to be located. Office space is provided at locations where it is anticipated that leases will be in demand and in an open land market, such as exists in a few United States cities like Houston, the developer can continue to supply space at 'safe' locations or 'lead' demand by shifting the supply of office space to locations which will improve the capital values and yields from development. In most countries, however, the client–development company interface is complicated by the development company–planning system interface (see Moor, Ch. 8; Schwartz, Ch. 9), whereby at the local level, zoning and development control procedures can be used to direct development to specified areas and at the inter-regional or national level, incentives and controls can be used to achieve a more balanced distribution of office activities.

The influence of development companies on the location of office space is inextricably linked with the sources of finance upon which most speculative office development depends. Merchant banks, insurance companies, pension funds and other financial institutions, many of which themselves require substantial quantities of prime office space, contribute to as well as benefit from office development. Many construct their own buildings and provide space well beyond their own requirements and then sublet to other clients. The office development industry is, therefore, partially involved in providing accommodation for itself. Does this mean that the financial institutions can preempt the most accessible and often most profitable locations and leave other organizations to reconcile their location requirements elsewhere in the CBD or at other locations in the city? This line of reasoning is clearly an oversimplified representation of reality, but it lends itself to the observation that office location patterns are not simply a product of easily accessible opportunities for information gathering and exchange (communications) but are also determined by complex financial and other vested interests which are on both the demand and supply side, directly or indirectly, of the office market and preferably with company profits and capital information in mind (Ambrose and Colenutt, 1975; Davidson and Leonard, 1976). Even organizations large enough to consider investing in custom-built office premises may prefer to borrow money from the financial institutions, which may well assess the viability of a proposal in the context of the long-term prospects of the office building on the assumption that the client may choose to sell or to sublet it in the future. Should this happen then the choice of location for the building becomes crucial and the lending institutions may look unfavourably upon schemes which abandon 'conventional' location practices. To this degree organizations will tend to conform with the highly agglomerated and centralized pattern of the office industry (cf.

Jeans, 1967). Development inertia therefore leads to locational inertia. If this is significant for private sector office development then it will also to some extent shape the location of public sector organizations such as government departments who are major tenants of office space provided by development companies in most large cities. Even if the public sector provides its own office space (*via* the Property Service Agency in Britain, for example), the reliance on interaction with private sector office activity again ensures that space is provided near to or within existing major concentrations. The process of providing office space has received only limited attention, apart from the work of Barras and Catalano (1975) who view it as a production process in which the main agents are local authorities, financial institutions and property companies. It would be useful to know how the processes vary in a spatial sense since this would help to predict the effects of alternative policies for office development in one region or city rather than another.

While the precise influence of finance and development companies on office location is elusive, the supply of labour is axiomatic. It is likely that it has become more important through time because of the trend towards increasing specialization in the occupation skills required of the office labour force. A symptom of this is the reduced growth rate in clerical occupations during recent decades but an accelerating growth of technical and professional occupations (Daniels, 1975a). It remains an open question whether increasing specialization of labour reduces the locational choices available to office organizations. Companies requiring a wide range of skilled computer personnel, business analysts, or commodity brokers and dealers must locate in urban agglomerations where they can easily attract the personnel required. Professional and other higher-level office workers are more prepared to accept long-distance residential change than clerical workers and it should not therefore be difficult to assemble suitable candidates at a number of locations which are some distance apart, but a key consideration is the ability to replace staff when the need arises and, in many cases, to avoid the costs of training staff to the levels required. In this way large metropolitan labour markets subsidize part of the labour costs borne by individual organizations although there are diseconomies in terms of higher salaries and turnover rates because of the competition between employers. If office occupations continue to become more specialized, it seems likely that headquarters and regional offices will continue to search for locations in those areas, mainly urban, able to meet their requirements in spite of improvements in long-distance communication which technology now permits (see Pye, Ch. 10). Programmed office functions may become more footloose because of changes in communications technology but technical developments will probably decrease the demand for employment of this kind (Thorngren, 1970). On the other hand, growth of employment will continue in those types of planning and orientation functions which are strongly dependent on each other and where telecommunications are difficult to apply.

Intra-Organization Location Factors

Some of the forces affecting the location of office establishemnts which have been outlined thus far are largely a product of the relationship between office activities and their external environment. But there are also a large number of internal variables which must be considered part of the location process. These include: the type of industry (Gudgin *et al.*, Ch. 5); policies defined by the management; the nature of control, which can range from an individual in a single office suite through to the national headquarters of a multinational, multiproduct organization; the effect of mergers, takeovers and acquisitions on organizational structure and distribution of plants and offices; the objectives of organizations with reference to rapid growth, stability or planned shedding of certain activities; or whether organizations are mainly concerned with satisfier rather than optimizer solutions to their operations. The latter depends, for example, on the degree of responsibility to shareholders, to employees and to the public; the personal characteristics of individual or corporate entrepreneurs; or management and investment policies. Many of these variables only provide a basis for classifying a company and its offices and occur irrespective of any spatial considerations, but all are relevant for location behaviour in the way that Townroe (1969) has demonstrated with reference to the location decisions made by firms for their manufacturing plants. He suggests that this 'approach recognizes that the result of locational analysis can affect a wide range of other management decisions from factor proportions to the size of the plant (*office*) and that there is a continuous inter-relating of all influences on the operation and development of the enterprise' and notes that the decision-making unit under which a plant (*office*) operates does not conform to classic economic premises but 'is subject to a multitude of conflicting motives, pressures and valuations' (Townroe, 1969, pp. 16, 24).

This line of approach has yet to receive the attention it deserves but there have been a number of studies which are relevant, if only indirectly, to this theme. Firstly, locational changes by offices such as those of publishers within limited areas of towns and cities, primarily the CBD, have been examined (Goddard, 1967; Cowan *et al.*, 1969; Bannon, 1972; Pritchard, 1975). Secondly, Rhodes and Kan (1971) have demonstrated the complexity of office location changes at the regional scale by listing six alternative ways in which a large organization may change the distribution of its office employees. These range from establishing new branch offices in regions where the company is under-represented and withdrawing from regions in which it is over-represented to moving work previously undertaken in regional offices to head office or *vice versa* and to undertaking partial dispersal of head office activities to another location in the same region or into a completely new region. Finally, Thorngren (1970) and Goddard (1973; 1975) take the view that an organizational/behavioural approach to the analysis of office location problems as they relate to regional development is a prerequisite for successful results (see also Goddard, Ch. 2). All three types of analysis involve elements of the approach advocated by Townroe and others.

Studies of intra-CBD migration (Goddard, 1967; Cowan *et al.*, 1969; Bannon, 1972; Pritchard, 1975; Hughes and Price, 1977) indicate that organizations pass through a sequence of office premises and locations which are occupied at various stages during their growth or contraction. Most location changes are triggered off by mismatch between the number of employees and the volume of office space available. The usual response to this is retention of existing premises and the acquisition of additional space to accommodate staff overflow. This is only a temporary expedient, however, since the process of subdivision may go on indefinitely until a company or government department may have 10 or more different address in the city centre (Civil Service Department, 1973). At some point along this continuum a decision may be taken to rationalize the number and location of office premises, perhaps because of increasing internal communications costs, operational inefficiencies resulting from fragmentation (Daniels, 1975a) or the cost of leases for so many separate buildings. A single office may be acquired in which all employees can be housed or, alternatively, some of the employees in the fragmented premises can be centralized at some location outside the CBD altogether, leaving a reduced number of offices in the CBD where the cost of centralizing all staff in one building may be prohibitive. Other events such as mergers and acquisitions may also lead to changes in office requirements. Where premises are owned by companies, the need to capitalize their assets in order to cover losses in business earnings could also lead to the sale of some premises and leasing of others. The permutations are many but these simple examples demonstrate the role of behavioural variables. Both Goddard (1967) and Bannon (1972) have shown how the centres of gravity of office functions shift within city centres for no other apparent reason than the need to respond to, or keep in touch with, location changes by competitors. Hence, Hughes and Price (1977) found that almost 70 per cent of the offices in 'new' buildings in Glasgow CBD had relocated during the last 10 years; 49 per cent had relocated in the old office sector.

The CBD also performs a vital role as a seedbed (Taylor, 1973) for small-scale business activities which operate from office premises: an entrepreneur requiring office space is not just attracted to the CBD by the advantages of access to clients and professional expertise but also by the ready availability of low-cost office space around the fringes as well as within the area. Residential areas outside the CBD also provide low-cost opportunities for new offices, provided that local authorities will permit the changes of use which are necessary. Once established such offices will move on, often over very short distances and at frequent intervals, usually into more spacious and more expensive premises. The distances moved tend to increase with size of centre, mainly because alternatives are more restricted in the central areas of small towns. It has been estimated that 50 per cent of the organizations which begin life in the CBD will not survive (Pritchard,

1975). Statistics of this kind, based on evidence from directories of various kinds, must be interpreted carefully, however, since mergers, takeovers, changes in company registration, may all mask the longevity of individual offices which have apparently disappeared from directories. Over a 10-year period Prichard found that half of the remaining offices did not change location while the remainder moved to intermediate locations and those offices which sacrificed the advantages of absolute centrality had the greater chance of survival. There has been virtually no research on the 'life-cycle' of office establishments and the role played by different areas within cities as 'incubators' for office-based enterprises (Struyk and James, 1975). Inner cities certainly have a crucial role in this respect for the emergence of production establishments; perhaps the recent research initiatives taken by the Department of the Environment will eventually provide some of the answers in the context of office development.

Internal behavioural variables are also significant at the national and regional scale as enterprises have become larger and increasingly organized along hierarchical lines. Decision-making functions become more remote from lower-order functions in offices and manufacturing plants (Gudgin et al., Ch. 5) which comprise a multiplant, multinational corporation, and Törnqvist (1968), Thorngren (1970) and Westaway (1974) have all drawn attention to the way in which the incidence of highly concentrated control of business functions is directly related to the correspondence between levels in organizational and urban hierarchies. The number of levels of control is related to the size of organizations, and as they become larger it is more likely that high-level decision-makers will be located at headquarters in one high-order urban area. It is then argued that this perpetuates or fuels the problems for regional development, although more work is still required on the precise influence of this effect relative to factors such as corporate strategy and structure (Dicken, 1976). Certainly there is accumulating evidence which shows that offices which are the headquarters of manufacturing and service industry enterprises in Sweden (Wärneryd, 1968), Britain (Parsons, 1972; Evans, 1973; Westaway, 1974; Daniels, 1975a), and the United States (Pred, 1974; Quante, 1976; Burns, 1977; Burns and Pang, 1977) tend to be concentrated in large metropolitan areas from which they exert control over the location, investment and other business decisions made by executives located in places lower down the urban hierarchy. While there is scope for much more research into the effects of corporate structure and change on office location at the regional and urban scale (cf. Hughes and Price, 1977), there is little doubt about the congestion, high accommodation costs, difficulties of recruiting suitable labour, and various other diseconomies of scale attached to office concentration.

Office Relocation

A natural response has therefore been to relocate office activities away from congested high-cost city centres to suburban areas and beyond; this process is now well established (Armstrong, Ch. 3; Goddard, Ch. 2; Schwartz, Ch. 9). A substantial volume of research has been stimulated by this process which is rather less concerned with understanding office location and more with evaluating the effects of these changed locational distributions on individual organizations, for their employees, and for urban and regional development policies (Goddard, Ch. 2). It should be stressed that these are not mutually exclusive lines of research since promotion of a successful regional policy, for example, depends on a proper understanding of office location behaviour in general. Continuing decentralization of residences and office jobs within major cities (Daniels, 1977a) poses a number of strategic planning problems (Alexander, 1977; Daniels, 1975b; 1977b) related to the best distribution of these activities in the interests of the community and the organizations involved. A number of the chapters in this book (Sidwell, Ch. 13; Goddard, Ch. 2; Bateman and Burtenshaw, Ch. 12; Daniels, Ch. 14) reflect a long-standing interest, especially in Britain, in this aspect of office location studies. In Britain the relocation of offices has not just been a voluntary response to the diseconomies of overconcentration, but has been reinforced by controls on office development in areas of excess demand such as the London Metropolitan Region in the hope that offices will be diverted to the Assisted Areas, for example. It is perhaps surprising that similar research in the United States is the exception rather than the rule even though a number of observers were drawing attention to office suburbanization during the early 1950s, some years before its significance was appreciated in Britain (Shehan, 1952; Carroll, 1953; Walker, 1957). Later work by Sternlieb (1961) and Schwartz (1963) also failed to incite more than a passing interest in the wider social and economic consequences of relocating headquarters offices from central cities, although location-specific studies of suburban office development which do not seem directed towards a common objective continue to be undertaken (Kersten and Ross, 1968; Deutermann, 1970; Jones and Hall, 1972; Hartshorne, 1973; Abler, 1974; Vahaly, 1976).

A possible explanation for the paucity of American research in this field, despite some notable individual contributions in recent years by Armstrong (1972), Pred (1974) and Manners (1974), is that the changes in office location are not perceived as a problem worthy of national or regional public policy (see Armstrong, Ch. 3). There is no equivalent of the Location of Office Bureau (LOB) which was established in 1963 specifically to promote relocation of offices from London and, more recently, to encourage offices to locate in provincial cities and to attract foreign companies prepared to locate their offices in Britain rather than elsewhere in Europe (Manners, 1977). The Bureau has undoubtedly given impetus to office location research which might not otherwise have been achieved. It possesses the most complete, although still imperfect (Hall, 1972), source of basic data on offices which have moved from London or which intend to do so. While the Bureau has no executive power, its work has been facilitated by the use of office development permits in clearly defined areas of the country to limit the construction of new and replacement office space. This task has been the responsibility of various government departments, and the effectiveness of the controls has been under constant scrutiny by researchers (Daniels, 1969; Rhodes and Kan, 1971; Burtenshaw et al., 1974; Goddard, 1977). The role of central government in office relocation has long been recognized in Britain and since the 1940s, when strategic requirements dictated redistribution, there have been a number of dispersal programmes which have provided scope for empirical research into selected aspects of the impact of these changes (Hammond, 1967; 1968; Bateman and Burtenshaw, 1971; Bateman et al., 1971; Daniels, 1972; 1973) and attempts to assess the costs and benefits of moving various departments as a basis for subsequent decisions about which should remain in London and which should be moved elsewhere (Civil Service Department, 1973). Few other nations have adopted such comprehensive policies towards office location: Sweden is currently engaged in relocating government offices employing 11,330 office employees between 1972–80 (Thorngren, 1973); dispersal of government offices in the Netherlands has been relatively unsuccessful (Toby, 1973; Grit and Korteweg, 1976); in France office redistribution within the Paris region now seems to be having some effect but inter-regional movement is not given much credibility (Bateman, 1976); in Ireland the possibilities for setting up an Office Executive to assist and advise public and private sector offices relocating from Dublin to regional centres have been fully examined in a recent study by Bannon et al. (1977; Ch. 4); and the role of office activities in urban decentralization policies in Australia has been considered by Sorenson (1974). Elsewhere there seems to be considerable scepticism about the ability of public controls to influence the location of privately initiated office development (Schwartz, Ch. 9) although there is often virtually no research evidence to support this assumption.

There has also been considerable interest in the more systematic aspects of the office relocation process both from the viewpoint of the organization and its effects on employees. A number of contributions to this book are drawn from this sphere of applied enquiry which seeks to identify and to measure the impact of dispersal and to establish whether existing policies should be modified or replaced (Sidwell, Ch. 13; Bateman and Burtenshaw, Ch. 12; Daniels, Ch. 14). Office dispersal policies provide an excellent laboratory for testing assumptions about the ability of organizations to 'stretch' or to 'substitute' communications needs without damaging their efficiency or their ability to adjust to changes in communications requirements through time. Places between 60 and 80 miles from central London are the optimum location for decentralized offices (Goddard and Morris, 1976; Goddard and Pye, 1977) in terms of communications costs, the costs of accommodation and staff (Rhodes and Kan, 1971) or improvements in the journey to work (Daniels, 1972; 1973). But this situation will prevail only as long as the financial incentives available to offices moving to the Assisted Areas are not really large enough to persuade organizations to discriminate between locations much further from the centre of gravity of office activity in Britain. Equally important is the recognition that the communications complexes in cities more distant from London are still not comprehensive enough to support the day-to-day needs of many decentralized offices; major provincial cities such as Manchester, Newcastle, Leeds or Glasgow require greater functional diversity in order that offices do not continue to depend upon 'irreplaceable' contacts in London. Further dispersal of government agencies, especially policy-making staff, might persuade private sector offices to consider provincial cities, but public sector dispersal has largely ignored the importance of concentrated dispersal, which Goddard (Goddard, 1975; Goddard and Morris, 1976), among others, has been advocating for some years. This strategy does not mean that lower-order urban areas will lose vital office employment, since telecommunications now make dispersed organizational structures in which several offices in small towns in a subregion can be connected to a central location perfectly feasible (Goddard and Pye, 1977; Harkness, 1972). There is a limit, however, to the pool of mobile office employment and problem regions should try to encourage expansion of indigenous office activity wherever possible (Daniels, 1978).

The latter is important for the journey to work of office staff affected by dispersal programmes since daily travel to provincial locations is sometimes longer than expected because of scattered settlement patterns and low population densities. Travel could be reduced by wider intra-regional dispersal of some office functions although higher-order tasks and control functions should still be concentrated in major regional centres. Changes in travel behaviour, particularly by staff moved from London, also affect the balance of modal choice at reception areas and the results of studies used to monitor these changes can be employed to predict more accurately the likely transport consequences of choosing between alternative location strategies (Schwartz, 1963; Harkness, 1973; Daniels, 1975b; Ch. 14). A similar case can be made for other research into the socio-economic effects of relocation such as residential changes and Bateman and Burtenshaw (Ch. 12) and Sidwell (Ch. 13) examine some of the important issues. All this work on communications, housing, journey to work, social contacts, and the more general economic impact of office development (Yannopoulos, 1973) is based mainly on cross-sectional surveys using small samples and there is a danger that the broad generalizations subsequently made become accepted without the benefit of continuous monitoring of research findings. Longitudinal surveys would be ideal but are costly to implement and not without problems (Wall and Williams, 1970) and the best compromise seems to be cross-sectional surveys at intervals appropriate to the rate of change anticipated for the variables under examination (Carey, 1969; 1970). Such an approach to office relocation research is important for two reasons: firstly, the recognition that it is a relatively recent activity and previous experience may be modifying the locational response by organizations and their employees which are only now beginning to consider dispersal seriously, and secondly, the valuable contribution which this work is making to the wider problem of advancing our understanding of office location; in particular, our ability to create a general model. This must be one of the principal objectives for office location research during the 1980s.

Conclusion

This brief review suggests that much work remains to be undertaken if office location theory is to become more substantive. At the present time there are a number of 'dominant' themes which are centred on the role of communications and an evaluation of the role of office location in urban and regional development. Both these interests have developed because of location changes which have been taking place during the last 20 years; the highly centralized location patterns typical of office activities until the last war seen almost to have created an academic, as well as policy-making, indifference derived from the feeling that central location dominated all other location requirements. There was therefore little to understand and to require explanation. Suburbanization and regional redistribution of office activities has changed all that and the need for a more rigorous and comprehensive statement of office location theory is greater than ever.

In order to achieve this it appears that there are a number of avenues along which office location research needs to proceed. Firstly, there seems to be a good case for more work on the location behaviour of individual office establishments: the factors and forces which interact to determine location. Microscale studies of this kind will assist with more effective analysis of the problem of distributing office activities in a more equitable way at the inter-regional or the intra-urban scale. Secondly, it seems important to recognize that office location must be examined with due reference to the long- and short-term problems which confront individual organizations whether they are small, one-man operations or multinational, multioffice enterprises. In the short term, the location of office premises can be taken as fixed, and the problem is how to distribute functions between locations in order to permit efficient operation and quick reaction to structural or contextual changes in the business or administrative environment. In the long term, the problem is how, when and where location adjustments should be made and how office activities should be fully integrated into urban and regional policies and plans. Thirdly, it is necessary to know much more about the location characteristics of office activities attached to manufacturing industry since this is important for the continued diversification of employment opportunities in problem regions. Fourthly, there is scope for further work designed to confirm or modify the findings of the one-off studies upon which most aspects of our current understanding of office location depend. Fifthly, more studies in contrasting urban and regional systems which would lend support to concepts and ideas derived mainly from research in western Europe and Scandinavia would give office location theory a much firmer base upon which to build. It is assumed, for example, that office location in the developing countries is subject to the same constraints as those evident in advanced economic systems but there is virtually nothing published which helps to confirm or deny this basic assumption.

Office location research may yet be in its infancy, but there seems to be plenty of scope for advancing well beyond this stage in its development provided that the number of practitioners can be retained or, preferably, increased.

References

Abler, R. F. (1974), *Employment Shifts and Transportation Policy: Changes in the Locations of Corporate Headquarters in Pennsylvania, 1950–1970*. Philadelphia: Pennsylvania Transportation Institute.

Alexander, I. (1977), *Offices in the Suburbs: A Study of Private Sector Office Establishments in Sydney's Suburban Centrès*. Canberra: Department of Environment, Housing and Community Development.

Ambrose, P., and Colenutt, B. (1975), *The Property Machine*. Harmondsworth: Penguin.

Armstrong, R. B. (1972), *The Office Industry: Patterns of Growth and Location*. Cambridge, Mass.: The M.I.T. Press.

Bannon, M. J. (1972), The changing centre of gravity of office establishments within Central Dublin, 1940 and 1970, *Irish Geography*, **6**, 480–84.

Bannon, M. J. (1973), *Office Location in Ireland: the Role of Central Dublin*. Dublin: An Foras Forbartha.

Bannon, M. J., Eustace, J. G., and Power, M. (1977), *Service-type Employment and Regional Development*. Dublin: The Stationery Office.

Barras, R., and Catalano, A. (1975), *Investment in Land and the Financial Structure of Property Companies*. London: Centre for Environmental Studies (mimeo).

Bateman, M. (1976), Office location policy in the Paris region. Keele: I.B.G. Urban Study Group Autumn Meeting, September.

Bateman, M., and Burtenshaw, D. (1971), Sponsored white-collar migrants, *Town and Country Planning*, **39**, 554–57.

Bateman, M., Burtenshaw, D., and Hall, R. K. (1971), *Office Staff on the Move*. London: Location of Offices Bureau, Research Paper No. 6.

Bell, D. (1974), *The Coming of Post-industrial Society*. London: Heinemann.

Britton, J. N. H. (1975), Environmental adaptation of industrial plants: service linkages, locational environment and organization, in F. E. I. Hamilton (Ed.), *Spatial Perspectives on Industrial Organization and Decision Making*. London: Wiley, pp. 363–90.

Burns, L. S. (1977), The location of the headquarters of industrial companies: a comment, *Urban Studies*, **14**, 211–214.

Burns, L. S., and Pang, W. N. (1977), Big business in the big city: corporate headquarters in the CBD, *Urban Affairs Quarterly*, **12**, 533–44.

Burtenshaw, D., Bateman, M., and Duffett, A. (1974), Office decentralization—ten years' experience, *The Surveyor*, **143**, 22–25, 21–23.

Carey, S. J. (1969), *Relocation of Office Staff: A Study of the Reactions of Staff Decentralized to Ashford*. London: Location of Office Bureau, Research Paper No. 4.

Carey, S. J. (1970), *Relocation of Office Staff: A Follow-up Survey*. London: Location of Offices Bureau, Research Paper No. 4a.

Carroll, J. D. (1953), The future of the central business district, *Public Management*, **35**, 150–153.

Christie, B., and Elton, M. C. J. (1975), *Research on the Differences Between Telecommunication and Face-to-Face Communication in Business and Government.* Paper P/75180/CR. University College London: Communications Study Group.

Civil Service Department (1973), *The Dispersal of Government Work from London.* London: HMSO.

Collins, L., and Walker, D. F. (Eds.) (1975), *Locational Dynamics of Manufacturing Activity.* London: Wiley.

Cooke, A. (1975). *A More Detailed Comparison of the Costs of Travel and Telecommunications.* Paper P/74225/CN. University College London: Communications Study Group.

Cowan, P., Fine, D., Ireland, J., Jordan, C., Mercer, D., and Sears, A. (1969), *The Office: A Facet of Urban Growth.* London: Heinemann.

Croft, M. J. (1969), *Offices in a Regional Centre: Follow-up Studies on Infra-Structure and Linkage.* London: Location of Offices Bureau, Research Paper No. 3.

Daniels, P. W. (1969), Office decentralization from London: policy and practice, *Regional Studies,* **3**, 171–78.

Daniels, P. W. (1972), Transport changes generated by decentralized offices, *Regional Studies,* **6**, 273–89.

Daniels, P. W. (1973), Some changes in the journey to work of decentralized office workers, *Town Planning Review,* **44**, 167–88.

Daniels, P. W. (1975a), *Office Location: An Urban and Regional Study.* London: Bell.

Daniels, P. W. (1975b), Strategic office centres in London, *Town and Country Planning,* **43**, 209–14.

Daniels, P. W. (1977a), Office location in the British conurbations: trends and strategies, *Urban Studies,* **14**, 261–75.

Daniels, P. W. (1977b), Office policy problems in Greater London, *The Planner,* **63**, 102–105.

Daniels, P. W. (1978), Service Sector office employment and regional imbalance in Britain, 1966–71, *Tijdschrift voor Economische en Sociale Geografie,* **69**, 286–95.

Davidson, A. W., and Leonard, J. E. (1976), *The Property Development Process.* London: College of Estate Management, Centre for Advanced Land Use Studies.

Deutermann, E. P. (1970), Headquarters have human problems, *Federal Reserve Bank of Philadelphia Business Review,* 3–22.

Dicken, P. (1971), Some aspects of the decision-making behaviour of business organizations, *Economic Geography,* **47**, 426–37.

Dicken, P. (1976), The multiplant business enterprise and geographical space: some issues on the study of external control and regional development, *Regional Studies,* **10**, 401–12.

Economist Intelligence Unit (1964), *A Survey of Factors Governing the Location of Offices in the London Area.* London: Economist Intelligence Unit.

Evans, A. W. (1973), The location of headquarters of industrial companies, *Urban Studies,* **10**, 387–95.

Facey, M. V., and Smith, G. B. (1968), *Offices in a Regional Centre: A Study of Office Location in Leeds.* London: Location of Offices Bureau, Research Paper No. 2.

Fernie, J. (1977), Office linkages and location: an evaluation of patterns in three cities, *Town Planning Review,* **48**, 78–89.

Fuchs, V. R. (1968), *The Service Economy.* New York: Bureau of Economic Research.

Gad, G. H. K. (1975), *Central Toronto Offices: Observations on Location Patterns and Linkages.* Toronto: City of Toronto Planning Board.

Goddard, J. B. (1967), Changing office location patterns within Central London, *Urban Studies,* **4**, 276–84.

Goddard, J. B. (1971), Office communications and office location: a review of current research, *Regional Studies*, **5**, 263–80.

Goddard, J. B. (1973), *Office Linkages and Location*. Oxford: Pergamon.

Goddard, J. B. (1975), *Office Location in Urban and Regional Development*. London: Oxford University Press.

Goddard, J. B. (1975), The pressures for a revision of office policy, *Town and Country Planning*, **45**, 15–19.

Goddard, J. B., and Morris, D. (1976), The communications factor in office decentralization, *Progress in Planning*, **6**, 1–80.

Goddard, J. B., and Pye, R. (1977), Telecommunications and office location, *Regional Studies*, **11**, 19–30.

Goodwin, W. (1965), The management center in the United States, *Geographical Review*, **55**, 1–16.

Greenhut, M. L. (1956), *Plant Location in Theory and Practice*. Chapel Hill: University of North Carolina Press.

Grit, S., and Korteweg, P. J. (1976), Perspectives on office relocation in the Netherlands, *Tijdschrift voor Economische en Sociale Geografie*, **67**, 2–14.

Haig, R. M. (1927), *Major Economic Factors in Metropolitan Growth and Arrangement*. New York: Committee on Regional Plan for New York and Its Environs, Regional Survey Volume 1.

Hall, R. K. (1972), The movement of offices from Central London, *Regional Studies*, **6**, 385–92.

Hamilton, F. E. I. (Ed.), (1974), *Spatial Perspectives on Industrial Organization and Decision-Making*. London: Wiley.

Hammond, E. (1967), Dispersal of Government offices: a survey, *Urban Studies*, **3**, 258–75.

Hammond, E. (1968), *London to Durham: A Study of the Transfer of the Post Office Savings Certificate Division*. Durham: Rowntree Research Unit.

Harkness, R. C. (1972), *Communication Innovations, Urban Form and Travel Demand: Some Hypotheses and a Bibliography*. Seattle: University of Washington, Department of Urban Planning and Civil Engineering Research Report No. 71–2.

Harkness, R. C. (1973), Telecommunications substitutes for travel: a preliminary assessment of their potential for reducing urban transportation costs by altering office location pattern. Unpublished Ph.D. Thesis, University of Washington.

Hartshorne, T. A. (1973), Industrial/office parks: a new look for the city, *Journal of Geography*, **72**, 33–45.

Hoover, E. M., and Vernon, A. (1959), *Anatomy of a Metropolis*. Cambridge, Mass.: Harvard University Press.

Hughes, J. T., and Price, S. F. (1977), Urban services: locational dynamics and sectoral stability. Keele: C.E.S. Urban Economics Conference, July.

Isard, W. (1956), *Location and Space Economy*. Cambridge, Mass.: M.I.T. Press.

Jeans, D. (1967), Competition, momentum and inertia in the location of commercial institutions: case studies in some London commodity markets, *Tijdschrift voor Economische en Sociale Geografie*, **58**, 11–19.

Jones, D. E., and Hall, R. K. (1972), Office suburbanization in the United States, *Town and Country Planning*, **40**, 470–73.

Kersten, E. W., and Ross, D. R. (1968), Clayton: a metropolitan focus in the St. Louis area, *Annals Assoc. Amer. Geogr.*, **58**, 637–49.

Llyod, P. E., and Dicken, P. (1972), *Location in Space: A Theoretical Approach to Economic Geography*. London: Harper and Row.

Lösch, A. (1954), *The Economics of Location*. New Haven, Conn.: Yale University Press.

Malamud, B. (1971), The economics of office location. Unpublished Ph.D. Thesis, New School for Social Research, University of Nevada.

Manners, G. (1974), The office in metropolis: an opportunity for shaping metropolitan America, *Economic Geography*, **50**, 93–110.

Manners, G. (1977), New tactics for LOB, *Town and Country Planning*, **45**, 444–46.

Martz, D. C. (1976), The location research program at the Bank of America, *Geographical Review*, **66**, 469–76.

Mason, R. S. (1928), *Should the Factory and Office be Separated?* New York: American Management Association.

Meier, R. L. (1962), *A Communications Theory of Urban Growth.* Cambridge, Mass.: The M.I.T. Press.

Melman, S. (1951), The rise of administrative overhead in the manufacturing industries of the U.S., *Oxford Economic Papers*, **3** (New Series), 62–112.

Parsons, G. F. (1972), The giant manufacturing corporations and balanced regional growth in Britain, *Area*, **4**, 99–103.

Pred, A. (1973), The growth and development of systems of cities in advanced economics, in A. Pred and G. Törnqvist, *Systems of Cities and Information Flows.* University of Lund: Lund Studies in Geography Series B, No. 38.

Pred, A. (1974), *Major Job-Providing Organizations and Systems of Cities.* Washington D.C.: Association of American Geographers, Commission on College Geography Resource Paper No. 27.

Pred, A. (1977), *City Systems in Advanced Economies.* London: Hutchinson.

Pritchard, G. (1975), A model of professional office location, *Geografiska Annaler*, **57B**, 100–108.

Pye, R. (1977), Office location and the cost of maintaining contact, *Environment and Planning*, A, **9**, 149–68.

Quante, W. (1976), *The Exodus of Corporate Headquarters from New York City.* New York: Praeger.

Rannells, J. (1956), *The Core of the City.* University of Columbia Press.

Rees, J. (1974), Decision-making, the growth of the firm and the business environment, in F. E. I. Hamilton (Ed.), *Spatial Perspectives on Industrial Organization and Decision-Making.* London: Wiley.

Rhodes, J., and Kan, A. (1971), *Office Dispersal and Regional Policy.* London: Cambridge University Press.

Schwartz, L. E. (1963), From core to ring: an econometric study of the relocation of the central office and its workers. Unpublished Ph.D. Thesis, Harvard University.

Semple, R. K. (1973), Recent trends in the spatial concentration of corporate headquarters, *Economic Geography*, **49**, 309–18.

Shehan, R. (1952), Should management move to the country, *Fortune*, **56**, 142–143, 164.

Simon, H. A. (1956), Rational choice and the structure of the environment, *Psychological Review*, **63**, 129–38.

Simon, H. A. (1960), *The New Science of Management Decision.* New York: Harper and Row.

Soederman, S. (1975), *Industrial Location Planning.* New York: Halsted Press.

Sorenson, A. D. (1974), Office activities as an economic base for urban decentralization in Australia, *Royal Australian Planning Institute Journal*, **12**, 51–57.

Sternlieb, G. (1961), Is business abandoning the big city?, *Harvard Business Review*, **39**, 6–25.

Struyk, R. J., and James, F. J. (1975), *Intra-metropolitan Industrial Location.* Lexington: D. C. Heath.

Taylor, M. J. (1973), Local linkage, external economies and the iron-foundry industry of the West Midlands and East Lancashire conurbations, *Regional Studies*, **7**, 387–400.

Thorngren, B. (1970), How do contact systems affect regional development?, *Environment and Planning*, **2**, 409–27.

Thorngren, B. (1973), Communication studies for government office dispersal in Sweden, in M. J. Bannon (Ed.), *Office Location and Regional Development*. Dublin: An Foras Forbartha.

Toby, J. (1973), Regional development and government office relocation in the Netherlands, in M. J. Bannon (Ed.), *Office Location and Regional Development*. Dublin: An Foras Forbartha.

Törnqvist, G. E. (1968), Flows of information and the location of economic activities, *Geografiska Annaler*, **50**, 99–107.

Törnqvist, G. E. (1970), *Contact Systems and Regional Development*, University of Lund: Lund Studies in Geography, Series B, No. 38.

Townroe, P. M. (1969), Locational choice and the individual firm, *Regional Studies*, **3**, 15–24.

Ullman, E. L. (1958), Regional development and the geography of concentration, *Papers and Proceedings, Regional Science Association*, **4**, 179–198.

Vahaly, J. Jr. (1976), The location of service and office activities in Nashville-Davidson County, 1970, *Land Economics*, **52**, 479–92.

Walker, M. (1957), The plant, the office and the city: III, Trends in office location, *Tax Policy*, **24**, 1–40.

Wall, W. D., and Williams, H. L. (1970), *Longitudinal Studies and the Social Sciences*. London: Social Science Research Council.

Wärneryd, D. (1968), *Interdependence in Urban Systems*. Gothenburg: Regionkansult Aktiebolog.

Webber, M. N. (1964), The urban place and non-place urban realm, in D. L. Foley *et al.* (Eds.), *Explorations into Urban Structure*. Philadelphia: University of Pennsylvania Press.

Weber, A. (1909), *Theory of the Location of Industries*. Chicago: University of Chicago Press.

Westaway, E. J. (1974), The spatial hierarchy of business organizations and its implications for the British urban system, *Regional Studies*, **8**, 145–155.

Yannopoulos (1973), Local income effects of office relocation, *Regional Studies*, **7**, 33–46.

2

Office Development and Urban and Regional Development in Britain

J. B. GODDARD

Introduction

Evidence continues to accumulate which indicates that in many respects British regional policies have been highly successful in diverting manufacturing investment and employment to peripheral regions of the country. For example, Keeble (1977) has recently highlighted the growth of manufacturing employment in these areas compared with considerable declines elsewhere, while McDermott (1977a) has pointed to the increasing shift of new overseas manufacturing investments towards the periphery. The work of Moore and Rhodes (1976) and MacKay (1977) clearly suggests that such shifts may be largely attributed to the operation of regional policy controls and incentives on manufacturing industry.

These successes are even more remarkable given that they were achieved in a period during which manufacturing employment was declining nationally. In contrast, office employment, which was growing rapidly, was relatively unin-fluenced by public policies, at least at the inter-regional scale. It will be argued subsequently that the success of regional policy in dispersing manufacturing employment has been more than offset by a failure of public policies to deal with increasing centralization within parts of the office sector. Moreover, it will be suggested that centralization of office activity and decentralization of manufac-turing are both part of the same process of spatial functional separation operating within the large organizations that have come to dominate the UK space economy. It follows that aspatial policies which have influenced the corporate organization of economic activity, such as those relating to take-over and merger activity, have perhaps been as important in shaping the distribution of office employment as more overtly spatial policies. It also follows that a successful regional policy for the future must not only take account of the importance of the office sector, but must set this within the overall context of policies designed to influence the spatial organization of economic activity as a whole, encompassing both manufacturing and the service sector and public and private corporations. In other words, office policy and by implication studies of office location need to be placed in a broader context than in the past.

These themes will be illustrated by reference to recent empirical studies of office employment trends in Britain seen particularly from the viewpoint of one peripheral area, the Northern Region. This Region has been selected because a recently produced strategic planning study for the Region has identified a poorly developed office sector as one of the chief impediments to the Region's economic and social development (Northern Region Strategy Team, 1977). Wherever possible employment trends in the Region and elsewhere will be related to the corporate organization of industry under the hypothesis that it is the division of administrative functions within multisite organizations that is one of the major determinants of spatial variations in the distribution of different types of office employment. Moreover, since several writers (e.g. Wärneryd, 1968; Pred, 1977; Goddard, 1975; 1977a) have stressed the need to relate the corporate hierarchy and the urban hierarchy, office employment trends will also be examined in terms of their impact on the British urban system. The urban perspective is given further relevance in view of the declining economic base of large urban areas in Britain, a decline which has given rise to new government initiatives designed to attract economic activity back to the inner parts of large cities, and also by national and international suggestions that broad-brush regional policies need to be replaced by more spatially selected policies relating to the national system of cities (e.g. Chisholm, 1976; Manners, 1976; Bourne, 1975; EFTA, 1975).

Regional Office Employment Trends

One indicator of the relative neglect of the office sector in British public policy is the absence of up-to-date statistics on office employment—although here British data are probably far superior to those availabe in most other developed countries, with the possible exception of Sweden. The only source is the *Census of Population*, which collects information on the occupations of the workforce. Unfortunately the latest date for which information is available from the *Census* is 1971. Other bodies responsible for the collection of regular employment statistics, such as the Department of Employment, obtain no information on the occupational structure of employment (although they do collect a great deal of information on the occupational structure of *un*employment). Office employment data from the *Census* also have their limitations in that cross-classifications of occupation by industry are only available for large Economic Planning Regions; for smaller areas it is impossible to separate out, for example, office employment in the public and private sectors.

Notwithstanding these limitations, the pattern of regional disparities revealed by the *Census* is clear cut. Table 2.1 indicates that office occupations account for 38.3 per cent of all employment in Greater London, and 25.3 per cent in the rest of the South East, compared with only 19.4 per cent in the Northern Region. All

Table 2.1. Regional Distribution of Total Office Employment, England and Wales, 1971

Region	Total office ('000)	% of total employment	Total	Location quotients* Clerical	Managers	Prof.
Greater London	156.5	38.3	1.51	1.53	1.47	1.61
Other South East	98.8	25.3	1.00	0.97	1.03	1.08
East Anglia	14.4	20.2	0.79	0.82	0.85	0.79
South West	34.1	21.9	0.88	0.86	0.82	0.88
East Midlands	30.7	20.6	0.81	0.81	0.88	0.80
West Midlands	52.3	22.2	0.88	0.85	0.98	0.90
Yorks. & Humberside	41.8	20.1	0.79	0.81	0.86	0.66
North West	69.2	23.4	0.92	0.99	0.92	0.82
Wales	20.1	18.7	0.74	0.76	0.62	0.70
North	26.3	19.4	0.76	0.81	0.66	0.70
England and Wales	544.0	25.2				

*Location quotients are defined as the regional share of employment in each occupation group divided by the regional share of total employment.
Source. *Census* 1971, Economic Activity Sub-Regional Tables. Table 2. Persons in employment by area of workplace and occupation.

Table 2.2. Regional Distribution of Office Employment by Occupation Groups, 1971

Region	Clerical % total office	Professional % total office	Administration & managerial % total office	Actual – expected*	% total office †
Greater London	62.4	12.7	14.7	− 8900	− 0.6
Other South East	59.5	12.9	15.9	3650	0.4
East Anglia	62.2	11.4	16.3	1100	0.8
South West	61.0	12.2	14.6	− 3100	− 0.9
East Midlands	60.9	11.7	16.6	3510	1.1
West Midlands	60.0	12.4	17.2	8770	1.7
Yorks. & Humberside	63.0	10.0	16.6	4680	1.1
North West	63.7	10.7	15.3	− 1470	− 0.2
Wales	62.9	11.4	13.0	− 1060	− 1.9
North	64.9	10.9	16.6	− 4910	− 0.5
England and Wales	61.9	12.0	15.5	—	—

*'Expected employment' is calculated on the basis of each region having the same proportion of administrators and managers as nationally.
†Actual–expected as % total office employment.
Source. *Census* 1971, Economic Activity Sub-Regional Tables. Table 2. Persons in employment by area of workplace and occupation.

other regions fall at least 15 percentage points behind London. Moreover, in every region outside the South East the share of national office employment is less than the share of total employment (indicated by location quotients of less than 1.0). This shortfall is particularly concentrated into the higher-grade administrative and professional occupations. Thus Table 2.2 indicates that routine clerical occupations form a larger proportion of the total office workforce in the North than nationally (64.9 per cent compared with 61.9 per cent), a situation which may partly be attributed to major dispersals of routine government clerical work to the Region. For the administrative and managerial grades, Wales is the only other region to have a location quotient lower than the North (0.62 compared with 0.66), while only Yorkshire and Humberside has a lower location quotient for professional occupations (0.66 compared with 0.70). These figures should be compared with the concentration in London of the administrative and technical grades as indicated by location quotients of 1.47 and 1.61 respectively. Nevertheless, Table 2.2 does indicate that administrative and managerial occupations do account for a smaller proportion of total office employment in London than in the nation as a whole: this is largely due to the size of the capital's clerical labour force. Peripheral regions, notably Wales, the North West and North, all have shortfalls in these higher grades.

Changes between 1966 and 1971 did little to ameliorate inter-regional differences, although at the intra-regional scale the growth of office employment in the South East outside Greater London was dramatic (Table 2.3). Nevertheless, it is clear that during a period when all employment declined by − 1.7 per cent and office employment increased by 9.1 per cent, office activity was a major component in the changing distribution of job opportunities in Britain. Much of this growth was concentrated in administrative and managerial grades

Table 2.3. Office Employment Change 1966–71, by Region and Occupation Groups

Region	Total employment	Total office	% Change		
			Clerical	Admin. & managerial	Profes- sional
Greater London	− 5.6	2.4	− 3.0	11.0	8.8
Other South East	5.0	21.5	15.2	33.4	29.0
East Anglia	4.3	23.5	17.3	42.5	27.5
South West	1.1	12.5	6.1	26.3	17.7
East Midlands	− 1.7	12.9	9.0	21.7	17.5
West Midlands	− 2.6	6.5	3.1	18.1	6.9
Yorks. & Humberside	− 3.8	6.7	5.3	12.1	2.2
North West	− 4.2	6.3	2.8	18.8	5.6
Wales	− 1.4	10.8	6.3	4.7	10.7
North	− 2.7	9.1	7.2	20.0	10.1

Source. *Census* 1971, Economic Activity Sub-Regional Tables. Table 2. Persons in employment by area of workplace and occupation.

(+ 18.9 per cent), while clerical employment increased by only 4.9 per cent. Significantly, however, clerical employment grew more rapidly in peripheral regions like the North (+ 7.2 per cent), than nationally. Within the South East the decline of clerical employment in London of − 3.0 per cent was more than offset by a 15.2 per cent increase in the rest of the Region. Unlike the peripheral regions, the growth of clerical employment in the South East outside London was also paralleled by major increases in managerial and professional jobs (+ 33.4 per cent and + 29.0 per cent respectively). Regions adjacent to the South East, notably East Anglia and the South West, also experienced significant increases in all office grades, while the rate of change in the capital lagged well behind the national average.

These regional patterns have to be interpreted with some caution since the data refer to office occupations in all industries. Clearly the location requirements of office functions in local governement are different from those in central government, which in turn are different from manufacturing industry. Thus much of the significant growth of office employment outside London may be attributed to the local government sector and to population-orientated service functions generally. At the same time, certain industries which have a small office component in their total workforce, like shipbuilding, are concentrated in particular regions such as the North East, while other industries such as insurance, banking and finance, in which office occupations predominate, are concentrated in other regions, notably the South East. It is therefore not unreasonable to assume that the regional shortfalls and surpluses in office employment that have been described may be explained solely in terms of the industrial structure of the different regions.

In practice, however, industrial structure is only a partial and a secondary reason for the shortfall of office employment in the Northern Region. The Northern Region Strategy Team have suggested that the lower proportion of office workers in the Region relative to the national average may be broken down into two components (Northern Region Strategy Team, 1976). The first component is the occupational structure within each industry, that is, the degree to which there is a difference in the proportion of office workers in each industry in the Region relative to the national average. These differences can be summed across all industries. The second component is the industrial structure, that is, the extent to which the Region specializes in industries which nationally have a high or low proportion of office workers. In the case of the Northern Region, of a total shortfall of 73,000 office jobs (calculated on the basis of the Region having the same proportion of office workers to total employment as the nation), a 50,000 deficit could be attributed to the occupational structure of employment in the region and 23,000 to the industrial structure. Table 2.4 indicates that the shortfall due to occupational structure is much more pronounced in the managerial and professional grades than in the clerical grades. Indeed, in only two out of 27 industries (clothing and footwear and public administration) was a

Table 2.4. Actual and Expected Office Employment, Northern Region, 1971

Grade	Actual ('00)	Expected ('00)	% difference
Clerical	171.3	191.9	88.7
Sales	7.4	7.7	95.9
Managerial	35.7	49.8	71.6
Senior professional	28.7	39.0	73.5
Junior professional	19.8	24.4	80.9

Expected office employment is calculated on the assumption that each industry has the same occupational structure as nationally.
Source. Northern Region Strategy Team, unpublished.

higher proportion of office workers recorded than in Britain as a whole. In some industries, even those well represented in the North, the gap was considerable. For example, in coal and petroleum products only 10.7 per cent of employment in the Region was in the office sector compared with 30.7 per cent nationally.

The implication of this simple standardizaton exercise is that for many industries, including those with significant amounts of manufacturing activity in the Region, either the office function within them is carried on elsewhere, or the office function is weakly developed. The truth or otherwise of both of these explanations can be established only at the level of the individual enterprise. Evidence on this point for the Northern Region will be presented later, but first, the regional trends that have been described will be re-examined at the urban scale.

Urban Trends in Office Employment

It has frequently been hypothesized that office employment is essentially an urban phenomenon, being able to derive maximum advantages of agglomeration in large urban centres. Central locations within large cities offer ease of personal communication between senior office staff both within the city and to places in its hinterland, and also ready access to a large potential supply of clerical labour. And, insofar as the office sector provides a service function, it would be reasonable to hypothesize that the size of the office workforce should increase in line with city size (i.e. in relation to increase in size of hinterland and the local population served).

It is possible to test this hypothesis for the UK using data for 126 Metropolitan Economic Labour Areas (MELAs). These functional urban areas are composed of administrative units (pre-1974 local authority areas) with an employment density of over five workers per acre (12.5 per hectare) or a minimum of 20,000 jobs (an urban core) together with contiguous areas from which more than 15 per

Table 2.5. Office Employment and City Size, 1966 and 1971

	1966	1971
Constant	0.832	0.711
Log total employment (beta)	1.048	1.045
R^2	0.949	0.948
Standard error	0.091	0.089

$N = 126$.
Source. Urban Change Project, Dept. of Geography, London School of
   Economics.

cent of the economically active population commute to the core (the Metropolitan Ring) and from which more persons commute than to any other core (the Outer Metropolitan Ring) (Drewett *et al.*, 1976). Table 2.5 describes the result of the regression of the logarithm of total office employment (Y) against the logarithm of total employment (X) for each MELA for both 1966 and 1971. One would hypothesize that the alpha coefficient from this regression should be between 0 and 1 and the beta coefficient be greater than zero if there was any tendency towards clustering of office employment in large cities; indeed, the greater the beta value the steeper the hierarchy of office employment. Table 2.5 indicates that there is indeed a close relationship between city size and total office employment in both 1966 and 1971 ($R^2 = 0.95$ for both dates) and that the relationship is of the hypothesized form. Significantly, however, the degree of concentration in large cities has declined marginally between the two dates as indicated by a small reduction in the alpha coefficient.

Although total employment is an important factor in accounting for variations in the absolute amount of office employment within a town, the relative importance of office jobs in the overall employment structure is more strongly related to regional factors. Table 2.6 highlights the extremes of the distribution of towns in terms of the proportion of employment accounted for by office occupations. The towns with the highest proportions are all in the South East peripheral to London and do not include any of the largest cities. Towns at the bottom of the ranking are primarily centres of heavy industry. Amongst the different types of office employment, the greatest variation is for clerical jobs, from 21.1 per cent of total employment in London to 7.9 per cent in Rhondda. Again, because of definitional problem, the range for managerial employment is smaller—from 5.8 per cent in Letchworth to 2.3 per cent in Barrow. The ranking of towns according to each type of employment is similar, with the notable · exception of the large proportion of clerical jobs in places that have received government office dispersal, notably Blackpool (17.2 per cent clerical, ranked fifth) and Liverpool (16.7 per cent clerical, ranked tenth).

Table 2.6. Office Employment by Occupation Groups, Metropolitan Economic Labour Areas (MELAs), Great Britain, 1971

Ten MELAs with highest proportions of office workers as % total employment		Ten MELAs with lowest proportions of office workers as % total employment	
	%		%
1. London	36.3	117. Doncaster	16.4
2. Crawley	34.6	118. Port Talbot	16.2
3. Hemel Hempstead	32.3	119. Scunthorpe	15.9
4. Stevenage	32.2	120. Ayr	15.4
5. Watford	30.8	121. Workington	15.0
6. Walton & Weybridge	30.8	122. Kings Lynn	14.7
7. Letchworth	29.7	123. Barnsley	14.7
8. Harlow	29.6	124. Hartlepool	13.8
9. Worthing	29.0	125. Mansfield	13.2
10. Reading	28.5	126. Rhondda	12.9

Source. Urban Change Project, Dept. of Geography, London School of Economics.

Table 2.7. The Localization of Office Employment, City Size and Distance from London, 1971

Step No.	Standardized beta coefficients		R^2	Standard error	F ratio
	Log distance (X_1)	Total employment (X_2)			
1	−0.669		0.448	0.136	100.6
2	−0.638	0.092	0.455	0.135	51.4

Fig. 2.1 indicates that regional factors strongly influence the localization of office employment. It shows that only five labour market areas outside the South East (Bristol, Bath, Cheltenham, Harrogate and Edinburgh) have location quotients for total office employment in excess of 1.0. Moreover, the six largest cities after London, all with populations in excess of one million (Birmingham, Glasgow, Manchester, Liverpool, Newcastle and Leeds), all have smaller shares of national office employment than of total employment. That regional factors are more important than city size in explaining the localization of office employment is clearly demonstrated in Table 2.7. This table describes the results of a multiple regression model which attempts to explain the location quotient for total office employment in each MELA (Y) by the logarithm of its road distance from London (X_1) and its total employment (X_2). The model reveals that the localization of office employment is, not surprisingly, inversely related to distance from London; this factor is also a more powerful explanatory variable than city size. The relatively poor performance of the model ($R^2 = 0.46$) suggests that a number of other factors are at work accounting for variations in the localization of office employment.

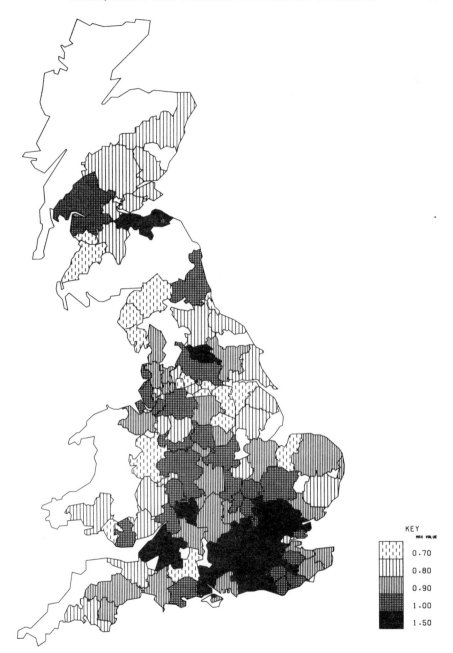

KEY

MAX VALUE

0.70
0.80
0.90
1.00
1.50

Fig. 2.1. Location quotients for total office employment, Metropolitan Economic Labour Areas, 1971

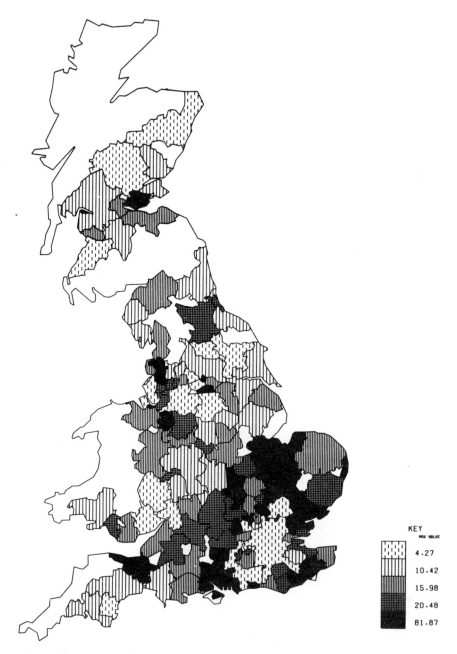

KEY

MAX VALUE

4.27

10.42

15.98

20.48

81.87

Fig. 2.2 Percentage change in total office employment, Metropolitan Economic Labour Areas, 1966–71

Examination of office employment changes between 1966 and 1971 again reinforces the importance of labour market areas in the South East, together with parts of East Anglia and the South West. Fig. 2.2 shows that few towns south and west of a line between the Severn and the Wash recorded significant increases in office employment, while some of the largest cities, including London, had relative increases well below the national average. Although some of the largest absolute increases in office employment were recorded by major cities, a number of medium-sized towns, such as Portsmouth, Southampton, Edinburgh, Cardiff and Leicester, also figure prominently in the list of leading towns in terms of absolute office employment increase (Table 2.8). Given that relatively slow-growing employment forms a larger component of the total office workforce in the largest cities, one might expect a decline here relative to the rest of Britain.

This is confirmed by the results of a shift/share analysis. This analysis breaks down the difference between the actual growth of total office employment and that which might have been expected if employment had grown at the national rate into two components. First, the proportionality shift identifies the amount

Table 2.8. Absolute Office Employment Change, Metropolitan Economic Labour Areas, Great Britain, 1966–71

Ten MELAs with largest absolute and relative increase in total office employment			
Absolute change (tens)		Relative change (%)	
1. London	6852	1. Basingstoke	81.8
2. Birmingham	1665	2. Milton Keynes	60.1
3. Portsmouth	1335	3. High Wycombe	45.5
4. Southampton	1055	4. Dunfermline	44.4
5. Bristol	1023	5. Worthing	41.6
6. Edinburgh	937	6. Harlow	40.3
7. Newcastle	936	7. Hemel Hempstead	36.8
8. Glasgow	900	8. Dewsbury	33.1
9. Cardiff	859	9. Great Yarmouth	32.6
10. Leicester	812	10. Crewe	32.2
Ten MELAs with smallest absolute and relative increase/decrease in total office employment			
117. Southport	60	117. Newport	3.1
118. Barrow	58	118. Sheffield	1.7
119. Torquay	57	119. Liverpool	1.6
120. Harrogate	44	120. Manchester	0.9
121. Perth	− 15	121. Perth	− 1.7
122. Rhondda	− 15	122. Hereford	− 2.3
123. Hereford	− 22	123. Halifax	− 2.5
124. Halifax	− 38	124. Aberdeen	− 3.9
125. Ayr	− 60	125. Rhondda	− 4.7
126. Aberdeen	− 92	126. Ayr	− 5.7

Source. Urban Change Project, Dept. of Geography, London School of Economics.

Table 2.9. Components of Office Employment Change, Metropolitan Economic Labour Areas, Great Britain, 1966–71

	Ten MELAs with highest absolute differential shift 1966–71			Ten MELAs with smallest absolute differential shift 1966–71		
		Abs.*	%†		Abs.	%
1.	Portsmouth	933	20.2	117. Halifax	− 177	− 11.7
2.	Southampton	642	13.6	118. Coventry	− 241	− 3.2
3.	Oxford	481	12.1	119. Aberdeen	− 301	− 13.0
4.	Cambridge	462	16.7	120. Leeds	− 415	− 3.1
5.	Dunfermline	423	36.1	121. Glasgow	− 472	− 2.8
6.	High Wycombe	387	36.1	122. Sheffield	− 712	− 7.0
7.	Northampton	383	19.7	123. Liverpool	− 1010	− 6.4
8.	Preston	366	12.9	124. Birmingham	− 1072	− 3.5
9.	Reading	365	10.3	125. Manchester	− 1974	− 7.6
10.	Worthing	348	33.0	126. London	− 7695	− 4.6

*The differential shift identifies the difference between actual and expected employment growth with expected growth based on the assumption of each type of office employment (clerical, managerial and professional) growing in each MELA at the same rate as nationally.
†The percentage differential shift is the absolute shift expressed as a percentage of total office employment 1966.
Source. Urban Change Project, Dept. of Geography, London School of Economics.

by which employment has grown or declined as a result of specialization in nationally slow- or fast-growing components of the total office labour force (clerical, managerial or professional). Second, the differential shift reflects the surplus or deficit of employment resulting from each category of office employment growing at a faster or slower rate than nationally. Table 2.9 demonstrates that some of the major cities experience less office employment growth than might have been expected, principally because of slower growth rates in each type of office employment locally than nationally (negative differential shift). Owing to the small variation between cities in the proportion of managerial and professional workers, the proportionality shift accounts for only a small part of the total shift. Again, substantial positive differential shifts are to be found in the South East, notably in the larger centres, such as Portsmouth, Southampton, Cambridge, Oxford and Reading.

The overriding conclusion of this analysis is that office employment is not only moving away from London to smaller and particularly medium-sized towns in the South East, but is also declining relatively in other major urban centres. These inter-urban trends are undoubtedly an extension of a well-established tendency for office activity to decentralize from the inner to the outer parts of large cities. This is clearly demonstrated in Table 2.10, which shows office employment changes 1966–71 for the constituent zones of MELAs. In the urban cores of cities with a population of over a million the decline of total employment,

Table 2.10. Office Employment Change by Urban Zone, Great Britain, 1966–1971

	Million cities		Rest of Britain	
	Abs.	%	Abs.	%
Urban cores				
Total employment	− 621	− 8.2	− 33	− 0.5
Total office	8	0.4	174	10.8
Clerical	− 64	− 4.5	89	8.9
Managerial	32	10.7	46	22.8
Other office	40	7.5	46	11.4
Metropolitan rings				
Total employment	75	3.3	131	4.4
Total office	94	19.9	103	23.3
Clerical	47	16.7	48	19.4
Managerial	21	26.7	24	30.7
Other office	27	23.1	31	26.7
Outer metropolitan rings				
Total employment	5	0.8	− 47	− 1.7
Total office	13	11.8	61	15.2
Clerical	9	14.6	23	9.5
Managerial	4	22.4	15	23.5
Other office	− 0	− 0.3	17	18.1

Figures in 000's.
Source. Urban Change Project, Dept. of Geography. London School of Economics.

contrary to popular belief, has not been compensated for by an increase in office employment. Clerical employment has declined by − 4.5 per cent in the cores of the 'million cities', compared with an 8.9 per cent increase in urban cores elsewhere. Likewise, managerial employment was growing less rapidly in the cores of the larger cities than elsewhere (+ 10.7 per cent compared with + 22.8 per cent). In the case of all cities, clerical and especially managerial employment has been the principal component of the growth of jobs in metropolitan rings and outer metropolitan rings. As has already been noted for the largest cities, especially London, this process of net decentralization has spilled over the outer metropolitan rings into free-standing peripheral towns.

In the case of London, it is likely that decentralization is creating space for new highly specialized office activities which are able to take advantage of the capital's key position in a strong regional economy (as well as its national and international role); however, the same cannot be said of most of the major provincial cities. Historically, the growth of these cities was partly related to their role as business service centres for regional economies; with the expansion of large multisite companies and improvements in communications, together with the increasing involvement of national government based in London in industrial affairs, this regional role is now threatened. Yet the considerable investment in infrastructure, particularly centrally focused public transport systems, suggests that these cities are well placed physically to function as major centres for office activity. It is in this context that prospects for office development in regions outside the South East will now be considered.

Industrial Organization and Regional Variation in Office Employment

In their work on the office sector in the Northern Region, the Northern Region Strategy Team identified four types of office activity.

> 1. Offices concerned with the planning and control of the production of goods and services. Such planning and control functions are distributed throughout organisations and in general tend to be concentrated in the upper end of the organisational hierarchy, most particularly in company and corporation head offices.
> 2. Offices which provide services to the business community, for instance, banking, insurance, market research and advertising. In some organisations, especially large ones, these may be internalised but generally they are provided by external agencies.
> 3. Offices which provide services to individuals. These personal services may be either public or private, for instance, employment exchanges, many local authority services, estate agencies or solicitors, though numerically the public sector predominates.
> 4. The headquarters offices of Central Government Departments, i.e. civil service offices serving a national rather than a local or regional need (Quince, 1977).

In the Northern Region the last two categories are not under-represented largely due to past dispersals of routine headquarters office work from London (for example, social security payment); also, personal services to individuals do not vary much throughout the country owing to uniform standards of provision in the public sector and fairly small inter-regional variations in personal income. However, planning and control and business services offices are under-represented in the North. Regarding planning control offices the Northern Region Strategy Team note that three factors have been important.

> First, as a result of industrial concentration largely brought about by merger activity, more and more of the national output of goods and services is controlled by fewer and fewer enterprises, most of which are based in the South East. The attractions of the South East are access to the national and international communications networks and sources of high level information, in particular that disseminated by the government policy-making machine, itself concentrated in the South East, and by other planning and control offices. Second, in areas like the North, many enterprises with locally based planning and control functions are in declining sectors, such as shipbuilding or heavy engineering, so that over a long period there has been a contraction in indigenous industry. Third, in the main, this has been replaced not by the establishment and growth of other locally based industry, but, with the encouragement of regional policy, by branch plants, most of which have head offices in the South, and which themselves carry out a narrow range of production-related functions. While such branch plants, in absolute terms, have undoubtedly directly increased office employment in the development areas, there can be no doubt that his gain would have been much greater if these plants had carried out a wider range of functions (Quince, 1977).

Table 2.11. Ownership Status, Manufacturing Establishments, Northern Region, 1963 and 1973

Status group	Establishments*				Employment			
	1967		1973		1963		1973	
	No.	%	No.	%	No.	%	No.	%
Independent	228	27.2	184	16.6	413.0	10.6	184.4	4.4
Regional branch	89	10.6	73	6.6	519.3	13.3	333.2	7.9
Regional parent	133	15.8	107	9.7	931.6	23.9	416.6	9.9
External subsidiary	127	15.1	305	27.5	668.6	17.2	1330.0	31.4
External branch	262	31.2	439	39.6	1365.3	35.0	1953.2	46.3
Totals	839	100.0	1108	100.0	3897.8	100.0	4217.4	100.0

*Classification of establishments:

Independent = establishment owned by a company with only one manufacturing site.

Branch = establishment of a parent company based outside the Region which has *never* previously been locally owned.

External subsidiary = establishment which previously has been owned by a firm based in the Region.

Regional Branch = establishment owned by a parent company with headquarters inside the Region.

Regional parent = regional headquarters establishment with control over other establishments in the Region.

Source. Northern Region Strategy Team and I. J. Smith, Department of Geography, University of Newcastle-upon-Tyne. Data refer to establishments employing more than 50 persons and cover approximately 95 per cent of total manufacturing employment.

Some empirical evidence can be found to support these generalizations. The first point to note concerns the increasing external control of employment in the Northern Region. According to Table 2.11, in 1973 only 22.2 per cent of employment in manufacturing establishments employing more than 50 persons was in plants controlled from within the Region. This compared with 47.8 per cent in 1963. The number of establishments internally controlled fell from 53.6 per cent of the total in 1963 to 32.9 per cent in 1973. During the period, the number of branch plants, many of which arrived in the Region during a period of active regional policy, increased from 262 to 439, representing an increase in the share of manufacturing employment of + 11.3 per cent. However, by far the largest component of the growth in external control is attributable to the increase of the share of employment in subsidiary companies whose ultimate ownership is located outside the Region. This component is related chiefly to takeover and merger activity. This process has also been operating within the Region, as is indicated by the increase of employment in intra-regionally controlled subsidiaries.

Further analysis of the data in Table 2.11 suggests that 45.6 per cent of manufacturing employment in the Northern Region was controlled from the

Table 2.12 Percentage Change in Regional Turnover Share 1971/2–1976/7, Top 1000 Companies in the United Kingdom

Planning region	71/72 turnover*			76/77 turnover			72–77 % change
	£m	%	Rank	£m	%	Rank	
Greater London	48,829	77.24	1	109,311	76.69	1	−0.55
Rest of South East	2298	3.64	3	8976	6.30	2	2.66
East Anglia	271	0.43	10	510	0.36	10	−0.07
East Midlands	888	1.40	7	1445	1.01	8	−0.39
West Midlands	3080	4.87	2	6794	4.77	3	−0.10
North West	2223	3.52	5	3848	2.70	6	−0.82
Yorks. & Humberside	1894	3.00	6	4097	2.87	5	−0.13
South West	728	1.15	8	1504	1.05	7	−0.10
Wales	120	0.19	11	76	0.05	11	−0.14
Scotland	2243	3.55	4	4840	3.40	4	−0.15
Northern Ireland	8	0.01	12	68	0.05	12	0.04
North	635	1.00	9	1075	0.75	9	−0.25
United Kingdom	63,217	100	—	142,544	100	—	0.0

*Turnover figures have been rounded to nearest million.
Source. *Times 1000* and Smith and Goddard (1978).

South East. The dominant position of London is clearly demonstrated by Table 2.12, which is based upon an analysis of the location of the headquarters of the 1000 largest companies by turnover in the UK (the *Times 1000* list). The table shows that more than three-quarters of the turnover of these companies was controlled from London in 1977. Changes in the preceding five years have been at the expense of all other regions, except the South East outside London. In fact, London's share of turnover has declined marginally as larger companies have decentralized their headquarters to the rest of the South East. To counteract this, however, a number of smaller companies have moved headquarters into London from other regions, while firms based in the South East have grown more rapidly than elsewhere in the country. Detailed examination of the changes underlying Table 2.12 suggests that decline in regions like the North and Wales may be related to acquisitions activity resulting in a transfer of headquarters control out of the region, while in the intermediate areas (Yorkshire and Humberside and the North West and the Midlands) the decline may be related to the relatively poor growth performance of companies headquartered there (Smith and Goddard, 1978).

Research into the regional impact of takeover and merger activity by Leigh and North suggests that some of the most significant immediate consequences occur in the distribution of administrative functions (Leigh and North, 1977). Service functions like accounting previously supplied at different locations within separate organizations before merger may be centralized in the acquiring company's headquarters, while external services that were subcontracted to local firms may subsequently be provided either by the head office of the acquiring company or by a service firm near to it.

But what of the relationship of these organizational factors to the distribution of office employment? By far the most comprehensive cross-sectional evidence comes from a sample survey of non-manufacturing activity in UK manufacturing industry recently completed by Crum and Gudgin (Crum and Gudgin, 1977). Details of non-manufacturing employment were obtained from 484 establishments in 80 companies; these establishments included branches, manufacturing plants to which the company head office was attached, and detached head offices of companies with more than one site. Twenty-two of the establishments were located in the Northern Region. Table 2.13 confirms the marked contrast between manufacturing establishments with head offices attached and branch plants in terms of the proportion of employment to be found in different managerial functions, with the greatest difference being in marketing and distribution functions. Although based on a very small sample, the contrast between similar status establishments in the North and the UK as a whole is striking. With the exception of activities related to production, office functions in Northern Region branches and locally controlled companies account for a smaller share of total employment than nationally. Again, marketing and distribution is particularly poorly developed in the North. The converse of this situation is to be found in the South East, where marketing and distribution is over-represented relative to the national average.

A number of factors account for the limited range of functions performed in branch plants. Chief amongst these is the extent to which office services are provided at the establishment or obtained either from elsewhere in the

Table 2.13. Employment in Non-Production Functions in Manufacturing Industry, Northern Region, United Kingdom, 1976

| Department/Function | Branch | | Non-detached HQ | | Detached HQ |
	NR	UK	NR	UK	UK
(No. of cases)	(15)	(352)	(7)	(64)	(32)
General management	1.2	4.5	3.3	5.2	28.9
Specialist services	2.4	3.7	4.1	5.8	17.6
Personnel & maintenance	6.2	6.2	5.2	6.9	6.4
Production	10.7	7.6	10.6	8.4	7.1
Research & development	0.3	0.7	2.0	1.7	5.4
Marketing & distribution	2.5	7.2	4.8	13.3	30.0
Total non-production as % establishment total*	23.5	30.4	30.7	41.7	96.1

*Including others not listed above.
Source. Crum and Gudgin (1977).

organization (usually the head office) or from other firms frequently close to the head office. Various studies of service linkages have demonstrated this phenomenon (e.g. Britton, 1974; East Midlands Economic Planning Council, 1971). Crum and Gudgin's survey confirms this. They found that the use and provision of services was in turn related to the degree of autonomy given to managers in different decision areas. Thus, with the exception of scientific and technical employees, the average proportion of employment devoted to non-production functions in plants where managers had maximum autonomy was twice that in plants where most decisions were made elsewhere.

Regional shortfalls of office employment in manufacturing industry are not entirely attributable to the existence of a large number of branch plants. It has already been noted how industries which are 'indigenous' to the Northern Region have relatively fewer office workers than nationally. The Northern Region Strategy Team have commented upon the weakly developed range of office functions, particularly those concerned with marketing, in indigenous industries. This may partly be related to the nature of the products and markets involved (for example, one-off heavy engineering goods for specific monopoly-buying customers). The Team went on to associate the under-representation of office functions with the poor competitive performance of many of the region's indigenous manufacturing industries, particularly in terms of the industrial innovation and diversification which must form the basis for self-sustained regional economic growth. According to the Team, 'offices make a vital contribution to the generation of new economic activity, to the search for, and development of, new processes, markets and management systems. It is generally in offices too that decisions are taken as to how, when and where ideas for new goods and services should translate into action. It follows that an area deficient in office activity and thus lacking these crucial skills and capabilities will find it difficult to increase and sustain economic growth' (Northern Region Strategy Team, 1976).

In contrast to the Northern Region, Crum and Gudgin found that companies based solely in the South East Region generally possessed a wider range of office functions and higher proportions of non-production workers than nationally. Significantly, these higher proportions were associated with higher labour productivity (output per worker). The direction of causality connecting office workers with productivity is difficult to ascertain. Does higher productivity lead to more office workers or *vice versa*? High levels of productivity should increase profitability, which in turn may allow resources to be devoted to the development of new products and processes, thereby affecting the long-term survival possibilities of the firm.

The critical question is why are firms which are based in the South East generally more competitive than firms based elsewhere? Although many forces are at work, one factor that is frequently mentioned but seldom directly incorporated into any empirical analysis is the better access to specialist information in this region as compared to more peripheral areas. The role of office functions information exchange within and between organizations is well established in the regional literature (e.g. Thorngren, 1970; Tornqvist, 1970; Goddard, 1975). However, few empirical studies have explicitly sought to relate information flows to organizational considerations, particularly corporate structure and strategy and the economic and technological dimensions of the organization's environment. Perhaps the most relevant recent study has been McDermott's investigation of the information linkages related to the sales functions of electronics firms in three contrasting regions of the UK—Greater London, the Outer Metropolitan Area and Scotland (McDermott, 1977b).

McDermott's investigation of the contacts of marketing managers confirms the findings of other studies concerning the dominance of the local environment in information flows, especially those external to the organization. He considered this result to 'place Scottish firms at a disadvantage as their local region does not coincide with or adjoin the current centre of market-related information for the electronics industry as it does for London and Outer Metropolitan Area respondents' (McDermott, 1977b, p. 233). Moreover, the contact fields of marketing managers in the Outer Metroplitan Area were less localized than for their counterparts in other regions. This finding takes on added significance when consideration is given to the quality of the information flows, with the more routine contacts tending to be places over *longer distances*. Thus, although the local environment is relatively more important to the Scottish-based firms, the quality of non-routine information obtained from that environment is likely to be poorer than for those firms based elsewhere. McDermott concludes, 'in day-to-day external communications the marketing sub-system maintains relatively wide spatial horizons with respect to those functions for which it holds primary responsibility, the maintenance and monitoring of customer relations. However, in less routine functions, functions which may well be more critical in terms of general firm management and alignment, respondents were, on average, considerably more constrained in their spatial interaction, suggesting a greater degree of dependence upon local information' (McDermott, 1977b, p. 247).

While the information fields of Scottish firms were more locally peaked, their spatial extent was more extensive, reflecting a peripheral location *vis à vis* the rest of the UK; so as far as information *via* personal contacts is concerned, marketing managers in Scottish-based firms are inevitably involved in extensive business travel. What generalizations follow from this finding? An information theory of regional development would suggest that firms based solely in peripheral regions would also be peripheral to the dominant flows of information in the space economy. Because of the time involved in travel, fewer business contacts will be maintained than by equivalent firms in core regions, thus possibly resulting in the loss of new business opportunities. This may be particularly so in industries in which managers perceive there to be a relatively stable market and technological environment. In contrast, in multisite organizations with regional establishments, information flows would be predominantly internal to the organization and confined to lower levels of the managerial hierarchy. Research is currently in hand within the Northern Region which is attempting to explore the relationship between information flows *via* personal contact and the corporate structure of the organization and the characteristics of its economic and technological environment. The work is proceeding both at the level of the enterprise (Rabey, 1977) and the region in aggregate (Marshall, 1977). In this latter respect, data relating information flows into and out of the regional economy as a whole have been obtained by means of a two-week survey of business travellers by rail and air between the North East and South East regions.

The analysis of the business travel data lends some support to an information theory of regional development. Table 2.14 indicates that office employment is a reasonably good predictor of the proportion of business travel originating from different sectors in the South East and North East regions. Nevertheless, certain sectors generate significantly more or less business travel than might be expected in terms of their share of each region's total office employment. For example, in

Table 2.14. Business Travel and Office Employment, North East England and the South East Region, 1977

(*Y*) % total travellers by sector	Constant	(*X*) % total office employment by sector	R^2	Standard error *Y*
North East origins*	0.884	0.846	0.51	3.40
South East origins	0.621	- 0.835	0.75	2.25

*For North East origins only:
Sectors with more travel than expected

Greater than one standard error
  Chemicals
  Professional & business services
  Electrical engineering
  Mechanical engineering

Less than one standard error
  Coal
  Metal manufacture
  Other manufacturing

Sectors with less travel than expected

Greater than one standard error
  Insurance, banking & finance
  Coal
  Food
  Vehicles
  Metal goods
  Textiles
  Construction
  Gas, electricity & water
  Transport
  Miscellaneous services
  Publishing

Less than one standard error
  Instrument engineering
  Shipbuilding
  Clothing
  Leather
  Bricks
  Timber

Source. Marshall (1977).

Table 2.15. Occupational Status of Business Travellers from North East Origins

Sector	Occupation						Total
	Top management	Support staff	Technical and related	Production management	Clerical occupations	Selling occupations	
North East origin							
More contact-intensive sectors	121 (8.1)	469 (31.6)	737 (49.6)	120 (8.1)	10 (0.7)	28 (1.9)	1485 (49.2)
Less contact-intensive sectors	281 (18.3)	661 (43.0)	318 (20.7)	180 (11.7)	33 (2.1)	63 (4.1)	1536 (50.8)
Total	402 (13.3)	1130 (37.4)	1055 (34.9)	300 (9.9)	43 (1.4)	91 (3.0)	3021 (100.0)

Table 2.16. Departmental Functions of Business Travellers from North East Origins

Sector	Major functions							Total
	Production management	Technical services	Marketing	Sales	Financial services	General administ.	Education	
North East origin								
More contact-intensive sectors	210 (14.4)	336 (23.0)	91 (6.2)	170 (11.7)	99 (6.8)	77 (5.3)	188 (12.9)	1459 (53.0)
Less contact-intensive sectors	117 (9.0)	132 (10.2)	65 (5.0)	291 (22.5)	183 (14.1)	176 (13.6)	25 (1.9)	1295 (47.0)
Total	327 (11.9)	468 (17.0)	156 (5.7)	461 (16.7)	282 (10.2)	253 (9.2)	213 (7.7)	2754 (100.0)

the North East, the professional and business services sector, chemicals, electrical and mechanical engineering all generate more travel, and the public sector, insurance and shipbuilding less travel, than might be expected. For South East origins, the relationship between business travel generation by sector is more closely related to the distribution of office employment than in the North East, but with a broadly similar pattern of residuals, that is with the notable exception of chemicals, which generates fewer South East than North East based trips relative to its respective shares of total regional office employment.

The explanation for these residuals can partly be found in contrasts between sectors in the occupational and functional mix of office employment, with certain occupations and types of department generating more travel than others, and also in contrasts in the organizational status and size of workplaces in different industries. Table 2.15 indicates that there is a highly significant difference between the occupational mix of the more and less travel-intensive sectors from North East origins. Technical and related staff are more important in the contact-intensive sectors, while top management and their support staff are more important in the less contact-intensive sectors. This suggests that in those industries which communicate less, travel tends to be confined to high levels in the organization. This is confirmed by Table 2.16, which indicates that in the more travel-intensive sectors, the sales, financial and general administrative functions are more important as compared with production management and technical services in the less travel-intensive sectors. In other words, in those industries generating a great deal of business travel, communication is principally concerned with routine production-related matters, while in those producing less travel, communication is related more directly to commercial and administrative issues. This is consistent with the view that those industries which have less well-developed organizational hierarchies are characteristically composed of smaller indigenously controlled establishments. Table 2.17 confirms that the travel-intensive sectors contain proportionately more smaller establishments and fewer with over 500 employees. Finally, Table 2.18 suggests that in terms of organizational status a higher proportion of the travellers in the less contact-intensive sectors come from head offices and branch plants, while travellers from the more contact-intensive sectors are characteristically from divisional head offices of multisite companies.

Further analysis of other information from the travel surveys suggests that the bulk of travel from the more contact-intensive sectors is internal to the organization, while the professional and business service sector in the South East is the principal destination for travellers from the less contact-intensive sectors in the North East. This is a reflection of the under-representation of business and professional services in the North and their concentration in the South. In terms of the characteristics of the meetings to which businessmen are travelling, there are significant differences between meetings held in the North and South East regions, with the former being more routine in character. This suggests that

Table 2.17. Employment Size of Workplace of Business Travellers from North East Origins

| Sector | Employment size of normal workplace | | | | | | |
	10 or less employees	11–49 employees	50–99 employees	100–299 employees	300–499 employees	500 or more employees	Total
North East origin							
More contact-intensive sectors	111 (7.5)	203 (13.7)	137 (9.2)	197 (13.3)	135 (9.1)	701 (47.2)	1484 (49.0)
Less contact-intensive sectors	256 (16.5)	319 (20.6)	210 (13.6)	235 (15.2)	103 (6.7)	424 (27.4)	1547 (51.0)
Total	367 (12.1)	522 (17.2)	347 (11.4)	432 (14.3)	238 (7.9)	1125 (37.1)	3031 (100.0)

Table 2.18. Corporate Status of Workplace of Business Travellers from North East Origins

Sector	Head office	Divisional head office	Branch establishment	Total
		Corporate organizational status of normal workplace		
North East origin				
More contact-intensive sectors	221 (22.6)	448 (45.7)	311 (31.7)	980 (51.6)
Less contact-intensive sectors	301 (32.7)	265 (28.8)	354 (38.5)	920 (48.4)
Total	522 (27.5)	713 (37.5)	665 (35.0)	1900 (100.0)

travellers from the South East are in the main bringing relatively low-level information, for example in the form of instructions and advice; in contrast, businessmen based in the North have to travel to the South East to seek higher-level information, for example concerning marketing and finance. This dependence of the North East on the South East is reflected in a basic asymmetry in the number of travellers generated by each region; thus in absolute terms, for every one traveller originating in the South East two originate from the North.

The Corporate Hierarchy and the Urban Hierarchy

The preceding review has suggested that organizational considerations are an important factor in accounting for inter-regional variations in office employment. Moreover, these variations may be linked to more fundamental processes of regional economic development, particularly concerning inter-regional flows of information. The question now arises as to whether there is an urban dimension to organizational structure which can be related to the urban employment trends already described. More specifically, is there a corporate hierarchy which matches the hierarchy of office employment in relation to city size that has already been noted?

In order to answer this question, the headquarters of the 1000 leading companies have been allocated to the 126 MELAs defined for a project on urban change in Britain (Department of Environment, 1976), and the total turnover of all firms headquartered in each MELA calculated. This provides the basis for the MELA ranking shown in Fig. 2.3. The logarithmic rank-size graph, markedly steepening at its upper end, reflects the dominance of the London MELA with a turnover share considerably above that expected by its rank size. A slight steepening of the graph between 1972 and 1977 suggests a relative increase in

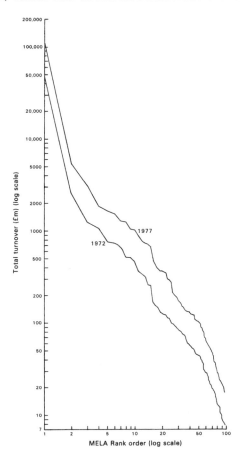

Fig. 2.3. Rank-size distribution of Metropolitan Economic Labour Areas according to total turnover controlled, 1972 and 1977 (source: *Times 1000*)

London's share. Another marked steepening of the 1972 graph occurs at rank order 15 (Coventry) but this has considerably diminished by 1977, suggesting that lower-ranked MELAs have relatively gained ground. The general rounding of the 1977 graph is also an indication that higher-ranked MELAs (2–15) have relatively lost ground. These for the most part are the provincial capital cities. For example, Edinburgh, Newcastle, Bristol, Nottingham, Leicester and Coventry all fell in the rankings between 1972 and 1977, all except Edinburgh being overtaken by Basildon and Reading. The rapid growth of some London satellite MELAs as control centres is best illustrated by Walton and Weybridge, unrepresented in the rankings in 1972 but ranked 20 in 1977.

However, as the majority of MELAs contain less than four headquarters of the leading 1000 companies, even small changes in turnover produce large variations in the rankings at the lower end of the scale. A more satisfactory method of showing control changes at the city-region level is to calculate the total turnover of each MELA as a percentage of the total turnover of all 1000 companies in each year. On this basis the MELAs can be classified into three main types: those in which there has been an absolute decrease of total turnover, those in which there has been a relative decrease in turnover share, and those in which there has been a relative increase in turnover share. Only a minority of MELAs experienced an increase greater than 0.1 per cent and these have been mapped as a separate category because their geographical distribution is significant to the issue at stake (Fig. 2.4).

MELAs experiencing absolute decline in turnover share are mainly the smaller city regions of the older industrial areas, particularly South Wales, North East Lancashire, and the West Riding of Yorkshire. MELAs experiencing relative decline are the most numerous category and include all the major city regions with the exception of London and Glasgow. The Northern Region is distinguished by every constituent city region either relatively or absolutely losing ground, although relative decreases are general throughout all the traditional manufacturing regions.

MELAs showing a marginal relative increase in turnover share are, for the most part, peripheral to the traditional manufacturing regions, suggesting a limited degree of local control decentralization. Thus Humberside has gained at the expense of the West Riding and North Lancashire at the expense of South Lancashire and Cheshire. The changes here, however, represent less than 0.1 per cent of total turnover and MELAs with substantial gains are limited to London and its satellites, Glasgow and Kidderminster. Gains exceeding 0.2 per cent were experienced only by London itself, Basildon, Reading, Slough, Southampton and Walton and Weybridge. As in the previous section, Scotland and in particular the Glasgow MELA stands out as the only significant counter-magnet to the centripetal forces emanating from the core region.

The Influence of Public Policy on the Distribution of Office Activities

What impact have public policies had on shaping the distribution of office activities within the UK? As with regional industrial policy, office policies have taken the form of physical controls and more recently financial incentives designed to encourage the physical movement of office activities. Thus, the Industrial Development Certificate (IDC) has been paralleled by the Office Development Permit (ODP). The office controls first came into operation in 1965 but were not complemented by significant incentives to encourage office activity to relocate to peripheral areas until 1973. This was largely because the office problem was initially seen as essentially one of intra-rather than inter-regional

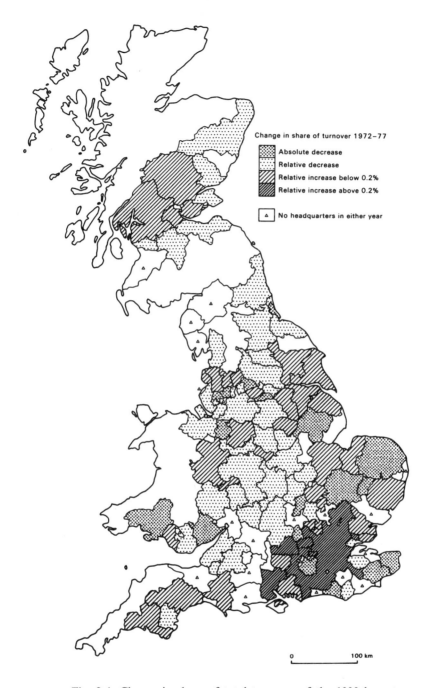

Change in share of turnover 1972–77

Absolute decrease
Relative decrease
Relative increase below 0.2%
Relative increase above 0.2%

△ No headquarters in either year

0   100 km

Fig. 2.4. Change in share of total turnover of the 1000 largest companies by Metropolitan Economic Labour Areas, 1972–77 (source: *Times 1000*)

distribution, with the primary objective being simply to move office activity away from central London.

Unlike the industrial aspects of regional policy, few attempts have been made to assess the effectiveness of these office policy instruments. However, some figures have been produced by the Department of Environment which suggest that the direct effects of the ODP system have been limited. Thus of all the 41 ODPs refused to named user applicants for 10,000 sq. ft or more of space in the Greater London Council area between 1965 and 1972, 11 firms remained in the same premises and 20 subsequently obtained on ODP at the same or another site in London. Only six of the applicants had in the event moved out of London, and all of these stayed within the South East Region (Department of the Environment, 1976).

Of course, one of the difficulties of the office control system is that unlike the industrial field most office space is built speculatively, with no particular occupier in mind. This is because most firms prefer to rent their office accommodation owing to uncertainties about their future demand for space. A system of controls operating on the provision of space can therefore only influence the occupiers of the vast majority of space indirectly through limiting the supply of accommodation and thereby affecting rental levels generally. However, it is extremely difficult to quantify the exact nature of this effect since so many other factors are at work influencing the general level of rents. In addition, there is also a considerable lag between the application of the control and when its effects are felt on the property market, during which time considerable changes in economic circumstances could have occurred.

Nevertheless, in spite of these limitations, the general consensus is that the existence of ODPs has been a significant factor *indirectly* contributing to increases in the price of office accommodation in London and thereby encouraging firms to relocate in search of lower-cost space. Most of this general movement has been confined to the South East, although within this region it has been spread about amongst a large number of locations. In addition, significant concentrations of dispersed offices can also be found just outside the South East control area (for example, Swindon in the South West Region). This latter fact illustrates another problem of an area-based control system in that places just beyond the control zone become highly attractive for office development. At the same time, major cities, such as Birmingham, in which a considerable amount of speculative office space has been built, have received few relocated commercial offices because prices there exceed those in smaller places nearer to London.

The effectiveness of office incentives is also difficult to judge since they only came into operation in 1973, by which time the UK was in the grip of a serious recession during which the incidence of both industrial and office mobility is likely to be low anyway. Thus, up until the 31st March 1977, only 7633 office jobs are estimated to have been moved to or created in the Assisted Areas as a result of the service industries incentive scheme. The average cost in 1976/77 was approximately £1240 per job, amounting to less than 1 per cent of the total regional aid in that year—or £3.2 million out of £600 million (Department of Industry, 1977). In contrast to the controls, incentives apply to office employers directly, be they in the manufacturing or service sectors; there are no incentives directly for the *provision* of a space, even though in some reception areas there may be significant shortages of appropriate office accommodation. The incentives take the form of a fixed grant for each employee moved with his work up to 50 per cent of the total number of jobs created, a grant to cover the whole cost of rental for up to seven years, and an additional grant per employee for each new job created. Although grants are availabe for firms starting up in the Assisted Areas, these must be for projects which have a genuine choice of location between Assisted and non-Assisted Areas. In other words, office activities serving local markets (e.g. business services to local industry) are not eligible for aid. This aspect of the policy has been criticized by the Northern Region Strategy Team on the grounds that the present shortfall of business services in the Region could be a considerable impediment to the efficient operation of indigenous industries—industries which may be serving national and international markets (Quince, 1977; Goddard, 1977b).

To what extent are existing controls and incentives of the right type and at the right level to fundamentally affect the future distribution of office activity in Britain? On strictly economic grounds, it has been demonstrated elsewhere that the pattern of office dispersal from London to places in the South East has been consistent with spatial variations in the operating costs of office activity (Goddard and Pye, 1977). The three critical items are office rentals, clerical wages and communication costs for executives involved in business travel. In comparison with central London, where most office employment is still concentrated, the savings on rents and wages level off after about 60 miles from the capital. Indeed, these savings fall off again as the large provincial conurbation with their higher wages and accommodation costs are reached. In contrast, communication costs continue to increase with distance, jumping particularly once day-return trips to London are no longer possible, thereby necessitating the additional cost of an overnight stay.

In order to compensate for these increased communication costs, it has been demonstrated that present incentives would have to be increased substantially to make moves to the Assisted Areas attractive. For example, for an office in which the average member of staff needed to travel to London 0.3 times each week and valuing travel time at £2.50 per hour, the incentive would have to be increased more than threefold to make Sheffield more preferable than Coventry (Goddard and Pye, 1977, p. 26).

The basic realities of the spatial organization of the UK economy, particularly the focus of the national passenger transport network on London, are such that any changes in these relative cost advantages are unlikely in the foreseeable future. It has been suggested that in future telecommunications technology might be able to substitute for some face-to-face meetings which currently involve business travel, thereby making peripheral locations more attractive for office development. However, preliminary results from research in progress suggest that far from acting as a force for decentralization, telecommunications could encourage centralization of higher-level decision-making functions. The results from the survey of business travel referred to earlier suggest that meetings held in the Northern Region and which involve people travelling from the South East are generally more routine in character and therefore more eligible for substitution than those attended by businessmen from the North who travel South (Marshall, 1978). The more ready availability of new telecommunications facilities for internal communications on the private wire network of large multisite organizations as compared with the public switched network is another factor potentially favouring centralization. At the same time, the local de-centralization of head offices of some of the largest organizations in the country from central London to places within the South East may have further disadvantaged firms based in the periphery; while a day-return trip to central London may have been feasible, the additional journey to places elsewhere in the South East may be impossible. Thus intra-regional decentralization may be favouring inter-regional centralization.

While geographical factors are clearly of major importance in accounting for the distribution of office activity within the UK space economy, organizational considerations are also at work which are tending to reinforce existing spatial patterns. The limited range of functions performed by branch plants in peripheral regions is not simply a reflection of geography; aspatial forces encouraging industrial concentration which have as their corollary a con-centration of headquarters functions in the South East Region are equally important. The current relatively crude controls and incentives applied to broad swathes of territory are unlikely to make significant impacts on the way in which large multisite enterprises distribute their office functions over geographical space. Although it may be desirable on social grounds for manufacturing activity to perform a wider range of office functions in branch plants in the Northern Region, for a large organization, with a number of plants operating throughout the UK, there could be considerable direct and indirect costs involved in splitting up central functions like accounting and marketing between several sites. On strictly economic grounds, branch plants only require office functions directly related to production.

Thus the opportunity for public policy to influence this situation is ex-tremely limited. One possibility is for more sophisticated forms of control on office development. Thus consideration has been given by the Department of the Environment to replacing the Office Development Permit system by something akin to the French Occupation Permit system which applies to users of office space in the controlled area. Under this system, any office user requires a permit to extend the total space he occupies in this controlled area beyond 1000 square metres. It is recognized that the chief advantage of such a control is that it will encourage 'earlier consideration of the possibility of moving to the Assisted Areas and in a manner which would bring organization and location considerations closer together' (Department of the Environment, 1976). However, even if such a system were applied it does not recognize the fact that considerable changes in organizational structure—which may affect the distribution of office functions over space more profoundly than the distribution of manufacturing—may frequently by recurring within the given stock of accommodation without any of the physical manifestations upon which the present types of control are principally based (Goddard, 1977b). Takeover and merger activity is only one form of such change. New organizational arrangements, for example the establishment of a divisional structure, may imply significant reallocation of office functions between different locations within the company.

If policy were to move more towards influencing the geographical distribution of functions within multisite enterprises, by whatever means, it is quite clear that the present spatial framework of Assisted Areas and non-Assisted Areas would be inappropriate. In particular, the present pattern of incentives and controls gives insufficient weight to the older provincial conurbations which have the necessary infrastructure to support office activity but which have recently been losing out to settlements lower down the urban hierarchy. In part these changes may be related to the organizational considerations already mentioned. But if office policy were to be restructured on the basis of a geography of enterprise approach, the national urban system could provide an appropriate spatial framework. However, such a restructuring of office policy would need to be set within the wider context of a fundamental overhaul of policies designed to influence the distribution of economic opportunities throughout the country (Manners, 1976). It is therefore of paramount importance that office policies are set within this wider context and not seen as a separate set of instruments designed to influence a form of economic activity unrelated to the operation of the rest of the UK space economy.

References

Bourne, L. S. (1975), *Urban Systems: Strategies for Regulation*. London: Oxford University Press.

Britton, J. N. H. (1974), Environmental adaption of individual plants: service linkages, locational environment and organisation, in F. E. I. Hamilton (Ed.), *Spatial Perspectives on Industrial Organization and Decision-Making*. London: Wiley, pp. 363–90.

Chisholm, M. I. (1976), Regional policies in an era of slow population growth and higher unemployment, *Regional Studies*, **10**, 201–14.

Crum, R., and Gudgin, G. (1977), *Non-Manufacturing Activities in U.K. Manufacturing Industry*. University of East Anglia: School of Social Studies (mimeo).

Department of the Environment (1976), *The Office Location Review*. London: Department of the Environment (mimeo).

Department of Industry (1977), *Annual Report, 1972 Industry Act*. London: HMSO.

Drewett, J. R., Goddard, J. B., and Spence, N. A. (1976), *British Cities: Urban*

Population & Employment Trends, 1951–71. London: Department of the Environment, Research Report No. 10.

East Midlands Economic Planning Council (1971), *Office Services in the East Midlands.* London: Department of the Environment (mimeo).

European Free Trade Association (1975), *National Settlement Strategies: a Framework for Regional Development.* Geneva: European Free Trade Association.

Goddard, J. B. (1975), Organisational information flows and the urban system, *Economie Appliquée,* **28,** 125–64.

Goddard, J. B. (1977a), Urban geography: city and regional systems, *Progress in Geography,* **1,** 296–301.

Goddard, J. B. (1977b), The pressures for a review of office policy, *Town and Country Planning,* **45,** 15–19.

Goddard, J. B., and Pye, R. (1977), Telecommunications and office location, *Regional Studies,* **11,** 19–30.

Keeble, D. (1977), Spatial policy in Britain: regional or urban, *Area,* **9,** 9–14.

Leigh, R., and North, R. (1977), The spatial consequences of takeovers in some British industries and their implications for regional development, in F. E. I. Hamilton (Ed.), *Contemporary Industrialisation—Problems for Spatial Analysis and Regional Policy.* London: Longman.

Manners, G. (1976), Regional policy rethink, *Town and Country Planning,* **44,** 208–14.

Marshall, N. (1977), *Business Travel and Regional Office Employment.* University of Newcastle-upon-Tyne: Centre for Urban and Regional Development Studies, Discussion Paper No. 8.

McDermott, P. (1977a), Overseas investment and the industrial geography of the United Kingdom, *Area,* **9,** 200–208.

McDermott, P. (1977b), Regional variations in enterprise: the electronics industry in Scotland, London and the Outer Metropolitan Area. Unpublished Ph.D. Thesis, University of Cambridge.

MacKay, R. R. (1977), *Important Trends in Regional Policy and Regional Employment.* University of Newcastle-upon-Tyne: Department of Economics, Discussion Paper No.21.

Moore, B. C., and Rhodes, J. (1976), A quantitative analysis of the effects of the regional employment premium and other regional policy inducements, in A. Whiting (Ed.), *The Economics of Industrial Subsidies.* London: HMSO.

Northern Region Strategy Team (1976), *Office Activity in the Northern Region.* Newcastle-upon-Tyne: Northern Region Strategy Team, Technical Report No. 8.

Northern Region Strategy Team (1977), *Strategic Plan for the Northern Region.* London: HMSO.

Pred, A. (1977), *City Systems in Advanced Economies.* London: Hutchinson.

Quince, R. (1977), A regional view of office policy, *Town and Country Planning,* **45,** 21–25.

Rabey, G. F. (1977), *Industrial Linkage and Communications Flow: An Organisational Communications Approach to the Geography of Enterprise.* University of Newcastle-upon-Tyne: Centre for Urban and Regional Development Studies, Discussion Paper No. 5.

Smith, I. J., and Goddard, J. B. (1978), Corporate control changes in the British urban system 1971–77 (forthcoming).

Thorngren, B. (1970), How do contact systems affect regional development? *Environment and Planning,* **2,** 409–27.

Törnqvist, G. (1970), *Contact Systems and Regional Development.* University of Lund: Lund Studies in Geography, Series B, No. 38.

Wärneryd, O. (1968), *Interdependence in Urban Systems.* Göteborg: Regionkonsult Aktiebolag.

3

National Trends in Office Construction, Employment and Headquarter Location in US Metropolitan Areas

REGINA B. ARMSTRONG

Introduction

Office work, or white-collar jobs performed in office buildings, represents the most rapidly growing economic activity in the United States, with significant impact on the physical structure of the nation's metropolitan areas. Because office jobs are eminently suited to city centres, they offer a chance to provide a new economic base for deteriorating central cities, to make them attractive to a mix of economic and ethnic groups, and to improve public transportation and urban finances. Office growth enables burgeoning suburbs to concentrate non-residential development in clusters that introduce urban form and amenity, require less land consumption, and create less auto-dependent urban regions. The centripetal forces of location that distinguish office activity from other urban economic activities have implications not merely for the future of commercial districts, but for the entire structuring of a more resource-conserving urban environment.

Yet despite its prime importance, the office sector has received relatively little analytical investigation in the American disciplines of urban economics or city and regional planning. The paucity of research in part reflects the dearth of quantitative information on office employment and floorspace in the voluminous statistics available from government agencies. We lack a national inventory of land use or an accounting of stock in non-residential structures, even though a comprehensive enumeration of residential buildings is taken with every decennial census. Moreover, compulsory employment-reporting by business establishments follows an industrial system of classification along major product lines,

61

whereas office work is performed by a cross-section of white-collar occupations in every industry group and is legally organized into firms, divisions, or departments of firms, but rarely detached establishments. The exception is, of course, central administrative offices (CAOs) or detached headquarter establishments, and for these reporting units a quinquennial economic census is taken.

For the researcher or policy analyst who requires an accurate assessment of office employment locally or for the nation as a whole, the data deficiencies are numerous, time-consuming to correct, and when available as estimates rarely consistent in measurement or definition between geographic areas. Neither standard series of employment reporting, those residence-based occupational reports or establishment-based industry reports, will provide a reliable estimate of office employment when used independently. At the local level, estimates should initially be constructed from the decennial metropolitan enumeration of detailed occupations by industries, and these household-based matrices must then be adjusted for a place of work definition by applying the skill coefficients to establishment-based industry employment. Though laborious, this procedure can explain such anomalies as central city mining employment, an office function, account for the office labour force in newspaper or book publishing, a manufacturing activity, and eliminate professional skills such as artist or teacher from services and government, which are typically white-collar industries.

At less than city scale, especially for the central business districts, data deficiencies and errors tend to increase. For one, the skill composition of industry varies with employment density of the work site, and some adjustment of the intra-industry occupational matrix, towards more white-collar participation at higher densities, is in order. Then again, small area industry employment at work site is generally not available from standard sources with the exception of the journey to work reporting of the decennial census, or by accessing private data sources that provide partial industry estimates of employment on a firm basis. In several instances, localities have assisted state employment services in disaggregating citywide data to mail code delivery areas, although the industry grain of this information can be sharply curtailed by disclosure regulations.

Once the size, skill, and industry composition of office employment is known, much information pertaining to the function, costs, and inter-industry linkages of office work is required for more than a cursory analysis of the employment impact of this activity. A functional stratification of office work would consider the headquarter role separately because its export orientation towards regional, national, or international markets has far larger multiplier implications for the economy than purely residentiary office functions or detached, labour-intensive back offices and business support services to major corporations. This chapter analyses trends in headquarter location from the only government source of data, the enterprise statistics of the quinquennial economic census. In scope, the source is limited to reporting characteristics of detached central administrative offices and auxiliaries of multi-establishment firms in mining, construction, manufacturing, trade, and selected service industries. Published data are minimal at the metropolitan and county scale, while special tabulations are both costly and edited of much industry detail to avoid disclosure of identifiable operations on a small area basis. Excluded from coverage are headquarter offices in transportation, communications, utilities, finance, insurance, real estate, securities, trusts, and non-profit service industries, a deficiency which can be rectified only by accessing business directories and reports to regulatory agencies. Often, major government offices and large single establishment firms of covered industries, such as law firms, function in a headquarter manner; these omissions require further research and judgment on the part of the analyst. As tedious and somewhat subjective is the task of compiling a functional stratification of office employment, the undertaking is necessary for analysing inter- and intra-urban patterns of spatial preference, for assessing exogenous impacts on the economy from headquarter relocations, and for policy targeting of critical activities which may respond to locational incentives.

Still more elusive than an employment profile of office work are data pertaining to the income and output, or the costs of performing the business of offices, and to the inter-industry ties upon which offices are dependent. By convention, central office employment reported by the economic census is not assigned a value added measurement and, as is true also of government, productivity is assumed equal to labour payments. Much more research is called for on the issue of office production, and this research could be accomplished through the well-formulated procedures of income and product accounting. Similarly, the principles of input–output accounting may prove to be a useful technique in measuring inter-industry dependencies of office activities, or what is more commonly referred to as the centripetal force of face-to-face communication in office locational decisions. Both undertakings would require access to the income statements filed by major corporations and supplementary survey or diary methods for assigning purchases to the headquarter establishment.

Lastly, relatively little is known in the United States about the volume and location of detached office space, although government data sources provide annual statistics for investment in office buildings and private sources compile the square footage of new and altered construction on a local area basis. Estimates of office stock in the largest central business districts can be purchased from a private mapping concern, based upon building dimensions recorded by field surveyors, and a trade association of office building owners and managers regularly monitors changes in the stock, rental value, and operating costs of its sample owners. Local measurements taken under urban or regional land-use planning and municipal building permit auspices vary greatly in quality, geographic coverage, and definition, as this chapter will later show. But the bulk of decentralized office stock, constructed over the past few decades along highway strips, in suburban subcentres, or isolated campus locations, falls largely outside the geographic coverage provided by this loose-knit network of sources. A national system of asset or stock accounts, tied to the local area reporting of the economic census, would correct many of these deficiencies and could be undertaken with the low marginal costs of expanding the comprehensive mail-back survey of firms by the addition of several questions pertaining to occupied space and the nature of capital investment. For those industries not covered by the census, similar information ought to be required by the regulatory agencies to which most remaining firms submit annual income and asset statements.

The data on office activity presented in this chapter are derived essentially from three sources: (1) the best available public and private documentation on trends in office construction, selected office employment, and establishments; (2) the author's estimates based on detailed industry–occupation matrices, occupancy rates, unpublished information, and a prior publication (Armstrong, 1972); and (3) a survey of the 100 largest city planning agencies in the nation, conducted expressly for the purposes of this study in 1976. The analysis begins with a brief perspective on national trends, followed by a discussion of regional shares and the relationship with scale. It subsequently examines major metropolitan levels of office employment and growth, changes in the pattern of headquarter location, office construction, and floorspace stock in central business districts.

The National Perspective

In a quarter century of rapid economic growth, during which total employment increased by half as much again, virtually all of the expansion in the American economy was attributable to increase in white-collar and service workers, and to growth in the tertiary industries of trade, finance, services, transportation, and government. To be sure, farm and manufacturing output rose in real terms, at annual average rates of 5.9 and 3.0 per cent respectively, but capitalization and technological innovations enabled production gains to take place within a relatively stable workforce. Owing in part to the recent deep recessions, full-time employment in the extractive and goods-producing industries has now returned to the level of 26 million jobholders recorded in 1950 (Table 3.1).

Tertiary activities, which are service-performing and thus more labour-intensive and income-responsive by nature, surged ahead during this period—from 30.4 million to 57.1 million employed, and from 54 to 69 per cent of the nation's workforce by 1975. Translated into manpower requirements by occupation, these structural shifts in the economy fuelled an accelerating demand for white-collar and service skills (Table 3.2). Over the 25-year period, seven in every 10 new labour force participants offered white-collar skills, and nearly one in five were in service occupations.

Before 1980, white-collar work will account for more than half of all job

Table 3.1. United States Workforce by Industry Characteristics, 1950–1975

Industry	1950	1960	1970	1975
		Millions		
Tertiary (trade, finance, services, transportation, government)	30.4	38.3	50.9	57.1
Secondary (manufacturing, construction)	18.1	21.3	23.1	22.6
Primary (agriculture, forestry mining)	7.9	5.0	3.3	3.4
Total	56.4	64.6	77.3	83.1
Tertiary as per cent of total employment	54	59	66	69

Source. US Bureau of the Census.

Table 3.2. United States Labour Force by Occupational Characteristics, 1950–1975

Occupation group	1950	1960	1970	1975
		Millions		
White-collar (professional, managerial, clerical, sales)	21.6	28.7	38.3	44.0
Blue-collar (craftsmen, operatives, labourers)	24.3	25.6	29.5	32.0
Service (household, other)	6.2	8.3	10.4	12.4
Farm	6.9	5.4	2.4	2.2
Total	59.0	68.0	80.6	90.6
White-collar as per cent of total labour force	37	42	48	49

Source. US Bureau of the Census.

opportunities. As Table 3.3 shows, total employment in white-collar activities, including part-time employed, numbered 42.6 million in 1975. Of these, 24 million jobs or 28 per cent of the total were in office work. Clerical positions dominated the office sector, with support-staff clerical and sales jobs outnumber-

Table 3.3. Employment in White-Collar Occupations and Office Work in the Nation, 1950, 1960, 1970, 1975

| Year | White-collar occupations (millions) | | | | |
	Prof.	Mgrl.	Cler.	Sales	Total
1950	4867	6646	7292	3775	22,580
1960	7280	7140	9655	4386	28,461
1970	11,287	8002	13,791	4982	38,062
1975	13,032	8386	15,384	5756	42,558
	Office workers (millions)				
	Prof.	Mgrl.	Cler.	Sales	Total
1950	1563	1863	6657	988	11,071
1960	2293	2574	8965	1333	15,165
1970	3781	3281	12,757	1605	21,424
1975	4457	3682	14,230	1920	24,289
	Distribution of office occupations				
	Prof.	Mgrl.	Cler.	Sales	Total
	%	%	%	%	%
1950	14.1	16.8	60.1	8.9	100.0
1960	15.1	17.0	59.1	8.8	100.0
1970	17.6	15.3	59.5	7.5	100.0
1975	18.3	15.2	58.6	7.9	100.0

Detail in percentages may not add to totals because of rounding.
Source. US Bureau of the Census and Bureau of Labor Statistics.

ing professionals and managers by roughly two to one. Despite the infusion of capital into office activity—notably, the proliferation of electronic computers, calculators, photocopiers, and the introduction of telecommunication transmission—the demand for office skills has not yet undergone radical change. Some slackening is evident in the overall rate of growth, from 3.5 per cent annually in the 1960s to 2.5 per cent in the 1970s, accompanied by a gradual shift in the relative composition that masks skill upgrading or replacement of more detailed occupations. The emergence of computer specialists and programmers among professionals, growing from 1.2 to 2.55 million employed over the past decade, accounts for one of the more dramatic changes.

From an urban planning perspective, capital investment in office structures has had a more visible and immediate impact on the office sector than the infusion of new technology and equipment. Most office work is performed in detached office buildings, although nearly half of the 24 million office jobs may be located in factory, retail, institutional and other facilities. Nationally, the true level and growth of office employment in public and private office buildings is unknown, though some informed estimates can be made. Table 3.4 portrays

Table 3.4. Office Building Employment, Floorspace, and Construction in the Nation, 1957–1976

	Office bldg. employment (millions)	Gross square feet (millions)	
		Floorspace	Construction
1957		1850	76
1958			71
1959			71
1960		2000	76
1961			76
1962			89
1963		2200	104
1964	8.76		95
1965			108
1966			109
1967		2600	121
1968			153
1969			192
1970	11.25	3000	171
1971			172
1972			188
1973			195
1974			159
1975	12.90	3700	107
1976			108

Office building floorspace is total stock of public and private detached office buildings in gross dimensions, including vacant and non-rentable space. Construction includes additions, alterations, and conversions in private buildings as well as new construction by year of start.
Sources. Author's estimates for employment and floorspace (including those previously published in Armstrong, 1972) and F. W. Dodge Company for construction.

these and other estimates of the free-standing stock of gross office floorspace in the nation, along with the actual volume of new construction recorded in office and bank buildings over a 20-year period. Table 3.5 compares office construction to residential and non-residential totals by valuation and number of structures at the height of the office building boom.

About 3.7 billion gross sq. ft of detached office building floorspace exists in the United States, accommodating roughly 13 million office jobs or 15 per cent of total employment in 1975. Both the demand for new employment and space were a dominant feature of the past decade, the imprint of which altered many urban skylines, transformed farmlands and increased commutation flows within major metropolitan areas. Nearly 2.5 billion gross sq. ft of private office space were newly constructed, altered, or converted between 1957 and 1976. This level was equivalent to the entire stock of public and private floorspace available in the mid-sixties which had taken over a half century to accumulate.

The actual building boom, spanning 12 years from 1963 to 1974, put in place

Table 3.5. Office Construction as a Share of Total Private Construction in the Nation, 1966–1976*

	Office buildings	Total non-resid. buildings	New housing units
	$	$	$
1966	1758†	9984	13,081
1967	1755	9886	15,004
1968	2465	11,395	18,319
1969	2847	13,061	18,623
1970	2806	12,503	19,169
1971	3718	14,108	28,306
1972	3758	16,201	35,857
1973	4058	19,604	33,669
1974	3872	19,242	23,479
1975	2965	14,985	23,855
1976	2917	17,152	34,832

	Office buildings	Number of structures Total non-resid. buildings	Apartment buildings
1966	10,536	136,075	18,721
1967	10,256	133,628	23,330
1968	10,348	142,343	30,431
1969	11,030	148,536	36,478
1970	10,135	150,557	35,016
1971	12,642	153,382	51,197
1972	16,264	183,091	59,170
1973	17,495	199,225	46,008
1974	15,537	193,652	21,027
1975	13,242	183,300	13,158
1976	14,971	215,530	19,959

*Based on reports from 13,000 permit-issuing places until 1972, on 14,000 places from 1972 to 1976.
†Valuation in current million dollars.
Source. US Bureau of the Census.

an average 147 million sq. ft per year for private, largely speculative purposes. Under average occupancy conditions, this addition would be sufficient to accommodate 6 million office jobs; in fact, about 4 million more jobs, or half as many again, were created between 1964 and 1975. At the peak of the boom, office activity accounted for 22 per cent of total non-residential building by valuation, with the investment of an average $3.4 billion in 13,350 new structures annually between 1968 and 1974. Moreover, the volume of office construction during the boom diverted some capital from the housing market, contributing to a growing shortage in new residential space. New apartment structures outnumbered offices by only three to one, and expenditures for office buildings averaged over 13 per cent of all single and multi-family housing investment.

Towards the end of the office building boom, vacancy rates of over 10 per cent were not uncommon in the nation, as a result of the overbuilding from projects in the pipeline when back-to-back recessions brought white-collar layoffs and reluctance on the part of firms to expand quarters or to relocate. In Boston, it is estimated that nearly half of the new stock is still vacant, while in Atlanta, a quarter remains unoccupied.[1] And in New York, about 30 million gross sq. ft of office space are available, an amount sufficient to accommodate demand for at least the remainder of the decade.[2] Since 1974, few new office buildings have been built in the city centres, construction has declined nationwide to the mid-sixties rate, and scattered evidence from realty surveys indicates pockets of shortage which may worsen in the coming years. In two decades, the nation doubled its stock of public and private detached office space. At least that amount of net addition can be expected over the remainder of the century, but economic conditions will probably not converge to support a resurgence in building until the 1980s.

Trends in Major Regions of the Nation

Population growth has slowed considerably in the United States since 1970. Resettlement of inhabitants has, however, accelerated. As Table 3.6 shows, the nine states of the Northeast which housed one-quarter of the nation's population in 1960 have experienced virtually no population gain, a net migration loss from the export of residents to the South and West, and a marginal decline in total employment since 1970. Until recently, this region contained the major

Table 3.6. The Distribution of Selected Activities in Major Regions of the Nation, 1960–1975

	North-east	North Central	South	West	Nation
Resident population (millions)					
1960	44.8	51.7	55.2	28.3	180.0
1970	49.1	56.7	63.0	35.0	203.8
1975	49.3	57.7	68.3	37.8	213.1
% anl ave chge					
as % of nation	0.6	0.7	1.4	2.0	1.1
1960	24.9	28.7	30.7	15.7	100.0
1975	23.1	27.1	32.1	17.7	100.0
Net migration (millions)					
1960–70	0.4	− 0.7	0.7	2.8	3.2
1970–75	− 0.9	− 0.9	2.8	1.5	2.5
% anl ave rate*	− 0.7	− 2.0	3.8	8.7	1.9
As % of nation	− 8.7	− 28.1	61.0	75.8	100.0

Table 3.6. (*Contd.*)

	North-east	North Central	South	West	Nation
Total employment (millions)					
1960	18.1	19.7	19.3	10.4	67.5
1970	20.8	23.4	24.8	13.8	82.8
1975	20.6	24.2	28.0	15.9	88.7
% anl ave chge	0.9	1.4	2.5	2.9	1.8
As % of nation					
1960	26.8	29.2	28.6	15.4	100.0
1975	23.2	27.3	31.6	17.9	100.0
Tertiary employment (millions)					
1960	11.1	11.5	11.9	6.9	41.4
1970	13.8	14.7	16.2	10.0	54.7
1975	14.5	15.8	19.1	11.8	61.2
% anl ave chge	1.8	2.1	3.2	3.6	2.6
As % of nation					
1960	26.8	27.8	28.7	16.7	100.0
1975	23.7	25.8	31.2	19.3	100.0
White-collar occupations† (millions)					
1960	7.5	7.5	7.0	4.6	26.6
1970	9.9	9.9	10.4	6.8	37.0
% anl ave chge	2.8	2.8	4.0	4.0	3.3
As % of nation					
1960	28.1	28.3	26.4	17.2	100.0
1970	26.8	26.9	28.0	18.3	100.0
Production Employment (millions)					
1963	3.89	3.95	3.00	1.39	12.23
1967	4.16	4.58	3.61	1.60	13.95
1972	3.58	4.33	4.00	1.62	13.53
% anl ave chge	−0.5	0.6	1.9	1.0	0.7
As % of nation					
1963	31.8	32.3	24.5	11.4	100.0
1972	26.4	32.0	29.6	12.0	100.0
CAO & A employment ‡ (millions)					
1963	0.45	0.41	0.22	0.13	1.21
1967	0.51	0.47	0.27	0.15	1.40
1972	0.60	0.57	0.39	0.21	1.77
% anl ave chge	3.1	3.7	6.4	6.0	4.3
As % of nation					
1963	37.5	33.8	18.3	10.4	100.0
1972	33.9	32.1	22.0	12.0	100.0

* Net migration rate represents annual average net flow per thousand mid-period population.
† White-collar occupations represent employed persons and differ from those reported in Table 3.2 by the volume of white-collar unemployed.
‡ CAO & A employment is comprised mainly of detached headquarter office employees in manufacturing and selected non-manufacturing industries.
Sources. US Bureau of the Census, National Planning Association.

concentration of office building activity, anchored by the headquarter and financial capital of the nation in New York. Since the early 'sixties, the detached headquarter element, represented in Table 3.6 by central administrative and auxiliary (CAO & A) employment, has grown less rapidly here than elsewhere in the nation. Only 11 per cent of the rise in tertiary employment nationwide, over the 1970 level, has been captured by the Northeast, while an offsetting amount of production employment has been lost because of disinvestment in goods-producing facilities. The out-movement of manufacturing is of serious consequence to the headquarter role of the region, for some firms, now sufficiently large to internalize many support services that concentrate here, follow their production facilities or find less reason for remaining in the Northeast as they expand in other markets of the nation.

The 12 North Central, or midwestern, states have been net losers of population from out-migration over a longer span of time. On average, two per thousand residents have annually resettled from the manufacturing centres and rural areas of this region since 1960. Yet unlike the Northeast, population and employment continue to increase, albeit at a decelerating pace. For one thing, the population base is replenished by higher rates of fertility, and a much less rapid erosion has taken place in the region's disproportionately large production base. Because of ties to this manufacturing concentration, the North Central states, with the major metropolitan areas of Chicago and Detroit, have traditionally housed the second largest share of detached central office employment. Firms headquartered here often have New York offices, but the ties to production facilities appear stronger. Residents of the Midwest have fewer white-collar skills *per capita*, yet the rates of increase in the region's tertiary and headquarter activity exceed those of the Northeast. Although both areas declined relatively in their share of the nation's office employment indicators since the early 'sixties, the spread between them has narrowed to the advantage of the North Central region.

The resettlement of population, the migration of firms, and the flow of capital investment, including public expenditures, have been directed to the South and West, with the South gaining in the most recent period. Long the most populous region in the nation, the South's economic resurgence was built initially on the attraction of goods production facilities. Over three-quarters of the increase in production employment nationwide was located in the South between 1963 and 1972. Lower factor costs, such as cheaper labour, less unionization, fewer taxes, more plentiful and less costly energy sources, were a prime incentive for firms to move. The South also benefited from heavy public investment in the aerospace industries and the spin-off of related research and development activity. Since 1970, a massive influx of population, amounting to nearly three million net in-migrants, has stimulated the expansion and diversification of a residence-based service economy. Much room for growth remains for, overall, a less than proportionate share of tertiary employment than population has been added to the South in the 1960 to 1975 period. The region now provides the largest share of

Table 3.7 Regional Shares of Office Building Construction* by Valuation in the Nation, 1966–1976

Year	Northeast		North Central		South		West	
	Office	Non-resid.	Office	Non-resid.	Office	Non-resid.	Office	Non-resid.
	$	$	$	$	$	$	$	$
1966	338.8†	1835.2	427.6	2280.4	444.8	2238.4	419.3	1891.9
1967	415.4	1789.3	341.3	2286.1	436.4	2477.4	417.5	1827.3
1968	828.2	2397.1	474.0	2564.2	554.0	2973.8	426.4	1965.5
1969	672.8	2447.1	688.9	2886.2	602.6	3128.6	565.8	2365.2
1970	577.3	2456.9	469.3	2353.2	806.2	3301.9	627.6	2329.8
1971	515.5	2177.6	854.8	2928.8	1108.4	3790.3	952.9	2822.2
1972	529.5	2151.6	689.3	3174.7	1276.4	4863.2	857.2	2896.7
1973	524.4	2506.7	632.3	3732.7	1433.1	6260.2	926.3	3564.1
1974	428.3	2781.2	738.8	3871.1	1285.4	5312.7	808.1	3426.3
1975	357.3	1720.9	629.4	3047.4	767.2	3759.4	826.1	3196.2
1976	211.1	1779.6	563.8	3511.6	956.2	4396.6	831.3	3528.5
Period total	5398.6	24,043.2	6509.5	32,636.4	9670.7	42,502.6	7658.5	29,813.7
As % of non-resid.	22.5	100.0	19.9	100.0	22.8	100.0	25.7	100.0
As % of nation	18.5	18.6	22.3	25.3	33.0	33.0	26.2	23.1

*Based on all authorized construction in 3014 permit-issuing places; the sum of regions will therefore differ from nation totals in Table 3.5.
†Valuation in current million dollars.
Source. US Bureau of the Census.

white-collar skills in the nation. Headquarter employment, which was least represented here, has grown more rapidly than elsewhere, particularly in the most recent five-year period. The development of headquarter-based office economies in Atlanta, Dallas, and Houston, and the enormous growth of government employment in Washington DC, attest to the dominant role emerging for the South in the nation's distribution of office activity.

In contrast to the South, the West has been more oriented towards white-collar and away from primary or secondary activity over the long history of its settlement, largely for reasons of topography and accessibility. It remains the fastest growing region in employment and working-age population, although its lead in total residents and migration has now been overtaken. Tertiary functions provide about three-fourths of all job opportunities; production activity less than one-tenth. With further growth in the economy, inevitable with the West's continued attraction to resettlers, this region will soon overtake the Northeast in the level of tertiary and white-collar activity. The composition of the office sector, however, should remain more broadly based, with fewer of the elite industrial headquarter functions that retain spatial linkages to production facilities or to national and international centres of finance and corporate or public decision-making. San Francisco offers a higher density of opportunity for interaction between firms or with capital markets, and contains the largest concentration of CAO & A activity in total employment. Denver, which provides amenity and a quality labour force, competes statistically in relative share, but the greatest number of office job opportunities are available in the massive Los Angeles–Anaheim area.

Further evidence of the shifting pattern of office location nationwide is provided by construction data in Table 3.7 for the 1966 to 1976 period. It shows that the volume of office and non-residential building, measured by construction valuation, has been heaviest in the South, highest on *per capita* terms in the West, and least overall in the Northeast. During the last 10 years, nearly $10 billion in office construction was invested in the South, or fully one-third of the national total. About one in every four dollars expended on non-residential building in the West, or $7.7 billion, was for private office structures. The Northeast put in place $5.4 billion, or merely half of the office investment occurring in the West in *per capita* measures. Although more oriented towards office development than the North Central states, the Northeast was nonetheless outpaced by this region in total and *per capita* expenditures on private office construction.

A Shifting Relationship to Scale

Behind the regional shifts in the distribution of office employment and floorspace is a pattern of location that relates to scale, and which is in itself undergoing some structural change. Nearly three-fourths of the population in the United States, or 147 million people, is concentrated within 265 standard metropolitan statistical areas (SMSAs) which encompass 12 per cent of the nation's land. SMSAs are comprised of counties, or towns in New England, with at least one central city of 50,000 or more residents and any contiguous counties (towns in New England) that are socially or economically integrated with the central city. For 50 years, metropolitan settlements have accommodated virtually all the increase in the nation's population. Over half of the rural residents now live in ex-urban counties which border SMSAs or fill the interstices of multimetropolitan urban regions, such as the Boston-to-Washington corridor. This population overspill is but the third wave of a pattern of migration which relates to scale. The rural to urban concentration has ended, leaving only 10 million farm population. The urban to suburban decentralization continues to dominate resettlement, with virtually all growth occurring in SMSAs outside central cities between 1950 and 1970. The dispersion of population into ex-urban areas, which are growing faster than SMSAs since 1970, will further change the shape of metropolitan development across the nation by causing most SMSAs to coalesce into several dozen belts of low-density urban regions.

The pattern of employment location tends to be more concentrated with scale than the spreading population. As the data in Table 3.8 show for 134 of the 265 SMSAs, 67 per cent of the nation's employment is housed in the largest metropolitan areas, in contrast to 64 per cent of resident population. Per hundred persons, SMSAs over 250,000 population offer 43 jobs, smaller urban and rural areas provide 37, and the nation as a whole averages 41 jobs per hundred population. The major difference is due, of course, to net in-commutation, rather than to variation in labour force participation. By sector, the availability of job opportunities varies. Manufacturing is located more evenly with respect to population, the largest SMSAs providing 10 jobs per hundred in contrast to 9 per hundred population elsewhere in the nation. Factory-site production, which accounts for roughly 70 per cent of manufacturing employment, exhibits a virtually one-to-one relationship. Tertiary activity intensifies with scale: the largest SMSAs offer 30 white-collar opportunities per hundred residents while the rest of the nation provides 22. And clustering is most apparent in the distribution of central administrative office employment. Nearly 90 per cent of all detached headquarter jobs are situated in metropolitan areas over 250,000 population, with 1.2 front office jobs per hundred as opposed to 0.3 per hundred in smaller urban or rural areas of the nation.

Within the large metropolitan class, SMSAs can be stratified into four size ranges that magnify the central location tendency of office-type employment. The nine foremost SMSAs, those over 2.5 million inhabitants accounting for 22 per cent of the nation's population, retain 27 per cent of tertiary employment and 39 per cent of headquarter activity. The next largest, or 25 SMSAs in the 1.0 to 2.5 million range, contain 19 per cent of population, 20 per cent of employment, 21 per cent of tertiary jobs and 28 per cent of headquarter activity. As scale of metropolitan area is reduced to the half million and quarter million base, the

Table 3.8. The Distribution of Selected Activities by Metropolitan Size Range in the Nation, 1960–1972

	Metropolitan area population size (millions)					Rest of nation	Nation
	2.5 +	1.0–2.5	0.5–1.0	0.25–0.50	Total		
Number of SMSAs	9	25	35	65	134	131 & rural	265 & rural
Population (000's)							
1960	39,636	31,673	20,738	18,782	110,829	69,150	179,979
1970	44,794	38,702	24,314	21,948	129,758	74,052	203,810
% anl ave chge	1.2	2.0	1.6	1.6	1.6	0.7	1.3
As % of nation							
1960	22.0	17.6	11.5	10.5	61.6	38.4	100.0
1970	22.0	19.0	11.9	10.8	63.7	36.3	100.0
Net migration (000's)							
1960–70	812	3050	943	687	5,492	−2286	3206
% anl ave rate	1.9	8.7	4.2	3.4	4.6	− 3.2	1.7
As % of nation	25.3	95.1	29.4	21.4	171.3	−71.3	100.0
Total employment (000's)							
1970	20,282	16,306	10,023	8854	55,465	27,336	82,801
As % of nation	24.5	19.7	12.1	10.7	67.0	33.0	100.0
Per 100 population	45	42	41	40	43	37	41
Manufacturing employment (000's)							
1970	4585	3855	2626	2166	13,232	6509	19,741
As % of nation	23.2	19.5	13.3	11.0	67.0	33.0	100.0
As % of employment	22.6	23.6	26.2	24.5	23.8	23.8	23.8
Per 100 population	10	10	11	10	10	9	10
Tertiary employment (000's)							
1970	14,670	11,274	6636	5857	38,437	16,289	54,726
As % of nation	26.8	20.6	12.1	10.7	70.2	29.8	100.0
As % of employment	72.3	69.1	66.2	66.2	69.3	59.6	66.1
Per 100 population	33	29	27	27	30	22	27

Table 3.8. (Contd.)

	Metropolitan area population size (millions)					Rest of nation	Nation
	2.5 +	1.0–2.5	0.5–1.0	0.25–0.50	Total		
Production workers (000's)							
1963	2900	2173	1517	1304	7894	4340	12,234
1972	2824	2403	1798	1502	8527	5001	13,528
As % of nation							
1963	23.7	17.8	12.4	10.7	64.5	35.5	100.0
1972	20.9	17.7	13.3	11.1	63.0	37.0	100.0
Per 100 population	6.3	6.2	7.4	6.8	6.6	6.8	6.6
CAO & A employment (000's)							
1963	528	299	139	103	1069	144	1213
1972	695	502	240	136	1573	198	1771
As % of nation							
1963	43.5	24.6	11.5	8.5	88.1	11.9	100.0
1972	39.2	28.3	13.6	7.7	88.8	11.2	100.0
Per 100 population	1.6	1.3	1.0	0.6	1.2	0.3	0.9
Value of construction*							
1972 *per capita*							
Office	$21	$25	$37				$18
Non-residential	$68	$100	$127				$78
Office as % of non-residential	30.9	25.3	29.0	N.A.	N.A.	N.A.	23.2

*Derived from information for selected metropolitan areas within each size range. Comprehensive valuation data by SMSA are not available.
Source. Based on US Bureau of the Census for population, migration, and ranking; and on US Bureau of the Census and National Planning Association for employment and construction.

share of tertiary employment to population is normalized, while headquarter activity becomes disproportionately low. Thus surplus office employment, or the agglomeration of headquarter and other office jobs in disordinate shares that signal an export function, truly characterizes only the million-plus metropolitan areas at present.

Over the past decade, a significant number of locational decisions were made by central administrative offices. CAO & A jobs increased by nearly half as many again nationwide between 1963 and 1972, and a rash of detached headquarters relocated within and between metropolitan areas. Their production facilities continued to gravitate outwards from big cities to suburbs and smaller metropolitan areas. The data in Table 3.8, which show net changes and shifts in shares for the most recent period, indicate that the multimillion SMSAs acquired 66 per cent of the total increase in central office jobs but the nine foremost areas declined relatively in share, from 44 to 39 per cent of nationwide headquarter employment. Over half of the gain was captured by the second largest million-plus range, while below one million population, SMSAs above 500,000 also increased in relative share. Growth in the rest of the nation, amidst smaller metropolitan and rural areas, was weak which intensified the concentration of major office functions in areas over the half million population scale.

Central office expansion and locational decisions since the early 'sixties have thus reflected the pattern of population resettlement by size of metropolitan area. Most migrants to or between urban areas now select residence in the 1.0–2.5 million size range, followed by the 0.5–1.0 million SMSAs. The nine multimillion metropolitan areas rank third in preference and, though twice as populated as 65 in the 0.25–0.50 million scale, they retain only a modest edge in attracting new residents. This trend, which is another reflection of the spread of development into continuous bands of low-density settlement, has significance for the future location of office activity. Most urban region corridors are comprised of several commuter sheds. Working-age resettlers tend to be youthful, educated, relatively affluent, and skilled in white-collar occupations. As smaller metropolitan areas grow in the shadow of major metropolitan centres and the interstices between SMSAs are settled by white-collar workers, the density of the available labour force at decentralized locations increases while the tolerance for lengthened work trips declines. In the New York Urban Region, which encompasses the New York–NE New Jersey SCA and nine other SMSAs midway on the Boston-to-Washington corridor, many more corporations relocated to the smaller regional metropolitan areas and outlying suburbs than moved to other parts of the nation.

Office-type Employment in Selected Metropolitan Areas

The nation's major metropolitan areas achieved population growth from some initial economic specialization, but once scale is attained, the degree of office orientation is determined more by the nature of this specialization. Thus the disproportionate share of office activity found to characterize the million-plus size range is borne out in some, but not all, of the respective SMSAs. Indeed, the recent employment shifts away from the very largest SMSAs towards the million size range tend to reinforce this relationship with economic base. Traditional production areas such as Philadelphia, Detroit, Pittsburgh, St Louis and Cleveland, all in excess of two million population, have fared less well in the growth of office-type employment over the past decade. The largest office centres—New York, Los Angeles, San Francisco, Washington, and Boston—essentially retained their rank as areas of export office activity, while regional centres or large trading nodes, such as Atlanta, Kansas City, or Denver, rose to office centres stature.

Table 3.9 provides population and office-type employment data for 20 of the 34 SMSAs over one million population. Those excluded had less than proportional shares of office-type activity to population, while several included also fell below the norm but displayed above average shares of headquarter activity.[3] The data show that the selected metropolitan areas engaged 17.6 office-type jobs per hundred residents in 1970, while elsewhere in the nation 14.5 office jobs serviced a population of one hundred. Assuming that the average for areas outside the largest SMSAs basically reflects local office demands which must be satisfied at a nearby location, then 18 per cent of the respective areas' employment is surplus office activity, or functions for export beyond the limits of any one metropolitan area. Those areas of strongest export orientation, by rank order of descent, are: Washington, Boston, Atlanta, New York SCA, Minn.–St Paul, Dallas, Denver, San Francisco, Los Angeles, and Kansas City. SMSAs with less than average surplus office activity follow by rank: Chicago SCA, Houston, Cleveland, St Louis, Philadelphia, Cincinnati, Detroit, and Pittsburgh. Considering recent growth in addition to the relative strength of the office sector, the data suggest that the areas most specialized in office-type economies in the nation are, by descending size: New York SCA, Los Angeles, Washington, San Francisco, Boston, Dallas, and Atlanta.

A shift in the relative share of surplus office employment for any metropolitan area reflects the fact that export activity is linked to national requirements, and alternative metropolitan areas actively compete for or are available as locations for this activity. The major identifiable component of export office employment is CAO & A activity—the detached headquarters of multi-establishment enterprises (mainly corporations) in mining, construction, manufacturing, trade, and selected services. Table 3.10 summarizes this pattern of location by selected SMSAs over an 18-year period. Major financial, business or non-profit services, and federal government functions are important elements of the national market excluded from this data source. They display even more compact patterns of location that favour the largest office centres; particularly in places such as Washington and New York, the omission of these national office functions from

Table 3.9. Population, Office-Type Employment, and Estimates of 'Surplus' Office Activity in Selected Metropolitan Areas with Populations over One Million, 1960 and 1970

	Population		Office-type employment		Derived surplus employment per 100 population		
	1960	1970	1960	1970	1960	1970	% surplus
United States	179,323.2	203,211.9	21,948.8	31,465.1	12.2	15.5	0
New York–NE N.J. SCA	14,759.4	16,178.7	2391.6	3237.1	16.2	20.0	Over 25
New York SMSA	10,694.6	11,571.9	1884.2	2165.4	17.6	18.7	15–25
Nassau–Suffolk SMSA	×		×		×	×	×
Newark SMSA	1689.4	1856.6	254.7	325.5	15.1	17.5	15–25
Chicago–NW Ind. SCA	6794.5	7612.3	999.6	1212.2	14.7	15.9	5–15
Chicago SMSA	6220.9	6978.9	942.3	1146.4	15.1	16.4	5–15
Los Angeles SMSA	6742.7	7032.1	1050.8	1236.8	15.6	17.6	15–25
Philadelphia SMSA	4342.9	4817.9	519.5	690.2	13.3	14.3	Under 5
Detroit SMSA	3762.4	4199.9	454.3	564.7	12.1	13.4	Under 5
San Francisco SMSA	2783.4	3109.5	452.2	576.9	16.2	18.6	15–25
Washington SMSA	2001.9	2861.1	408.7	654.5	20.4	22.9	Over 25
Boston SMSA	2589.3	2753.7	430.4	572.0	16.6	20.8	Over 25
Pittsburgh SMSA	2405.4	2401.2	282.2	319.1	11.7	13.3	Under 5
St Louis SMSA	2060.1	2363.0	270.2	361.4	13.1	15.3	5–15
Cleveland SMSA	1796.6	2064.2	255.8	318.8	14.2	15.4	5–15
Houston SMSA	1243.2	1985.0	176.7	313.8	14.2	15.8	5–15
Minn.–St Paul SMSA	1482.0	1813.6	241.5	348.4	16.3	19.2	15–25
Dallas SMSA	1083.6	1556.0	181.0	295.2	16.7	19.0	15–25
Atlanta SMSA	1017.2	1390.2	155.8	278.9	15.3	20.1	Over 25
Cincinnati SMSA	1071.6	1384.9	151.3	197.7	14.1	14.3	Under 5
Kansas City SMSA	1039.5	1253.9	160.6	221.1	15.4	17.6	15–25
Denver SMSA	929.4	1227.5	151.3	231.7	16.3	18.9	15–25
Total SCAs and SMSAs	57,905.1	66,004.7	8793.5	11,630.5	15.2	17.6	15–25

Detail may not add to totals because of rounding. × indicates SMSA did not exist in period. Standard Consolidated Areas (SCAs) and Standard Metropolitan Statistical Areas (SMSAs) are established by the Office of Management and Budget. Geographical boundaries are revised periodically to reflect changes in the land areas falling within the metropolitan classification. For following tables and analysis, the year of data collection is taken to specify the geographical definition of the metropolitan area. Office-type employment includes professional, managerial, and clerical.
Sources. US Bureau of the Census, *Census of Population, Journey to Work, 1970 and 1960.*

Table 3.10. Employment in Central Administrative Offices and Auxiliary Units in Selected Metropolitan Areas, 1954–1972

	1954		1963		1972		Growth rate(%)1954–72	
	Emplymt (000's)	% of nation	Emplymt (000's)	% of nation	Emplymt (000's)	% of nation	CAO & A	Non-agr. emplymt
United States	771.3	100.0	1213.4	100.0	1771.5	100.0	129.7	48.4
New York–NE N.J. SCA	160.7	20.8	231.1	19.0	299.6	16.9	86.4	22.5
New York SMSA	130.6	16.9	174.9	14.4	212.4	12.0	62.6	7.3
Nassau–Suffolk SMSA	×	×	×	×	13.7	0.8	×	×
Newark SMSA	18.1	2.3	30.1	2.5	45.1	2.5	149.2	56.3
Chicago–NW Ind. SCA	78.5	10.2	99.9	8.2	130.3	7.4	66.0	25.9
Chicago SMSA	76.0	9.9	98.3	8.1	128.4	7.2	68.9	25.4
Los Angeles SMSA	(22.8)	3.0	45.4	3.7	65.0	3.7	185.1	62.6
Philadelphia SMSA	26.9	3.5	40.3	3.3	53.6	3.0	99.2	22.3
Detroit SMSA	63.5	8.2	89.6	7.4	109.0	6.2	71.7	14.4
San Francisco SMSA	(21.8)	2.8	30.5	2.5	42.7	2.4	95.9	49.5
Washington SMSA	4.9	0.6	13.1	1.1	20.6	1.2	320.4	34.5
Boston SMSA	(10.4)	1.4	35.5	2.9	49.4	2.8	375.0	29.4
Pittsburgh SMSA	34.6	4.5	42.8	3.5	48.3	2.7	39.6	9.2
St Louis SMSA	(17.4)	2.3	25.5	2.1	34.2	1.9	96.6	28.9
Cleveland SMSA	16.3	2.1	25.0	2.1	31.2	1.8	91.4	27.7
Houston SMSA	9.5	1.2	18.6	1.5	45.1	2.5	374.7	215.7
Minn.–St Paul SMSA	14.5	1.9	23.4	1.9	38.2	2.2	163.4	65.5
Dallas SMSA	9.4	1.2	15.1	1.2	32.8	1.9	248.9	188.5
Atlanta SMSA	6.6	0.9	11.9	1.0	29.8	1.7	351.5	82.6
Cincinnati SMSA	(5.7)	0.7	13.2	1.1	18.7	1.1	228.1	28.4
Kansas City SMSA	8.5	1.1	12.3	1.0	16.7	0.9	96.5	53.8
Denver SMSA	3.6	0.5	7.5	0.6	16.1	0.9	342.7	121.9
Total SCAs and SMSAs	515.6	66.9	780.7	64.2	1081.2	61.0	109.7	37.2

Metropolitan areas are ranked by descending population size, according to the 1970 *Census of Population* SMSA definition. Only those SMSAs with greater than class-size employment per hundred population were included. Data series are not strictly comparable over the period because of areal redefinition of selected metropolitan areas. ( ) are estimated. × did not exist in period.
Sources. US Bureau of the Census, *Enterprise Statistics: 1972 and 1963, Part 2*; US Bureau of Labor Statistics, *Employment and Earnings*, 1975.

the business headquarter data understates, by more than half, the magnitude and change in export activity.

The data in Table 3.10 show that the selected SCAs and SMSAs, with 37 per cent of the nation's office-type employment, contain 61 per cent of the central administrative activity. It is a rapidly expanding category which, nationwide, grew 130 per cent between 1954 and 1972 and decentralized, somewhat, out of and within the selected areas. SCAs and SMSAs gained over half a million headquarter jobs for a 110 per cent increase, in contrast to a 37 per cent rise in a non-agricultural employment over the period. The most specialized office economies—New York SCA, Los Angeles, Washington, San Francisco, Boston, Dallas, and Atlanta—accounted for more than half of the group performance and attracted nearly one-third of the national growth in CAO & A activity. Excepting New York and San Francisco, the five other highly specialized areas increased in relative as well as absolute terms. Boston led the 20 areas by nearly a fourfold growth, with Atlanta and Washington marking a close third and fifth in rate of increase over the 18 year period. The New York SCA's gain of 130,000 headquarter jobs represented a substantial portion of the nation's, but in contrast with its past pre-eminence New York declined in share from 21 to 17 per cent of the total by 1972.

Six of the seven largest metropolitan areas more specialized in goods production, yet with a substantial volume of headquarter activity, grew less rapidly in CAO & A employment than the combined SCAs and SMSAs or the nation. Chicago SCA, Philadelphia, Detroit, Pittsburgh, St Louis, and Cleveland were twice disadvantaged: from regional locations in the declining Northeast and North Central portions of the nation, and from a slowdown in their manufacturing sectors which generated much of the export office function. Over the period, the seven areas (including Cincinnati) provided one-third of the SCAs' and SMSAs' growth. Apart from furthering the concentration of headquarters in office-specialized economies, diminishing the shares attributable to multimillion production areas, and decentralizing a portion to smaller SMSAs, the pattern of CAO & A employment location over the period exhibited one other trend worthy of note. Several of the major regional centres with balanced economies or a trading orientation, such as Houston, Minn.–St Paul, Denver, and in previous years Atlanta, captured disproportionately large shares of central office employment growth. Houston ranked second, Atlanta third, and Denver fourth in rate of increase over the period, while Minn.–St Paul more than doubled its level of headquarter employment. Most of these SMSAs benefited from favourable intra-national locations that support rapid economic development, and all were characterized by the scale and density of population that attracts preferential settlement.

Table 3.11 provides information on CAO & A activity as a per cent of non-agricultural employment by metropolitan area. Central office jobs in the selected SCAs and SMSAs rose from 2.6 to 4.0 per cent of local employment between

Table 3.11. Growth of CAO & A Employment as a Share of Total Non-agricultural Employment in Selected Metropolitan Areas, 1954–1972

| | CAO & A as % of non-agr. employment | | | | |
	1954	1958	1963	1967	1972
United States	1.6	1.9	2.1	2.1	2.4
New York–NE N.J. SCA	3.0	3.6	3.9	3.9	4.6
New York SMSA	3.3	4.0	4.0	4.1	5.0
Nassau–Suffolk SMSA	×	×	×	×	1.8
Newark SMSA	3.3	3.8	4.4	4.8	5.3
Chicago–NW Ind. SCA	3.1	3.2	3.7	3.7	4.1
Chicago SMSA	3.2	3.4	3.9	3.9	4.4
Los Angeles SMSA	1.3	1.6	1.9	1.9	2.2
Philadelphia SMSA	1.8	2.5	2.7	2.6	3.0
Detroit SMSA	5.1	6.7	7.4	7.1	7.4
San Francisco SMSA	2.6	2.6	3.0	2.9	3.4
Washington SMSA	0.8	1.0	1.5	1.4	1.7
Boston SMSA	1.1	2.7	3.2	2.9	3.9
Pittsburg SMSA	4.4	5.5	5.8	5.7	5.6
St Louis SMSA	2.6	3.0	3.4	3.1	3.9
Cleveland SMSA	2.5	3.1	3.6	3.1	3.7
Houston SMSA	2.5	3.5	3.5	4.0	5.5
Minn.–St Paul SMSA	3.0	3.8	3.9	5.5	4.8
Dallas SMSA	3.4	3.6	3.4	3.6	3.4
Atlanta SMSA	2.2	2.5	2.8	3.0	4.5
Cincinnati SMSA	1.4	2.4	3.3	3.3	3.7
Kansas City SMSA	2.5	2.7	2.9	3.3	3.2
Denver SMSA	1.4	1.7	2.1	1.9	2.9
Total SCAs and SMSAs	2.6	3.2	3.6	3.5	4.0

Sources. US Bureau of the Census, *Enterprise Statistics: 1972 and 1963, Part 2*; US Bureau of Labor Statistics, *Employment and Earnings*, 1975.

1954 and 1972. Nationally, the increase was less steep, from 1.6 to 2.4 per cent of all non-agricultural job opportunities. The trend towards larger shares of local activity devoted to headquarter functions was apparent among all SMSAs, but the deepest inroads were made essentially in the balanced regional economies which also sustained the fastest overall rate of employment growth. Production centres followed, although a strengthened role for central office activity in these localities more often than not resulted from flagging growth in other functions. The specialized office centres exhibited the least average increase in headquarter activity as a share of all non-agricultural employment. They also displayed the smallest role for CAOs, ranging in share from 1.7 to 4.6 per cent of local employment in 1972. The anomaly exists because strong office SMSAs have extensive development in other office functions, such as finance or government of an export nature, a host of ancillary business services, or the back office white-collar operations that must remain accessible to headquarter concentrations. Specialized office centres are not less dependent on central administrative offices, for these headquarters represent the cornerstone of their office industry. Rather, the development of related office functions eventually overtakes headquarter employment requirements.

In other respects, the composition of a local economy's office sector may prove advantageous or limiting to its future prospects. A brief inspection of the CAO & A data in selected SMSAs by manufacturing and non-manufacturing components provides some clues to past growth and the direction of future development. Table 3.12 shows that in the nation as a whole, 57 per cent of the central administrative employment belongs to manufacturing, and 43 per cent to non-manufacturing. Since 1958, however, non-manufacturing headquarters have been generating employment more rapidly, so that, in absolute numbers, the two sectors are growing about equally. In the SCAs and SMSAs, administrative manufacturing jobs comprise a slightly larger share of CAO & A activity than nationwide, or 58 per cent of the respective areas' headquarter employment. Yet the shift towards non-manufacturing central offices has essentially kept pace with the nation over the long term, so that the SCAs and SMSAs show no competitive disadvantage in capturing new headquarter growth that will probably draw more heavily upon the non-manufacturing sector.

Within SMSAs, as Table 3.13 indicates, no clear-cut pattern emerges over time

Table 3.12. Industry Composition of CAO & A Employment in the Nation and Selected Metropolitan Areas, 1954, 1958, 1963, 1967, 1972

Year	Manufacturing			Non-manufacturing		
	All jobs (000's)	Interim change Absolute (000's)	%	All jobs (000's)	Interim change Absolute (000's)	%
The nation						
1954	451.2			320.0		
1958	602.2	+150.9	33.5	384.8	+64.7	20.2
1963	726.5	124.3	20.6	486.9	102.2	26.6
1967	819.5	93.0	12.8	576.6	89.7	18.4
1972	1013.7	194.2	23.7	757.8	181.2	31.4
The SCAs and SMSAs						
1954	307.1			208.5		
1958	410.1	+103.0	33.5	242.7	+34.2	16.4
1963	472.9	62.8	15.3	307.8	65.1	26.8
1967	517.5	44.6	9.4	367.8	60.0	19.5
1972	628.1	110.6	21.4	453.1	91.1	23.2

Detail may not add to totals because of rounding. See footnote in Table 3.10 for qualifications of data.
Source. US Bureau of the Census, *Enterprise Statistics: 1972 and 1963, Part 2.*

Table 3.13. Growth in Manufacturing and Non-manufacturing Employment in CAO & A Units in Selected Metropolitan Areas, 1958–1963, 1967–1972

| | Growth rate (%) | | | |
| | 1958–1963 | | 1967–1972 | |
	Mfg	Non-mfg	Mfg	Non-mfg
United States	20.6	26.6	23.7	31.4
New York–NE N.J. SCA	12.3	21.6	23.6	17.0
New York SMSA	3.4	12.7	13.6	9.2
Nassau–Suffolk SMSA	×	×	×	×
Newark SMSA	34.7	0.0	30.1	−4.1
Chicago–NW Ind. SCA	18.9	22.1	25.4	2.7
Chicago SMSA	20.4	21.9	25.5	1.5
Los Angeles SMSA	12.8	61.3	23.6	25.4
Philadelphia SMSA	5.7	15.3	29.6	5.3
Detroit SMSA	14.7	33.8	6.5	3.1
San Francisco SMSA	27.9	38.0	23.7	28.1
Washington SMSA	235.3	65.9	70.4	35.1
Boston SMSA	20.0	42.2	53.0	18.8
Pittsburgh SMSA	−2.4	12.4	−1.7	10.1
St Louis SMSA	13.8	31.3	25.4	30.4
Cleveland SMSA	20.9	13.9	18.1	30.3
Houston SMSA	53.8	10.5	39.2	100.3
Minn.–St Paul SMSA	28.8	4.7	10.1	45.3
Dallas SMSA	−11.6	36.3	60.2	66.8
Atlanta SMSA	173.0	20.2	78.5	92.0
Cincinnati SMSA	41.3	31.6	15.3	30.9
Kansas City SMSA	43.1	13.3	−6.3	11.8
Denver SMSA	30.3	55.8	143.1	90.6
Total SCAs and SMSAs	15.3	26.8	21.4	23.2

× Indicates SMSA did not exist in period. 1958–1963 data based on 1964 areal definition of SMSAs; 1967–1972 data based on 1972 areal definition of SMSAs.
Source. US Bureau of the Census, *Enterprise Statistics: 1972 and 1963, Part 2.*

or between specialized areas as to the sectoral composition of CAO & A growth. Rates of manufacturing increase tend to decline as size of area increases, yet even among the smaller SMSAs that experienced the fastest rate of administrative manufacturing growth, the pace or domination of the industrials is not maintained over several periods. Only in the Washington SMSA, which was vastly under-represented in manufacturing headquarters, did these growth rates exceed non-manufacturers' in both the 1958–1963 and 1967–1972 periods. Rapid non-manufacturing rise characterized office-oriented and balanced economies, across the range of scale, and consistently excluded the traditional production areas. Yet the New York SCA and Boston displayed mixed responses while Pittsburgh and St Louis underwent more non-manufacturing than industrial headquarter expansion in both periods.

Table 3.14 portrays the sectoral composition of headquarter growth in the SCAs and SMSAs as a share of the nation's total. Worthy of note here are the strong gains in manufacturing office expansion captured by the New York SCA in recent years, or 19.3 per cent of the national growth located in the SCA as opposed to 18.3 per cent in seven combined production areas over the 1967–1972 period. Part of New York's increase is attributable to the performance of smaller SMSAs and non-metropolitan areas that lie within the confines of the SCA, but part is also due to the heterogeneity of the area's mix of manufacturing offices, many of which are solely for export and not linked to the production base. It appears that the more narrow industrial profile of production centres, such as Detroit and Pittsburgh, eventually weakens their prospects for administrative office employment, while other specialized office centres, with the recent

Table 3.14. Share of Nation's Growth in Manufacturing and Non-manufacturing Employment in CAO & A Units in Selected Metropolitan Areas, 1958–1972

	Share of nation's growth (%)					
	1958–1963		1963–1967		1967–1972	
	Mfg	Non-mfg	Mfg	Non-mfg	Mfg	Non-mfg
United States	100.0	100.0	100.0	100.0	100.0	100.0
New York–NE N.J. SCA	13.5	13.5	5.5	12.2	19.3	8.3
New York SMSA	3.0	6.8	9.4	6.7	8.5	3.4
Nassau–Suffolk SMSA	×	×	×	×	×	×
Newark SMSA	2.8	1.6	3.8	3.2	4.5	−0.2
Chicago–NW Ind. SCA	6.9	8.2	3.7	12.1	7.5	0.8
Chicago SMSA	7.1	8.1	4.4	12.0	7.4	0.5
Los Angeles SMSA	1.6	10.2	0.5	7.0	2.2	4.7
Philadelphia SMSA	1.0	2.2	1.2	4.4	3.7	0.6
Detroit SMSA	7.4	4.5	9.7	4.9	2.7	0.4
San Francisco SMSA	3.2	3.4	−1.3	5.1	2.1	2.7
Washington SMSA	1.8	3.9	−1.1	9.5	0.7	2.5
Boston SMSA	2.9	4.1	−1.4	1.8	5.5	1.6
Pittsburgh SMSA	−0.7	0.8	6.3	−0.5	−0.4	0.4
St Louis SMSA	1.5	2.4	1.9	−0.4	2.2	1.6
Cleveland SMSA	2.5	0.9	0.2	0.6	1.7	1.3
Houston SMSA	1.7	1.2	4.9	2.9	2.1	8.4
Minn.–St Paul SMSA	2.6	0.4	8.8	0.2	1.2	2.3
Dallas SMSA	−0.4	3.0	2.3	3.0	1.8	5.2
Atlanta SMSA	1.5	1.5	2.3	2.1	2.1	5.5
Cincinnati SMSA	2.2	0.9	1.9	0.8	0.9	0.8
Kansas City SMSA	1.0	1.0	1.7	2.3	−0.2	0.6
Denver SMSA	0.4	1.9	0.5	−0.3	1.9	2.6
Total SCAs and SMSAs	50.4	63.7	48.0	66.9	56.9	50.3

Detail may not add to totals because of rounding. × indicates SMSA did not exist in period. 1958–1967 data based on 1964 areal definition of SMSAs; 1967–1972 data based on 1972 areal definition of SMSAs.
Sources. US Bureau of the Census, *Enterprise Statistics: 1972 and 1963, Part 2.*

exception of Boston, hold little appeal for the expansion of manufacturing front offices.

Also evident in the most recent period is the concentration of non-manufacturing growth in other specialized and balanced economies, and the concomitant failure of production areas to compensate for limited manufacturing headquarter prospects by acquiring non-manufacturing administrative employment. Together, the office and balanced economies captured 44.4 per cent of the nation's total as opposed to 5.9 per cent shared by the production areas. Compared to previous periods, there is a discernible shift on the part of non-manufacturers to locate headquarters in the smaller million-plus metropolitan areas. The largest SMSAs, including New York, Los Angeles, San Francisco, and Washington, underwent substantial reductions in share of the nation's non-manufacturing headquarter growth. Although, as noted earlier, this sector of export office activity is especially under-represented by the nature of CAO & A data, the decentralization of non-manufacturing administrative offices away from the largest areas is cause for concern about office-specialized economies should it continue.

Another measure of the export role of major SMSAs and changing preferences in the pattern of headquarter location is the distribution of the nation's 500 largest industrial corporations by headquarter address, as determined annually by *Fortune* magazine. These elite firms, which command more than half of the commodity sales and nearly three-fourths of the profits earned each year, make an exceptional contribution to the creation of an environment which is amenable to the success of other office operations. Table 3.15 provides data on their location for selected years since 1958. It shows that the number of elite corporations headquartered in the SCAs and SMSAs peaked in 1963 at 71 per cent of the total, and declined to 63 per cent, or 313 firms, by 1975.[4] Forty-eight of the 44 net firm losses over the period can be attributed to the New York SCA; however, the Connecticut suburbs and smaller SMSAs of the New York Urban Region, which are excluded from the SCA definition, have now acquired nearly 30 of the 500 elite corporations. Other notable losses, in these instances entirely out of the respective regions, are ranked by SMSA: Pittsburgh, 7; Chicago SCA, 6; Philadelphia, 3; San Francisco, 3; Detroit, 2; and St Louis, 2. Major gains were scored by: Houston, 8; Los Angeles, 5; Atlanta, 5; Cleveland, 3; Washington, 2; Boston, 2; Minn.–St Paul, 2; and Denver, 2. On the whole over the 12 years, office economies outside New York increased by 11 corporation headquarters to a total of 55, production centres declined by 18 to 117, and balanced economies nearly doubled with 11 added for a total of 26.

Two hundred and forty of the 313 corporations are housed in central city locations of the metropolitan areas. Headquarter suburbanization is most prevalent in SMSAs above the 2.5 million population scale. In the New York SCA, 25 or 22 per cent of the total are located outside Manhattan; in Chicago, 15 or one-third; in Los Angeles, seven or one-third; in Philadelphia, six or nearly

Table 3.15. The Location of Headquarters for the Largest Industrial Corporations, 1958, 1963, 1969, 1975

	Corporate headquarters				CAO & A establishments	
	1958	1963	1969	1975	1963	1972
United States	500	500	500	500	17,569	24,780
New York–NE N.J. SCA	151	163	148	115	2246	2769
New York SMSA	142	147	131	104	1738	1983
Nassau–Suffolk SMSA	×	×	×	1	×	183
Newark SMSA	4	7	7	6	235	327
Chicago–NW Ind. SCA	50	50	49	44	987	1355
Chicago SMSA	50	50	49	44	965	1315
Los Angeles SMSA	17	16	21	21	780	1178
Philadelphia SMSA	17	16	14	13	431	600
Detroit SMSA	16	15	13	13	392	540
San Francisco SMSA	13	12	11	9	512	718
Washington SMSA	—	—	1	2	264	413
Boston SMSA	7	10	9	12	355	413
Pittsburgh SMSA	23	22	14	15	287	346
St Louis SMSA	14	14	10	12	282	363
Cleveland SMSA	15	14	17	17	276	330
Houston SMSA	1	3	2	11	242	513
Minn.–St Paul SMSA	7	10	11	12	264	394
Dallas SMSA	6	6	7	6	306	665
Atlanta SMSA	—	—	3	5	252	484
Cincinnati SMSA	4	4	4	3	149	215
Kansas City SMSA	3	2	2	1	251	323
Denver SMSA	—	—	1	2	194	283
Total SCAs and SMSAs	344	357	337	313	8470	11,899

Excludes large privately owned companies that do not publish sales. All 500 companies must qualify by deriving 50 per cent of their revenues from mining or manufacturing for fiscal years ending not later than December 31 of year stated. CAO & A establishments are the total number of central administrative offices and auxiliaries.

Sources. *The Fortune Directory*, 1959, 1964, 1970, and 1976; US Bureau of the Census, *Enterprise Statistics: 1972 and 1963, Part 2.*

half; in Detroit, eight or over three-fifths; in San Francisco, three or one-third; and in Boston, six or one-half of the corporations have suburban addresses. The rapidly growing centres of the South—Houston, Dallas and Atlanta—all retain elite corporations in inner city locations.

Office Space and Construction in the Nation's Major Central Business Districts

Shifting spatial patterns in office and headquarter location between and within metropolitan areas have an impact on the distribution of office space, occupancy rates, and the demand for office construction in the downtowns and suburbs of the largest SMSAs. The dispersion of some office activity out of these areas to smaller SMSAs, and even ex-urban places, has caused some outlying construction, but essentially these office structures are modest or, if large, built for non-speculative purposes. While it is impossible to inventory the extent of metropolitan office space, even at the largest scale, a survey was undertaken of central business district (CBD) stock and recent construction in the 100 largest SMSAs. Perhaps the single most important finding is the paucity of information on the size, physical composition, and recent development in the downtowns at nearly every level of metropolitan scale. As a result, the information provided in Tables 3.16 and 3.17 represents, in part, the author's estimates based on partial reporting of data, or local estimates for downtown retail areas that are definitionally smaller than commercial business districts.

Bearing these data deficiencies in mind, Table 3.16 shows that the downtowns in the selected SMSAs acquired 370 million gross sq. ft of office space, or 22 per cent of the nationwide net addition between 1960 and 1975. As such, CBD office construction virtually kept pace with the nation's by retaining a 23 per cent share of detached office stock over the 15 year period. The increase of 170 million sq. ft in the 1970s as opposed to 200 million sq. ft in the 1960s represents an accelerated pace and share (24 per cent) in office building. This trend is also borne out by partial figures reported for current authorizations or construction underway, if taken as a share (31 per cent) of private office building in the nation in 1976.

The primacy of Manhattan among the nation's major CBDs is readily apparent in viewing the distribution of downtown stock between metropolitan areas. In a nine square mile CBD, Manhattan provides 290 million gross sq. ft of public and private office space, or over one-third of the selected areas' 838 million gross sq. ft and about 8 per cent of the nation's 3700 million sq. ft of detached office space. The construction of 111 million sq. ft of office building in Manhattan since 1960 comprises 30 per cent of the areas' net addition and roughly 7 per cent of the nation's increment. The second largest downtown office market in the United States, the Chicago Loop, offers 84 million gross sq. ft of public and private office stock, or 29 per cent of the Manhattan total. Despite Chicago's orientation towards goods production and the more limited prospects afforded for non-manufacturing headquarter expansion in the area, a full 10 per cent of the SMSAs' office increment was constructed in the Chicago CBD. Downtown Washington, with its massive complex of government offices, ranks third in office stock and recent construction, having doubled over the 15-year period. The CBDs of Boston, Philadelphia, and Los Angeles offer near equivalent space of 40+ million sq. ft and follow successively in rank.

San Francisco and Houston have grown equally over the period to 37 million sq. ft of floorspace each in 1975, yet Houston's development is a more remarkable achievement in view of disparities between metropolitan scale and the greater office orientation of the Bay area. Nearly twice the office-type

Table 3.16. Office Floorspace and Construction in the Central Business Districts of Selected Metropolitan Areas With Populations Over One Million, 1960–1975

	Gross land area (sq. m)		Gross office space (in 000,000 sq. ft)			Other non-res. space (in 000,000 sq. ft)		Net add'n office space		
	CBD	city	1960	1970	1975	Retail	Total	1960–70	1970–75	Under constr.
New York SMSA	9.0	300	179	240	290	36	588	61	50	2.6
Los Angeles SMSA	3.5	464	16	33	42	13	79	17	9	1.0
Chicago SMSA	1.2	223	47	63	(84)	n.a.	n.a.	16	21	n.a.
Philadelphia SMSA	2.5	129	26	34	(43)	n.a.	n.a.	8	9	0
Detroit SMSA	n.a.	138	13	18	22	n.a.	n.a.	5	4	2.5
San Francisco SMSA	4.0	45	16	26	(37)	n.a.	n.a.	10	11	1.5
Washington SMSA	1.7	61	36	54	71	7 (73)	89 (73)	18	17	n.a.
Boston SMSA	2.7	46	24	34	(45)	6	n.a.	10	11	5.4
Pittsburgh SMSA	0.9	55	15	22	(26)	n.a.	n.a.	7	4	n.a.
St Louis SMSA	1.3	61	(9)	(17)	20	8	41	8	3	0.5
Cleveland SMSA	n.a.	76	8	11	15	n.a.	n.a.	3	4	0
Houston SMSA	1.5	434	(15)	(25)	37	7	61	10	12	1.5
Newark SMSA	3.0	24	12	14	14	6	51 (70)	2	0	n.a.
Minn.–St Paul SMSA	0.9	55	(8)	(10)	13	6	n.a.	2	3	n.a.
Dallas SMSA	1.4	266	(15)	(21)	24	3	61	6	3	1.8
Atlanta SMSA	1.2	132	8	17	21	4 (70)	n.a.	9	4	1.1
Cincinnati SMSA	n.a.	78	10	12	13	n.a.	n.a.	2	1	n.a.
Kansas City SMSA	0.8	316	6	9	10	3	30	3	1	0.5
Denver SMSA	0.8	95	(5)	(8)	11	3	25	3	3	4.7
Total office in SMSAs			468	668	838			200	170	

( ) estimated by author from partial data supplied by city planning agencies. (73) year of retail or non-residential floorspace estimate if other than 1975.
Data pertain to downtowns or central business districts as locally defined in survey responses.
Source. Armstrong (1972), *The Office Industry*, MIT Press, for 1960 and 1970 data; 1975 office, retail and other floorspace estimates from a survey of respective city planning agencies in 1976.

Table 3.17. Office Floorspace and Construction in the Central Business Districts of Metropolitan Areas Without Major Office Concentrations, 1970 and 1975

	Gross land area CBD (Sq. m)	Gross office space (in 000,000 sq ft) 1970	Gross office space (in 000,000 sq ft) 1975	Other non-res. space (in 000,000 sq. ft) Retail	Other non-res. space (in 000,000 sq. ft) Total	Net add'n office space 1970–75	Net add'n office space Under constr.
Over 1.0 million population							
Baltimore SMSA	0.3	8.4	10.2	5	30	1.8	2.4
Seattle SMSA	0.3	8.6	12.5	8 (66)	31	3.9	1.0
Milwaukee SMSA	1.7	9.4	11.0	6 (72)	28 (72)	1.6	0.3
Paterson SMSA	1.0	1.4	1.6	3	12 (70)	0.2	n.a.
San Diego SMSA	2.1	n.a.	8.1	n.a.	23	n.a.	0
Miami SMSA	0.4	(4.0)	(6.5)	2	n.a.	2.5	0
Indianapolis SMSA	4.5	10.4	12.5	5	31	2.1	0.5
San Jose SMSA	0.9	2.0	3.5	1	n.a.	1.5	0.1
New Orleans SMSA	n.a.	(6.2)	(9.8)	n.a.	n.a.	3.6	1.3
Tampa SMSA	0.5	(3.0)	3.7	3	n.a.	0.7	0.2
0.5–1.0 million population							
Pheonix SMSA	n.a.	n.a.	(7.0)	n.a.	n.a.	n.a.	n.a.
Dayton SMSA	n.a.	4.9	5.9	2	16	1.0	0.6
Louisville SMSA	1.1	(7.8)	10.0	4	26	2.2	0.2
Sacremento SMSA	n.a.	n.a.	3.7	2	n.a.	n.a.	0.3
Memphis SMSA	n.a.	n.a.	1.5	n.a.	n.a.	n.a.	n.a.
Fort Worth SMSA	0.8	(2.5)	3.1	2	n.a.	0.6	0.8
Birmingham SMSA	1.3	(1.9)	3.0	n.a.	n.a.	1.1	n.a.
Toledo SMSA	n.a.	2.3	2.6	n.a.	n.a.	0.3	0.1
Akron SMSA	0.4	5.3	5.9	2	11	0.6	0.4
Hartford SMSA	0.6	4.1	7.2	n.a.	n.a.	3.1	0.1
Honolulu SMSA	0.1	4.1	5.7	1	n.a.	1.6	0.2
Salt Lake SMSA	0.3	(2.2)	2.3	3	n.a.	0.1	0.1
Springfield SMSA	0.2	n.a.	2.0	2	6	n.a.	0.1
Wilmington SMSA	n.a.	3.0	3.0	n.a.	n.a.	0	n.a.

Table 3.17. (Contd.)

	Gross land area CBD (Sq. m)	Gross office space (in 000,000 sq. ft)		Other non-res. space (in 000,000 sq. ft)		Net add'n office space	
		1970	1975	Retail	Total	1970–75	Under constr.
0.25–0.50 million population							
Orlando SMSA	1.2	(2.2)	2.9	5	10	0.7	0.2
Fresno SMSA	n.a.	0.5	0.6	n.a.	n.a.	0.1	0.1
Charlotte SMSA	2.9	3.0	7.5	2	n.a.	4.5	0
Lansing SMSA	0.3	4.0	4.1	1	7	0.1	n.a.
El Paso SMSA	0.4	2.9	3.2	3	n.a.	0.3	0
Peoria SMSA	0.3	1.8	1.9	2 (72)	6 (73)	0.1	0
Columbia SMSA	1.7	2.5	4.0	2	23	1.5	n.a.
Albuquerque SMSA	0.5	1.6	2.9	1	7	1.3	0
Austin SMSA	1.6	n.a.	3.3	n.a.	n.a.	n.a.	n.a.
Spokane SMSA	0.6	3.9	4.2	3	13	0.3	0
Des Moines SMSA	1.0	6.0	7.2	3 (72)	29 (72)	1.2	0

( ) estimated by author from partial data supplied by city planning agencies. (73) year of retail or non-residential floorspace estimate if other than 1975.
Data pertain to downtowns or central business districts as locally defined in survey responses.
Source. Survey of respective city planning agencies in 1976.

employment is available in the metropolitan area for concentration in the San Francisco CBD. Similarly, Pittsburgh and Dallas have each increased CBD office stock from 15 to roughly 25 million gross sq. ft by 1975. Here, the underlying differences are less in the magnitude of SMSA office-type employment or the degree of office suburbanization, and more in population scale or economic specialization. Lastly, it should be noted that Detroit, St Louis, and Atlanta, SMSAs that range in size from 4.2 to 1.4 million population, afford the same scale of downtown office space, an average of 21 million gross sq. ft in 1975. Atlanta's rapid economic development and emergence as an office centre in the most recent period underpin its first-place ranking, with Los Angeles, among the SMSAs in overall rate of downtown office construction.

An indication of the strength of a metropolitan area's central business district in the regional office market can be derived in rough measure by the relationship between downtown office floorspace and SMSA office-type employment. For the SMSAs as a whole, 62 gross sq. ft of CBD office floorspace were available per metropolitan office employee in 1970. Using average urban office occupancy rates of 155 sq. ft per worker, one can assume that about 40 per cent of SMSA office employment was located in the downtown areas. New York, Washington, Houston, and Dallas—ranging from 111 to 71 CBD sq. ft per metropolitan employee, or averaging about 60 per cent of areawide employment in downtown offices—were the leading SMSAs in the degree to which office activity is centralized in strong downtown areas. Atlanta, Boston, and Chicago were fairly representative of the group average, with about 40 per cent of metropolitan office space and employment located in downtown areas. Los Angeles, Detroit, and Cleveland were the most dispersed, with weak CBDs capturing only 20 per cent of metropolitan office activity. It should be noted that these estimates, in general, concur with *Census of Population* responses on work destinations.

In the order of 2 billion gross sq. ft of the nation's 3.7 billion sq. ft of public and private office floorspace are located in the selected SCAs and SMSAs. About 500 million sq. ft are situated in the downtowns of all other metropolitan areas over 250,000 population. Survey responses from a sampling of these areas are provided in Table 3.17. In comparison to the major SMSAs where CBDs outside Manhattan averaged 30 million gross sq. ft of office floor space in 1975, around one-fourth or 8 million sq. ft were offered in other million-plus SMSAs lacking significant office concentrations. Residentiary requirements declined gradually thereafter, with roughly 5 million sq. ft provided in downtowns of SMSAs in the 0.5–1.0 million population range, and 4 million sq. ft in CBDs of the 0.25–0.50 million SMSA scale. Across the range, some noteworthy exceptions are production centres, such as Baltimore or Milwaukee; state capitols, such as Indianapolis or Des Moines; and emerging regional office centres, such as Charlotte or Pheonix. The extent to which the latter areas—as prototypes of several with climate, amenity, low density, and regional advantages—can compete effectively for export office activity and thereby threaten the future of some major central cities depends, ultimately, on whether the need for face-to-face communication can co-exist or thrive in an era of rapidly expanding telecommunications technology.

Notes

1. Survey conducted in 1977 by Howard Ecker Real Estate Co., Chicago; verified by Julien J. Studley, Inc., Washington.

2. Vacancy estimated by Tri-State Regional Planning Commission, New York. Demand based on author's estimates of recession-related employment cutbacks in Manhattan CBD, and forecasts for full employment growth, as contained in *The Office Industry* (MIT Press, 1972).

3. Details of occupational employment, necessary for a computation of office building workers, are not available by job site location. In their absence, the major occupations of professional, technical, managerial, and clerical (excluding sales from white-collar total) were tabulated by place of work as a proxy for office industry employment.

Two SCAs (Standard Consolidated Area) are defined by the Office of Management and Budget, in addition to the 265 SMSAs (Standard Metropolitan Statistical Area) in the nation. The New York–NE N. J. SCA is comprised of the New York SMSA, Nassau–Suffolk SMSA, Newark SMSA, Jersey City SMSA, Paterson–Clifton–Passaic SMSA, New Brunswick – Perth Amboy – Sayreville SMSA. The Chicago–NW Ind. SCA is comprised of the Chicago SMSA and Gary–Hammond–East Chicago SMSA.

4. SMSA losses can consist of corporate mergers, acquisitions, or decline in sales rank below the 500th firm, in addition to headquarter relocation.

References

Armstrong, R. B. (1972), *The Office Industry: Patterns of Growth and Location.* Cambridge, Mass.: MIT Press.

Regional Plan Association (1975), *Growth and Settlement in the U.S.: Past Trends and Future Issues.* New York: Regional Plan Association.

4

Office Concentration in Dublin and its Consequences for Regional Development in Ireland

MICHAEL J. BANNON

Introduction

One of the dominant features of the labour statistics of developed countries in the twentieth century has been the movement of labour away from direct involvement in the production of goods into work associated with the creation and processing of an immaterial output. The growth in employment associated with the handling or exchange of information and the related expansion of the office industry has been well documented in the case of the larger and more developed Western economies (Gottmann, 1974; Armstrong, 1972; Törnqvist, 1970; E.F.T.A., 1973; Davey, 1972). Considerably less attention has been focussed upon the less spectacular growth of information and related office occupations in smaller or the less developed economies. Recent research into office activities in the Republic of Ireland (Ireland) has clearly demonstrated the important role of office occupations in the development of the Irish economy and in influencing the distribution of population and urban growth, particularly after 1961 (Bannon, 1972; Bannon et al., 1977). These studies may have a wider significance for occupational trends in other small or less developed economies.

From 1958 until 1973 the Irish economy experienced a period of sustained and unprecedented economic growth, resulting in a growth of total population, expansion of non-agricultural employment and an accelerated trend towards urban living (Eustace and McKee, 1973). Because of the small size of the country, its relatively underdeveloped economy and the primate nature of the urban structure, it is hardly surprising that Dublin, the capital city, benefited substantially from the overall expansion of the economy. Thus, most of the population growth and expansion of employment occurred within Dublin or its surrounding region. But it was in the management of the economy, and in spite of regional industry policies favouring the less developed regions, that Dublin exerted its greatest influence. Because of the growing complexity of corporate management and marketing systems, the widening scope and nature of public service involvement in social and economic life, the growth of the media and the growing need for speedy and reliable professional advice, the period of economic growth after 1958 was accompanied by a rapid growth of personnel engaged in the handling or exchange of information, particularly office occupations. From 1961 to 1971 office occupations in Ireland increased by 37.4 per cent; but within central Dublin, comprising approximately the CBD and transition zone (Griffin and Preston, 1966), office occupations increased by 46.0 per cent in the same period (Bannon, 1973).

But the growth of Dublin's office functions was not simply a passive reaction to economic growth; through the expansion of existing offices or the establishment of new office activities, Dublin exerted a control over the continued growth of the economy. Through its relatively rich milieu of office communications, research facilities, financial institutions and headquarters offices, Dublin became an increasing source of innovation; thus Dublin office organizations often enabled dispersed firms to innovate, to attain new markets and to retain a competitive edge. Throughout the 1960s a growing proportion of major industrial, commercial, social and government institutions were located in central Dublin from whence decisions were transmitted to executive agencies or production units throughout the country. This dominance of central Dublin in the management of the economy has been intensified through the processes of innovation diffusion whereby new ideas, technologies and customs are first adopted in Dublin, the centre of greatest information exchange, and only later diffuse to other cities and towns following the diffusion process suggested by Pederson (1970).

The growth of office occupations within central Dublin, coupled with a demand for improved office accommodation for existing office workers and the replacement of obsolete accommodation, resulted in a dramatic growth in the absolute and relative importance of office space in the area (Dublin Corporation, 1975). This growth in demand for office space forced the outward expansion of the central area into residential districts, generated a major property boom in the Irish context and also contributed to the escalation of land costs and occasionally resulted in socially destructive land speculation.

Within central Dublin the growth of employment in office activities took place against a background of increased levels of labour specialization required in all types of work. Consequently the labour scarcity which sometimes affected the Dublin office industry was paralleled by a growing level of redundancies and unemployment in unskilled or semi-skilled occupations. This mismatch of labour and opportunities was reversed in other parts of Ireland; there, the success of the regional industrial policies created a large number of jobs in goods production

(McMenamin, 1975), while those with a higher occupational aspiration were often forced to migrate to Dublin in search of suitable white-collar opportunities. By and large, this mismatch of occupations and opportunities, which has intensified since 1973, was largely ignored in the labour statistics, which were more concerned with the branch of economic activity in which people worked rather than their job function or occupational status and requirements within the different activities.

Drawing upon recent research in Ireland, this chapter examines four interrelated aspects of the growth of office activities: the regional pattern of office occupations; the concentration of office decision-making; the interdependent nature of office linkages with Dublin; Dublin's role in the Irish office industry. Before examining these four interrelated aspects of office activities, it is necessary to look at the growth of office occupations within the context of overall employment change.

Overall Employment Trends

Unlike most Western countries, the Republic of Ireland experienced almost uninterrupted population decline between 1926 and 1961; since 1961 there has been an upward trend in population, with a growth of 2.3 per cent from 1961 to 1966 and 3.3 per cent between 1966 and 1971. In 1974 Ireland had a population of just over three million and a labour force just in excess of one million (EEC 1974); only Luxembourg among the EEC member states had a smaller population or labour force. Table 4.1 shows that between 1961 and 1971 there was an annual percentage growth in employment of only 0.4 per cent; this resulted from a continuing rapid decline in the agricultural labour force and an annual growth of 2.3 per cent within the industrial sector. The service sector, which had an employment growth rate of 0.4 per cent per annum from 1926–1961, grew by 1.0 per cent per annum from 1961 to 1971. Estimates of employment for 1975 confirm a continuation of the overall trend of employment away from production of material goods (Table 4.1).

As can be seen from Table 4.2, the principal areas of employment growth were the industrial sector and in the insurance–banking–business services, public administration–defence, and professional services subsectors within the service sector. The gains in these activities were offset by the employment losses in the agricultural sector and in old services, including the retail distribution and personal service subsectors (*Census of Population, 1961* and *1971*). Within the service sector the principal areas of employment expansion occurred in new and complementary services as identified by Sabolo (Sabolo, 1975).

The changes taking place in employment between 1961 and 1971 are more easily understood if they are also examined by occupation. In terms of occupation, a dominant feature of change in the labour force has been the growth of white-collar occupations within all economic sectors and almost all subsectors

Table 4.1. Changes in Population and Employment by Sector, 1961–75

Sector	Numbers employed			Percentage share by each sector			Annual % change	
	1961	1971	1975	1961	1971	1975	1961/71	1971/75
Agriculture	379,491	273,079	252,000	36.1	25.9	24.2	−3.23	−1.98
Industry*	257,178	322,749	307,000	24.4	30.6	29.5	2.28	−1.24
Service	415,870	459,011	483,000	39.5	43.5	46.3	0.99	1.28
Total employed population	1,052,539	1,054,839	1,042,000	100.0	100.0	100.0	1.11	0.31
Total population	2,818,341	2,978,248	3,100,000	—	—	—	0.42	1.01

*Includes mining, manufacturing, building and construction and workers in electricity, gas and water.
Source. *Census of Population*, Stationery Office, Dublin, 1961 and 1971, and *Economic Review and Outlook*, July, 1976, p. 38.

Table 4.2. Change of White-Collar Employment by Branch of Economic Activity, 1961–71

Sectors and subsectors	Total employment			Total white-collar occupations			White-collar occupations as percentage of total employment	
	Numbers		Percentage change 1961–71	Numbers		Percentage change 1961–71	1961	1971
	1961	1971		1961	1971			
Agriculture	379,491	273,079	− 31.3	765	1046	+ 36.7	0.2	0.4
Industry	257,158	322,749	+ 25.5	35,351	51,049	+ 44.4	13.7	15.8
Insurance, banking, business services	16,396	23,992	+ 46.3	15,250	22,464	+ 47.3	93.0	93.6
Commerce	142,695	148,286	+ 3.9	108,732	109,722	+ 0.9	76.2	74.0
Transport and communications	54,167	60,122	+ 11.0	11,879	14,285	+ 20.3	21.9	23.8
Public administration & defence	40,580	48,869	+ 20.4	17,437	22,738	+ 30.4	43.0	46.5
Professional services	85,913	109,078	+ 27.0	71,079	91,109	+ 28.2	83.4	83.5
Recreational services	10,986	10,851	− 1.2	6459	6333	− 2.0	58.8	58.4
Personal services	63,314	54,441	− 14.0	4256	6845	− 60.8	6.7	12.6
Other services	2539	3372	+ 32.8	1064	2007	+ 88.6	41.9	59.5
Total service sector	415,870	459,011	+ 10.4	236,156	275,503	+ 16.7	56.8	60.0
Total all industries	1,052,539	1,054,839	+ 0.2	272,272	327,598	+ 20.3	25.9	31.1

Source. *Census of Population* Vol III, Tables 7A & 7B, Stationery Office, Dublin, 1966 and 1971. Adjusted figures for white-collar employment include commerce, professional, clerical and administration workers actually employed.

(Table 4.2). Within the total employed population white-collar occupations increased by 20 per cent between 1961 and 1971; in 1971 these occupations accounted for 31.1 per cent of the working population. The largest percentage increases in white-collar employment occurred in the industrial sector and in the insurance–banking–business services, public administration–defence and professional service subsectors. White-collar employment in the industrial sector increased by 3.0 per cent per annum; in the professions it grew by 2.5 per cent; and by 3.9 per cent in insurance–banking–business services (Bannon *et al.*, 1977). In public administration–defence the annual growth rate was 1.9 per cent. The greatest absolute increases in white-collar employment were in professional services, the industrial sector, insurance–banking–business services and in the public administration–defence subsectors. While many of the subsectors of the service sectors are almost exclusively white-collar, only 15.8 per cent of industrial sector jobs and 30 per cent of manufacturing subsector jobs are white-collar. Within the service sector employment decline was associated principally with those subsectors containing a low number and proportion of white-collar occupations.

Growth of Office Occupations

Much of the growth of white-collar employment was confined to office activities, with non-office white-collar activities such as nursing, teaching, religion and sales experiencing little employment growth after 1961 (Bannon, 1973). Most of the growth of office occupations between 1961 and 1971 resulted from the expansion of professional and administration opportunities, with a relatively slow growth of routine office occupations.

As in the more developed European and North American countries, there has been a rapid growth of office employment. Office occupations accounted for approximately 80,000 jobs or only 6.0 per cent of the labour force in 1946. By 1961 there were 123,928 office workers accounting for 11.2 per cent of the labour force. A growth of 37.4 per cent in office jobs between 1961 and 1971, with the growth rate increasing after 1966, led to a total of 170,276 office jobs by 1971, accounting for 15.2 per cent of the employed population. Between 1961 and 1971 office occupations accounted for one in every three additional jobs provided in the manufacturing subsector and for eight out of every 10 additional jobs in the service sector. Both the scale and rate of growth in office employment may be regarded as slow by international comparisons (Daniels, 1975); but within Ireland, the expansion of office opportunities made a distinct contribution to employment policies and contributed to the shift of population and jobs into urban areas, particularly into the Dublin area.

Regional Pattern of Office Jobs

While there has been rapid and consistent growth of office employment, much of this growth has been concentrated in and around Dublin. Table 4.3 provides

Table 4.3. Office Employment by Region, 1961–71

	Number of office workers			Regional share of office work		% change
			Change			
Region	1961	1971	1961–71	1961	1971	1961–71
East	74,458	100,391	25,933	60.1	59.0	34.8
South West	15,550	20,869	5319	12.6	12.3	34.2
South East	8479	11,978	3499	6.8	7.0	41.3
Mid West	7219	11,212	3993	5.8	6.6	55.3
West	4962	7170	2208	4.0	4.2	44.4
Midlands	4597	6660	2063	3.7	3.8	44.9
North East	4696	6642	1946	3.8	3.9	41.4
Donegal	2026	2724	698	1.6	1.6	34.4
North West	1941	2630	689	1.6	1.6	35.5
Total all regions	123,928	170,276	46,348	100.0	100.0	37.4

Source. *Census of Population, 1961 and 1971.*

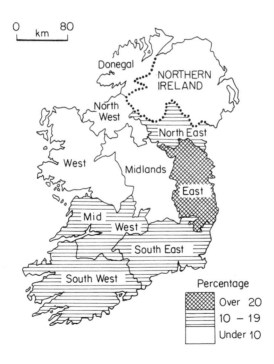

Fig. 4.1. Office occupations as a proportion of
total gainfully occupied population
by region, 1971

an overview of the regional distribution of office jobs in the decade 1961–1971.

Using the nine planning regions of the country, Fig. 4.1 illustrates the regional pattern of office work in 1971. Almost 60 per cent of all workers in office occupations were resident in the East Region in 1971, with only 12 per cent in the South West Region including Cork city. Less urbanized peripheral regions had a very low proportion of office jobs and most of the jobs in such regions were of a routine nature.

Even allowing for the small size of Ireland, the degree of office employment concentration in the capital city and its region is relatively high. While the decade 1961–1971 witnessed a slight reduction in the East Region's share of routine office workers (those engaged in information handling), there was a growing concentration of professional and administrative occupations (those in information exchange). The East Region's share of professional occupations increased from 40.1 per cent of the total to 43.7 per cent between 1961 and 1971; the share of the state's administration workers in the East Region increased from 57.5 per cent in 1961 to 61.4 per cent in 1971. Professional and administrative occupations account for an increasing proportion of both the office and total employment of the East Region. The slight decline in the proportion of total office workers resident in the East Region has been offset by the continued expansion of that region's share of higher-level office work.

Office Employment in the East Region

To understand the overall pattern of office employment it is necessary to look more closely at office functions within the East Region, a region consisting of metropolitan Dublin and a tributary area of 30–40 miles radius whose development is in the hands of 14 separate planning authorities (Wright, 1967). The East Region has experienced a continued growth of both population and employment over the past 50 years. By 1971 the East Region contained 36 per cent of the total population and 37 per cent of the total employment in the country; office employment acounted for 25.8 per cent of the region's employment as compared to 21.6 per cent in 1961. No data are yet available for occupational structure after 1971.

Employment growth in the East Region is almost synonymous with expansion of the Dublin subregion (Dublin city, Dunlaoghaire and County Dublin), which by 1971 accounted for 81 per cent of the both the region's population and employment as well as 82.4 per cent of all office occupations in the region. Within the subregion the growth of office functions has been further largely confined to the central area of the city, with the exception of those professional services provided on a population basis, for example local banks and the airport office complex to the north of Dublin as well as offices attached to production units on the industrial estates, mostly to the southwest of the city.

Office Employment Growth in Central Dublin

A 10 per cent sample survey of central Dublin offices involving respondents from 203 office establishments revealed that, while many of the Dublin offices were branches of international organizations, they functioned as independents within Ireland, many having responsibility for branches throughout the country (Bannon, 1972). The results of the survey show that while there had been some growth in the number of office establishments, most of the office employment growth was accommodated in larger establishments. Table 4.4 indicates the scale of growth of office employment, allowing for establishments which had either ceased trading or commenced operation between 1961 and 1971.

Office employment within the area grew by 46 per cent, with growth being particularly rapid in commercial–industrial and public sector categories. This growth in office employment resulted in a continuous growth in the size of office establishment, based upon evidence from establishments still existing in 1971 (Table 4.5). There has been a growth in the average size of office establishment, with growth being limited in the case of professional establishments but going up by 175 per cent in the public sector establishments between 1950 and 1971. While the growth of office employment accounted for one in every three new industrial sector jobs provided between 1961 and 1971, a survey of 14 of the largest public

Table 4.4. Estimated Total Office Employment in Central Dublin, 1961–71

Office group	1960	1971	% growth 1961–71
Professional	10,670	15,320	43.6
Financial	13,140	19,420	47.8
Commercial	10,640	18,830	77.0
Public sector	7770	18,820	142.2
Total office employment	42,220	72,390	46.0

Source. M. Bannon (1972).

Table 4.5. Average Number of Office Workers per Establishment, 1950–71

Office group	1950	1960	1971
Professional	9.4	10.0	13.6
Financial	25.9	41.4	57.1
Commercial	11.4	13.2	19.2
Public sector	48.1	69.2	132.1
Total office employment	16.4	20.2	30.7

companies indicated that in the same period office jobs accounted for one in every two additional jobs (Bannon, 1973).

In the decade 1961–1971 employment outside the agricultural sector increased by 108,712 jobs of which 59,664 or 59 per cent were white-collar. Office employment grew by 46,348 jobs in the same period and accounted for 46.2 per cent of all employment growth outside agriculture and for 77.7 per cent of all employment growth in white-collar work. The pattern of office work remained highly concentrated within the East Region, with higher-level office jobs congregating within Dublin. In the decade 1961–1971 office employment made a considerable contribution to national objectives of increased employment. However, most of these new jobs, especially at higher level, were created in the Dublin area, requiring migration of office workers into Dublin from the rest of the country.

Regional Pattern of Decision-Making

While the number and distribution of office workers is relevant to regional development, it is also necessary to have regard to the pattern of higher decision-making office functions. It is difficult to isolate from census data precise quantifiable groups of occupations which can be described as decision-makers. In the present context the number and distribution of persons engaged in higher-level white-collar work (i.e. the professions and administration) is taken as indicative of the pattern of decision-making power. Table 4.6 shows the regional distribution of both professional and administrative workers. In the case of professional and technical occupations there has been a growing concentration in the East Region, while these occupations account for a growing share of total white-collar work in each region. But only the East Region substantially increased its share of the national total from 1961 to 1971. The degree of concentration in the East Region becomes even more pronounced if teaching and religious professions are excluded. Administrative, executive and managerial occupations increased in all regions from 1961 to 1971 and in all but one region, the South West, accounted for an increased share of total white-collar work by 1971. Between 1961 and 1971 72.7 per cent of all growth in administration occurred in the East Region which, once again, was the only region to substantially increase its share of the national total, increasing by 3.9 percentage points.

The high degree of concentration of decision-making occupations in the East Region reflects the dominant role played by Dublin within the Irish economy. Dublin is the focus of decision-making in government, commerce, industry, the arts, the media and even by voluntary organizations (Bannon et al., 1977). The concentration of executive agencies and executive power indicated by Table 4.7 is fundamental to an understanding of the pattern of higher-level office workers engaged in information exchange and in decision-making.

Table 4.6. Regional Trends in Professional and Technical and Administrative, Executive and Managerial Occupations, 1961–71

Region	Professional and technical						Administrative, executive and managerial					
	1961		1971		total regional white-collar %		1961		1971		total regional white-collar %	
	Number	% distribution	Number	% distribution	1961	1971	Number	% distribution	Number	% distribution	1961	1971
East	31,605	40.1	45,190	43.7	24.7	27.6	7698	57.5	10,996	61.4	6.0	6.7
South West	11,841	15.0	14,849	14.4	30.1	32.2	1935	14.5	2188	12.2	4.9	4.8
South East	8130	10.3	9805	9.5	31.9	32.9	948	7.1	1150	6.4	3.7	3.9
Mid West	6401	8.1	8468	8.2	31.3	33.4	873	6.5	1193	6.7	4.3	4.7
West	6710	8.5	8280	8.0	37.9	40.1	497	3.7	615	3.4	2.8	3.0
Midlands	5430	6.9	6473	6.3	33.9	34.9	433	3.2	555	3.1	2.7	3.0
North East	4279	5.4	5266	5.1	30.3	32.6	551	4.1	717	4.0	3.9	4.4
Donegal	2342	3.0	2592	2.5	32.7	33.1	225	1.7	267	1.5	3.1	3.4
North West	2096	2.7	2393	2.3	33.9	38.8	220	1.7	235	1.3	3.6	3.8
Total all regions	78,834	100.0	103,316	100.0	28.7	30.9	13,380	100.0	17,916	100.0	4.9	5.4

Source. *Census of Population, Occupation Volumes, 1961 and 1971.*

Table 4.7. Miscellaneous Measures of Concentration

Headquarters offices of:	Total number	Percentage in East Region
Central government departments	17	100
Embassies accredited to Ireland	22	100
State-sponsored companies	87	86
Commercial state companies	20	90
Trade, professional and other organizations	503	93
Trade unions	65	93
Largest public quoted companies	50	90
Banking institutions	41	95
Hire-purchase firms	41	71
Insurance companies	31	100
Publishing companies	47	89
Advertising agencies	36	97

Sources. IPA *Administration Yearbook and Diary*, Dublin, 1976; *Sunday Independent's* Companies' League, January 4, 1976.

Dublin's role as a focus of power within all aspects of the Irish economy is intimately related to the primate nature of the national urban system (Fig. 4.2a), the regional distribution of professional and administrative occupations (Fig. 4.2b), and the pattern of information flows (Fig. 4.2c). There exists an almost identical correspondence in the ranking of the nine planning regions when ranked on the basis of the number of office workers per 1000 population (1971) or on the share of total regional population in towns of 10,000 population or over (1971). The high and increasing concentration of power within Dublin is both the cause and the consequence of the low 'contact potential' of regional centres relative to Dublin (Fig. 4.2d).[1] In turn, Dublin itself has a low contact potential relative to many European cities (Sahlberg and Engström, 1973).

The degree of concentration in Dublin is high in both public and private sector decision-making. In the case of the public sector in 1976 all general civil servants with principal officer or higher rank worked in Dublin. Private sector decision-making patterns are well illustrated by the growing agglomeration of the largest public companies in the Dublin subregion (Bannon, 1974). The concentration of decision-making may explain the variation in the structure of the East Region's manufacturing employment when compared with the national structure of manufacturing work (Table 4.8).

In all sectors of the economy, most major decisions appear to be taken in Dublin or outside Ireland and transmitted down the urban hierarchy for implementation at local level, in a manner resembling the hypothetical graphical model outlined by Wärneryd (Wärneryd, 1971). Particularly in the case of larger organizations, control functions are highly concentrated in Dublin while routine

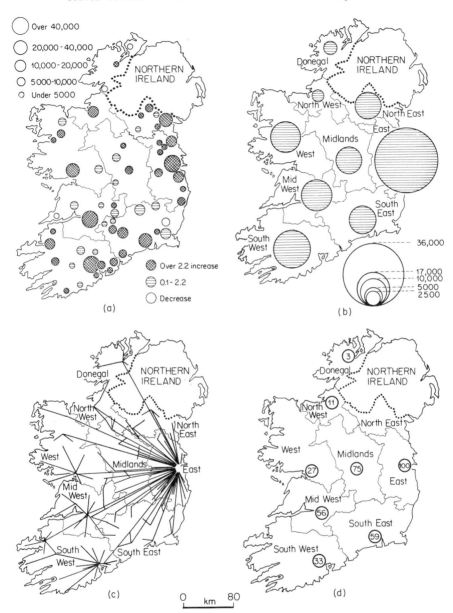

Fig. 4.2. (a) Urban pattern, 1971. (b) Regional distribution of workers in professional, technical, managerial and administrative occupations, 1971. (c) Urban nodal structure defined by telephone traffic (after O'Sullivan, 1968). Reproduced by permission of Pergamon Press Ltd. (d) Contact potential of regional centres, 1971

Table 4.8. Occupational Structure of Manufacturing Employment in State and East Region, 1971

	% Producers, etc.	% Transport, etc.	% Clerical	% Commerce	% Professional, technical	% Others, incl. managers	% Service	Total (%)
State	69.2	9.8	9.3	2.2	2.9	4.6	1.4	100
East Region	67.8	10.4	5.4	3.4	4.2	7.4	1.4	100

Source. *Census of Population, 1971* Vol. III, Tables 7A and 7B, and unpublished Census Data for East Region.

and production work is more widely distributed throughout the regions of the country. The pattern and structure of office organizations is indicative of both information flows and decision-making within the country as a whole.

Office Information Linkages

The previous sections dealt with the growth of office employment and the expansion of decision-making work within the labour force. The regional variation in the pattern of decision-making job functions was related to the pattern of organizational control, which is highly concentrated in Dublin. International research has demonstrated that paralleling the hierarchy of job functions within organizations, there exists a range of links relating each level to its external environment (Törnqvist, 1970; 1973). Production units are related to the outside world through the movement of physical goods before and after processing. Administrative units are related to the external world by means of information flows which may be both infrequent or of routine nature for junior staff but which involve senior personnel in numerous wide-ranging face-to-face meetings. Following upon work by Thorngren (1970), Westaway suggests that it is possible to distinguish three levels of organizational administration, three time horizons, three levels of task and three levels of decision-making, all of which influence the location of a firm's office employment (Westaway, 1974). Information linkages may be either controlled or uncontrolled. Controlled linkages are those for which a reverse payment is made, while uncontrolled information flows arise often from chance or accidental contacts. Both types of information linkages contribute to the growth of capital city regions often at the expense of development in peripheral areas.

In the case of controlled linkages, research suggests that the location of the head office has distinct bearing upon the spatial pattern of service linkages regularly utilized by an organization. In exploring the relationship between corporate structure and development processes, Pred has shown that the spectral structure of linkages within an organization can steer the spread of non-local multiplier effects (Pred, 1973). Since service contacts are often made by the head office in its own immediate environment, many of the benefits of expansion of regional branches accrue to the region in which the head office is located. Such a pattern of multiplier leakage to Toronto has been demonstrated in a study of firms throughout the province of Ontario (Britton, 1974). On the other hand, through uncontrollable information flows firms can derive important external economies and access to innovative stimuli, thereby enhancing the competitive edge of the whole firm (Thorngren, 1967). The centralization of organizational control in a large or capital city brings many benefits, including prestige, availability of a diverse and skilled labour pool and direct penetration into a milieu of inter-organizational exchanges. Because of the high contact potential of large urban centres, firms find it advantageous to locate there, thus intensifying contact differentials between these large centres and regional cities, which are increasingly characterized by limited contact possibilities, low levels of decision-making and few job opportunities in higher-level job functions.

Office units within organizations may be regarded as having both a hierarchy of job functions and a variety of information linkages. These information linkages are fundamental to the viability of the organization. But, in turn, the spatial pattern of contacts may intensify rather than ameliorate regional differentials. Fig. 4.2(d) illustrates the wide differential in contact possibilities between Irish urban centres. In order to understand the nature of inter-organizational contacts in Ireland and their spatial patterning, the following sections outline the results of some pilot studies which broadly confirm the findings of similar research work in other countries.

An initial investigation of communication patterns between offices in central Dublin was based upon management perception of communication flows (Bannon, 1972). From this investigation it appeared that intensity of contact varied with type of office, that office inter-connectivity depended highly on face-to-face contacts and that Dublin offices could be clustered into four groups on the basis of contact intensity and the diversity of contact sources. While the results from this study proved interesting and could be compared with those from other studies (Fernie, 1976), they depended heavily upon management's knowledge of the organization; they also revealed little about contact variations within organizations and provided little information about the nature and location of external contact sources.

Consequently, it was decided to initiate a programme of more detailed communications studies. These studies sought to investigate Dublin office communications within the framework of international communications research and to provide quantifiable data on the mode, duration and complexity of contact. They also sought to investigate the relationship between contact intensity and job status and to establish evidence as to the location and nature of external contact sources.

Communications studies were initiated in a number of Dublin public sector offices, using the contact diary method of recording. A separate diary record of each business communication was obtained and, over two survey periods of 3–4 days, approximately 360 respondents recorded over 6500 communications of which 2629 were over two minutes duration and involved contact with members of other organizations. Almost 70 per cent of the external contacts were made by telephone, with the remaining 821 contacts involving meetings (Table 4.9). These 2629 business communications exhibited characteristics broadly in line with the findings of international studies (Daniels, 1975). As a rule, telephone communications were of short duration, not prearranged, used to discuss a single subject and to provide or to receive information. By contrast, meetings tended to be of longer duration, with 15 per cent lasting more than two hours. Almost half of the recorded external meetings were prearranged; they were usually initiated by a person from another organization and 36 per cent of all meetings involved at least three persons. Over half of the meetings involved initial contact and, therefore, people who, at least in business terms, were not familiar to one another. Most meetings were concerned with a single subject, but over 8 per cent involved wide-ranging discussions. Whereas only 15.8 per cent of total telephone communication was concerned with information exchange, negotiation or general discussion, 26.9 per cent of all recorded meetings professed to involve knowledge exchange and a two-way flow of information.

The analysis of the results demonstrated that contact intensity varied with rank in the organizations, i.e. occupational status. From Table 4.9 it can be seen that these organizations had little dependence upon contact sources outside Dublin. Most of the telephone communication related to other state agencies, while only a small proportion of participants in meetings stated that they came from outside Dublin. Even the larger cities of Cork or Limerick were shown to have little involvement in the contact network outlined in these studies. Most of the participants in meetings worked within central Dublin and 80.3 per cent of all travel to meetings involved less than 30 minutes journey time. These communications characteristics bear out the international findings that office communications are highly concentrated and involve a complex network of information flows between geographically proximate organizations (Thorngren, 1973). The findings show that there is only limited involvement with contact sources from outside the Dublin area.

In an attempt to test the comparability of these results with other findings, the 2629 responses were subjected to latent profile analysis. In particular, the analysis sought to isolate broad communication types similar to the 'programming', 'planning' and 'orientation' processes identified by Thorngren. Fig. 4.3 and Table 4.10 show the results of this analysis using almost all of the 2629 responses. Approximately two-thirds of all communication had the identifiable characteristics of programme-type processes, i.e. predominantly short, unarranged, telephone communications between two persons and relating to a specific subject and involving little or no feedback. At the other extreme, some 10.6 per cent of communications were normally arranged in advance to discuss a wide range of subjects involving information exchange. These communications were almost exclusively meetings, often involved three or more persons and exhibited the identifiable characteristics of orientation processes. The programme allocated the remainder of all communications (25 per cent) to class III or planning processes, which had many of the characteristics of programming processes but were of more frequent occurrence and also involved a greater degree of feedback and complexity of subject-matter. Orientation, or class I communications, were confined almost exclusively to the most senior grades. Most of the class III (planning) processes were associated with middle-level administrators and with technical staff. Most of the staff covered by the surveys were engaged in only limited communication which had all the characteristics of programming processes, i.e. routine, standardized, one-way information flows, usually by telephone.

Table 4.9. Communications Characteristics

	Telephone	Meetings
Total no. of contacts	1808	821
Length of communication	%	%
Less than 10 min	90.8	50.6
11–30 min	8.8	16.6
31–60 min	0.2	6.6
1–2 hr	0.2	11.2
More than 2 hr	—	15.0
	100.0	100.0
Arrangement of communication		
Not prearranged	83.7	56.5
Arranged same day	7.7	5.3
Arranged previous day	3.5	5.5
Arranged 2–7 days in advance	4.1	16.4
Arranged more than 1 week in advance	0.6	16.0
Not stated	0.4	0.3
	100.0	100.0
Initiation of contact		
Person within own office	50.4	30.9
Person in other organization	49.2	68.8
Not stated	0.4	0.3
	100.0	100.0
No. of persons involved		
One other person	100.0	64.3
2–4 other persons	—	16.4
5–10 other persons	—	10.6
Over 10 other persons	—	8.5
Not stated	—	0.2
	100.0	100.0

Telephone only

Nature of organization contacted	%
Other government dept.	15.5
State-sponsored body	2.4
Other state agency	26.1
Local authority	1.6
University/regional technical college	1.1
Labour organization	3.2
Professional firm	15.3
Industrial concern	3.0
Commercial concern	2.7
Hospital	14.2
Outside Ireland	0.9
General public	13.6
Other	0.4
	100.0

Meetings only

For external meetings only: *Principal mode of travel to meeting*	%
Walk	25.1
Bus	11.1
Private car	58.8
Taxi	1.5
Train	3.5
	100.0
Journey time to meeting	
Less than 10 min	28.1
10–30 min	52.2
31–60 min	4.9
1–2 hr	0.5
Over 2 hr	13.8
Not stated	0.5

Table 4.9. (Contd.)

Frequency of contact	Meetings with one other person	Meetings with more than one other person
Occasionally	44.7	22.2
About once a month	11.3	10.7
About once a week	14.2	4.8
Daily contact	4.0	4.1
Initial contact	25.6	57.5
Not stated	0.2	0.7
	100.0	100.0

Range of subject-matter	Meetings with one other person	Meetings with more than one other person
One particular subject	87.4	76.4
Several individual subjects	10.8	14.5
Wide-ranging discussion	0.4	8.2
Not stated	1.4	0.7
	100.0	100.0

Main purpose of contact	Meetings with one other person	Meetings with more than one other person
Giving order/instruction	5.7	3.1
Receiving order/instruction	2.4	2.3
Providing information	31.5	28.3
Receiving information	31.8	28.6
Providing advice	5.5	4.5
Receiving advice	3.3	1.8
Exchanging information	11.6	10.5
Negotiation	2.3	5.7
General discussion	1.9	10.7
Not stated	4.0	4.5
	100.0	100.0

*Work address of participants in meetings**

	Meetings with one other person %	Meetings with more than one other person %
Dublin: inner city (PO areas 1, 2, 4)	21.3	51.4
Remainder of Dublin area	6.3	22.2
Rest of Ireland	7.4	13.7
Outside Republic of Ireland	0.7	0.7
Not stated	64.3	12.0
	100.0	100.0

*Nature of business of participants in meetings**

	Meetings with one other person %	Meetings with more than one other person %
Government dept.	6.6	7.8
State agency	1.1	4.3
Research agency or university	2.3	4.2
Local authority	0.7	0.5
Regional agency	6.4	20.1
Labour organization or prof. society	10.0	29.4
Industrial concern	1.6	0.9
Commercial firm	2.1	0.2
Professional consultancy	1.6	3.6
Other	7.4	25.6
Not stated	60.2	3.4
	100.0	100.0

* Includes only about 75 per cent of responses.

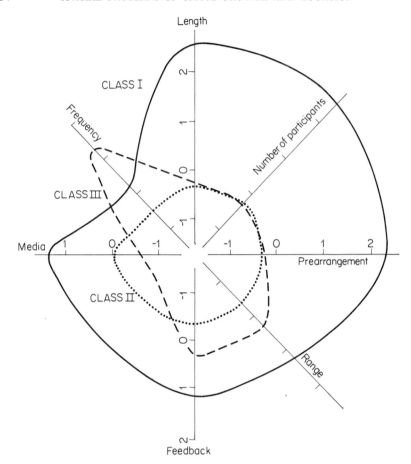

Fig. 4.3. Latent profiles of observed external communications in Dublin office establishments

Table 4.10. Class Means in Standardized Units for Each of Three Profiles

Characteristic	Class I	Class II	Class III
Media	1.4	− 0.2	− 1.2
Length	2.4	− 0.3	− 0.6
Prearrangement	2.3	− 0.3	− 0.4
No. of persons	2.4	− 0.2	− 0.6
Frequency	0.5	− 0.6	1.4
Subject-matter	1.6	− 0.5	0.4
Feedback	1.5	− 0.3	0.1

Source. Pilot studies of office communications in Dublin.

These findings are broadly similar to the findings of other studies (Goddard, 1973) and they have several policy implications. While routine office staff account for the largest share of total communication, these communications are usually routine, standardized and are often made by telephone. In terms of the nature of the work involved, much of this communication could be conducted from any location with adequate telecommunications facilities. The routine communications involve little negotiation, information exchange or interaction with the local environment. For this reason, such job functions could be relocated out of Dublin relatively easily; however, the routine nature of the communication processes involved would be unlikely to generate any serious interactive response from the reception area. While relocation of such routine work would create employment benefits for the reception area, it would do little to counter the existing serious inadequacy of the contact environment of peripheral areas.

Most of the recorded complex interactive communication involved the small number of senior technical and administrative staff. Senior staff both had the highest intensity of business communication and also spent much of their time in meetings with persons from other organizations. The relocation of such contact-intensive job functions would prove difficult and could not be considered in isolation; movement of such job functions would have to be accompanied by the concurrent movement of at least some of the contact sources in related organizations. Relocation of higher-order job functions could stimulate wide-spread interlinkage with the firms in the reception area and thus improve the overall development potential of the area. Relocation of higher-level public sector functions might stimulate parallel relocations by private sector firms. However, relocation of such public sector work would have to be considered in the context of administrative reform and might involve decentralization, devolution or delegation to regional agencies. These pilot investigations did not reveal a high degree of inter-communication or inter-dependence between the public and private sectors (Table 4.9). Further studies, especially within government agencies involved in economic development, might reveal a higher level of interaction with the private sector and identify work whose relocation would closely affect the location of private sector activities.

The results of these pilot surveys highlight the contact importance of a small number of senior job functions within the organizations. Relocation of such complex functions would have clear social, economic and structural benefits for reception areas. Such relocation of decision-making could be expected to create more demand for local services and to retain the benefits of relocation in the reception areas.

Service Contacts by Office Firms

In the previous section mention was made of the role of the head office in directing the pattern of service linkages and controlled contacts. As indicated, there now exists a considerable volume of international evidence to show that offices located in or near large urban centres obtain most of their supplies and services within the immediate environment, while office firms located in small towns or isolated regions often utilize major city services or else have to rely on lower-order service facilities in their immediate locality (Britton, 1974; Goddard, 1975). Studies of the nature and location of services utilized by offices in Ireland bear out the role of the national capital in the provision of 'controllable' services, i.e. services for which a reverse money payment is made.

In the case of central Dublin, office organizations provided information on the nature and location of services made use of in both 1961 and 1971. At both dates the network of service firms used by the offices in the survey was highly concentrated, not only in Dublin, but especially within central Dublin. It was evident that Dublin offices relied increasingly upon firms in their immediate locality for the supply of controllable services. Even when offices relocated within central Dublin they retained their highly centralized network of services. Only when contracting for a new or additional service did the office seek out a service supply source adjacent to its new location. Out of the total network of services utilized by Dublin offices, less than one per cent were located in some part of Ireland outside the Dublin subregion, even though most of the offices served the whole country. More importantly, the study showed that a smaller proportion of Dublin office contacts were with non-Dublin firms in 1971 than in 1961 (Bannon, 1973). In terms of controllable services, Dublin represents a highly self-contained network of contacts with little leakage to parts of Ireland outside the Dublin subregion. Office service firms located outside Dublin appear to face very strong competition from Dublin firms and to have little hope of breaking into the Dublin network.

By contrast, a study in Limerick city showed that offices in Limerick served the regional hinterland, few served areas beyond the Mid West Region, but many were controlled from Dublin. Only 62.9 per cent of controllable services were provided within the Mid West Region and 32 per cent were provided from Dublin. The reliance upon Dublin was particularly strong in regard to the provision of specialist skills, accountancy and insurance services. Approximately one-third of Limerick offices also appear to rely on Dublin suppliers for the provision of stationery, office equipment, printing and other office supplies (Connell, 1976).

A study of offices in Cork revealed similar results to the Limerick study (McCarthy, 1975). Out of a sample of 72 respondent establishments, 87 per cent were either branch offices or local independents; of these, only 12.5 per cent indicated that they provided services beyond the hinterland of Cork city. Contact frequency for services appears similar to the structure of such contacts by Dublin establishments, but unlike Dublin office establishments, which have little reliance on firms outside the Dublin area, 60 per cent of respondents in Cork indicated at least irregular contact with Dublin firms and a quarter of the respondents stated that they maintained weekly contact with Dublin firms for services.

While Dublin offices serve the whole country, they recruit almost all their required services from within their immediate environment with little leakage to the regions. By contrast, Limerick and Cork office firms are often controlled from Dublin; they serve the local region but import a high proportion of their services from Dublin firms, thus leaking many of their benefits out of the region and back to the capital. The concentration of organizational control and decision-making in Dublin induces the direct and indirect growth of Dublin office employment. Apart from the growth of employment in the major firms themselves, their demand for geographically proximate services leads to expansion of service firms in Dublin rather than in regional centres.

The Office Fabric

A major consequence of the expansion of office employment has been the changing demand for and requirements of office accommodation, not only in Dublin but also in regional centres. The changing office accommodation requirements are reflected in both the changing volume of accommodation and the changing pattern of that provision within cities. In Dublin and the other urban centres, offices are usually housed in buildings erected in the Georgian idiom and converted from residential use. Many of these buildings contravene office standards (Bannon, 1972), while planning in relation to office functions remains excessively concerned with negative and restrictive control aspects of the office accommodation factor alone.

As indicated above, much of the growth of office employment in Dublin occurred in expanding rather than in new establishments. Allied to the growing size of establishments, there was a desire for greater functional clustering and a demand for greater variations in the type of office environment. By a complex process involving the 'deaths' of some office establishments, the 'births' of others and the migration of still more, the pattern of office establishments has shifted southwards into the zone of 'active assimilation' within central Dublin. Spacious nineteenth-century residences have been converted to office uses, while large tracts of blighted property remain to the north of the business area in zones of 'passive assimilation' (Griffin and Preston, 1966). The evolving pattern of office functions derives from a complex succession of short-distance moves; through these short moves districts within the centre are increasingly specializing in particular office functions. Pivotal to this has been the expansion of the financial centre in Dame Street to the exclusion of other office uses which have migrated southwards, inducing in turn further relocations of other office functions. Apart from offices attached to the airport and to peripheral industrial estates, there has been little suburbanization of office functions and even less suburban office development. Attitudes to relocation out of the central area to fashionable suburbs are positive, but there is a reluctance to entertain proposals for relocation to less fashionable areas of the city or, more especially, to towns outside Dublin (Bannon, 1973).

The rapid expansion of office employment in Dublin, the need to replace obsolescent space coupled with a need to properly house new office equipment, and the desire to meet the changing requirements and tastes of office staff have led to an office property boom within central Dublin. Approximately five million sq. ft of commercial office space has been erected within central Dublin, most of it since 1965. The geographic pattern of office building follows and derives from the evolving pattern of office establishments (Fig. 4.4). Major office investment tends to be confined largely to locations which are perceived as safe office locations in

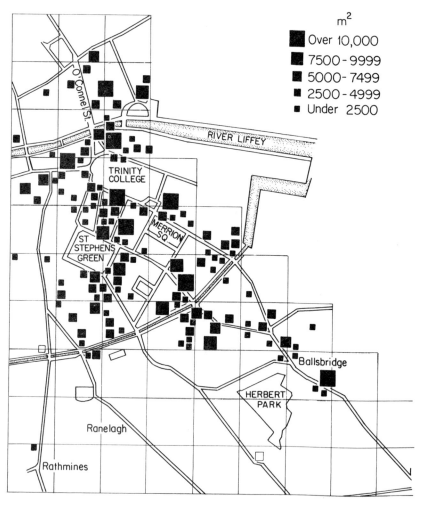

Fig. 4.4 Modern office buildings erected in central Dublin, 1960–76

which a demand for office space already exists and where change of use has taken place. Table 4.11 sets out the salient characteristics of the Dublin office market in recent years.

The amount of commercially developed office space being erected or rented is related to the volume of private office development. The period of recession after 1973 has seen an increased interest in office development for owner occupation. Nevertheless, the volume of commercial office space provision remains high, with over 600,000 sq. ft due for completion in 1976–77.

Table 4.11 shows that the volume of new office development remained high from 1970 to 1975, with a steady increase in the rental per square foot and the state sector renting an increasing proportion of the total available space. Having regard to the high level of government involvement, it is particularly unfortunate that more of this investment has not been directed to the 'passive assimilation' area requiring renewal (Fig. 4.4). In urban centres outside Dublin, there is relatively little demand for office space and much of the existing stock is old and often in contravention of legal standards. The provision of commercial office space has been inhibited in cities outside Dublin as a result of the limited office market deriving from the relative lack of office employment, by the low level of office rents which barely compensate for construction and site costs, and by the imposition of a uniform rate of stamp duty on office development in all major towns except Galway and Sligo. While over five million sq. ft of commercial office space has been erected in Dublin since 1960, the total provision of new commercial office space in centres outside Dublin would not exceed 500,000 sq. ft. Also, in contrast to developments in Dublin, commercial developments tend to be on a small scale, with few in excess of 50,000 sq. ft.

Regional centres are thus deprived of the construction and other direct benefits arising from office development, while the local economy has to forego the multiplier benefits of an expanding office industry. More important, however,

Table 4.11. Commercial Office Development in Dublin, 1969–75

Year of completion	Total floor space	Median rent	State sector	Type of tenant	
				Financial	Commerce/ Professional
	sq. ft	psf	%	%	%
1969	473,000	1.23	40	27	33
1970	180,000	1.34	39	47	14
1971	190,000	1.66	40	44	16
1972	756,000	2.08	40	46	14
1973	617,000	2.26	70	10	20
1974	572,000	2.75	82	9	9
1975	380,000	3.15	65	8	27

Source: Reports by Dublin estate agencies.

may be the very high degree of leakage back to the capital from much of the office development which actually occurs in regional centres, whether the development is built for owner occupation or for rental. A feature of much of this type of work has been the tendency to employ specialist services from outside the region or from abroad. Many of the architectural, engineering and surveying consultants are based in Dublin or London, while many of the construction companies are also based in Dublin. The impact of the limited office market outside Dublin is thus further restricted as a result of the leakage of benefits back to the capital; much of the local benefit derived from such activity is confined to the provision of skilled and semi-skilled construction jobs which are controlled from outside the region.

Thus in terms of both the amount of office construction activity and also the leakage from existing work back to Dublin, regional centres are seriously deprived of both the direct and indirect benefits of an expanding local office property market.

Future Trends in Office Employment

The previous sections of this chapter have examined four inter-related aspects of office activities each of which testifies to the importance of central Dublin within both the regional and national contexts. From these past trends it is necessary to identify the consequences of future developments and, in addition, to examine the potential for policy intervention. Projection of employment trends into the future by whatever means is fraught with many difficulties. Projection of office employment trends is especially hazardous since occupational forecasting is in its infancy and since short-run variations may more easily be exaggerated in the long term. In addition, the quality of occupational data and their comparability over time also leave much to be desired. In attempting to project future trends in office employment three possible approaches were considered. Office employment in Ireland in the future might reasonably be expected to increase its share of the total labour force in line with present levels in the more developed EEC countries. Secondly, from international data it is possible to suggest desirable or feasible limits for office occupations in each sector and to use these as targets to be attained at some future date in Ireland. Thirdly, a simple trend projection of office employment provides an indication of what might happen if past trends continue and if deliberate interventionist policies are not adopted. In the absence of earlier comparable data, Table 4.12 provides the results of a trend projection of office occupations, professional/technical and administration/managerial occupations from 1971 to 1986 based upon trends which occurred in the decade 1961–1971. The resultant figures can be relied upon with some confidence since they come within the levels which might be achieved using either of the other possible methods of projection mentioned above and since there are indications that the growth in information will continue.

Table 4.12. Trend Projection of Professional/Technical, Administration/Managerial and Office Employment, 1971–86

Region	Office occupations		Administrative/ managerial		Professional/ technical	
	Number 1986	% change 1971/86	Number 1986	% change 1971/86	Number 1986	%change 1971/86
East	157,180	+ 56.5	18,700	+ 70.1	77,260	+ 80.0
South West	32,445	+ 55.5	2620	+ 19.7	20,850	+ 40.4
South East	20,110	+ 67.9	1550	+ 34.8	12,980	+ 32.4
Mid West	21,700	+ 93.5	1900	+ 59.3	12,980	+ 52.2
West	12,455	+ 73.7	850	+ 38.2	11,370	+ 37.3
Midlands	11,615	+ 74.4	800	+ 44.1	8420	+ 30.1
North East	11,175	+ 68.2	1070	+ 49.2	7190	+ 36.5
Donegal	4245	+ 55.8	350	+ 31.1	3010	+ 16.1
North West	4150	+ 57.8	260	+ 10.6	2920	+ 22.0
Total all regions	275,075	+ 61.5	28,100	+ 56.8	156,890	+ 51.9

Source. Trend projection derived from *Census of Population, 1961, 1971.*

A continuation of past trends would lead to a 61.5 per cent growth in office occupations between 1971 and 1986. Table 4.12 shows that by 1986 the East Region's share of total office employment might be expected to decline slightly to 57.1 per cent of the national total. While the number of office workers in each region might be expected to increase, only five regions, the South East, Mid West, West, Midlands and North East, would be likely to increase their share of total office employment. In absolute terms, 54 per cent of all expected growth in office occupations would occur in the East Region, with most of it still within central Dublin.

Table 4.12 also presents the results of a trend projection of workers in administration and professional occupations which, though not exclusively office occupations, are likely to indicate the general trend in higher-level office occupations. On the basis of 1961–71 trends, the East Region's share of both occupational groupings might be expected to increase substantially. However, in both administration and professional occupations, only the East Region alone would substantially exceed the national level of increase in this type of work; the Mid West Region would also perform slightly better than the national rate and considerably ahead of trends in the other seven regions. Sixty per cent of all the projected increase in professional occupations and 76 per cent of total growth in administration work between 1971 and 1986 would occur in the East Region, particularly within Dublin.

The decline in the East Region's share of total office work derives from a reduction in its share of total routine office occupations. Similar tendencies have been identified in the United Kingdom's office employment structure (Department of the Environment, 1976). While the workforce in information handling is likely to expand more rapidly outside the East Region, higher-level office work on the basis of past trends will continue to expand rapidly within Dublin and to account for an increasing proportion of both the office employment and the total labour force of the Region. Analysis of the trend projection suggests that, without intervention, decision-making functions are likely to remain highly concentrated in the East Region, particularly within central Dublin.

While a trend projection provides some indication of the development implications of future growth along past lines, such a projection depends upon many assumptions and, in addition, may not concur with either the objectives or the requirements of policies for future development. Thus, in the case of Ireland, the national objective of providing full employment for the 1986 labour force would demand a more rapid rate of job creation and an even faster growth of office and white-collar work. Similarly, it can be argued that regional policies seek to ensure that the future regional sharing of total employment will reverse the past trend towards concentration, particularly in the case of decision-making. This, in turn, may depend largely on whether the government pursues a policy of dispersal or seeks to develop selected key centres as office reception areas.

In the case of a small 'developing' economy such as Ireland, several exogenous factors may inhibit development along historical lines. Membership of the EEC may adversely affect development by attracting decision functions to more centrally located European capitals. Conversely, however, other firms might be attracted to establish a trading base in the Community by setting up an Irish outlet. Of crucial importance to small and developing countries is their need to have control over their own production processing. Ireland has successfully attracted foreign manufacturing firms to set up in the country, thereby creating a substantial amount of new employment (McMenamin, 1975). However, many of these foreign firms are branches of multinational organizations and all are controlled from abroad. Consequently, decisions may be made without regard to the environment in which the branch plant is located, while many of the benefits may be leaked to other countries through the vertical pattern of linkages to head office and the pattern of horizontal contacts maintained by the head office in its own immediate environment. In addition, the developing economy, such as Ireland, is deprived of the considerable employment benefits and the multiplier effects associated with high income, and prestigious managerial and other research and development functions. This problem becomes all the more pertinent for Ireland in view of the recent development of natural resources.

In recognition of the importance of increasing employment outside the area of goods production, Ireland has since 1973 extended development policies and incentives to incorporate some categories of 'service industries' (Bannon *et al.*,

1977). However, in the light of future employment needs at both national and regional level, this policy requires to be strengthened by the provision of more attractive incentives to foreign firms and the pursuit of a clearly defined and logical location strategy for both private and public sector office functions within Ireland. The pursuit of such policies could be expected to generate more office jobs than' the non-interventionist assumptions implicit in Table 4.11 would suggest; a different spatial pattern of inter-urban office location might also emerge. A positive policy of developing a limited number of adequately equipped and serviced office centres could facilitate a new pattern of decision-making and stimulate the greater integration and development of the regions. Were relocation of office functions from Dublin to be considered within the broader context of organizational restructuring and administration reform, then wider social, economic and organizational benefits would also accrue. In addition, the mismatch between labour skills and employment would be reduced through the operation of comprehensive regional policies which promoted office opportunities in regional centres while also creating unskilled jobs in Dublin for a large pool of existing unemployed.

Future Research

Research into employment structures is dependent upon reliable and up-to-date information. The available data on occupational aspects of employment are both inadequate and seriously out of date. There is an urgent need to refine and expand the type of information available on occupational structure within each branch of economic activity at both national and local level. Development policies in the office field urgently require research into a number of separate aspects of office employment. Firstly, it is important to investigate the long-run implications of economic recession for white-collar jobs, especially in the public service; will a continuation of the recession lead to retrenchment in the private sector or to an acceptance of lower levels of state involvement and, ultimately, to a need for fewer jobs in the public service? Secondly, from the inadequate international data which do exist, is it possible to identify thresholds for office occupations for each industry? If so, how do these vary between countries of differing size or at different stages of development?

Within Ireland, development policies could be pursued with greater confidence in the area of office functions if there existed adequate information about the inter-linkage between the public and private sectors. The pilot studies quoted in this chapter relate to public service offices in the welfare area of government and, not surprisingly, the volume of inter-linkage was limited. How typical are these findings of other government agencies and, if they are found to be typical, could relocation of such functions be expected to stimulate private sector relocations?

Perhaps the single most important requirement is to further develop the concept of contact potential and to understand more clearly how the components of the contact potential model interact. Fig. 4.2(d) illustrated the wide variation in inter-urban contact potential within Ireland; by what means and to what extent must the contact potential of cities such as Cork or Limerick be enhanced or enlarged to enable such centres to compete with Dublin and also to evolve as self-sustaining, viable office centres? Is it possible to identify any catalyst to foster such developments? At the regional level, the most urgent problem is the specification of a strategy for physical development incorporating those elements conducive to the more equitable spatial patterning of decision-making and office functions in general. Such a strategy needs to evolve in the light of research into the issues outlined above.

Conclusion

This chapter has demonstrated that through decision-making functions and the related pattern of office linkages, Dublin exerts a very strong control over the development of the Irish economy. As a result, Dublin has benefited from a rapid growth of office jobs, especially higher-level jobs. The pattern of office linkages maintained by Dublin offices is spatially concentrated; in consequence, there is little leakage out of Dublin to regional centres, while offices in regional centres depend heavily upon Dublin firms and, thereby, leak many of their benefits out of the local economy in favour of Dublin. On the basis of past trends, Dublin can be expected to intensify its control of the social and economic development of the country and to attract an increasing share of head office functions and higher-level office work. However, it is the objective of regional policies to foster new patterns of development. The success of regional policies depends in large measure on the spatial development patterns which have been adopted and which can only be justified in the light of rigorous research findings, including further research into the development of office functions. Development planning at both local and national level must have greater regard for communication factors in location and the role of inter-organizational contacts in development generally.

References

Armstrong, R. B. (1972), *The Office Industry: Patterns of Growth and Location.* Cambridge, Mass.: MIT Press.

Bannon, M. J. (1972), *The Development and Organization of Office Activities in Central Dublin.* Unpublished Ph.D. Thesis, Trinity College, Dublin.

Bannon, M. J. (1973), Office location and regional development in Ireland, in M. J. Bannon (Ed.), *Office Location and Regional Development.* Dublin: An Foras Forbartha, pp. 9–18.

Bannon, M. J. (1974), The changing role of the office in the industrial firm, *Management*, **21**, 39–44.

Bannon, M. J., Eustace, J. G., and Power, M. (1977), *Service-Type Employment and Regional Development.* Dublin: The Stationery Office.

Britton, J. N. H. (1974), Environmental adaptation of industrial plants: service linkages, locational environment and organisation, in F. E. I. Hamilton (Ed.), *Spatial*

Perspectives on Industrial Organization and Decision-making. London: Wiley, pp. 363–390.

Connell, J. (1976), *Some Aspects of Office Activities in Limerick* Unpublished M.Phil. Thesis, Department of Urban Design and Regional Planning, University of Edinburgh.

Daniels, P. W. (1975), *Office Location: An Urban and Regional Study.* London: Bell.

Davey, J. (1972), *The Office Industry in Wellington.* Wellington: Ministry of Works.

Department of the Environment (1976), *The Office Location Review.* London: Department of the Environment.

Dublin Corporation (1975), *Land Use in the Inner City Area.* Dublin: Dublin Corporation.

EFTA (1973), *National Settlement Strategies: A Framework for Regional Development.* Geneva: European Free Trade Association.

European Economic Community (1974), *Basic Statistics,* Brussels.

Eustace, J., and McKee, S. I. (1973), Ireland, in M. Broady (Ed.), *Marginal Regions.* London: Bedford Square Press, pp. 28–45.

Fernie, J. (1976), Office linkages and location: an evaluation of patterns in three cities, *Town Planning Review,* **48**, 78–89.

Goddard, J. B. (1973), Office employment, urban development and regional policy, in M. J. Bannon (Ed.), *Office Location and Regional Development.* Dublin: An Foras Forbartha, pp. 21–35.

Goddard, J. (1975), *Office Location in Urban and Regional Development.* London: Oxford University Press.

Gottmann, J. (1974), *The Evolution of Urban Centrality: Orientations for Research.* Oxford: University of Oxford School of Geography, Research Paper No. 8.

Griffin, D. and Preston, R. E. (1966), A restatement of the transition zone concept, *Annals, Association of American Geographers,* **56**, 339–350.

McCarthy, J. (1975), *Office Location in Cork City.* Unpublished B.A. Thesis, Department of Geography, University College Dublin.

McMenamin, P. (1975), The industrial development process in the Republic of Ireland, 1953–72, in J. Vaizey (Ed.), *Economic Sovereignty and Regional Policy.* London: Gill & MacMillan, pp. 165–198.

O'Sullivan, P.M. (1968), The spatial structure of the Irish economy, *Regional Studies,* **2**, 199.

Pederson, P.O. (1970), Innovation diffusion within and between national urban systems, *Geographical Analysis,* **2**, 203–54.

Pred, A. (1973), The growth and development of systems of cities in advanced economies, in A. Pred and G. Törnqvist (Eds.), *Systems of Cities and Information Flows.* University of Lund: Lund Studies in Geography, Series B, No. 38, pp. 9–82.

Sabolo, Y., *et al.* (1975), *The Service Industries.* Geneva: International Labour Office.

Sahlberg, B., and Engström, M. (1973), *Travel Demand, Transport Systems and Regional Development.* Lund: Lund Studies in Geography, Series B, No. 39.

Thorngren, B. (1967), Regional interaction and flows of information, *Proceedings of the Second Poland-Norden Regional Science Seminar.* Warsaw: Polish Academy of Sciences, pp. 175–86.

Thorngren, B. (1970), How do contact systems affect regional development?, *Environment and Planning,* **2**, 409–427.

Thorngren, B. (1973), Communication studies for Government office dispersal in Sweden, in M. J. Bannon (Ed.), *Office Location and Regional Development.* Dublin An Foras Forbartha, pp. 47–58.

Törnqvist, G. (1970), *Contact Systems and Regional Development.* University of Lund: Lund Studies in Geography, Series B, No. 35.

Törnqvist, G. (1973), Contact requirements and travel facilities, in A. Pred and G.

Törnqvist (Eds.), *Systems of Cities and Information Flows.* University of Lund: Lund Studies in Geography, Series B, No. 38, pp. 83–121.

Walsh, B. (1975), *Population and Employment Projections, 1971–86.* Dublin: The Stationary Office.

Wärneryd, O. (1971), An operational model for regional planning and development control, in T. Hägerstrand and A. R. Kuklinski (Eds.), *Information Systems for Regional Development.* University of Lund: Lund Studies in Geography, Series B, No. 37, pp. 230–245.

Westaway, J. (1974), The spatial hierarchy of business organizations and its implications for the British urban system, *Regional Studies,* **8**, 145–155.

Wright, M. (1967), *The Dublin Region: Advisory Regional Plan and Final Report.* Dublin: The Stationery Office.

Woodward, V. H. (1975), A view of occupational employment in 1981, *Department of Employment Gazette,* **83**, 619–622.

Notes

1. Contact Potential (Face-to-Face) of Irish Regional Centres

	Score	Scale
Dublin*	172,419	100
Cork	57,574	33
Limerick	107,482	56
Waterford	101,212	59
Dundalk	101,957	59
Galway	57,049	27
Sligo	19,212	11
Athlone	129,000	75
Letterkenny†	5000	3

*Based on:

$$V_i = \sum_{j=i}^{9} (T_{ij} - D_{ij}) K_j$$

where V_i = contact potential of centre i; T_{ij} = staying time in centre j as based on eight-hour day; D_{ij} = resistance factor or return travel time to centre j as calculated in road travel time as estimated for the 30th highest hour (see *The National Primary Route*, An Foras Forbartha); K_j = the number of contact-intensive occupations in region j as calculated for the regional centre.

†In the case of Letterkenny since negative potential is not possible the equation was altered to

$$V_i = \sum_{j=i}^{1} \frac{(T_{ij})}{(D_{ij})} K_j.$$

5

White-Collar Employment in UK Manufacturing Industry

G. Gudgin, R. Crum and S. Bailey

Introduction

The fact that employment in service activities is greater than employment in manufacturing is a well-known aspect of advanced industrial economies. It is perhaps less commonly appreciated that similar activities also account for more than a third of all employment within the manufacturing sector itself. In Great Britain in 1971 nearly three million people were employed in office and other non-production occupations within the manufacturing sector.

In addition to the numerical significance of this employment, its regional distribution is an important aspect of the subject-matter of this book for several reasons. Firstly, while direct, or production, employment is in long-term decline within the UK, the non-production jobs tend to increase. Until the current recession at least, non-production employment has also fluctuated less over the business cycle. Regions with high proportions of non-production employment thus have had some built-in stability against the rigours of employment fluctuation. Non-production workers are more highly paid on average than are production workers, and any regional impact of differences in occupation composition is multiplied to this extent. Finally, these occupations include all of the decision-makers in manufacturing above the level of foreman, and it is sometimes argued that any regional concentration of control and authority will have serious implications for future regional development. In particular, worries are expressed about the growing threat of a UK economy in which a strong core–periphery element exists, with most control vested in the South and Midlands while branch plant economies typify the North and Wales.

This chapter is a summary of parts of a longer report (Crum and Gudgin, 1978)

127

which will serve as a source for those interested in a more extended discussion of the points raised here. In this chapter the nature and numerical importance of white-collar activities in manufacturing is described. This is followed by a consideration of influences on the occupational composition of employment at individual establishments as a prelude to an analysis of the nature and causes of the uneven regional distribution of non-production employment.

The main sources of data on which this chapter is based include both questionnaire/interview surveys and official statistics. There were four main surveys, aimed at headquarters sites, R & D sites, subcorporate organizations within large companies, and branch plants respectively (with some overlap between the last two). The numbers of establishments surveyed were 130, 30, 450 and 1200 respectively. Official statistics were drawn predominantly from the 1971 *Census of Population*, which was considered the most comprehensive and reliable source, but also from the *Census of Production* and *Census of Employment*.

The Functions of Non-Production Departments

Although the major concern is with white-collar activities, it is convenient for what follows to set these within the context of non-production activities as a whole. We shall refer to the latter as NP activities and retain the official abbreviation ATC (administrative, technical and clerical) for white-collar occupations. The difference between the NP and ATC categories is made up of manual employees in transport, warehousing and ancillary jobs such as cleaning canteens and security which together comprise 23 per cent of NP employment.

To some extent the role played by NP staff in manufacturing is self-evident, concerned as it is with management, administration, sales and distribution, research development and design, security and welfare. It is interesting to describe these functions in a little more detail, however, and it is important to specify their relative numerical importance.

Ideally, statistics would be available with employment classified by functions or departments, and also by levels in the organizational hierarchy, with categories such as production management or advertising. No official statistics are collected in this way, and all that is available to us is sample information collected in surveys. Complete figures are available by occupation and in great detail. Although occupation is not quite the same thing as function, the two do overlap to an extent.

In Table 5.1 the large number of occupations used in the *Census of Production* have been condensed into seven groups and 26 subgroups. Clerical workers (who are predominantly females) are easily the most numerous group, accounting for one-third of all NP employment and almost one in eight jobs in manufacturing as a whole. Next most numerous among the white-collar occupations are the scientific and technical occupations, dominated by engineers and associated technicians. Only 25 per cent of this group work in research and development

Table 5.1. Numbers Employed in Non-Production Occupations in Manufacturing Industry in Great Britain, 1971

Occupation category	Numbers employed	Percentage of total employment in manufacturing industry
General manager	264,720	3.25
Sales managers	79,000	0.97
Personnel managers	12,680	0.16
Specialist managers	64,830	0.80
Other professional workers	16,750	0.21
Accountants & company secretaries	32,920	0.40
Total: Managerial & professional	470,900	5.79
Typists/secretaries	229,230	2.82
Clerks & cashiers	623,280	7.66
Communications workers (telephonists)	27,930	0.34
Office machine operators	68,740	0.84
Office supervisors & managers	21,940	0.27
Total: Clerical	971,120	11.94
General engineers	123,180	1.51
Scientists	52,520	0.65
Technicians	139,040	1.71
Methods & planning engineers	42,020	0.52
Instructors/teachers	15,990	0.20
Draughtsmen	102,730	1.26
Total: Scientific & technical	475,480	5.85
Warehousemen	240,680	2.96
Transport workers	162,910	2.00
Salesmen, etc.	169,380	2.08
Cleaners	56,740	0.70
Service workers (canteen)	85,830	1.05
Maintenance & ground staff	116,500	1.43
Medical & social welfare workers	13,070	0.16
Total: Service	272,140	3.34
Workers specific to certain industries	55,930	0.69
Total: Non-production workers	2,818,540	34.64
Total employment in manufacturing industry	8,135,790	100.00

Source: *Census of Population, 1971.*

(Department of Trade and Industry, 1975), with the remainder in production engineering or design departments. Scientists are proportionately more heavily engaged in research than are engineers and are also concentrated in the chemicals industry.

Almost as numerous are managers and professional workers. Table 5.1 reveals something of the structure of managerial occupations, although well over half are described simply as general managers, a category including the owner-managers of small firms, production managers and managing directors. Specialist managers include departmental managers, other than those in production, sales or personnel, in such departments as transport, purchasing or advertising. The 'other professionals' category includes surveyors, architects, lawyers, economists and interpreters among others, and together with accountants and company secretaries comprises only a tiny fraction of NP employment.

The final white-collar occupation, other than the very small medical and welfare category, is salesmen. If these are added to the sales managers then sales, even with the omission of associated clerical support can be seen to employ nearly 10 per cent of NP staff, although this amounts to only 3 per cent of all manufacturing employment.

With the exception of the manual NP activities, it is not possible to gain much information on functions from figures on occupation alone. In particular, the distribution of clerical workers between functions is unknown. Table 5.2 provides the best information available to us, although even then it presents a somewhat biased picture in that the figures relate only to relatively large, multiplant, firms. Indeed, in small firms it is often impossible to measure individual functions since one person will usually assume several roles. There is some evidence (Wool Industry Economic Development Council, 1969) that differentiation of functions becomes marked by a size threshold of about 200 employees, and Table 5.2 is likely to be reasonably representative of firms larger than this, and thus of the majority of manufacturing industry.

Table 5.2 contains a differentiation between establishments on the basis of status within organizations to introduce some idea of location. Detached head offices account for only about 1 per cent of manufacturing employment and this should be born in mind in weighting the relative importance of the columns in Table 5.2. In research and development, for instance, the total figure is known to be 2.3 per cent, and this would represent a weighted average of the columns of Table 5.2, but would also include a minority employed in separate R & D establishments.

The major feature of Table 5.2 is the variety of functions and the wide dispersion of employment among them. No department in the branch plants includes more than one-sixth of NP employment, or 5 per cent of total employment. The largest white-collar departments are production planning (including engineering) and sales, with the remaining ones being individually small. General management (usually including factory managers and assistant

Table 5.2. Average NP Function Proportions by Status of Establishment

Department (or function)	Branch	Production site including head office	Detached head office
		% of total employment	
Number of observations	352	64	32
1. General management	2.1	2.0	12.0
2. Public relations	0.03	0.09	1.3
3. Data processing	0.3	0.9	5.5
4. Office services	2.0	2.2	10.1
Subtotal: General management	4.5	5.2	28.9
5. Wages and salaries	0.9	1.0	1.1
6. Accounts and finance	1.9	3.4	11.9
7. Legal, insurance, etc.	0.1	0.2	2.3
8. Purchasing	0.8	1.2	2.3
Subtotal: Specialist services	3.7	5.8	17.6
9. Personnel, etc.	0.6	0.8	3.1
10. Health, welfare, etc.	1.1	1.4	1.9
11. Security and maintenance	4.4	4.6	1.4
Subtotal: Personnel & maintenance	6.2	6.9	6.4
12. Product design	1.4	2.1	2.7
13. Production planning	4.1	4.1	3.7
14. Quality control	2.1	2.2	0.7
Subtotal: Production-related departments	7.6	8.4	7.1
15. Research and development	0.7	1.7	5.4
16. Market research, etc.	0.5	1.6	5.6
17. Sales	2.4	6.2	14.7
18. Sales servicing	0.5	1.9	3.8
19. Distribution	3.8	3.9	5.9
Subtotal: Marketing and distribution	7.2	13.3	30.0
20. Other	0.6	0.4	0.6
Total: NP functions	30.4	41.7	100.0

Source: *Organization Survey.*

managers and directors) and finance, which together make up the nerve centre of the administration, are shown to be functions carried out by a surprisingly small number of people.

The functions most likely to be concentrated at head office level are very apparent in Table 5.2. They include general management with clerical support, accounts and finance, but not wages and salaries, public relations, data processing and the company secretary's department (legal, pensions, etc.), personnel, marketing and sales. In some cases a hierarchical split is common. Within personnel, for instance, it is common to maintain a personnel director plus a small team of specialists at head office while one or a few personnel officers deal with day-to-day matters at individual plants.

If the evidence of Table 5.1 and 5.2 is taken together then the hierarchical, occupational and functional subdivisions of employment can all be ascertained to some extent. In particular, it is obvious that although functions are numerous and individually small, they often include a majority of clerical workers or technicians within them, as opposed to managers, professional workers, scientists or engineers.

Trends Over Time and International Comparisons

Although white-collar workers perform a variety of functions, they mostly have in common the fact that their numbers increase over time. Fig. 5.1 shows how ATC employment as a whole has increased from around 10 per cent after the first world war to almost 30 per cent now. In the period up until the early fifties the rate of increase was around a quarter of 1 per cent per annum, but after that

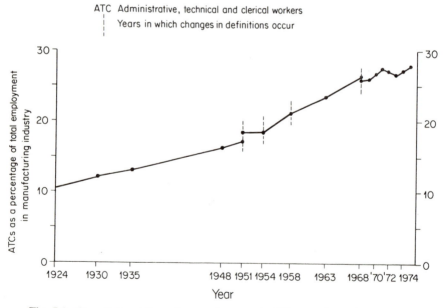

Fig. 5.1. Growth in white-collar employment in UK manufacturing industry (source: British Labour Statistics, *Department of Employment Gazette*)

the rate of increase doubled until 1968. Since then the increase appears to be back to interwar levels, although the increased amplitude of cyclical fluctuations in business activity in the 1970s makes it premature to decide whether the slowdown is due to a real change in long-term trends or to the effects of an incomplete cycle. Production workers are typically laid off in greater numbers and sooner with the onset of a recession. The next two years should suffice to tell us whether a break in the rapid growth of the fifties and sixties has indeed occurred.

The most probable explanation of changes in long-term rates of growth in the ATC percentage is connected with productivity. Despite a view occasionally advanced that white-collar, or indirect, workers reduce average productivity because they do not directly produce anything, the opposite seems the more accurate state of affairs. Across industries high ATC percentages are most closely associated with high productivity ($r^2 = 0.72$ for 118 industries). The connection between the ATC percentage and productivity is due to several factors. Firstly, managers must manage machines, goods and materials as well as workers, and hence any increase in the former relative to the latter will tend to increase the ratio of managers to production workers as long as economies of scale in management do not nullify the increase. More important in quantitative terms is the fact that increased output per operative produces more goods which then need to be sold, distributed, recorded and invoiced. In addition, the necessity for production engineers and computer staff (e.g. with numerically controlled machine tools) among others is increased if the productivity increase is due to increased capital intensity.

The relevance of the relationship to changes over time is as follows. High unemployment means less pressure to substitute capital for labour giving a lower rate of productivity increase, and hence a lower rate of increase in the ratio of ATC workers to operatives. This type of mechanism probably explains the change between the interwar and postwar periods, and if a real change has occurred since the late 1960s then this too may be associated with the higher unemployment which has characterized the UK economy since 1966. The relationship is not only important in explaining temporal change. As will be seen below, it is also important in the regional dimension. The general increase in the proportion of ATC workers is true of most broad categories of NP workers, although at a greater level of detail there are examples of decline. One example is provided by draughtsmen, whose function is being increasingly automated. Table 5.3 shows that the strongest increase has been among professional and scientific staff. The existence of definitional changes make it unwise to examine small changes too closely, but sales and warehouse staff appear not to have increased their proportions after 1966 and the increase in clerical staff slackened considerably in the sixties. The pattern is broadly what might be expected in that the more routine tasks, especially those employing large numbers, are automated and replaced first, with the result that clerical or manual occupations disappear at the expense of highly skilled occupations which service and operate the new

Table 5.3. Trends in Certain Occupations in Manufacturing Industry, 1921–71

| Occupation groups | Percentage of total employment | | | | | | Nos. employed (000's) |
	1921	1931	1951	1961	1966	1971	1971
Managers	N/A	N/A	2.7	2.4	2.6	3.2	264.7
Professional staff (incl. scientists)	N/A	N/A	3.2	5.5	6.1	7.1	574.4
Clerical & secretarial staff	4.8	5.6	9.2	11.0	11.3	11.6	943.5
Sales staff	N/A	N/A	1.8	2.1	2.3	2.1	169.4
Warehousemen & storekeepers	N/A	N/A	2.4	3.2	3.3	3.0	240.7
Road goods vehicles drivers	N/A	N/A	1.2	1.5	1.6	1.7	135.4

Sources. *Censuses of Population, 1951, 1961, 1966* and *1971*; Department of Employment, *Growth in Office Employment*, Manpower Studies No. 7.

technology. Typewriters, photocopiers, calculators and even vending machines are all labour-saving innovations affecting NP numbers, but the most important current innovations are obviously computers (Stoneman, 1975) and telecommunications.

The Causes of Variations in NP Proportions Between Establishments

Later in this chapter we shall want to explain regional variations in the distribution of white-collar workers and other NP workers. As with most spatial distributions, the important causal factors will be the geographical incidence of essentially non-spatial processes, and as a result it is necessary to examine these processes, albeit briefly, before proceeding.

The main factors can be viewed as belonging to one of two groups. One very important type of influence is connected with the type of product and process of manufacture. Different products and processes require different degrees of technical input, storage, paperwork and also marketing and distribution arrangements. In addition, the scale of production will influence the proportions in various occupations, particularly in management. The second group reflects the organizational status of an establishment within its company. Although the constraints of type of production and market will influence the occupational composition within a company, larger companies are left with considerable discretion on how to locate the NP functions between the various production (or other) sites. Hence branch plants, single-plant subsidiary companies, main factories, detached offices, will all have different compositions even if the end-product is identical. A third category consisting of other, or random, factors might also be inserted, since a considerable variation exists between companies even in producing the same product for similar markets at the same scale of production. This can be due to the contracting out of white-collar activities to specialist non-manufacturing firms, but more often appears to be due to variations in efficiency or internal organization.

The nature of products, processes and markets are all encompassed in describing an establishment's industry, although it should be realized that the commonly used standard industrial classification (SIC) is just one of many ways in which the hundred thousand or so establishments in the UK could be classified. Table 5.4 describes the variation of NP categories between industries, with the coefficients of variation indicating which occupations are most variable in numerical importance across industries. Managerial and professional workers form a relatively uniform proportion of employment in all industries, although in fact the uniformity is contributed by the managers rather than by the other professionals. Clerical workers have a similar degree of uniformity, and in both cases this is a result of the relatively constant managerial and clerical inputs required in the manufacture of almost all products. Technical sales and distribution occupations all exhibit greater variability reflecting the different demands of the various products, processes and markets. In distribution the variability is concentrated in transport rather than in warehousing and is contributed largely by four industries in which distribution is both an important element and also highly internalized within the industry rather than being contracted out.

Explanations which go beyond the catch-all industry classification need to divide occupations into those primarily dependent on production or marketing conditions and those which in contrast are largely dependent on other NP activities. Clerical and service workers largely fall into the latter category, and to some extent managers do also. A difference in marketing arrangements, for example, may have a direct effect on the size of the sales force and distribution staff, but will also have multiplier effects in terms of the additional clerical staff who pay the wages of the extra salesmen, and also personnel officers, managers, canteen staff, cleaners and others.

Table 5.5 lists those occupation groups which can be considered largely dependent on such external circumstances, and indicates the relevant industrial factors with which they are most closely associated. The beta coefficients are standardized partial regression coefficients and indicate the number of standard deviations by which the dependent variable is changed for a one standard deviation change in an independent variable. The coefficient of determination is for the joint effects of all the variables indicated in the appropriate row. There are four general variables with, in some cases, two or more measures of the concept or of different aspects of the same general factor.

All of these occupations are positively related to productivity, measured in one way or another. The strongest relationship is for managers, other professionals and transport, and the weakest for technical occupations. In the latter case the

Table 5.4. Employment in Six NP Occupation Groups by Industry, Great Britain, 1971

Industry	Managers and professional workers	Typists/secretaries, clerical workers	Scientists, engineers and technical workers	Sales workers	Distribution workers	Service workers	Total NPs (000's)	Total no. of NPs
Food	4.3	11.2	2.5	8.7	7.9	4.0	38.7	216,050
Drink	6.2	16.1	2.5	6.3	17.6	6.4	55.1	79,190
Tobacco	3.4	18.6	4.8	4.7	4.4	5.5	41.3	15,280
Coal & oil products	6.6	15.2	11.0	2.6	6.7	6.3	48.6	28,630
Chemicals	6.2	16.4	12.5	6.0	5.8	5.0	52.3	239,100
Ferrous metal manuf.	3.3	10.4	5.2	0.9	4.3	5.1	29.2	122,100
Non-ferrous metal manuf.	5.0	11.4	5.6	1.9	4.1	4.1	32.0	42,630
Mechanical engineering	5.6	13.2	8.8	3.0	4.1	2.8	37.5	422,220
Instrument engineering	5.4	15.1	9.8	3.6	3.7	2.2	39.9	58,010
Electrical engineering	4.5	13.7	11.7	2.6	3.8	3.0	39.3	331,710
Shipbuilding	2.7	6.7	6.3	0.4	3.3	3.3	22.7	40,880
Vehicles	3.1	11.3	8.7	1.0	4.9	2.7	31.7	250,360
Metal goods nec	5.3	10.7	3.5	2.0	4.3	2.7	28.4	166,260
Textiles	4.6	8.4	2.2	1.9	4.6	3.2	25.1	148,610
Leather, fur	6.6	7.7	0.9	2.0	4.0	2.0	23.2	12,260
Clothing	4.3	6.4	0.4	1.8	2.7	2.2	23.5	88,010
Footwear	3.5	7.5	0.9	1.4	3.4	1.7	18.5	17,720
Bricks, pottery, etc.	4.8	10.8	3.7	2.3	6.9	6.4	35.0	106,920
Timber & furniture	5.4	8.9	1.0	2.5	4.6	2.4	25.0	75,530
Paper, printing, publ.	6.0	17.0	1.8	4.2	5.2	2.7	41.5	254,200
Other manuf.	5.7	11.3	3.5	3.4	4.9	2.8	31.5	102,230
Total manufacturing	4.8	11.9	5.8	3.0	5.0	3.3	34.6	2,818,540
Coefficient of variation	0.25	0.30	0.66	0.64	0.62	0.40	0.28	0.80

Source. *Census of Population, 1971.*

Table 5.5. Summary of the Significant Relationships Between NP Occupation Proportions and Independent Industry Variables

| Occupation | Independent industry variables (beta coefficients) | | | | | | | | Coefficient of determination |
| | 'Productivity' | | 'Size' | 'Markets' | | | 'Technology' | | |
	PROD	LAB	SIZ	TEL	EXP	CON	R & D	CAP	
Managers	0.55		0.61	0.35					0.59
Professional workers nec	0.56								0.26
Sales workers		−0.40	0.25	0.19					0.61
Warehousemen		−0.41		0.36	0.18				0.26
Transport workers	0.55				−0.36		−0.26		0.54
Engineers & draughtsmen						−0.30	0.30		0.77
Scientists & technicians							0.37	0.50	0.69

PROD, net output per operative 1971.
LAB, wages and salaries as a proportion of net output 1971.
SIZ, average number of employees per establishment 1971.
TEL, expenditure on postage and telecommunications as a proportion of net output 1971, used as a measure of contact intensity.
EXP, proportion of sales exported 1971.
CON, proportion of sales going to domestic final consumption 1971.
R & D, expenditure on research and development 1971.
CAP, average investment in plant and machinery for five years 1963, 1968, 1971, 1972, 1973.
All relationships significant at the 0.05 level.
Sources. *Census of Population, 1971; Census of Production; National Income Statistics, 1971.*

association is with measures of technological or capital intensity, but these are themselves very highly correlated with productivity. Economies of scale with increasing size of plant are only evident in the case of managers, where this is an important influence. Market characteristics not surprisingly have most influence on sales and distribution, although contact intensity also affects managers, while numbers of engineers reflect the degree to which the industry produces capital rather than consumer goods.

In considering the status of an individual establishment within a company there are a number of separate issues. The first is the distinction between branch plants and headquarters within the same company or division. Secondly, there is the question of whether the company is independent or subsidiary, foreign-owned or UK-owned. Thirdly, there is the organizational hierarchy of headquarters at subsidiary company, divisional or corporate levels, with at each stage the possibility that the location may be the same as a production site or other headquarters.

A complete consideration of all of these factors is difficult because of the complexity of company organization but it is possible to indicate some of the main contrasts. Considering factory sites alone, the contrast between branches and head office sites clearly emerges in the following figures derived from the site survey.

	ATC%
Branch site	18.8
Single-plant company	21.8
Head office at production site	27.5

In addition, single-plant companies lie in an intermediate position as might be expected. Drawing conclusions is complicated by the fact that it is really necessary to standardize for the influence of productivity, plant size, etc., before imputing an effect to the status of establishments. However, the ordering observed in the figures above is also seen in most individual industries and hence probably indicates the correct magnitude of difference.

The proportion of white-collar workers at a given production site is found to depend on the degree of decision-making autonomy of the management. Although the general conclusion is unsurprising, the details are less obvious since there is apparently little loss of white-collar employment when decision-making authority is shared between local management and headquarters; only when most authority was removed does the proportion fall sharply. This is shown in Fig. 5.2, in which autonomy has been measured using an index constructed on the basis of where decisions are made within 12 categories of decision. Not all occupations react in the same way to the degree of local autonomy, and in particular the proportion of managers falls fairly steadily as autonomy declines.

A more detailed picture of the effect of plant status on individual departments

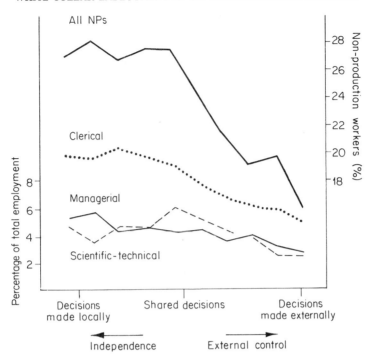

Fig. 5.2. The effects of the location of decision-making on average NP proportions (source: Site Survey)

has already been described for larger multiplant companies in Table 5.2, and the departments which are most likely to become located in detached headquarters have already been identified. Those most likely to be lost by branch plants to headquarters, whether detached or not, are in finance (but not wages), purchasing, sales, marketing and research and development. The retention of production-related functions, especially in engineering, at the factories might seem rational enough but by international standards is probably related both to the relative lack of concentration of *operational* control in UK companies, and to the relatively low status accorded to production management and engineering in this country. It was found that foreign-owned subsidiaries and also some of the very largest UK multinationals were more likely to concentrate such functions at corporate or divisional headquarters level.

The Spatial Distribution of Non-Production Employment

There is considerable variation between regions in the proportion of those working in manufacturing who are engaged in NP and particularly white-collar occupations. In 1971 the NP proportions varied from 45.7 per cent in Greater

London down to 28.9 per cent in Wales. In general, as can be seen in Table 5.6, the proportions engaged in white-collar occupations decline outwards from London, forming a pattern traditionally repeated by most indicators of economic performance or welfare within the UK.

Table 5.6 shows that outside the South East Region, only the South West has a proportion of NP employment which is above the national average, and even in this case the advantage is marginal. The next ranking area, East Anglia, is also adjacent to the South East. There is relatively little differentiation over the rest of the country, with all areas having NP percentages of between 30 and 34 per cent except for Wales and the two most northerly non-conurbation areas at close to 29 per cent.

The spatial distribution also contains an urban–rural dimension, although this is less marked than those conversant with the literature on office location might have been led to expect. In aggregate NP terms, the advantage of the six official conurbations over their respective hinterland areas amounts to two percentage points, although two of the six in fact have lower proportions. If attention is confined to administration functions (managerial and clerical), the conurbations have a more marked concentration of jobs and in this case all six conurbations have higher percentages than their hinterlands. In the case of managers, the conurbations have 16 per cent more than the rest of their regions. In general, however, the conurbation/non-conurbation distinction is less important than the regional contrasts, and particularly the dichotomy between the South East and the remainder of the country.

When the variation of occupations was examined across industries, managerial and professional staff had a notably even distribution. Across regions, however, this is the most unevenly spread of any group. This indicates what will be shown again below, namely, that the regional concentration has little to do with industrial structure. There are plainly processes operating to concentrate managerial and professional staff at both the regional and conurbation scales. Within the group the preeminence of London and also the other conurbations is greatest among sales managers, accountants, company secretaries and 'other professionals'. These, as we saw above, also represent activities likely to be concentrated in head offices. The remaining occupations in this group are all more intimately associated with day-to-day operations and thus somewhat less concentrated.

If occupational correlations are examined across industries, then clerical workers can be shown to be strongly associated in numerical importance with managerial, sales and technical workers. Although this does not necessarily imply that these groups will also be employed at the same locations, in fact the distribution of clerical workers is close to that of the remaining NP occupations combined. Those clerical occupations most closely associated with managers, namely typists and communications workers (telephonists, messengers, etc.), also have the most uneven distributions, with London occupying a similarly extreme position in both cases.

Table 5.6. Numbers Employed in NP Occupations by Region, Manufacturing Industry, Great Britain, 1971

	Managerial and professional	Clerical	Scientific and technical	Sales	Distri-bution	Service	Total NPs %	Total NPs No.
Tyneside conurbation	4.3	10.8	5.6	2.1	4.5	3.8	32.0	44,450
Other North	3.8	9.0	5.6	1.6	4.4	3.8	28.9	93,060
W. Yorkshire conurbation	5.6	10.2	3.4	1.9	5.1	3.2	30.3	109,820
Other Yorkshire & Humberside	4.7	10.6	4.5	1.9	6.0	3.9	31.1	136,760
Merseyside conurbation	4.8	11.2	4.9	1.9	4.9	3.7	31.8	59,770
SE Lancs. conurbation	5.6	11.3	5.5	2.1	4.8	3.6	33.7	162,940
Other North West	4.7	9.8	6.1	1.6	4.5	3.6	30.7	164,180
East Midlands	5.0	10.3	5.0	1.8	4.8	2.9	30.4	184,060
Birmingham conurbation	5.5	11.2	4.8	1.6	4.8	3.3	31.4	200,590
Other West Midlands	4.9	11.0	6.3	1.9	4.7	3.2	32.3	154,020
East Anglia	5.8	11.8	5.2	2.2	5.3	2.9	33.8	68,090
Greater London	9.3	17.3	6.3	2.7	5.2	3.2	45.7	499,950
Outer Metropolitan Area	7.1	14.6	9.1	2.4	5.0	3.2	41.9	313,370
Other South East	6.2	12.2	6.8	2.3	5.5	2.7	36.5	165,030
South West	5.5	11.6	7.2	2.6	5.2	3.0	35.6	149,760
Wales	3.8	9.1	4.9	1.7	4.8	4.0	28.9	97,500
Clydeside conurbation	4.6	11.8	5.3	2.4	5.2	3.7	33.7	95,460
Other Scotland	4.2	9.4	4.3	2.2	4.9	3.5	29.2	119,730
Great Britain	5.8	11.9	5.8	2.1	4.9	3.3	34.6	2,818,540
Coefficient of variation: all regions	0.23	0.17	0.21	0.17	0.08	0.10	0.13	0.64

Source. *Census of Population, 1971.*

Although the North–South contrast is exhibited in the distribution of scientific and technical workers, the degree of contrast is less than for managerial and clerical staff. More noticeable is the reversal of the advantage of the conurbations. In every case except Scotland, the hinterlands have higher levels than do their appropriate conurbations. This is most clearly demonstrated within the South East, where the belt around London has a high concentration of this category; indeed, almost one in 10 manufacturing employees in that area are scientific or technical workers. Outside the South East, the only region with a proportion significantly above the national average is predictably the South West with 7 per cent of manufacturing employees engaged in these occupations. Although there are no regional figures on R & D employment, it is the more research-oriented occupations within this group which have the most marked non-conurbation concentrations. Within the sales and distribution group salesmen have a marked concentration in the South East, with a declining proportion outwards except for an upturn in Scotland. Transport staff and warehousemen have regional distributions more or less in proportion to the numbers of operatives. Warehousemen are generally more important in conurbations, while the reverse is true of transport workers.

Although consisting largely of manual workers, the 'service' group is worthy of continued comment for the contrast it provides with the ATC occupations. Unlike any other NP group the proportion rises from South to North, although the regional variability is slight and in addition the smallness of this group means that the reversal does little to counteract the southern concentration in white-collar workers.

The overall pattern is clear, in that the higher-status occupations are the most likely to be concentrated in the South relative to the North and Wales. The manual NP jobs on the other hand are very evenly spread, with only the lowest paid occupations, notably cleaners, showing a sharp reversal of the general North–South trend.

The Employment Impact of Regional Imbalances

Although there are other consequences of regional imbalances in NP proportions, the most obvious and immediate is the direct loss (or gain) of employment. To calculate the numbers of jobs involved it is necessary to drop the practice of referring to those employed in NP occupations as a percentage of total employment, and instead to use a ratio of NPs to operatives. The choice of measure (i.e. ratio or percentage of total employment) is of considerable importance because each gives a widely different estimate of job excesses and deficits. The need for the NP ratio stems firstly from the fact that operatives, rather than all employees, form the most reasonable standard against which to compare the distribution of NP workers. Our basic *a priori* expectation is that any given number of operatives in a region will be accompanied by their full complement of NP workers. This is not of course a fully realistic expectation,

Table 5.7. Regional Employment Disparities of Non-Production Employment, Great Britain, 1971

Region	Actual employment 1	Expected employment 2	Actual minus expected employment 3	Industrial structure effect 4	Residual employment 5
North	137.6	171.5	−33.9	+7.0	−40.9
Tyneside conurbation	44.5	50.1	−5.6	+0.3	−5.9
Other North	93.1	121.1	−28.3	+6.7	−35.0
Yorkshire & Humberside	246.8	295.0	−48.2	−21.0	−27.2
W. Yorks. conurbation	109.9	134.1	−24.2	−16.0	−8.2
Other Yorkshire/Humberside	136.9	160.9	−24.0	−5.0	−19.0
East Midlands	184.5	223.4	−38.9	−22.9	−16.0
East Anglia	68.1	70.8	−2.7	+3.9	−6.6
South East	981.6	698.6	+282.0	+41.0	+242.0
Greater London	502.4	315.1	+187.3	+18.5	+168.8
Outer Metropolitan Area	314.1	230.8	+83.3	+18.6	+64.7
Other South East	165.1	152.7	+12.4	+3.9	+8.5
South West	149.9	144.0	+5.9	+1.8	+4.1
North West	387.4	435.1	−47.7	+7.1	−54.8
SE Lancs. conurbation	163.4	170.4	−7.0	−3.4	−3.6
Merseyside conurbation	59.8	68.2	−8.4	+6.5	−14.9
Other North West	164.2	196.5	−32.3	+4.0	−36.3
West Midlands	354.9	403.8	−48.9	−20.2	−28.7
Birmingham conurbation	200.8	232.5	−31.7	−14.9	−16.8
Other West Midlands	154.1	171.3	−17.2	−5.3	−11.9
Wales	97.5	127.3	−29.8	−2.1	−27.7
Scotland	215.5	254.2	−38.7	+5.5	−44.2
Clydeside conurbation	95.7	99.8	−4.1	+0.3	−4.4
Other Scotland	119.8	154.4	−34.6	+5.2	−39.8
Great Britain	2823.8	2823.7	0	0	0

The 'actual' figures differ slightly from those in Table 5.6 because they include an allowance for employment in detached head offices 'not allocable elsewhere' (from MLH 866) that belong to manufacturing industry.
Source. Research project calculations.

especially for salesmen or warehousemen, nor is it meant to be. It acts as an approximate but satisfactory standard for comparison. A second and more technical reason is that expectations based on percentages result in numbers of job excesses which, if they were to be redistributed back to the deficit regions, would still not produce an even distribution. The use of a ratio avoids this difficulty.

In 1971 the national ratio of NP workers to operatives was 0.530, a level of approximately one NP worker for every two operatives. If the number of operatives in each region in 1971 is multiplied by this ratio we then get a simple 'expected' number of NP jobs which can be compared with the actual number for the same year to give a residual deficit or excess. Employment figures constructed in this way are given in columns 1 to 3 of Table 5.7.

The outstanding figure in this table is the excess of over a quarter of a million jobs in the South East Region. This is largely concentrated within London itself, although the surrounding OMA has an excess of over eighty thousand jobs. The less urbanized regions adjacent to the South East have only small excess or deficit employment, but all of the remaining regions have employment shortfalls of between thirty and fifty thousand jobs. The development area regions (North, Wales, Scotland) have a joint deficit of over a hundred thousand jobs, but almost as large are those of the Midlands or of the North West plus Yorkshire and Humberside.

The pattern is again a clear one in which all regions not in the south of England lose significant numbers of jobs most of which end up in or around London. If allowance is also made for employment in trades dependent upon these additional jobs in the South East, then the total is even greater. A notional

Table 5.8. Regional Excess NP Employment in the South East Region, 1971

Occupation group	Total difference (actual − expected)		Industrial structure effect		Residual	
	No.	% of total	No.	% of total	No.	% of total
Managerial and professional	66,308	23.6	6974	16.7	59,334	24.8
Clerical	112,913	40.2	16,897	40.5	96,016	40.1
Scientific and technical	49,685	17.7	7488	18.0	42,197	17.6
Sales	15,395	5.5	2999	7.2	12,393	5.2
Distribution	20,141	7.1	538	0.7	19,606	8.2
Service	4052	1.4	− 3005	− 7.2	7057	2.9
Miscellaneous	12,542	4.5	9813	23.5	2729	1.1
Total	281,036	100.0	41,704	100.0	239,332	100.0

Source: *Census of Population, 1971.*

multiplier of 1.2 brings the excess employment in the South East up to 338,000 jobs. Similar calculations would also increase the deficits in the Central and Northern Regions.

From the previous section it was seen that the regional distribution of employment is most uneven in the ATC occupations. This fact is quantified in column one of Table 5.8, where it is shown that almost two-thirds of the South East regional gains are in managerial and clerical occupations. If technical and sales staff are included also, then ATC occupations account for 87 per cent of the region's residual excess. The manual NP occupations are relatively unimportant. The miscellaneous group although including some manual workers also includes a large number of journalists, and as a result the 'white-collar' element of the NP excess is close to 90 per cent. The converse of this is, of course, that the aggregate job losses of the deficit regions will be dominated to the same extent by white-collar occupations.

Time Trends in the Regional Distribution

In the last two sections it has been shown that the regional distribution of NP workers is markedly uneven, with important consequences in terms of national job losses and gains. A pressing question now is whether the degree of unevenness is increasing or decreasing, or alternatively whether it is a long-standing and essentially static state of affairs. Unfortunately, it is exceedingly difficult to obtain consistent time-series information for white-collar employment within manufacturing. The high prospensity of census constructors to change definitions is given full rein with the opportunity to work on industry, occupation and regional boundary definitions.

For the relatively short period between 1963 and 1971 data from the *Census of Production* give a picture of changes in ATC employment, although it is probable that the figures contain some underestimation of the lead of the South East over other regions, and also of the increase in the ATC percentage within the South East over the period. The figures in Table 5.9 show that there was little change in relative rankings over the short period. Proportionate rates of change were highest at the top and bottom of the league table, indicating convergence at the bottom but divergence at the top. The fastest proportionate rates of increase were in Yorkshire and the East Midlands, two regions which, as will be seen below, had particularly poor industrial structures in respect of white-collar employment. The South East and South West increased their advantage over the national average. Two regions, the North and most notably the West Midlands, increased their ATC proportions significantly more slowly than elsewhere. In both cases their 1963 proportions were below average and hence their position was one of trailing even further behind the national average.

The one longer-term series which it is possible to construct relates to managers and uses the *Census of Population* for the period 1951 to 1971. The group includes all those with managerial responsibility, excluding foremen but including office

Table 5.9. ATCs by Region, 1963–71

Region	Percentage total employment in manufacturing industry		Proportionate increase in ATC percentage 1963–71
	1963	1971	
North	22.7	24.6	8.3
Yorkshire & Humberside	19.6	22.7	15.8
East Midlands	20.8	24.1	15.9
East Anglia	23.6	26.6	12.7
South East	27.3	31.1	13.9
South West	25.9	29.4	13.5
West Midlands	22.3	23.9	7.2
North West	22.7	25.6	12.8
Wales	21.7	24.3	12.0
Scotland	20.9	23.9	10.1
Great Britain	23.4	26.4	12.8

Source. *Census of Production, 1963, 1971.*

managers. In 1951 3.1 per cent of manufacturing employees were in this category and by 1971 this had risen to 5.9 per cent. Taking account of major changes in regional and industrial classification the figures are listed in Table 5.10. The consistency of relative positions is quite striking over this period, in which the general proportion doubled, with two exceptions. The proportion of managers in the West Midlands slipped significantly downwards while that in Scotland rose sharply. In both cases the changes occurred predominantly during the 1950s, and in both cases in most industries, indicating that the causes were probably not merely due to changes of industrial structure. Both regions, it should be noted, also had slower than average growth rates for all ATC occupations between 1963 and 1971. With these two exceptions the rankings of regions are remarkably stable, indicating that the present uneven distribution of white-collar staff probably has long antecedents.

The Causes of Regional Imbalance

It has been estimated above that as many as a quarter or a third of a million jobs are currently located in the South East Region which would not be there if NP workers in manufacturing were distributed in proportion to the number of operatives. Conversely, a deficit of similar magnitude is shared between most of the remaining regions. It is both interesting and important to attempt an explanation of why this concentration should occur, and why it should be of this degree. Although space does not permit a full discussion, this section will briefly describe the causes and their quantitative effects.

Table 5.10. Time Trends in the Regional Distribution of Managers

Year	Managers as % of all employment in Great Britain	Regional percentage of managers expressed as a proportion of national percentage in the same year							
		Northern	East Midlands & Yorkshire–Humberside	North West	West Midlands	South East	South West	Wales	Scotland
1951	3.06	0.67	0.92	0.84	0.98	1.38	0.95	0.71	0.63
1961	4.46	0.68	0.91	0.83	0.91	1.34	0.98	0.75	0.74
1966	4.66	0.67	0.89	0.83	0.91	1.37	0.94	0.72	0.73
1971	5.89	0.68	0.87	0.86	0.89	1.36	0.96	0.68	0.76

It was argued above that the influences on NP employment at establishment level can be classified into structural and organizational groups. Paramount among the former are the effects of industrial structure, and thus it is likely that regional variations of industrial structure will contribute to the regional disparities in NP employment. Regions which have a high proportion of employment in, for instance, the chemical industry will tend to have high levels of NP employment because chemicals is an NP-intensive industry.

Industrial Structure

The importance of industrial structure can be examined by calculating the expected NP employment in each region assuming that each industry in the region has a ratio of NP workers to operatives which equals the national average. Working at the finest level of industrial disaggregation (Minimum List Headings), these expected values allowing for industrial structure were calculated and subtracted from the expected employment in Table 5.7 to give an industrial structure effect as listed in column 4 of that table. The difference between the actual minus expected employment (column 3) and the industrial structure effect is termed the 'residual' and is given in column 5.

The surprising fact which emerges from this table is how little of the pattern of regional disparities can be accounted for by invoking industrial structure. Indeed, several of the regions with high negative residuals in Table 5.7 have a favourable industrial structure. Their industries are of a type which together employ above average numbers of NP workers, and hence whatever is causing their employment deficit has nothing to do with industrial structure. Industrial structure does play a significant role in the midland regions and in Yorkshire, being proportionately most important in Yorkshire and the East Midlands, which are now Britain's major textile and clothing regions. Although industrial structure accounts for only a small part of the South East's employment excess, it is notable that this region does have a favourable structure and one which in itself contributes forty thousand jobs.

In fact, the South East does have the most favourable structure of any region, something which is made more explicit in Fig. 5.3. Although the effect can only be small, there may be an element of conscious selection in that NP-intensive industries choose locations in the South. In Fig. 5.3, the length of each arrow represents the difference between actual ratios of NP workers to operatives (N/P ratios) and the ratio expected on the basis of industrial structure. Upward pointing arrows indicate an excess of employment over expectation, downward pointing arrows indicate a deficit.

Once allowance is made for industrial structure the general decline in ratios outwards from London becomes most apparent. Overlaid on this pattern is the contrast between conurbations and hinterlands which again emerges much more strongly after allowance for industrial structure. In general, non-conurbation

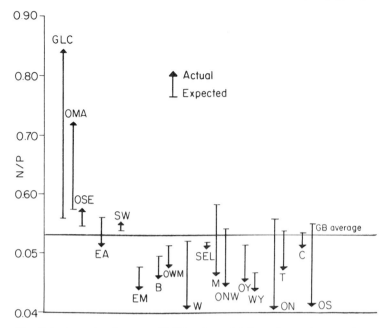

Fig. 5.3. Actual and expected N/P ratios: all NP workers, 1971. Regions are arranged in approximate rank order of distance from London. GLC, London; OMA, Outer Metropolitan Area; OSE, Outer South East; EA, East Anglia; SW, South West; EM, East Midlands; B, Birmingham conurbation; OWM, other West Midlands; W. Wales; SEL, South East Lancs. conurbation; M, Merseyside conurbation; ONW, other North West; OY, other Yorkshire–Humberside; WY, West Yorkshire conurbation; ON, other North; T, Tyneside conurbation; C, Clydeside conurbation; OS, other Scotland (source: *Census of Population1971*)

areas have relatively favourable industrial structure due to their shorter history of industrialization resulting in newer, more ATC-intensive industries; to the pattern of postwar industrial movement bringing many newer industries to northern non-conurbation areas; and finally to the land requirements of chemicals, the most ATC-intensive industry of all. The conurbations outside London mostly have neutral or poor industrial structures, but once this is taken into account their employment deficits are small. This really only follows for conurbations which are major regional centres and hence does not hold for Merseyside, which has a large deficit. The lowest residual N/P ratio of any area outside the two most southerly regions is in the South East Lancashire conurbation, which fits with Manchester's history as the industrial capital of England. The larger negative residual in the case of Birmingham also accords with that city's relatively small service sector given its size.

The pattern described in Fig. 5.3 after allowing for industrial structure can be divided into four elements.

(i) Positive residuals in South East and South West Regions amounting jointly to 246,000 jobs.

(ii) Small negative residuals in remaining conurbations (excluding Merseyside) with an aggregate deficit of 39,000 NP jobs.

(iii) Remaining non-conurbation areas outside Development Areas show a marked worsening in deficits away from London with the exception of East Anglia. The total deficit is 77,000 jobs.

(iv) Development Areas, excluding conurbations other than Merseyside, have the largest deficits, with a total shortfall of 117,000 jobs.

The regional distribution of industrial structure and residual effects can also be described for individual occupational groups. Ratios for managerial and professional workers decline strongly away from London but hardly any of the pattern is due to industrial structure, as can be seen in Fig. 5.4. Managerial proportions vary little between industries and hence variation in industry composition makes little difference. The regional concentration of managers into the southern areas and out of the Development Areas is thus likely to be due almost wholly to organizational rather than structural factors.

The pattern of regional variation in ratios for clerical workers is very similar to that for all NP workers and duplication of diagrams has been avoided. Aside from the difference in scale, which in this case rises from 0.13 for 'other North' to 0.31 for London, the only difference is that the South West has a small negative

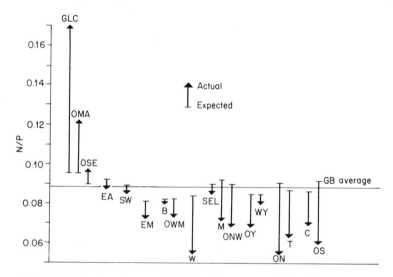

Fig. 5.4. Actual and expected N/P ratios: managerial and professional workers, 1971. Regions are arranged in approximate rank order of distance from London. (source: *Census of Population 1971*)

residual in place of the small positive one in Fig. 5.3. The similarity in pattern partly follows from the numerical importance of clerical workers within the NP category, but more importantly from the fact that clerical workers are located in the same places as administrative, technical and sales workers.

The distribution for scientific and technical workers (Fig. 5.5) has a rather different appearance although the contrast between southern areas and the rest remains as ever. Industrial structure explains more of the pattern than with managers because variation between industries is more marked, but it is still not the major factor. The main textile areas have low expected values, and in contrast the South East Region outside London has a favourable structure, again indicating some factor causing *production* in technical industries to become located in that area. Most Development Areas have favourable structures, but these are generally fully offset by large negative residuals, a characteristic which also afflicts Birmingham.

Space will not permit a discussion of the sales distribution and service categories, which are dominated by manual occupations not of direct relevance

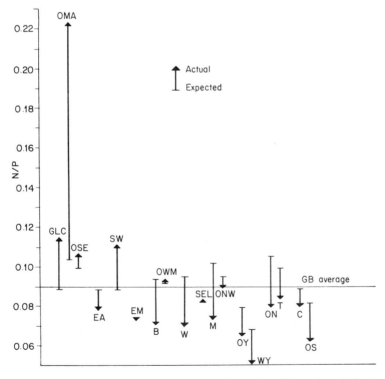

Fig. 5.5. Actual and expected N/P ratios: scientific and technical workers. Regions are arranged in approximate rank order of distance from London. (source: *Census of Population 1971*)

here. For the important case of the South East Region, a full breakdown is however contained in Table 5.8. In the South East, industrial structure accounts for one-sixth of the total excess, a little more than this for clerical, scientific and technical workers, and rather less for managerial, professional, sales and distribution workers. The small excess of service workers owes nothing to industrial structure, but the miscellaneous category dominated by journalists is naturally a reflection of London's preeminence in newspaper publishing.

Organizational Factors

Industrial structure explains relatively little of the pattern of NP employment, and other structural factors such as size of plant are insignificant. This leaves a collection of causes which can be loosely called organizational. In fact they include two distinct effects. One reflects the ways in which multiplant companies choose to locate their non-production departments between their various sites. The other, here termed managerial, reflects efficiency or productivity, or merely differences between companies in organizing the running of production and distribution. It is not obvious that these latter factors should have a regional dimension, but this does appear to be the case.

Within the locational category it is possible, indeed necessary, to subdivide the effects further. Only multiregional companies are relevant and within these an important distinction can be made between corporate and subcorporate levels in company hierarchy. Corporate level institutions are normally the company head office and perhaps also a corporate R & D facility. Such establishments are usually detached from production sites, especially within larger companies, and influences on their location may have relatively little in common with the normal factors influencing factory location. At subcorporate level most NP departments are at factories, although some headquarters of divisions or of large subsidiary companies may not be. In this case factors are still at work concentrating departments in some factories rather than others, and one important aspect is the distinction between factories with headquarters functions and branch plants. Forty years of regional policy has resulted in quite sharp differences in the regional distribution of these two types of factory and consequently of NP employment within them.

Subcorporate organizations, which may be divisions or subsidiary companies, may be internally composed of headquarters and branch plants. An alternative form of internal structure is that of subsidiary companies which are often small and may operate only a single plant. The former, or *branch-type* of organization appears to contribute considerably to the spatial concentration of NP employment, while subcorporate organizations consisting of subsidiary companies (*subsidiary-type*) contribute little.

The approach adopted in the East Anglia project towards explaining the concentration of NP employment was to attempt to estimate the amount of employment in corporate headquarters and R & D establishments, and also the degree of concentration occurring within subcorporate organizations. The organization, headquarters and R & D surveys were the principal means of achieving this, although prodigious use was also made of industrial directories and company reports.

One important aspect of the strategy was that of completeness, and to this end unpublished *Census of Production* figures were used to investigate employment concentration within single-region companies. These are dominated by smaller companies and complete the range of investigation, which in total encompassed the whole range of sizes and industries. Single-region companies were not expected to contribute much to the regional disparities, but surprisingly the figures show a distribution similar in both direction and degree to that of industry as a whole even after allowance for industrial structure. The reasons why single-region companies in the South East should have higher proportions of white-collar workers than other areas, and particularly more than Development Area regions, are not fully clear, but there is strong evidence suggesting that regional productivity differentials are responsible. In general, southern regions have higher productivity per operative than those further north.

The employment consequences of centralization within multiregional companies or of productivity variations among others are described in Table 5.11 for ATC workers. The industrial structure effect is also included to give a complete picture, and the other causes make allowance for industrial structure. The importance of industrial structure in the East Midlands and Yorkshire has already been noted. In East Anglia and the South West the single-region company effect which we ascribe to productivity is the major factor, although the total employment disparities are small in both cases. Productivity also has a major influence in two regions with large deficits, namely Scotland and the West Midlands. In the remaining regions the multiregion firms cause most of the disparities. These are the regions most involved in industrial movement either as sources or recipients. The South East gains 160,000 jobs because of its concentration of headquarters at both corporate and subcorporate levels. The North, North West and Wales all owe most of their deficits to multiregion companies, which in practice means to their high dependence on branch plants operated by companies with headquarters elsewhere.

The contribution of multiregion companies to the deficit of the West Midlands appears out of place when it is remembered that this region has been a major supplier of branch plants to other regions. In this case, as well as in other regions, relatively low productivity may lower ATC numbers in plants of multiregion companies as well as within those of single-plant companies. Although there are reasons to expect less regional variation in productivity within large multiregional companies, this factor should be borne in mind for all regions. There is in fact little more that can be done, since we know of no easy way of distinguishing this effect from that of centralization.

Table 5.11. The Components of Regional Disparities in ATC Employment

Region	Total excess or deficit		Explained by industrial structure	Explained by single region organizations	Explained by multiregion organizations
	No. (000's)	% of actual ATC	%	%	%
North	− 33.4	36	− 13.2*	28.7	84.3
Yorkshire–Humberside	− 48.7	29	45.0	23.2	31.8
East Midlands	− 30.9	24	54.0	10.4	35.6
East Anglia	− 4.7	10	− 10.6*	63.8	46.8
South East	+ 257.4	35	13.2	24.7	62.1
South West	+ 10.3	9	14.6	73.8	11.6
West Midlands	− 43.3	17	− 3.7*	47.6	56.1
North West	− 42.9	16	− 0.2*	7.0	93.2
Wales	− 27.9	43	6.8	20.8	72.4
Scotland	− 35.9	25	12.8*	41.2	46.0

*Minus signs in column 3 indicate that industrial structure explains none of the total deficit in the region in question. Instead, these regions have a better than average industrial structure despite their overall deficits. The minus sign indicates that the industrial structure effect is in the opposite direction from the overall deficit.

Source. Unpublished *Census of Production 1971*, figures.

The effect of centralization within multiregion companies has been further disaggregated for the important South East Region in Table 5.12. Once again the other components of the employment disparity have been included for comparison. The sources of the employment excess for NP workers prove to be surprisingly diverse, with no one factor accounting for as much as a quarter of the total. Detached corporate headquarters employ on our estimate about fifty thousand workers, reflecting the importance of London as a centre of communication and as a location for government and financial institutions. The importance of employment is, however, set in context by the fact that a similar magnitude of excess results from the productivity effect within single-region companies.

The largest single factor is concentration at subcorporate level (this also includes some corporate headquarters located at factories). The estimate of between sixty and a hundred thousand jobs includes head offices of divisions or major subsidiaries, as well as the effects of concentration of employment at headquarters sites below this level, and also the productivity effect. The location of headquarters of divisions or of subsidiary companies appears to owe little to factors connected with the proximity of governmental and financial institutions or international airports. Instead, proximity to plants is the major need, although communication with corporate head office or customers can be important. Currently important factors like communications needs are in many cases less important than the history of development of the division or subsidiary. In many cases it seems that the original factory was in the South East, and consequently the headquarters remains there. To this extent the concentration of subcorporate head offices in the South East reflects that region's

Table 5.12. The Components of the NP Employment Excess in the South East

Components	No. (000's)	% of total
Total excess	283.1	
Due to industrial structure	41.0	16.6
Due to single-region organizations	50.0	20.3
Due to multiregion organizations		
(a) Detached corporate headquarters	49.3	20.0
(b) Branch-type organizations (subcorporate level)	59.3	24.1
(c) Subsidiary-type organizations (subcorporate level)	13.7	5.6
Due to corporate R & D establishments	19.6	8.0
Due to detached sales offices & distribution depots	13.4	5.4
Total accounted for	246,300	100.0

Source. Project team calculations.

past economic performance and enterprise. Subcorporate organizations consisting of subsidiary companies often have a (small) detached headquarters in the South East, and it is estimated that these employ some fourteen thousand people. Corporate R & D establishments are heavily concentrated around London rather than within it and employ another twenty thousand, and proximity to the corporate headquarters appears to be a major location factor here. From the analysis of *Census of Population* figures it was finally estimated that thirteen thousand people were employed in detached sales offices and warehouses, although this figure should not be regarded as in any way a precise one.

The figures which have been derived from a number of independent survey and census sources add up to a total which is a reasonably close approximation to the total excess calculated from the *Census of Population*. Within the South East, multiregion companies appear to account for two-thirds of the employment excess. Within this component the corporate level accounts for rather under half and the subcorporate level rather more than half.

Conclusion

It is unnecessary to summarize the foregoing sections except to say that there are marked regional disparities in the proportionate importance of white-collar employment, in favour of the South East in particular, and that these have probably persisted over long periods. Although the question of causality has been dealt with only very briefly in this chapter, the most important facet to emphasize in conclusion is the multicausal nature of the forces acting to produce the disparities. In situations of this sort, which are extremely common in regional studies, it is important to attempt to disaggregate the total pattern into components for which the causes of the spatial variation are relatively self-evident or at least can be meaningfully tackled. The approach adopted in this study is an example of an 'accounting' approach, and in our view stands in marked contrast to the shotgun methods employed in, for instance, regression analyses.

In this study the causes of employment disparities have been clarified and directly or indirectly quantified by distinguishing the various sources of employment concentration. These include a wide range of influences. The effects of industrial structure and productivity differentials were made explicit above, but others include communications advantages of London as evidenced in the concentration of corporate headquarters, and to a much lesser extent headquarters at subcorporate level. The concentration of corporate headquarters in the South East has a multiplier effect in that these have also influenced the concentration of corporate R & D facilities around London. It should perhaps be emphasized at this point, however, that the great majority of R & D is carried on by subcorporate organizations within the large companies, is located at factories and is widespred across the country. Finally, one major contributor to the excess employment of the South East and the deficits elsewhere is the separation which exists between areas characterized either by main (i.e. headquarters) factories or independent single-plant companies and those, especially in the Development Areas, characterized by high proportions of branch plants. Although the long existence of an active regional policy has accentuated this contrast, an important underlying aspect is the greater prosperity of manufacturing in the South and Midlands. In this as in other respects the present disparities are the consequences of a long history of industrial development in this country, and this is probably more important than any current advantages or disadvantages which regions possess.

Acknowledgements

This chapter results from a research project funded jointly by the Department of Industry and the Regional Directorate of the EEC. Although the responsibility for opinions and errors is solely our own, we are grateful to the sponsors both for the financial assistance and for valuable criticisms made in the course of the research. In particular, Mr R. S. Howard of the Department of Industry suggested the adoption of operatives instead of total employees as a standard for comparing the regional distribution of white-collar workers, and thereby significantly improved the analysis.

References

Crum, R., and Gudgin, G. (1978), *Non-Production Activities in U.K. Manufacturing Industry*. Brussels: European Economic Commission.
Department of Trade and Industry (1975), Employment on scientific research and development in British industry, *Trade and Industry*, 13 Feb., 397–401.
Stoneman, P. (1975), The effect of computers on the demand for labour, *Economic Journal*, **339**, 590–606.
Wool Industry Economic Development Council (1969), *The Strategic Future of the Wool Textile Industry*. London: HMSO.

6

Office Activities as Activity Systems

Lars-Olof Olander

Introduction

It is a well-known fact that office activities play a more and more essential role in developed economies in comparison with the relative decline of the raw materials producing, manufacturing and service-oriented activities. The assignment of office activities within industry can be exemplified by formulation of ideas, exchange of information, information processing and planning with a view to guiding and coordinating other activities such as the physical production of goods. All these tasks are characterized by abstract work contents demanding different forms of theoretical competence and they are distinctively different from the tasks performed within the remainder of an organization.

Office occupations can either make up a small part of the total employment of a firm or they can dominate it throughout; a great deal depends on the type of activity and the kind and complexity of the production process. Further, they can be grouped into organizational units together with other types of employment or into entirely independent units. To a greater and greater extent ideas and information are circulated between these different administrative parts of a firm at a rate which is determined by the increasing specialization and complexity of production. Some of this information is aimed at guidance and coordination of units within organizations, whereas other information is exchanged between formally independent organizations. The most important information exchange in qualitative terms still demands that individuals travel and meet on a face-to-face basis, but a growing proportion of this information can profitably be transferred between locations by means of modern communications technology. Thus information and interaction are key words in the study of office location and, by logical extension, it must also involve the study of activity systems.

The research within this field has for some years been one of the more conspicuous problem areas in economic geography. The basic questions revolve

159

around administration and its role in production; the information content of activities and how they are carried out as events within an organization and in its environment under the influence of different structural possibilities and restrictions. This research has been aiming at the development of an *activity theory*, which is an understanding of how organizations operate as activity systems at a specific location in space.[1] Several social–scientific disciplines such as psychology, sociology, organization theory and economics constantly contribute new knowledge which must be accommodated within a geographical conceptual framework. It is very rare for researchers within these disciplines to cooperate directly with geographers, who tend to pick up, on their own initiative, a little knowledge here and a little knowledge there from adjacent disciplines in order to understand how different possibilities and restrictions exert an influence on the implementation of administrative activities, in time and space.

Hitherto the problem has been that there does not exist a consolidated geographical conceptual framework of how administrative activities are carried out as events in time and space and which is constructed in such a way that it can at the same time take into account the influence of several structural possibilities and restrictions. A number of different theoretical but fragmentary conceptual frameworks have been proposed and each of them have been adapted to account for the influence of one or the other possibility or restriction: for instance, the functional and spatial structure of organizations, the transport system, or the environmental structure. Such selective conceptions of reality often run the risk of overemphasizing now one, now the other aspect of the problem, and therefore they often manage to escape the fact that perhaps the essential insight lies in the joints between them, i.e. in the simultaneous cooperation or conflict between different possibilities and restrictions.

There follows a discussion about administration and its common role in production. Using this discussion as a point of departure, a fundamental definition of the contents and characteristics of activities will then be given. This is followed by a time–geographical model of how these activities could possibly be carried out as different kinds of events under the simultaneous influence of, and cooperation between, a number of different locational possibilities and restrictions.

Business Administration as a Project

The three principal tasks of administration are sometimes said to be to *initiate, plan* and *direct* production and distribution of goods or services. As a description of what administration is and how it is practised the statement is of course a little platitudinous. In one respect, however, the description does deserve some attention. It indicates a logical and sequential order between administrative activities which, perhaps surprisingly, is little noticed in the literature. The reason may be that it is difficult to describe clearly and unambiguously the meaning and mutual relations between activities whose contents are mainly of an abstract and information-processing nature but which have the common purpose of making possible the step-by-step production of goods and services. Nevertheless there are good theoretical reasons, tested in reality, for conceiving administration as a project consisting of sequential activities which certainly cannot always be predicted but which, notwithstanding closer consideration, are ordered with obvious logical and sequential connections. If this is the case, there is reason to conceive of a firm's administration as *administrative projects*, which run either parallel or with greater or lesser displacements in time in relation to each other.

Administrative projects cannot be given an absolute definition because the definition of them is in all respects dependent on which scale one chooses to start from. Theoretically, however, it is suitable to start from those that can be said to be *superior*, in the sense that when being undertaken they involve all or the major part of the firm's different administrative resources. A very schematic picture of an administrative project (of the superior kind) and its implementation as a series of events within a firm and between the firm and its environment will now be outlined. The purpose is to depict a background for the understanding of the administrative activity system that makes up the firm and of the contact system it participates in.

Orientation Moment

It can be assumed that administrative projects, in a superior sense, are introduced by a *moment* that is called an orientation moment because its activities are mainly of an orientating, scanning and preparatory character, and intended to smooth the way for further procedures. To this moment belong activities which include the conceptual initiation of a new or special production run and analysis of the prerequisites for production, financing, marketing and sales. Research and investigation work in connection with new production is also a possible inclusion. The activities of this moment are probably the most complicated in an administrative project and require penetrative judgment and processing of information about the firm and its environment. Therefore, the orientation moment's activities are accomplished both as individual work events and contact events within the firm and with its environment. The essential element of contacts from the viewpoint of contents is face-to-face contact. The information here is nearly always two-way and the contact time often lasts for hours. The number of participants is seldom less than three persons and the planning for the meetings can be time-consuming. Contacts of this kind are considered to cover only a few per cent of all contact work, but provide nearly all the new information needed about technology, market, and other essential conditions in the environment (cf. Thorngren, 1970).

Planning Moment

The orientation moment and its associated activities can fluctuate widely in time and content but the planning moment, which follows, probably becomes narrower and more objectively oriented with reference to contents. Moreover, the planning moment is to a large extent inescapable since it is a response to decisions taken earlier.

Thus, a planning moment comes next in the time sequence and is designed to make the contents of the orientation moment concrete and to plan the details for further procedures. Production planning and market preparation, for instance, as well as sales organization and financial planning, are activities that belong to this moment. Experiments and design work connected with new production can be considered as further examples. The work contents are usually not as uniformly complicated as in the orientaion moment. This does not, however, exclude a requirement for advanced preparation and judgement about information and its extensive exchange within the firm as well as with the environment. In this case the exchange of information between the firm and its external environment is most often carried out through better established information channels than in the preceding case. The contacts are not as wide-ranging as regards the information exchanged and the contact durations seldom exceed 30 minutes. Telephone contacts also occur to a greater extent and are mixed with personal contacts (cf. Thorngren, 1970).

Programme Moment

Last in the time sequence of an administrative project is a programme moment, which is most closely connected with production and distribution. Its contents can be described as guidance and follow-up of the production process; supervision of production, sales, delivery control and management of economic transactions are some examples of the various work contents of the activities within this moment. The tasks usually require routine and less advanced handling of information, and as far as the exchange of information within the firm and with the environment is concerned, this is also largely routine and is mostly realized through well-known and frequently used information sources. The contacts as a rule are of short duration and the information exchange one-way and well structured, with insignificant information breadth. The majority of contacts are by telephone and, as a rule, they are planned the same day that they are executed (cf. Thorngren, 1970).

It should be pointed out that administratively superior projects, orientation, planning and programme moments may quite well be a conglomerate of several subordinate projects with a similar threefold division of moments which should be looked upon as necessary building blocks in the creation of the whole. These administratively subordinate projects consequently touch only limited parts of the firm's administrative resources and can be discovered only if one watches the different activities and their contents again after having changed the scale.

Daily Perspective

If the administration of a firm is perceived in the way outlined above, i.e. composed of administrative projects which either run parallel to each other or which have greater or smaller displacements in time, the consequence should be that, in a daily perspective, the firm simultaneously carries out orientation planning and programme moments, but for *different* administrative projects which exist side by side.

The way in which a firm in its *daily* work carries out parts of such different moments as activities realized through individual work contacts within the firm and as contacts between the firm and its environment is shown schematically in Fig. 6.1. The figure shows, from left to right, three different parts of the firm's operations during one working day. At the extreme left the activities that can be considered parts of orientation moments have been separated; the middle section shows similarly the activities that belong to planning moments; and finally at the extreme right the different activities of the programme moment are represented. All the activities considered as events have fixed durations and specific positions in the 'time–space box', which is made up of the duration of the working day and the firm's spatial environment. The reason why the daily work has been divided into three different time–spaces in this way is exclusively technical. Even if there is reason to believe that activities belonging to different moments are carried out as different events in different parts of the environment, this, of course, happens in an environment that basically is the same for the whole organization.

Activities as events do not of course exist in a kind of vacuum in time and space, which the figure may possibly suggest, and they are not carried out independently. They are performed through the movements of the individuals in time and space and exist only through individuals. Fig. 6.2 mirrors how the activities described earlier can be coupled to the different individuals who have performed them. The activities as events can be threaded like pearls on to a string with different individual paths: the way in which an individual travels when moving in time and space. As long as the individual is on one and the same spot, the path moves only parallel to the time axis. Moreover, the individual path is indivisible, unbroken and continuous and cannot be interrupted in time or space. In order to reach a proper understanding and description of a firm's activities it is probably true to say that the observations must always start with these smallest constituents—the events and the individuals.

As already mentioned, the three different moments possess varying degrees of difficulty and complexity and this is also evident from the diverse ways in which they are carried out as activities and contacts. Therefore one can count on them to demand different kinds of competence from the individuals whose duties it is to realize them. Such competence–moment couplings will be referred to as *positions*. The individuals represented in Fig. 6.2 can therefore be looked upon as belonging to one of three different classes of position with responsibility to realize the respective orientation, planning and programme moments of different administratively superior projects. Of course, these three principal classes of positions can be divided further if one wants a detailed examination of the competence–moment couplings existing within the subordinate projects of which the different moments in the superior projects are considered to be built

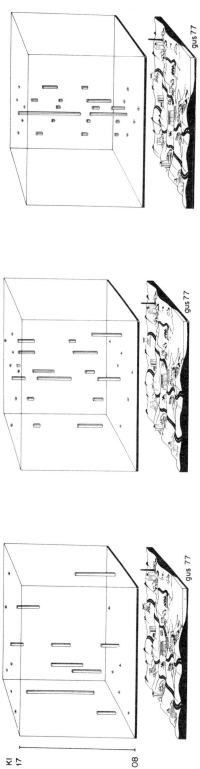

Fig. 6.1. Activities as events within a firm and in its environment (left to right, orientation activities, planning activities and programme activities respectively)

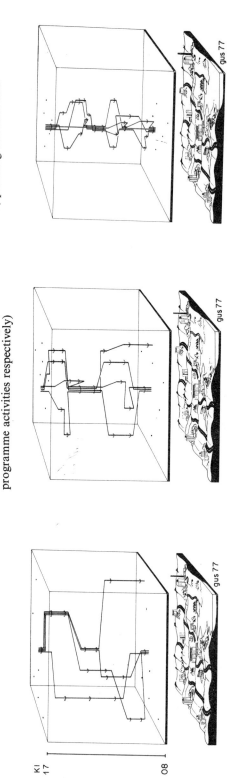

Fig. 6.2. Activities as events carried out by individual paths belonging to the firm's employees (left to right, individuals in orientation, planning and programme positions respectively)

up. Such a division does not, however, add anything to the investigation from the theoretical viewpoint. All the combinations of positions and classes of position that are necessary to realize superior administrative projects constitute *an organization*. This can be used as a general concept and can therefore include several different *organizational units*, which can be assigned to locations in different parts of the environment, and in consequence of this there may be considerable deviations from the simplified system (Fig. 6.1).

Structural Possibilities and Restrictions

The possibilities and restrictions confronting a firm attempting to complete the activities that are necessary are dependent on different conditions both within the firm and in the environment. Some of these possibilities and restrictions will now be considered.

Environmental Images of Individuals

The concept of environmental image is used for individual office workers' attitudes towards, and knowledge of, different abstract and concrete phenomena within the firm and its environment. The term need not necessarily mean that it is a picture in the common sense of the word; rather, the environmental image comprises a view on, and information about, details and entities of the environment. This image must be assumed to contain only a small part of an enormous number of phenomena and to be of great importance in respect of an individual's ability to find his bearings concerning the real possibilities and limitations in the environment. From theoretical points of departure at least there is reason to discriminate between the individual's professional and private environmental images. In practice it is, of course, difficult both for the observed individuals and for researchers to distinguish between professional and private impressions of the environment. The requirements of the research in hand must decide if it is the professional impression that is of interest. It is self-evident in this present context that the professional environmental image must be relevant. It is considered that this subjective image reflects the objective possibilities and restrictions within and outside the firm, and is therefore in itself a decisive factor in determining how the individuals can carry out their activities and contacts. In the cases where the contents of the activities require that the individuals shall receive, deliver or exchange information with other individuals within the firm or in its environment, the environmental images are of great importance for scanning the possibilities for coupling individuals to each other. In summary, the environmental images of individuals can be perceived both as possibilities and restrictions when carrying out activities as events in time and space (cf. Persson, Ch. 7).

Administrative and Other Rule Systems

By rule systems are meant all the administrative, legal and economic principles, routines, rules, contracts or laws that in various ways influence the implementation of activities and contacts within and between firms. Elements of these rule systems can be implicit or clearly expressed as verbal or written agreements and dictates. Further, they can be constant as general rule systems within or between firms, or more temporary as in connection with special projects. They all have in common that they can exist outside individuals and therefore have a formal and objective existence. The rule systems can, as with the environmental images of individuals, be perceived both as possibilities and restrictions.

Individuals as Indivisible Time Resources

The environmental images of individuals and the rule systems are both possibilities and restrictions which must be observed in order to 'arrange' the implementation of activities in their physical sense. This statement has implications for the movements of individuals in time–space, which have their special possibilities and limitations. For instance, individuals are indivisible and cannot be in more than one place at a time. It follows from this that the implementation of certain activities excludes the simultaneous implementation of others. Instead, activities and contacts must be ordered successively, and therefore events in progress withdraw time resources from other events also requiring completion. Certain events cannot take place because of the competition within a common time budget which is the working day of the individual. The indivisibility of the individuals and the total individual time that is at an organization's disposal therefore dictate physical possibilities and restrictions on how activities can be carried out as events in time and space.

Transport System

Transport systems comprise all the technical/physical possibilities and restrictions on the movement of information and individuals between an organization and its environment. Also belonging to this concept are possible temporal or other rules which influence the utilization of transport. Transport systems can be perceived as a physical possibility or restriction on the contacts implemented outside an organizational unit. As a rule, the transport alternatives restrict the outer potential frame of contact possibilities that is offered by the environmental structure.

Environmental Structure

By environmental structure is meant the individuals in various combinations of positions, working places, and organizations that surround an organization. Because of its composition, size and distribution the environmental structure can be looked upon as a potential frame of contact possibilities outside the different units of an organization.

All the activities and contacts which constitute the sequence of events in Fig. 6.2 are the result of the possibilities and restrictions connected to the individuals and their environment which have already been mentioned. Activities are realized through the *stepwise growth of individuals' paths* in time and space. This growth is *simultaneously* steered by all the constraints which have been outlined. Thus, when studying the realization of administrative moments *via* activities and contacts, one should not draw too far-reaching conclusions about the influence of one or the other possibility or limitation without relating them to their natural situation-dependent interaction within the individuals' paths.

Theoretical and Empirical Studies of Activity Systems

A large number of authors have emphasized the significance of studying administrative activities and contacts as regards their contents and importance for the existence and development of organizations. Moreover, in this context great attention has been paid to the external characteristics of the activities, such as time expenditure, scheduling time, number of participants and spatial distribution. For instance, Ehrlemark (1964) was one of the first researchers to draw attention to questions concerning different kinds of processes within firms. He discriminates between programme processes that comprise ongoing activities and transactions with the world around, and planning processes which are a response to changes in programme processes. Orientation processes are a third type whose function is to adjust the planning processes by means of changes in the specialization of the activity.

Thorngren (1970) has taken up these divisions and developed them further. He is of the opinion that control of 'production–sales' (programme), 'product development–marketing' (planning) and 'research–public relations' (orientation) should be discriminated from each other, since these processes can be expected to differ as regards stability and time horizon. In accordance with these views he has proposed three fundamental contact classes with which organizations are 'scanning' their environments, i.e. with programme, planning and orientation relations. Starting from different characteristic variables, Thorngren has managed to develop a technique by means of which the contacts of organizations can be assigned to one of the three contact classes. He has used latent profile analysis: a multivariate technique to show empirically that organizations situated in different parts of the Swedish urban system display considerable differences as regards the utilization of these three contact classes with the environment. Orientation contacts, and to a certain extent planning contacts, are, for instance, fewer in number in urban regions situated well down in the regional hierarchy but more common amongst organizations located higher up in the urban hierarchy. Similarly Goddard has studied the contact patterns of organizations in London (Goddard, 1973) and has also investigated how the contact relations with the environment have changed for organizations which have decentralized from London to other regions in England (Goddard and Morris, 1975). Both Thorngren and Goddard discuss a number of different possibilities and restrictions that can influence the contact behaviour of organizations and some are wholly identical to those touched on earlier in this chapter. A shortcoming of these studies, however, is that they concentrate on contact events rather than considering the activities which are carried out as individual work events. We probably need to combine activities that are individual work and contact events into a more *general framework* which takes account of their common meaning and purpose. The administrative project concept may be a useful starting point, since we could then consider it to be irrelevant whether, due to circumstances, different moments happened to be individual work or contacts. Closer concentration on the contents of activities must replace the classification of contacts on the basis of their outside characteristics only, as in latent profile analysis.

Numerous other researchers have carried out different kinds of investigations of administrative activities and contacts. Carlson started this research as early as 1951 by studying how senior managerial employees allocate their time to different activities. He clearly shows how these individuals devoted a large share of their time to information handling and interaction (Carlson, 1951). One of the most comprehensive studies in this tradition has been made by Stewart (1967), who investigated the time allocation of activities for a large number of individuals at various administrative levels within organizations. Within organization theory at the present time there is also a trend towards the introduction of activity-oriented realism into a subject which has hitherto been dominated by very abstract generalizations. Mintzberg (1973) is a prominent representative of this trend with comprehensive research about the different roles that individuals are playing in an organization when they carry out different activities. These three studies are, however, limited by the fact that they do not look upon activities as related to each other in the way advocated by Thorngren and Goddard and as explicitly proposed in this chapter. Moreover, these studies are aspatial and non-temporal and consequently they do not, and indeed cannot, take account of the influence of different possibilities and restrictions.

In Sweden, Hedberg (1970) has investigated the time expenditure of personal contacts and their functional and regional distribution for different work functions in a number of organizations. Sahlberg (1970) has also completed a study of the functional and regional structure of the contact work which different organizations in Sweden carry out *via* the Swedish domestic network of airlines. A pervading characteristic of these and other studies (cf. Thorngren and Goddard) is that the majority of the contacts of individuals and organizations are, as a rule, conducted with counterparts elsewhere in the same region. The remaining contacts are mainly distributed over a few other regions and most of these are with the most dominant urban region in the system. Another feature of these studies is that the time expenditure for transport and travel in connection with external contacts makes up a considerable proportion of the working hours of individuals. Hedberg's and Sahlberg's investigations, like the studies of Carlson, Stewart, and Mintzberg, lack theoretical or empirical attempts to fit contacts into an overall framework. However, they account very satisfactorily for variations in contact time for different work functions, but analyses of how different possibilities and restrictions are influencing contact work are again lacking.

Theoretical and Empirical Studies of Structural Possibilities and Restrictions

The importance of *environmental images* for office activity systems has only been recognized relatively recently and therefore it is not possible to discuss any empirical results here. A theoretical examination of the build-up and importance of the environmental image as possibility and restriction in the activity system is presented in Ch. 7 of this book (cf. Persson). *Administrative rules* as a possibility for, and restriction on, contact flows within or between organizations have been discussed by Thorngren (1973) and Horvath and Ramström (1971) from the theoretical point of view. Individuals as *indivisible time resources* and conflicts arising from this when contacts have to be carried out in different parts of the environment during the working day have been studied by Olander (1974). The *transport system* is a possibility and restriction that has been treated in voluminous studies. For instance, Persson had used a model to show how contact possibilities can be said to vary according to the transport facilities available to organizations located in different regions within a regional system (Persson, 1974). General contact and transport possibilities in a regional system have also been studied in so-called contact landscapes (Engström and Sahlberg, 1973; Törnqvist, 1973). Wärneryd (1968) has studied in detail the relationship between employment distribution, organizational structure and regional structure and has described theoretically and empirically how the structure of different organizations can be projected on to a hierarchical urban system. Different groupings of administrative work functions such as head office, divisional office or administration of production are located in separate regions within such a system (Wärneryd, 1968). Pred (1973) has also devoted comprehensive research to the relationship between organizational structure and regional structure. These recent studies have, of course, been aimed primarily at the understanding of conditions behind localization and distribution of office activities and the description of their development, and in some respects they concern questions outside the current subject of this chapter. At the same time, however, these investigations are analyses of the type of possibility and restriction that has been referred to here as *environmental structure*, and they have, in many cases, been used for the interpretation of the results of activity studies.

In all the older geographical literature offices are mainly studied as elements of urban land use and as a component of the morphological development of the urban region. There exists a comprehensive literature on the localization and redistribution of such activities within individual urban regions and, as a rule, these studies are aimed entirely at an analysis of changes in the organization and extension of the town core, where of course offices now play such a central role. However, it is very rare that these CBD studies manage to combine their observations with a theoretical conception of the organization of the economic activity system. Some general observations, however, may be made. For instance, it seems to be a pervading characteristic that concentration in the town core tends to be higher for the more specialized and interaction-dependent office activities. Another characteristic is that decentralization to suburban areas increases over time and with the size of the urban region. Several studies from the USA and other countries indicate such tendencies for locational change; one of the most comprehensive reports has been produced by Armstrong (1972).

In recent literature more sweeping attempts at studies of localization and redistribution are beginning to emerge. As a rule, the extension and change of employment and organizational units between the whole system of urban regions in different countries are now being investigated. The most obvious observation in such studies is the extreme concentration in a few dominant urban regions within each system. The level of concentration, whether within private or public administration and services, is directly related to the degree of specialization of the office functions which have been investigated. Swedish studies of regional development have been completed with very precise data (Engström, 1970; Törnqvist, 1970; Engström and Sahlberg, 1973), while Westaway (1974) has described a similar development in Great Britain, and for the USA this subject has been examined by Armstrong (1972).

This review of the literature is not exhaustive and the different approaches have been discussed somewhat superficially with brief summaries of some empirical observation. But on the whole all existing approaches to office studies are mentioned and placed in some kind of order which demonstrates the fit between them or shows how they complement each other. A large number of individual research contributions have not been referred to, but with few exceptions they can be fitted into this overall schema.

Suggestions for Further Research

The first part of this chapter outlined administration and its common role in production. As a point of departure for this discussion a definition of the contents of activities was given. This was followed by a description of these activities as realized through the individual's paths in time and space, followed by a list of possibilities and restrictions that either stopped or made possible the growth of individuals' paths and thereby the realization of activities as physical events in time and space.

As a theoretical framework such a presentation is oversimplified and by no means exhaustive, but a large amount of work on the development of a conceptual network based on physical realism does seem very necessary before proceeding on a more comprehensive and fundamental basis with the practical work on a multitude of separate problems. We certainly need a common and consistent general view of the problem from which to start out empirical work and to provide a reference point to return to. Therefore, it is suggested that we start from a conceptual and intellectual vision of how organizations are built up as activity systems in time and space. From then on we should try to validate our conceptual network with empirical studies of *any* organizations, with *no other* purpose other than to see if we can capture the reality and understand it. Any specific or short-term practical problem, big or small, which surrounds us as planners or professionals must be excluded for a while.

Now, why should such pieces of academic work have priority over all the trends and up-to-date problems that everybody wants to have our professional views and assistance on in this field? This is simply because it is absolutely necessary not to make mistakes when interpreting these contemporary problems as well as the empirical data available to analyse them. Let us return briefly to the theoretical and empirical studies of activity systems and their restrictions and possibilities that were referred to in the second part of this chapter. It must be quite obvious that these fragmentary theoretical approaches and their corresponding empirical data do not give us any coherent picture which we can use to understand reality in relation to the office location problem. The reason, of course, is not that these were bad studies—quite the contrary, in most cases—but rather that they were all adapted to an examination of individual problems that reflected very specific research interests. Since the theoretical approaches to these different problems do not start from the basis of a common conceptual frame of the total reality, it is quite impossible to put them together in a helpful intellectual order.

It could be argued that it is not so much history that matters but future. Researchers should not go on sitting on two chairs at the same time as they have been doing so far and trying simultaneously to develop theory and elucidate or solve some specific problems. Many of the studies referred to above are of this kind in that the theoretical approaches are lacking in generality because they were applied to specific up-to-date problems within the area of urban and regional policy. Suppose we could find a theoretical frame that could both describe reality and make us understand the mechanisms behind the processes in it. In that case it would help us to better understand the various urban and regional problems that everyone wants us to tackle in practical life.

The theoretical frame presented in the first part of this chapter is just an exploratory version; it must be followed by better ones. However, at present it serves rather well as a guide to empirical work when trying to describe the administrative activity system that makes up an organization and to understand how different structural possibilities and restrictions work together to shape these processes.

Studies of specific administrative projects which last over a long period of time and studies of the daily administrative activity of an organization are currently going on side by side in Sweden. In both cases the point of departure is that the activity system of an organization cannot be described without being oriented towards the individual and that the influence of different possibilities and restrictions cannot be fully understood without observing how they interact when creating the physical events that are carried out by the growth of individual paths in time and space.

The studies mentioned are all divided into two separate parts. The first part involves a pure description of the activity system of an organization, whereas the second part is an analysis of the importance of different kinds of structural possibilities and restrictions to this system. When studying the activity system, individuals are asked to register all their individual work and contacts within and outside their organization during a period of time. For this purpose a specially designed diary is used with some complementary questions about the events registered. For instance, questions are asked about the activities performed with reference to their information content, and about the elements in individuals' environmental images or the administrative rule systems which influenced their decisions to get into contact with various individuals and organizations in different parts of the environment. The duration of events, their sequential location in time and space and the points in time when they were planned are other questions included in the diaries, which are completed during the working days of administrative workers. The information from these diaries serves as a pure description of what actually happened during a certain period of time (cf. Figs. 6.1 and 6.2).

Starting from the actual events registered in the diaries there follow analyses of the alternative locations where these events could be performed due to each of the separate possibilities and restrictions. Of course, the individuals studied have only been in contact with a limited number of other individuals and organizations in the external environment; it is of great interest to compare this limited number of individuals and organizations with the total contact potential in the environmental structure. Starting from the information content of activities and their functional linkages to other organizations, attempts are being made to describe alternative sets of contact possibilities in the environmental structure.

Only a limited part of these alternative sets of contact possibilities in the environment can probably be used if further possibilities or restrictions are regarded, such as the transport system. Starting from time–budget restrictions in the scheduling of actual events registered and combining them with the transport possibilities to different parts of the potential environmental structure, it is quite possible to delimit a new set of alternative contact possibilities which can be compared to the one actually used.

If we are to continue in this way it must be recognized that only a limited part of this new alternative set of contact possibilities can be used if administrative rule systems and environmental images of the individuals are regarded as possibilities and restrictions. Special investigations must be done on how compulsory different parts of the rule system are and whether there are alternative rules to follow which allow the individuals in various positions to make the same kind of contacts with other organizations in the environment. In the same way, special interviews must be undertaken to find out whether the environmental images of individuals contain alternative sets of contact possibilities in the environment. The new sets of alternative contact possibilities must of course be compared to the results of the previous studies of the other structural possibilities and restrictions. Offices attached to manufacturing industry and offices which provide non-physical services to industry are currently being studied in the Malmö region, which is one of the two subnational city regions in Sweden. Other studies involving similar offices in other city regions are also planned.

The conclusions from this kind of analysis can possibly begin to indicate something about the degrees of freedom to act which various possibilities and restrictions are giving the organizations studied and also the relative importance and influence which they exert when they are working together in the activity system that makes up an organization.

Notes

1. Parallel to these investigations of activity systems, comprehensive research is also being carried out on the factors which influence the growth and location of occupations and office establishments and their consequences for urban and regional development. This research on *location theory* is not treated in this chapter.

References

Armstrong, R. B. (1972), *The Office Industry: Patterns of Growth and Location*. Cambridge, Mass.: MIT Press.

Carlson, S. (1951), *Executive Behaviour: A Study of the Work Load and the Working Methods of Managing Directors*. Stockholm: Strömberg.

Ehrlemark, G. (1964), *Proceedings of International Labour Organization Advanced Management Seminar*, Ootacamund.

Engström, M. G. (1970), *Regional arbetsfördelning. Nya drag i förvärvsarbetets regional organization i Sverige*. Lund.

Engström, M. G., and Sahlberg, B. (1973), *Travel Demand, Transport Systems and Regional Development: Models in Co-ordinated Planning*. University of Lund: Lund Studies in Geography, Series B, No. 39.

Goddard, J. B. (1973), *Office Linkages and Location*. Oxford: Pergamon.

Goddard, J. B., and Morris, D. M. (1975), *The Communications Factor in Office Decentralization*. London: London School of Economics (Mimeo).

Hedberg, B. (1970), *Kontaktsystem inom svenskt näringsliv: En studie av organisationers externa personkontakter*. Lund.

Horvarth, D., and Ramström, D. (1971), *Organisationsuppdelning i samband med lokaliseringsöverväganden: En teoretisk föreställningsram!*. Umeå.

Mintzberg, M. (1973), *The Nature of Managerial Work*. New York: Harper and Row.

Olander, L. O. (1974), Företagens kontaktsituation, *Svensk geografisk årsbok*, **50**, 58–63.

Persson, C. (1974), *Kontaktarbete och framtida lokaliseringsförändringar: Modellstudier med tillämpning på statlig förvaltning*. Lund.

Pred, A. (1973), The growth and development of systems of cities in advanced economies, in *Systems of Cities and Information Flows, Two Essays*. University of Lund: Lund Studies in Geography, Series B, No. 38.

Sahlberg, B. (1970), *Interregionala Kontaktmönster: Personkontakter inom svenskt naringsliv–en flygpassagerarstudie*. Lund

Stewart, R. (1967), *Managers and their Jobs*. London: Macmillan.

Thorngren, B. (1967), Regional economic interaction and flows of information, in *Proceedings of the Second Poland-Norden Regional Science Seminar*. Warsaw: Polish Academy of Sciences, pp. 175–86.

Thorngren, B. (1968), External economies and the urban core, in M. Van Hulten (Ed.), *Urban Core and Inner City*. Leiden: Brill.

Thorngren, B. (1970), How do contact systems affect regional development?, *Environment and Planning*, **2**, 409–427.

Thorngren, B. (1973), Swedish office dispersal, in Bannon, M. (Ed.), *Office Location and Regional Development*. Dublin: An Foras Forbartha.

Törnqvist, G. E. (1970), *Contact Systems and Regional Development*. University of Lund: Lund Studies in Geography, Series B, No. 35.

Törnqvist, G. E. (1973), Contact requirements and travel facilities: contact models of Sweden and regional development alternatives in the future, in *Systems of Cities and Information Flows, Two Essays*. University of Lund: Lund Studies in Geography, Series B, No. 38.

Wärneryd, O. (1968), *Interdependence in Urban Systems*. Göteborg: Regionkonsult AB.

Westaway, J. (1974), Contact potentials and the occupational structure of the British urban system 1961–66: an empirical study, *Regional Studies*, **8**, 57–73.

7

Environmental Images and Decision Processes: Some Theoretical and Methodological Reflections

CHRISTER PERSSON

Post-industrial society is characterized by an accelerating growth of the quaternary sector, which contains large portions of information-processing activities of different kinds in both the private and public sectors. These activities, which are highly dependent on recurrent contacts with each other, have been located in and tend to be highly concentrated within the largest city regions all over the world. In the central parts of these city regions their presence is clearly marked by agglomerations of office establishments. Within these establishments we find the head offices of national and international corporations which employ labour from both domestic and foreign sources. Besides these corporations and smaller local companies there are various central agencies which belong to the public sector. All these units are involved in some sort of administrative work.

The increasing importance of office activities and their associated employment growth in the present societies of the Western world suggests that we need a better understanding of the structure and function of these activities. Office activities consist of decision-making units operating at different levels which are constantly interacting with each other and with their environment. To be able to describe and comprehend this interaction process, our studies need to employ a very broad approach of a kind which has not been used to date. As is pointed out by Olander, rather narrow approaches have been used for specific reasons by different researchers and he suggests that the absence of a broad and coherent approach is more or less consequent on the fact that there is not a consistent theory upon which to build. As an attempt to change this situation he discusses the prerequisites of an activity theory from the viewpoint of administrative units.

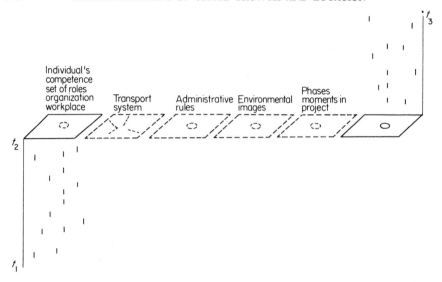

Fig. 7.1. Structural elements of the activity system arranged in a process-oriented time-space perspective

The main components which need to be included within any theoretical framework for the understanding of activity systems within administration are summarized in Fig. 7.1. This chapter concentrates on some of the problems attached to measuring the influence of environmental images on the behaviour of decision-makers in offices.

The Subjective View of the Environment

An individual's subjective view of the environment has been studied within the context of several disciplines: medicine, psychology, sociology, economics, geography and political science, for example. Specific problems in conjuction with this field of research are also treated within semantics, linguistics and media research.

In many ways geographers find themselves at the meeting-point of these different research lines. As early as the 1920s, Wright (1925) and Sauer (1925) treated themes of this kind, and their interest in the individual's subjective view of the environment was also apparent during the 1940s (Wright, 1947; Sauer, 1941). Wright proposed three ways to approach the study of behaviour, all of which had implications for geographical research. He thought that geographers should 'reconstruct the organized world that framed behaviour; compare the perceived with the real; and assess the influence of particular experiences and changes in knowledge on world views' (Bowden, 1976). The transition period between the 1950s and 1960s marks the beginning of the latest wave of geographical research on knowledge about, and attitudes towards, the environment; Lowenthal (1961) has presented a basic theoretical contribution on this subject, while Lynch (1960), Wolpert (1964), and Gould (1965) have contributed important empirical studies. A large number of papers by different researchers have subsequently appeared and these deal with varying parts of the environment, different types of objects and separate categories of individuals. A detailed summary of this geographical research and the output of related research fields within other disciplines is given in Downs and Stea (1973).

In his investigations Wolpert (1964) follows the traditions set by location studies within geography, and Pred (1965) discusses, from a theoretical viewpoint, the relationship between behaviour and location. There have also been a number of investigations concerned with the location decisions within firms with reference both to the location of new units and the relocation of existing units. The decision-makers' knowledge of, and views on, the environment and different phenomena within it have been mapped and are used in order to explain the final choice of location (Stafford, 1974; Green, 1974). McDermott and Taylor (1976) examine the decision-makers' knowledge of, and attitudes towards, different objects and conditions in the environment which can be expected to influence their decisions. These authors stress the fact that *each* decision made within a firm is influenced by the information received by the decision-maker. Moreover, the structure of the information received is dependent partly on the spatial context from which it emanates and partly on its subjective contents. In making these statements McDermott and Taylor have widened the perspective in that they are concerned with more than just locational decisions. As has been pointed out by Pred (1973), locational decision belongs to a category of decisions that are rather few and infrequently taken compared with all the other decisions that must be made within a corporation. The interest in the locational decision has of course to do with the ease with which it can be identified and its explicit spatial effects. Other categories of decisions should be more interesting because of their greater number, since they too often have spatial effects, although of a more implicit nature.

In post-industrial society one can see an increasing number of large enterprises which contain a head office and several branches of different kinds spread over large geographical areas. The growth of these organizations has meant an extended functional specialization. Decisions are constantly made that directly or indirectly affect the spatial organization of these enterprises: investment plans, mergers or the buying and selling of firms, for example. These decisions are not overtly locational decisions and in fact it is only very seldom that a new unit is created during the process of growth and expansion. It is the size of existing units and the spatial patterns of organization that are changed as a result of different kinds of decisions.

It is evident from this discussion that when studying the subjective view of the environment and its influence on the decision process it is necessary to pay attention to both current daily decisions and more dramatic and unique ones which may affect the medium- and long-term spatial arrangements within firms and organizations. It should be remembered, however, that current daily decisions are often of a routine character and therefore predictable and this means that the individual decision-maker's subjective view hardly affects the actual decision. In this case it is rather the 'rules' that govern decision-making which are important to observe. Such 'rules' are often the result of subjective views held by persons other than those who have to apply them.

The Concept of Environmental Image

A project involving one or more decision-makers and the setting in which it appears and operates can be described objectively. The decision processes taking place within a project are linked to, and have implications for, different phenomena in the environment. On the basis of knowledge about the sector of the environment that is involved or will be involved, its outer range can be defined (maximum range). Ideally, the decision-maker himself should make this delimitation but in certain cases it may well be that the researcher decides in advance, on the basis of his specific purpose and need, which part of the environment should be investigated. Both procedures are aimed initially at a geographical delimitation of an outer borderline which encloses all the possibly relevant elements. This procedure implies, simultaneously, that one chooses a certain geographical scale; this may coincide with units such as a neigh-bourhood, municipality, region or country, or consist of other types of units. In this context it should be stressed that the actual environment need not consist of a continuous area but may be composed of several non-contiguous parts.

Independent of which scale is chosen, the environment will contain an enormous number of objects and phenomena of which only a minority are relevant to a specific investigation. For this reason the elements that are to be investigated must be clearly defined. It has been stressed earlier that it is desirable to have the actors take part in the selection of the relevant objects. But for different reasons the researcher often has to determine beforehand which phenomena are to be included. The elements or the objects can be formally defined. They are given an *identity* by means of a proper name or a concept and their *position* in time and space can be fixed. Moreover, it should also be possible to describe *function*. After the environment has been delimited and defined in this way it will be possible to relate it to the individual actor's subjective image of it. The term *environmental image* is then used for the actor's knowledge of, and attitudes towards, different concrete and abstract elements in the defined environment. The concept does not imply that it is necessarily a picture in the current sense of the word; more likely the overall attitude towards the environment is contained in the concept. This image is a very complex phenomenon based on personal experience, knowledge, imagination and memories (Lowenthal, 1961).

If the elements which make up the environment can be defined it should also be possible, at least from a theoretical standpoint, to distinguish between one *private* and one *professional* environmental image. In practice, of course, it is difficult for the individual to distinguish between these impressions of the environment. The investigations discussed below deal with studies of decision processes within office organizations and this means that interest is focused on the professional environmental image, i.e. the image that is considered to influence decisions and actions during the course of the individual's office work.

On the basis of his role and his position in a project and an organization, the actor has to maintain a certain preparedness before the events he meets with and participates in. The environmental image can be said to contribute to this process; it is an aid to sort, classify and organize information and impressions from the environment. In this way it becomes both a support and a guide for different decisions and actions.

The image represents the individual's view of the environment at a specific point in time and it is of a general character since it comprises both old and new components. This arrangement is the result of a prolonged process during which information has been integrated, handled, stored, used, and perhaps finally replaced by new information which is more useful. The environmental image is of course, in certain respects, a very dynamic phenomenon which can lead to progressive corrections of the image. For example, the outer limits may be widened or contracted; new components may be recognized; or knowledge of existing components may be increased or decreased. Its dynamic character can be demonstrated by mapping the individual's environmental image at several different points in time. 'The risk of change' in the environmental image can also be manifest if the study is coupled to a concrete decision process where the structure and contents of the environmental image in question are confronted with the reality whose manipulation it should facilitate. The necessity of changing or completing the image can probably be observed during such decision processes.

It is natural for a geographer to look at the environmental image in the context of a spatial perspective. In a sense this is inevitable because the image concept in itself has a spatial character. Whether the spatial dimension is immediately present in the individual's view of the environment or not, it is of interest to link knowledge and attitudes to space, i.e. to describe how the environmental perception changes with regard to different geographical areas. In addition, one can try to analyse how these variations may have been affected by the life-histories of the actors, i.e. the experiential background that can be derived from *curricula vitae* containing data of places of residence, education, professions, and positions in firms or organizations.

The actor's image of the environment is built up successively, partly by the information obtained about the environment and partly by the acting in the environment (Fig. 7.2). This happens *via* the sensory system when the individual

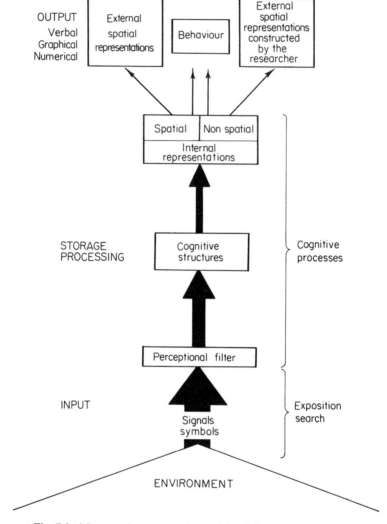

Fig. 7.2. Man–environment relationship; information processing and image construction

is in direct contact with a certain part of the environment or certain phenomena within it. In this context one speaks about *signals*, while the corresponding information can be received through *symbols* (Cassirer, 1957). In the latter case, the information is transferred indirectly *via* different types of information sources such as other persons, books or newspapers. Information supply in today's society is very strongly dominated by symbols, but except for a very limited sphere where the individual lives and works and a few other places, the individual principally receives indirect information about the environment. This means that most information is collected and assimilated through verbal, written or 'pictorial' statements made by other people; the mass media are probably the largest source of information regarding the general picture of the environment. Among office activities face-to-face contacts play an important role in image formation during the course of collecting and handling different pieces of information. Obviously the quality varies according to whether the environmental knowledge is derived from directly felt sensations or whether it emanates from secondary sources of information. The individual is subjected to a constant flow of information from the environment even though he may at the same time be seeking particular pieces of information.

Each piece of information is exposed to the perception and value filter that is an integral part of the individual. In this process, information that reinforces former knowledge and views has the greatest chance to permeate and be integrated, whereas non-reinforcing information is in all probability rejected and tends to be integrated only after repeated exposure.

Within the individual different impressions and elements of knowledge are stored and arranged as *internal representations*. These are interpretations and reproductions of elements and phenomena in the environment. Some are of spatial character, others are linked more to time and others are not directly associated with either time or space. These internal representations are unique to each individual actor but they probably have components in common, at least as far as individuals from the same culture and with similar backgrounds are concerned. In principle, internal representations are not really accessible to research scrutiny, but their external modes of expression certainly are.

External spatial representations directly reproduced by the individual are *one* essential manifestation. They can be of different kinds: verbal, graphical, and numerical representations may be made by using words, maps, or mathematical models. Another way of expressing internal pictures is *spatial representations constructed by the researcher* on the basis of cognitive and value elements stored in the individual's brain. A third manifestation is found in *observed behaviour*. Of these three, the first and third manifestations are probably most similar to the internal representation of an individual's environmental image. The first one is, however, not entirely without its problems, because the result of reproducing spatial representations is strongly dependent on the individual's ability to use the tools required for verbal, graphical, or numerical presentations. This is certainly true with cartographic reproductions (Francescato and Mebane, 1973). Irrespective of which mode of expression one chooses to study, it should be apparent that no given unambiguous relationship exists between the internal and external representations that are to be mapped and analysed. It is probable, however, that an acceptable approximation can be obtained.

Both types of external spatial representations mentioned above constitute examples of components creating environmental images. The environmental image that is primarily built up by spatial representations is probably more coherent and photographic the smaller the environment it covers. The images serves as an orientaion aid which can be used when repeating spatial behaviour. As the image 'screen' grows wider, the image tends to be dissolved into its single elements, and at the same time becomes more abstract. Such an image is often very stereotyped, as in the case of an individual who comes across a designation such as 'the South' or a common country name; a number of facts and views are actualized in his mind which represent his perception of these geographical notions. This latter type of image is probably very similar to that which the researcher can put together on the basis of the non-spatial cognitive elements stored in the individual. In general, it is probably the case that the similarities between the first and last-mentioned type of environmental image are greatest when they cover large parts of the environment.

The process in which the professional environmental image appears and functions can be regarded as a cycle (Fig. 7.3). It is methodologically possible to choose one's starting-point in any one of the boxes in the scheme, i.e. one can enter the process in separate phases. Moreover, it should be stressed that the process does not come to a natural conclusion after one round, but several rounds are probably needed before it can be regarded as logically finished. For the present discussion it seems reasonable to start from the box which represents the objective environment and which, to the actor, defines a field of possibilities and constraints. Different types of information reach the individual from the environment. This process is affected by the individual's prerequisite perceptions

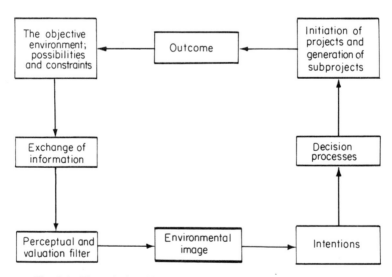

Fig. 7.3. The relationship between the objective environment, the environmental image and the initiation of projects

and values and the result leads to a certain view of the objective environment which has been named the environmental image. On the basis of the role played by the individual and the position held by him, the environmental image contributes to shape the individual's intentions as regards the activities he is engaged in. Intentions, however, can also emanate from other actors in the environment, but even in that case they are interpreted by the individual actor. Starting from the individual's intentions, different decision processes are initiated, often in cooperation with other actors. In many cases these lead to the initiation of new projects which, in their turn, bring forth different subprojects. The different projects start separate activities which link together people and material and prescribe different spatial and temporal solutions for their realization. These conditions, in conjunction with the final results of the work done within the separate projects, influence in different ways the structures originally observed in the objective environment. Thus, the prerequisites are different each time one runs through the cycle for the second, third, fourth time, etc., and therefore, in practice, the process cannot be considered to reach a natural end. One has to define a beginning and an end only from an operational viewpoint.

Decision Processes

Often one can use a broad definition of the decision process so that it becomes identical with a project or a subproject. In order to do this one has to decide when the project should start and end. The whole procedure may be facilitated if it is possible to link the decision process to a specific problem that has to be dealt with; in any event, the definition is made mainly for operational reasons.

Let us take the firm as an example. In the literature there is great consensus concerning the formal structure of decision-making and decision processes (cf. Shartle, 1956; Simon, 1957; Cooper, 1961; Folsom, 1962; Scanlan, 1973.) The references given are all connected with the study of administration in general without any special interest in quaternary activities as such. The course and outcome of a decision is strongly dependent on the first phase in the process–the definition of the problem (Fig. 7.4). The ability to discover different problems in due course, to make a fair interpretation of them, and to relate them to the general aim of the firm is of great importance to the handling of a problem within the decision process. A precise and clear formulation of a problem will facilitate later phases in the process. This is very much the case in the context of the second phase–the determination of alternative solutions. This phase begins with a search for information and a collection of data. Once a problem is clearly stated, it is much easier to delimit those subject fields from which relevant information is available. The third phase in the decision process involves the analysis of the actual alternatives, which, in this case, means an examination of the advantages and disadvantages of different solutions. Since the analyses are likely to reveal

Fig. 7.4. The process of decision-making

expected results and outcomes which will vary according to the decisions taken, the decision-makers are confronted with a choice situation. One of the presented alternatives has to be chosen, and once the choice has been made another phase begins. The decisions that have been made must be executed, and the execution must be followed up in order to check if intentions and real outcomes coincide. In this phase one usually can observe a feedback effect which consists of the generation of new problems which keep the 'machinery' going. The phases which are illustrated in Fig. 7.4 are bound together in a rather fixed time sequence which means that any changes of this sequence are hardly possible.

A decision process often involves several people in the firm. Typically, the executive is responsible for the formulation of the problems and then the search for information and data collection is delegated to experts and investigators who assist in the analysis of different alternatives and solutions. Once this work is complete the executive makes the final decisions and controls their execution.

As it has been described here the decision process is of course an idealization. It is obvious from the studies of real-world situations that only a few decisions will be made according to this model (cf. Townroe, 1971; Stafford, 1974). The scope, the complexity, and the importance of a decision affect the structure of the decision process. A great and complex problem which is of crucial importance to an organization probably generates a decision process which comes close to the ideal one, if the time factor permits. The basis upon which a decision is presented will reveal whether it is a simple or complex process; if it is the latter much more time is devoted to creating a basis that is as complete as possible. Routine matters, which dominate decision-making in most firms, are often solved by using simple and standardized decision processes.

The Environmental Image and a Hypothetical Decision Process

How does the environmental image relate to the decision process? This question will be examined in this section, which will provide the basis for a subsequent discussion of different methodological approaches to the study of images and their effects on decision-making. Once again it must be stressed that the decision-maker's image of certain parts of the environment is moulded by experiences that he has had at different times and in different parts of the environment. Social and professional relations have given the individual a unique set of values and norms which affect his behaviour and his relations to the environment. When a person enters a firm and is given a position he probably carries with him a professional image which is marked by the prerequisities that pertained in the 'old' firm. In the new firm he encounters a collective image which represents its outlook on its external environment. His own image is confronted with this collective image and this probably results in a successive adaptation of the former to the latter. This development occurs because the activities of a firm very much determine the construction of the collective image.

Whether one will get a totally one-sided adaptation or not is dependent on how strong a position the individual has within the firm. If he has a powerful position he may be able to influence the development of the collective image; there is reason to believe that there exists an overall consensus among most firms' executives regarding the general aim of the firm's activities and this creates the collective view on the environment. But in every single decision-making situation the individual images are also important factors to be considered. In fact, decision-making within an executive consisting of several persons means that a new collective image is created in connection with every important decision that has to be made. Thus, this image is the result of a confrontation of a number of individual images whose foci are all related to the activity of the firm which is, to some degree, perceived and interpreted differently by each person because of varying knowledge, values and earlier experiences.

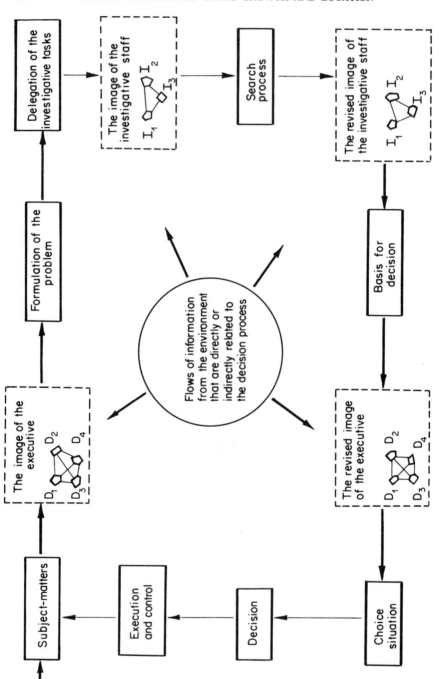

Fig. 7.5. The use of the environmental image in the decision process

The function of the environmental image in a hypothetical decision process in outlined schematically in Fig. 7.5. Decision-making can be regarded as a cycle which is constantly provided with new subject-matter, either from within the process itself or externally. Most subject-matter, and especially that with a spatial character, is filtered through the environmental image of the executive (Fig. 7.5: D_1, D_2, D_3, and D_4). According to the procedure described in the figure the problem is formulated and then interpreted by the investigators. This interpretation is dependent on the images of each single person (Fig. 7.5: I_1, I_2, and I_3). Usually they arrive at a joint view of the status of the problem and they also agree on how to deal with it. At the next stage a search procedure begins which includes collection of information and different types of data which help to build up a basis for the final decision. The search for relevant information often leads to a revised collective image; the outer limits of the image are widened and knowledge of different objects is increased. With the aid of this altered image the basis for a decision is produced by the investigating staff. This material will, in turn, affect the image of the executive. Senior staff gain an increased knowledge and comprehension of the elements in the environment that are relevant for the decision. This should facilitate the final choice from a number of different solutions, and when the decision has been made the process of execution and control can begin. As has been pointed out already, this phase often leads to the identification of new subject-matter and problems and these can be treated in the same way.

During the entire decision process both the executive and the investigating staff are exposed to a continuous flow of information from the environment which is directly or indirectly related to the decision process referred to. This means that the individual images as well as the collective image are constantly changing. Consequently, the environmental image is a rather dynamic phenomenon.

Suggestions for the Study of Environmental Images and Decision Processes

How do we go about studying the relationship between environmental images and decision processes? In order to understand fully how it all functions, it is essential to use strongly micro-oriented approaches. The individual decision-maker should be our object of investigation and through him we should try to map and analyse the image as well as the decision process, including the relations between them. In the ideal case such a study would represent one approach in a broad attempt to analyse and comprehend the structure and function of administrative projects (cf. Olander, Ch. 6).

The image can be used in two different ways by the decision-maker. It can be an auxiliary device when the individual needs to reactivate pieces of information that are already stored in his brain as spatial representations (cf. Fig. 7.1). In this instance the image produces first-hand information which can be directly useful to the individual working at this desk. For example, a buyer who wants a delivery of certain products and knows where he can find the subcontractors can immediately use this information, as it is a part of his image of the environment. The image can also be a support when seeking information that is not an integral part of the image. The individual may utilize his image when he needs to identify and choose from different sources of information that he judges to be relevant in a certain context. Taking the example of our buyer again, if he does not know of the existence or the names of any subcontractors who produce the goods demanded, he may use his image of the environment to locate different sources of information such as business contacts or professional journals which may provide assistance to find the relevant information. From the viewpoint of the decision-maker the former situation involves an easier and less time-consuming procedure, while the latter situation may create meetings and the need to travel which will take up considerably more of his time.

In order to understand how the image is constructed, how it changes over time, and then how it is used in the decision process, one has to delimit a project and register the individual's behaviour during the whole process. This can be done *retrospectively* in collaboration with the individual, although this type of investigation has many drawbacks resulting from the time lapse which exists between the actual course of events and the registration of these events. Instead, one would wish to observe the individual closely during the process that he is part of, an approach which McCall and Simmons (1969) call '*participant observation*'. It contains the following components: interaction with the tested objects in the field; direct observation of relevant events; informal interviews; systematic registration and collection of documents.

Let us look at the entire compostion of such a study and try to identify the different parts that have to be put together in order to achieve our objectives. The first step would be to decide, in collaboration with the respondent, which project or subproject is suitable for study. Ideally, the project chosen is not yet underway so that it is possible to determine when it actually starts and the individual is going to be engaged. One may choose a project that contains a pure location problem such as the creation of a new unit or the relocation of an existing unit, an investment problem, or a general growth problem. If one knows what type of project it is, the respondent may be able to indicate which parts of the environment will be of interest. At the same time, it will be necessary to find out what objects within the environment are of special importance in connection with the project.

The purpose of the next step is to map the individual's information and knowledge of the environment and those elements which are regarded as relevant. This can be done in different ways. A first possibility is to use a rather free mode of expression which means that the individual makes an attempt to summarize his information about each particular part of the environment and using content analysis it should be possible for the research worker to classify and describe the contents of such a summary.

The advantage of this approach lies in the fact that it allows the object of investigation, the individual decision-maker, to define and point out elements which he regards as of special interest. He is also free to describe these elements in his own words and to stress those aspects which he finds important. But at the same time there is a risk of the respondent omitting elements and facts which may later show up to be relevant and which the investigator would have included if he had had the opportunity to influence the decision-maker's description beforehand.

A second, but more limiting mode of expression is the listing of different geographical units. The respondent could be asked, in addition, to give the relative location of these geographical units; this can be done in words only or by drawing a map of the area. Besides these purely geographical matters the respondent can identify, describe and locate objects that will be of interest from the viewpoint of the chosen project. This technique has both advantages and disadvantages. On the credit side, all geographical areas and all elements that the investigator judges to be important can be included on the lists presented to the decision-maker. Moreover, these areas and elements can be described from different viewpoints. On the debit side, a clear disadvantage in using this technique is that one prevents the actual person from including other areas and elements which may be important as well as from using his own mode of description. Furthermore, varying skills, of map drawing for example, may affect the usefulness of this procedure.

All the methods already mentioned are example of *direct* ways of registering the respondent's information on, or familiarity with, a certain part of the environment. If only a rough measure which expresses the familiarity with an area is required, it is possible to use a more *indirect* method. To achieve this purpose it is possible to register meeting patterns and contact networks. Contacts both on a face-to-face basis and by telephone have already been mapped and analysed for office activities in Britain (cf. Goddard, 1973). But these studies have not examined office contacts within the context outlined in this chapter. It is suggested that the respondent could describe his visit pattern and contact net with reference to the defined environment. Ideally, one would also like to know about the frequencies of the contacts. The real business contacts made during the previous year may be registered in this way. The spatial patterns of visits and contacts will give a general picture of the individual's familiarity with different areas in the environment.

Besides the individual's information on and knowledge of the environment one would also like to obtain an idea of how he perceives each part of his own immediate environment. What are his attitudes towards different elements and objects? As this data collection precedes the start of the project work, it is primarily an attempt to catch the respondent's general view of the area and different objects in this area. Varying methods are available: the semantic differential technique (Osgood, 1962), the adjective list (Katz and Braly, 1933), and the repertory grid method (Bannister and Mair, 1968) are possibilities. All these techniques produce a rather generalized and stereotyped view of the environment, but in spite of this they can be regarded as a valuable complement to other pieces of information that are collected from the respondent.

The purpose of the data collection described above is to reveal the environmental image which the individual decision-maker possesses before he starts to work on the specific project that has been chosen. During the project work the respondent will be closely observed, and his image's role in the work will be scrutinized as well as changes in the image because of different demands which the work makes. Consequently, the methods of investigation must be adapted to these latter purposes.

The 'close-up study' of the individual's role in the project work will start with a personal description by the respondent of the task in hand. Coupled to this description there will be an account of how he intends to cope with his specific task; what is already prescribed and what is left to personal judgments? As his work progresses he is asked to register and summarize what he thinks and what he does. Now and then the research worker undertakes check-up interviews in order to account for different events and lines of development. Personal contacts, telephone contacts and other sources of information which are used such as letters, newspapers and journals are listed. Meetings and discussions with people inside and outside the firm are taped if at all possible. Formal minutes from different meetings are also secured and included as part of the research data, and if the research worker is allowed to be present at some meetings, and to make his own observations, it would be an advantage.

Besides the 'retrospective study' and the 'close-up study' there is the 'laboratory study'. The latter means that the research worker invents a project or a problem that is preferably constructed on the basis of real situations which the decision-maker may encounter in his work within the firm. Through this type of investigation, though somewhat artificial, it is easier to control and account for each step the individual takes in order to achieve his aim: the solution of the problem. The investigator must endeavour to present to the tested person a setting as real as possible so that the latter is able to use his special ability and experience to fulfill his task.

As background material and to complement the actual images, one may collect a 'life-history' of the individual decision-maker. This will contain the place of birth and all other places where he has lived; the time intervals of residence at each place will also be included. Educational background, including different forms of education, number of years at different schools, and the location of these schools will also be part of this material. Furthermore the professional 'life' will be documented, such as the names of employers, their location, number of years with each, and different positions. Eventually this material will include data on what newspapers, professional and other journals the respondent usually reads, and also his habits as regards viewing television programmes of an informative and factual nature.

All of this background material may be utilized in an attempt to discover how the construction of a presently observed environmental image has been affected by the life-history of the individual. It must be admitted, however, that there are many questions of both a practical and scientific nature that have to be answered before it is possible to make any basic statements regarding the relationship between life-histories and environmental images.

One question is how much and what things about the individual's life is it necessary to try to collect information on. Is the individual conscious of those experiences that have significantly shaped his general view of the environment? Are there any clearly observable relationships between, for example, educational status or working-life experiences on the one hand and perception of different parts of the environment on the other? If so, how can these be revealed and measured? Is it perhaps the case that one cannot describe scientifically what these relationships look like in the course of analysing the environmental image of one single person? Perhaps life-histories can only be used in connection with studies of several people's images. In this context one may discuss whether similar backgrounds or life-histories of different respondents also result in similar views or images of the environment.

All the different approaches which have been suggested and discussed above are attempts to map, analyse and comprehend images and their role in decision-making. They have been presented from a geographical viewpoint, which means that knowledge and perception of different areas and their contents are the focus of investigation. It must be stressed that investigations of this type should not be made exclusively for their own sake but rather as an integral part of a joint approach to studying how people on different levels within a firm perform their tasks both in a short and long time perspective. In this context environmental image studies are but one dimension of the quest for a better comprehension of the structure and function of activity systems in the world of administration.

References

Bannister, D., and Mair, J. M. M. (1968), *The Evaluation of Personal Constructs.* London: Academic Press.

Bowden, M. J. (1976), *The Cognitive Renaissance in American Geography: The Intellectual History of a Movement.* Clark University (Mimeo).

Cassirer, E. (1957), *The Philosophy of Symbolic Forms: Vol. 3. The Phenomenology of Knowledge.* New Haven: Yale University Press.

Cooper, J. (1961), *The Art of Decision-Making.* Garden City: Doubleday.

Downs, R., and Stea, D. (eds.) (1973), *Image and Environment: Cognitive Mapping and Spatial Behavior.* Chicago: Aldine.

Folsom, M. (1962), *Executive Decision Making.* New York: McGraw-Hill.

Francescato, D., and Mebane, W. (1973), How citizens view two great cities: Milan and Rome, in Downs, R., and Stea, D. (eds.), *Image and Environment: Cognitive Mapping and Spatial Behaviour.* Chicago: Aldine.

Goddard, J. (1973), Office linkages and location: a study of communications and spatial patterns in Central London, *Progress in Planning*, **1** (2), 109–232.

Gould, P. (1965), *On Mental Maps*. Ann Arbor: Michigan Inter-University Community of Mathematical Geographers, Discussion Paper No. 9.

Green, D. H. (1974), Information, Perception and Decision-Making in the Industrial Relocation Decision. Unpublished Ph.D. Thesis, University of Reading.

Katz, F., and Braly, K., (1933), Racial stereotypes of 100 college students, *The Journal of Abnormal and Social Psychology*, **28**, 280–290.

Lowenthal, D. (1961), Geography, experience, and imagination: towards a geographical epistemology, *Annals of the Association of American Geographers*, **51**, 241–260.

Lynch, K. (1960), *The Image of the City*. Cambridge, Mass.: MIT Press.

McCall, G. J., and Simmons, J. L. (1969), *Issues in Participant Observation: A Text and Reader*. Reading: Addison-Wesley.

McDermott, P. J., and Taylor, M. J. (1976), Attitudes, images and location: the subjective context of decision-making in New Zealand manufacturing, *Economic Geography*, **4**, 325–376.

Osgood, C. E. (1962), Studies on the generality of effective meaning systems, *American Psychologist*, **17**, 10–28.

Pred, A. (1965), Industrialization, initial advantage and American metropolitan growth, *Geographical Review*, **40**, 158–85.

Pred, A. (1967), *Behaviour and Location*. University of Lund: Lund Studies in Geography, Series B, No. 27.

Pred, A. (1973), The growth and development of systems of cities in advanced economies, in Pred, A., and Tornqvist, G., *Systems of Cities and Information Flows*. University of Lund: Lund Studies in Geography, Series B, No. 38.

Sauer, C. O. (1925), The morphology of landscape, *University of California Publications in Geography*, **2**, 19–53.

Sauer, C. O. (1941), Foreword to historical geography, *Annals of the Association of American Geographers*, **31**, 1–24.

Scanlan, B. (1973), *Principles of Management and Organizational Behaviour*. New York: Wiley.

Shartle, C. (1956), *Executive Performance and Leadership*. Englewood Cliffs: Prentice-Hall.

Simon, H. (1957), *Administrative Behaviour*. New York: Macmillan.

Stafford, H. (1974), The anatomy of the location decision: content analysis of case studies, in Hamilton, F. E. I. (Ed.), *Spatial Perspectives on Industrial Organization and Decision-making*. London: Wiley.

Townroe, P. (1971), *Industrial Location Decisions: A Study in Management Behaviour*. University of Birmingham: Centre for Urban and Regional Studies, Occasional Paper 15.

Wolpert, J. (1964), The decision process in spatial context, *Annals of the Association of American Geographers*, **54**, 537–553.

Wright, J. K. (1925), *Geographical Lore at the Time of the Crusades: A Study in the History of Medieval Science and Tradition in Western Europe*. New York: American Geographical Society. Republished as a paperback, Dover Publications Inc., New York, 1965.

Wright, J. K. (1947), Terrae incognitae: the place of the imagination in geography, *Annals of the Association of American Geographers*, **15**, 1–15.

8

The Contribution and Influence of Office Developers and their Companies on the Location and Growth of Office Activities

NIGEL MOOR

Introduction

The property development company is a key figure in the location of office activities. Figures are not available which indicate the proportion of office floorspace developed by property companies, but from observation, it can be confidently assessed as a major proportion. Although much of the recent local government expansion has been accommodated in offices developed by the local authorities themselves, central government has often leased office space from developers, so that they have been responsible not only for the location of much commercial office floorspace, but of space occupied by civil servants too. Despite this importance, there is little in the existing literature concerned with office development that deals with the role and influence of development companies in the provision of office space. This is in part due to the highly competitive nature of the development business, and the lack of published statistics. Much of what information is available is that contained in business and economic publications, written by journalists specializing in property matters. Such a journalist, Oliver Marriott, wrote what is still the definitive, although now out-of-date in terms of personalities and property companies, account of the property industry in 1967, *The Property Boom*. Nevertheless, the time is now right to survey the role of the developer in office location. Several commentators on the property scene have predicted that before the end of the decade, the conventional property development company will have disappeared and that development will be initiated by the insurance and pension companies who presently finance many of the schemes. This trend is already noticeable in the rapidly dwindling number of property development companies quoted on the London Stock Exchange. By 1964, which was the height of the office boom in London, the number had grown from 111 recorded in 1958 to 183, by 1967 it had fallen to 164, and 10 years later in 1977 it had declined to 105.

The classic property company has usually been started by an estate agent or solicitor, someone with intimate knowledge of land and property. He exercises his skill in purchasing land where he judges that development or redevelopment is possible and profitable. A property company can be any size. It can be a very small operation run by a few people or, like MEPC or Town and City, it can employ scores of people, including its own architects, surveyors and other skills. The size of the company has nothing to do with the size of a scheme that might be developed, although it will influence the number of schemes that can be underway at any one time. This is because the development finance is raised externally, from the same sources, the clearing banks, the secondary banking houses, the pension funds and the insurance companies, whatever the size of the company. It is primarily the skill and judgment exercised in borrowing capital, against the risks and profit inherent in a particular development, that character-izes the successful property developer. Inevitably, the property developer finds himself pitted against his chief obstacle: the planning authority. The authority determines in principle where and what quantity of floorspace the developer can construct, but the relationship is more subtle than this since the developer generally has one major advantage in that he is the initiator, and can attempt to change policies with regard to location and quantity of floorspace. The relationship is essentially that of a developer wanting to build offices where his commercial judgment tells him that they are required and hence profitable, influenced and in some instances cajoled, by a planning authority wishing to set office policy in the context of its whole plan for employment, housing, recreation and transport.

London was the centre of the office property boom, but as the then planning authority, the London County Council, became aware of the problems of congestion, it attempted to force the office developers into the provinces. Since the second world war, this relationship has had a considerable effect on the location of office premises in that it has kept in check the dominance of London and encouraged the development of office premises in provincial centres, which otherwise would not have witnessed development on such a scale. Nonetheless, for all the efforts of government, London still remains the dominant office centre in the country; to appreciate the factors behind this continuing momentum, we turn to a review of post-war office development trends.

Statistical Review of Post-War Office Development Trends

Dominance of London

London's dominance as a location for office development was already evident during the early post-war years. There was a strong demand for office space in the capital, due partly to the fact that between the wars relatively little office building had taken place and Victorian offices, many of them obsolete, were ripe for renewal. In addition, around 0.883 million sq. m of office space in central London (out of a total stock of 8.1 million sq. m in 1939) had been destroyed by wartime bombing. Yet these factors only partially explain the post-war upsurge in demand for office space in London. During the early 1950s London became increasingly popular as the chosen location for firms' prestige headquarters and cemented its position as an international centre. This, coupled with two crucial political decisions, namely the lifting of the development charge by Macmillan in 1953 and the dropping of building licences by the then Minister of Works in November 1954, led to an unprecedented boom in office development in London.

The extent of this boom is clearly illustrated by planning permission statistics relating to this period. In 1952 the London County Council granted planning permission for 0.223 million sq. m of office space, a figure which rose to 0.279 million during the following year. By 1954 this total had shot up to 0.530 million sq. m.

Policies for Restraint

During the period from then on until the mid 1960s, London's predominance in terms of office location became increasingly problematic. Policy-makers focused considerable attention on the central area of the city, and in 1957 the LCC revealed its *Plan to Combat Congestion in Central London*. This policy of decentralization—of attempting to restrain the growth of office employment in central London whilst encouraging it in outer areas, notably in Middlesex, Kent, Croydon and Essex—was reiterated in the LCC's 1960 review of the development plan. At this time voluntary decentralization was being advocated by the government, which had rejected the idea of office development certificates.

Yet by the early 1960s it was clear that the LCC's enthusiasm for its policy of suburban development was no longer shared by other local authorities. Doubts were soon translated into specific limitations on office development in Middlesex, Kent, Essex, Hertfordshire and Surrey; and in 1963 the government—in response to pressure from local authorities and other bodies such as the Town and Country Planning Association which issued a White Paper entitled *London—Employment: Housing: Land*, in which the problems resulting from the enormous growth of office employment in central London were discussed. Although rejecting the concept of licences, the government did introduce an important adjustment to the Town and Country Planning Act 1962 and advocate the dispersal of civil servants. The Location of Offices Bureau was set up as an agent of this decentralization policy. The government's *South East Study 1961–1981*, which followed in March 1964 (Ministry of Housing and Local Government, 1964), reiterated this emphasis on decentralization and suburban development, but also included a policy of providing office centres further away from the London conurbation.

Office Development Permits

Along with the change in government late in 1964 came changes in approach to the problems of office development. Stringent controls on office building were introduced in the form of Office Development Permits (ODPs), as a result of the Control of Office and Industrial Development Act 1965. Under the terms of this Act, every proposed office development (new buildings, rebuildings, extensions and changes of use) which involved an increase of 279 sq. m or more floorspace had to obtain an ODP from the Board of Trade, as well as a planning permission from the local authority. At first this requirement applied only to the London Metropolitan Area, but later during 1965 and 1966 was extended to Birmingham, and finally to all the South East, the East and the West Midlands. The result of the 'Brown Ban', as it came to be known, was a considerable slowing-down of office development in central London. Its consequences—a severely restricted supply of office accommodation which in turn led to soaring office rents—are well known.

Greater London Development Plan

During the early 1970s office location policy began to settle down. The administration of controls was simplified and incorporated into the Town and Country Planning Act 1971 and the government took a slightly more relaxed view of development in central London, recognizing that some firms were tied to the central area. The GLC, for its part, did not fully subscribe to this view, and through the medium of the *Greater London Development Plan* attempted to increase office development in outer London at the expense of central London. Its 'Locational Criteria', published in January 1972, aimed to achieve a balanced distribution of office space throughout London, in GLC terms, one goal being to improve the economic viability of boroughs outside the central area. Six types of development situations by means of which planning advantage could be attained were cited. These were:

1. Redevelopment of areas of poor layout or design;
2. Provision of residential accommodation in conjunction with the development;
3. Improvement of the public transport system, especially in relation to interchanges and railway termini;
4. Provision of specific benefits in the form of buildings, land or other facilities for the use of the public;
5. Conservation of buildings or places of architectural or historic interest;
6. Provision of small suites of offices, particularly if available on a rental basis.

The GLC document went on to state that growth might also be permitted, subject to the above conditions, in other locations. These would be in close proximity either to central London termini or to places providing significant passenger interchange facilities (with the caveat that the development should not cause passenger traffic exceeding the transport capacity), or where traffic generated would at all times be consistent with existing road capacity and flow requirements. 'Growth of offices in other locations or in other circumstances should generally be restricted' (Greater London Council, 1972).

The GLC's office development policy was taken one stage further when its new 5-year plan was revealed in February 1975–a plan which in essence banned the building of further offices in London but allowed a strictly limited construction programme well away from the centre of the capital (Greater London Council, 1975). This policy, covering the period 1976–1981, had been conceived back in 1973 when the overall building climate was significantly different. Two main criteria were used by the GLC in determining its new plan. Firstly, on the basis of projected population statistics, the corresponding number of office workers was calculated. This figure was then expressed in terms of office floorspace. Secondly, using the ratio of residents in a particular area of London to the present number of office employees, those areas with few office jobs were earmarked as priority zones for new office development under the 5-year plan. The GLC estimated that by 1981 the population of Greater London would be 6.8 million, and that there would be 60,000 more office jobs than in 1976. This would mean a total additional requirement of 1.6 million sq. m (a figure which included an allowance for an increase in the amount of working space allocated to each employee). Only 0.279 million sq. m was to be developed within central London, the other 1.3 million in the suburbs. The GLC was eager to see new office development in areas which had previously been bypassed, such as Enfield and Harrow in the north west; Brixton, Lewisham and Clapham Junction in the south; and Bromley, Woolwich, Ilford and Walthamstow in the east. The proposed effects of this GLC policy are summarized in Table 8.1.

Nevertheless the plan did not totally exclude the possibility of exceptions to

Table 8.1. GLC Office Floorspace Projections 1976–81

	New space 1976–81	Total space 1981
	million sq. m	million sq. m
Central	0.278	18.552
Inner NE	0.092	1.858
Inner S	0.241	1.737
Inner NW	0.111	1.607
Outer NE	0.213	1.254
Outer SE	0.222	1.263
Outer SW	0.148	2.601
Outer W	0.037	2.146
Outer NW	0.222	2.108
Total	1.564	33.126

such GLC rules, in the form of expansion schemes for central government offices in central London, to give one example. Indeed, such concessions highlight the problem of divided authority faced by the GLC.

Effect of Policies

Despite policies such as these, and regional growth in areas like the South West, London's predominance in terms of office location remains largely unchallenged. The government's *Office Location Review*, published in late 1976, revealed an imbalance in office and service employment in favour of the South East as a whole, and at the end of the same year some 1.9 million sq. m of office space were available outside central London, a figure that represents a capacity for a 3 per cent increase in office employment on a national basis.

Even so, policies in recent years aimed at restraining London's primacy have not been entirely without effect, as is shown by the Department of the Environment's *Statistics for Town and Country Planning—Series 11*, which cover the period 1967–1974 (Department of the Environment, 1976). Floorspace comparisons between the years 1967 and 1974 are given only for commercial offices; statistics relating to central government offices are unfortunately not available. The DOE's figures reveal that between 1967 and 1974 the number of commercial office properties in Greater London fell marginally from 49.1 to 48.3 thousand, compared with an increase in the rest of the South East region from 22.4 to 27 thousand. Overall in the remaining areas of England and in Wales, there was a smaller growth in the number of commercial office properties, generally in the region of one thousand or under.

Recent Trends

Floorspace comparisons over the period 1967–1974 (Table 8.2) reveal that although the North West Region and the South East (excluding Greater London) accounted for almost identical amounts of commercial office floorspace in 1974, and that the South East Region as a whole increased its total by one-third, the largest percentage growth over the period took place in the South West Region, where commercial office floorspace rose by more than 50 per cent. Nevertheless, in overall terms the latter still accounted for a relatively small proportion of total floorspace, with 2.0 million sq. m compared with 2.4 to 2.5 million in the West Midlands and in Yorkshire and Humberside, figures which fall well short of the totals for the North West and the South East (excluding Greater London), both with 5.3 million sq. m of commercial office floorspace.

A more detailed breakdown of net increases in floorspace between 1967 and 1974 is given in Table 8.3. These statistics show that in both the South West and the South East (excluding Greater London), there was a net increase in commercial office floorspace of 56 per cent during the period 1967–1974. The

Table 8.2. Commercial Office Floorspace (million sq. m) at 1 April 1967 and 1 April 1974

Region	1967		1974	
Northern	1.124		1.458	
Yorkshire & Humberside	1.839		2.461	
North West	3.660		5.267	
East Midlands	1.031		1.560	
West Midlands	1.876		2.508	
East Anglia	0.566		0.817	
South East	13.954		18.766	
Greater London		10.581		13.498
Other South East		3.372		5.258
South West	1.309		2.043	
Wales	0.798		1.170	
Total: England & Wales	26.157		36.050	

Table 8.3. Net Increase in Commercial Floorspace, 1967–74

Region	Million sq. m		Net increase as % of stock at 1.4.1967	
Northern	0.334		29.8	
Yorkshire & Humberside	0.622		33.8	
North West	1.607		43.9	
East Midlands	0.529		51.4	
West Midlands	0.631		33.7	
East Anglia	0.250		44.3	
South East	4.812		34.5	
Greater London		2.917		27.6
Other South East		1.885		55.9
South West	0.733		56.0	
Wales	0.371		46.5	
Total: England & Wales	9.889		37.9	

next largest growth was found in the East Midlands, where the stock rose by 51.5 per cent. At the other end of the scale, the smallest percentage increase—27.6 per cent—took place in Greater London.

Yet in overall terms regional shares of total commercial office floorspace have not shifted dramatically, as shown in Table 8.4. The figures reveal that the South East Region as a whole has retained its dominant position with more than 50 per cent of the total commercial office floorspace for England and Wales, and that Greater London remains in second place, even though its percentage share has fallen marginally.

The situation is similar in the case of central government offices. At 1 April

Table 8.4. Distribution of Commercial Floorspace by Regions (%), 1967 and 1974

Region	1967		1974	
Northern	4.3		4.0	
Yorkshire & Humberside	7.0		6.8	
North West	14.0		14.6	
East Midlands	3.9		4.3	
West Midlands	7.2		7.0	
East Anglia	2.2		2.3	
South East	53.4		52.0	
Greater London		40.5		37.4
Other South East		12.9		14.6
South West	5.0		5.7	
Wales	3.1		3.2	
Total: England & Wales	100.0		100.0	

Table 8.5. Office Floorspace at 1 April 1974 (million sq. m)

Region	Commercial offices		Central govt offices	
Northern	1.5		0.3	
Yorkshire & Humberside	2.5		0.3	
North West	5.2		0.6	
East Midlands	1.6		0.2	
West Midlands	2.5		0.3	
East Anglia	0.8		0.1	
South East	19.2		3.0	
Greater London		14.1		2.3
Outer Metropolitan Area		2.9		0.4
Outer South East		2.2		0.4
South West	2.2		0.4	
Wales	1.2		0.3	
Total: England & Wales	36.9		5.5	

1974, central government office floorspace in England and Wales totalled 5.5 million sq. m compared with 26.9 million sq. m of commercial office floorspace. Of this 5.5 million, more than half—3 million sq. m—was located in the South East Region, 2.3 million of this within the Greater London area. No other region accounted for more than 0.6 million sq. m. The situation is summarized in Table 8.5.

Regional Centres

An analysis of floorspace distribution *within* the various regions reveals the dominance of particular centres. Within the Northern Region, just under half (46 per cent) of the total commercial floorspace of 1.5 million sq. m is located in Tyne and Wear, which also accounts for 57 per cent of the region's central government office floorspace. In Yorkshire and Humberside, 48 per cent of the total commercial office floorspace is concentrated in West Yorkshire, where a slightly smaller proportion of central government office floorspace (44 per cent) is located. Within the North West, Greater Manchester accounts for more than half (53 per cent) of the total commercial floorspace—compared with only 24.5 per cent on Merseyside—but central government offices are spread more evenly throughout the region, 38.5 per cent being located in Greater Manchester and 30 per cent on Merseyside.

By way of contrast, in the East Midlands central government office floorspace is concentrated in Nottinghamshire, whereas commercial offices are fairly evenly distributed throughout the region. Within the West Midlands Region, nearly two-thirds of both commercial and central government office floorspace are concentrated in the conurbation. In East Anglia, commerical office floorspace is spread fairly evenly over the region, although Cambridgeshire has the largest proportion of central government office floorspace. Within the South West Region, Avon accounts for one-third of both commercial and central government floorspace, and in Wales, South Glamorgan occupies a similar position.

Greater London and the South East

Finally, in the South East, Greater London is clearly predominant, accounting for 73 per cent of commercial and 76 per cent of central government office floorspace. Yet there are stronger concentrations of office development in some boroughs compared with others, as the 'league table' (based on the DOE statistics already referred to) shows (Table 8.6). The 'bottom five' (i.e. the boroughs with the smallest amounts of office floorspace) are shown in Table 8.7. We have seen that despite considerable government initiatives and increased control on office development by planning authorities, there has not been a major change in office location patterns. The extent to which office developers have been able to resist these initiatives and controls is now examined.

Table 8.6. Greater London Boroughs: Major Office Locations, 1974

Commercial office floorspace		Central govt office floorspace	
	000's sq. m		000's sq. m
1. Westminster	4015.4	1. Westminster	961.0
2. City of London	3064.5	2. Camden	259.3
3. Camden	1294.2	3. Lambeth	141.3
4. Islington	608.6	4. Southwark	139.0
5. Croydon	479.5	5. City of London	109.4

Table 8.7. Greater London Boroughs: Non-Important Office Locations, 1974

Commercial office floorspace		Central govt office floorspace	
	000's sq. m		000's sq. m
1. Waltham Forest	54.9	1. Merton	4.5
2. Lewisham	61.4	2. Havering	4.8
3. Greenwich	73.7	3. Bexley	5.3
4. Haringey	74.9	4. Haringey	5.6
5. Barking	83.2	5. Barking	6.5

Discussion of the Effectiveness of Government Policies in Controlling Office Development, Emphasizing the Development Company Viewpoint

This examination is inevitably retrospective, with a strong emphasis on Greater London, office development in the capital being a prime influence on government policy. Several phases in office policy have already been recognized in this chapter and are designated as follows.

Phase 1. 1945–1953

The concern of government was with the movement of manufacturing industry away from Greater London; active policy in relation to office developments scarcely existed before the construction boom of the 1950s. Although mention of an 'office problem' and decentralization appeared in the 1944 Greater London Plan, control of office development was left to the statutory powers under the Town and Country Planning Act 1947 and by the system of building licences which existed up to 1954. The *LCC Development Plan* (London County Council, 1951) contained a reference to the need to reduce central congestion, but permissions for office development were given in considerable number. Other local planning authorities were almost completely unaware that office developments presented any problem for them. Although the planning authorities may not have been aware of the trends leading to a massive increase in demand for office space, many developers were. Oliver Marriott (1967) in his book recounts the story of an office site in the West End of London whose value almost doubled overnight with the end of licensing.

Phase 2. 1953–1955

This phase began with the relaxation and lifting of building controls in 1953 and 1954. The Ministry of Housing and Local Government warned of a large impending increase in office employment and effected amendments to the LCC's 1955 *Development Plan*. This rezoned some office development areas to residential uses and residential areas in the centre were protected. The government abandoned the financial provisions of the Town and Country Planning Act 1947 and there was an immediate rush by landowners to sell their land to office developers. In 1954 and 1955, more new office floorspace was approved by the LCC than in any other year before or since. These two years laid the basis for the great office development boom of the late fifties and the emergence of a score or so of new property development companies. Many of these companies appreciated that restrictions might again be applied and lost no time in obtaining planning permissions and commencing development.

Phase 3. 1956–1961

During this phase the problem was seen almost entirely as one of the London central area. The *Plan to Combat Congestion in Central London* (London County Council, 1957) marked the start of the LCC's policy of decentralization of offices to outskirt areas. In general, the affected local planning authorities (e.g. Middlesex, Kent, Croydon, Essex) welcomed the suburban solution. In its 1960 review of the development plan, the LCC reiterated its intention to restrain the growth of office employment in central London whilst encouraging it in the outer parts of the county and beyond in the remainder of the South East. The government, having rejected the idea of office development certificates, advocated decentralization on a voluntary basis. The LCC, however, tried to be more specific and reduced the plot ratios (the amount of development possible on a site) in many areas zoned for office use. This hardly deterred many developers who were busy exploiting a loophole in the Planning Act. Schedule 3 of the Town and Country Planning Act 1947 laid down that a building could be enlarged by up to 10 per cent of its cubic content. The purpose of this had been in 1947 to allow owners to make minor improvements to existing buildings without having to pay the development charge, but when the charge was abolished, the Third Schedule remained intact. Therefore when an existing building was redeveloped, the developer was allowed to put up a new building with a cubic capacity 10 per cent greater than the older building. Effectively, with the benefit of modern internal planning of the premises, the gain could be much greater than this. Oliver Marriott cites the example of New Scotland Yard, where the floorspace represented by a new office building, by virtue of the Third Schedule, gave the effect of a plot ratio of 7:1, compared with the LCC's zoning of 3.5:1. Office developers consequently sought out sites which could be effectively redeveloped on the basis of the Third Schedule. Developers too were pursuing sites in suburban locations. Rising rents in central London were forcing many office occupiers to consider a location in outer London, provided it was well located in relation to public transport. From 1956 to 1960, Middlesex gave permission for 0.85 million sq. m of offices. It is difficult to know how much developers were influenced by government exhortations in this tendency, as sanctions were minimal and office planning permissions were still being obtained in central

London. It is likely that developers were reacting to market trends caused by higher costs in central London, and government policy fortunately coincided.

Phase 4. 1961–1964

While the LCC remained with the policy of suburban development until about 1964, other local authorities first had doubts about the policy and then acted to halt suburban office development in their metropolitan areas. Middlesex, Essex, Hertfordshire, Kent and Surrey all imposed limitations of some form or another. After pressure from local authorities and bodies such as the Town and Country Planning Association, the government issued in February, 1963, the White Paper *London—Employment: Housing: Land*, which discussed the problems caused by the enormous growth of office employment in central London, but rejected the idea of licences. An important adjustment was made to the Town and Country Planning Act 1962 which nullified the effects of the Third Schedule, dispersal of civil servants was advocated, and the Location of Offices Bureau was set up as an agent of the now stated policy of decentralization. The emphasis on decentralization and suburban development remained in the government's *South East Study* 1961–1981 (Ministry of Housing and Local Government, 1964) but it also included a policy of providing office centres further away from the London conurbation. Although developers may have anticipated government policy on decentralization, what was not expected was the virtual total ban on office development announced on 4 November 1964.

Phase 5. 1965–1970

The era of the 'Brown Ban'. With the change in government late in 1964, government action over the problem of office development took another step. The Control of Office and Industrial Development Act 1965 introduced a series of Office Development Permits similar to the IDC system over industry which had been in operation since the war. Every proposed office development (new buildings, rebuildings, extensions and changes of use) involving an increase of 279 sq. m or more additional floorspace, in the London Metropolitan Area, now had to obtain on ODP from the Board of Trade, as well as a planning permission from the local authority. Later, during 1965 and 1966, this stringent control of office building was extended outside the GLC area to Birmingham, and finally to all the South East, the East and West Midlands. The ban had its effect, and new office development in central London slowed down considerably.

But its effect was welcomed by many developers. By artificially restricting supply, it helped to fill up the unlet blocks, which were becoming more frequent in and around London. It also sent rents soaring, and towards the end of this phase there was acceptance by the government that some relaxation of the policy was necessary in central London. The Location of Offices Bureau during 1967/68 was responsible for moving nearly 14,000 jobs; this represented its peak year of activity with the exception of 1973/74, which saw a reaction to the steep increase in office rents in central London in the form of a sudden increase in enquiries concerning relocation.

Phase 6. 1971–1973

A short period in which office location policy began to settle down. The administration of controls was simplified and incorporated into the Town and Country Planning Act, 1971 and government took a slightly more relaxed view of development in central London, recognizing that some firms were tied to the central area. The GLC, for its part, did not share this view so enthusiastically and through the medium of the Greater London Development Plan attempted to increase office development in outer London at the expense of central London. New provincial office centres, for example Leeds, Bristol and Newcastle, began to emerge during this period, as a direct result of government policy with its restrictions on new office building in central London. During this short period there appeared to be a convergence of viewpoint between government and developer: (a) there was a need for some new office space in central London, and (b) there was wisdom both in terms of planning policy and commercial realism in the development of provincial office centres. The only obstacle at the time was the GLC, which had begun to seriously question new office building in central London. At the time there was little to suggest the dramatic change in the fortunes of office developers that occurs in our seventh phase, with which we now deal.

Phase 7. 1974–

In November 1973, the government, faced with a record new £300 million trade deficit, announced that the minimum lending rate was to be increased to 13 per cent, and also that taxes on development gains were to be considerably increased. With these two initiatives the government effectively undermined the basis of the property development industry. In the spring of the following year, a new government announced measures for bringing land required for development into public possession and that it would introduce a development gains tax. Since that time, the Community Land Act has become law and the minimum lending rate increased even further, but November 1973 was comparable in its dramatic effect to the Brown ban nine years earlier. By January 1975 a number of property companies had collapsed and there was a virtual standstill on new developments. A year later in January 1976 the GLC had publicly announced that decentralization had been overtaken by events and that it was to critically reevaluate its policies. This was of little importance to office developers who had been caught by the property collapse with schemes either uncompleted or stillborn. Land cleared for office development in Covent Garden and in the City of London, and alongside the River Thames in Southwark, blighted by planning delays, now no longer had any prospect of redevelopment. The proposals of the GLC for decentralizing office space to the strategic centres of outer London had now been overtaken by events and was hopelessly out-of-date. Restrictions on rent increases, increased taxes on profits from property development, followed by the oil crisis, recession and high interest rates, have completely floored the property development industry, and particularly office development. In retrospect, it can be seen that government policy on office location was too slow in being formulated and, when finally administered, too severe in its application. Controls applied intelligently in the mid-fifties could have meant much more office development located in the regions than in fact happened. From the point of view of developers, the controls themselves were not necessarily a bad thing. Much more of a problem were planning delays once an ODP was obtained, and the increasing cost of money during these delays. Many developers with sites assembled for office development, having the benefit of an ODP but no complete development to let, were caught by the restrictions of this phase and were forced into liquidation. The example below shows the extraordinary effect of delay on the cost of money borrowed to finance a development scheme.

	£1,000,000 borrowed	
	15% interest	18% interest
Repayment in 3 years	1,521,000	1,643,000
Repayment in 6 years	2,313,000	2,700,000
Repayment in 9 years	3,518,000	4,435,000

The pattern of office development is now likely to be static for some time owing to the small amount of office development currently under construction. This situation is attributed to the interplay of four economic factors: inflation of building costs, the high cost of finance, uncertainty about trends in rental incomes and the relative weakness of the investment market. In the future, much of the office space being developed is likely to come about through the rehabilitation of existing properties, and this will tend to perpetuate existing location patterns. Furthermore, in the event of any revival in the property market, planning authorities will be in a poor position to oppose schemes proposed in existing areas, which will again tend to perpetuate existing locations. With the benefit of hindsight it can fairly be stated that had planning authorities anticipated the office boom much more quickly and dealt with schemes more quickly, developers would have responded to the new locational initiatives, with the result that more offices would have been built in outer London and in the provincial centres. In the future, developers are likely to be much more cautious and prefer locations close to established office centres, for example the City of London.

An Examination of the Factors Affecting the Developer's Choice of Site and the Variables which Lead to a Decision to Provide Speculative Development

There are not surprisingly a number of factors that influence the choice of site on which a developer will construct a speculative office scheme, and although by its nature such development is opportunistic, it is possible to categorize the various factors. In the first part of this section these factors will be described, and later a specific example will be used to demonstrate their significance. The factors are as follows.

(a) The opportunity and need for redevelopment. The office boom was originally fuelled by the need to rebuild after the war, but once bomb-damaged sites had been redeveloped, other sites where existing buildings were either obsolete or in poor repair were regarded suitable for office development. Little office development had taken place between the wars, and consequently in many areas redevelopment has primarily taken place to increase the stock of office floorspace available.

(b) Land needed for the development should be capable of being acquired with the minimum of delay and on favourable financial terms. Any considerable delay could jeopardize the scheme, as part of the site would already have been purchased and finance interest would be incurred in advance of building. Nevertheless, land acquisition for many schemes has taken place over a relatively long time, as sites have been purchased quietly, without the proposed scheme being publicized, in order to discourage any speculative selling or individual landowners 'sitting tight' in order to bid up the price paid for their sites. Where this has occurred, some developers have attempted to persuade local authorities to compulsorily purchase such sites, in return for road or other planning improvements that would be included in the scheme.

(c) The existence of favourable town planning policies regarding office development, or alternatively the anticipation that policies might become more favourable. This is obviously a matter of individual judgment, but many fortunes have been made where land has been purchased in anticipation of a policy change regarding office development.

(d) The suitability of an area from a marketing point of view. In both London and provincial centres there are confirmed office areas, but much recent speculative development has been on the fringes of these areas, on sites not already zoned for office use but which enjoy good access to financial and banking centres and public transport.

(e) The application of detailed planning factors, for example the permitted plot ratio (the amount of space permitted to be built relative to the ground floor area of the development site), daylighting angles, the maximum height of the building and car parking requirements, all of which will determine the amount of office development granted planning permission.

(f) The obtaining of an Office Development Permit, if in an area subject to

ODP restrictions. In April 1976 the exemption limit for Office Development Permits in the South East Economic Planning Region was raised from 929 sq. m. to 1394 sq. m following a review of office location policy by the Department of the Environment. The new policy places severe restriction on new permits for speculative building, even for replacement, but the Department undertook to give permits in a limited number of cases where the development would produce a 'substantial public benefit'. To help small firms, the Department would be ready to consider favourably proposals for speculative office space to be let in small suites, under 465 sq. m. An Office Development Permit of a 'speculative' nature, i.e. where there is no known tenant for the office space, is worth considerably more to a developer than one tied to a particular tenant. The tenant will not surprisingly use his ODP as a negotiating tactic in agreeing satisfactory rental terms, particularly as named-tenant ODPs often have a condition that the tenant must occupy the building for a period of at least five years. The Department has thus to assess the two types of ODP application quite differently. In the case of a named tenant, they must decide whether the amount and type of employment generated by that tenant should be permitted in that particular area; the speculative ODP has to be justified against the background of an overall office policy for an area. To assist itself, the Department does require a considerable amount of information not only about the project, but the present use of the site, intended occupiers, employment to be generated from the project, nature of the existing premises, particularly the existing amount of office space, and reasons for the need for new offices. Despite this impressive statistical requirement, considerable difference of judgment can centre around an ODP application, particularly where it involves a request for a replacement ODP, i.e. where new office space is to be built to replace existing obsolete office premises. The judgment of what constitutes an office and an office worker, and whether premises are a head office or a subsidiary office location, can be complex and have far-reaching financial implications. Extensive office and warehouse premises, on the north side of Pentonville Road, London, in an area not zoned for offices, were acquired by a developer in the belief that a good case could be made for a replacement ODP well in excess of the existing office-use rights granted on a previous planning permission. In this instance the developer was successful and a modern multistorey office building occupies what in part was once the distribution centre for a leading shoe retailer. In other instances the developer has not been so successful and the lack of an ODP has thwarted many office development schemes; it is for this reason that I have dealt at some length with the ODP system. The legislation of these controls has introduced yet another factor which affects the developer's choice of site.

The variables which lead to a decision to provide speculative development once a site has been chosen are inevitably of a financial nature, and concern principally the funding of a project. Whitbread Trafalgar Properties Ltd, for example, have spent some seven years in both the preparation of a scheme involving 48,000 sq. m of office space, at Chiswell Street, on the edge of the City of London, and the obtaining of the necessary planning permission and ODP.

The principal variable is that of yield, which in a classical economic sense represents the income from a security expressed as a proportion of its current market price. The concept of yield is very important to property development as it exerts a strong influence on the borrowing powers of development companies. In the past 10 years or so most long-term property development finance has been obtained from the insurance companies and pension funds by means of lease-back arrangements. By this method the institution purchases the development site, assembled by the property company, at its cost or at an agreed figure, enters into a lease for at least 125 years with the developer and provides the cost of development during the building period together with fees and expenses. Until the development is completed and let, interest is rolled up and forms part of the total development costs. Once the development is completed and let the institution receives an agreed income, the balance going to the developer. At this point the developer owns an asset which to all intents and purposes can be valued as virtually a freehold. In the valuation the concept of yield is paramount. It expresses the return an investor looks for from an investment, but obviously it is not only a function of the actual income that can be obtained from a property development at that time, but as property investment is a medium-term proposition, expectations about future rent increases. During the early part of 1973 yields for prime office developments fell from $4\frac{1}{4}$ per cent to $3\frac{3}{4}$ per cent over a period of months and this substantially influenced the capital valuation of assets. If in a particular instance a developer expects a substantial increase in rents from a development in the immediate future, he may be prepared initially to run an income deficit on a scheme in the expectation of a capital surplus in the future. What in fact has happened in the property collapse since November 1973 is that office rents have not increased at the levels budgeted by developers and companies have been faced with a permanent deficit situation as measured between income from rents against interest on borrowings, and with no help from the capital appreciation of assets, which ultimately would influence the share price upwards. As yields have increased, only companies that are in surplus can expect to obtain institutional finance.

A further point needs to be made regarding yields, and that is the difference in viewpoint between a developer and the institutional purchaser of a completed property development. A developer obviously wishes to maximize his own return, and this may result in a lower yield as far as the institutional purchaser is concerned. However, if the purchaser takes the view that the yield can be improved, by means of rent reviews for example, despite the low yield, a development will be purchased. Yields have therefore to be seen in the context of the prevailing investment climate. At the present time, institutions are looking for yields as high as 7 per cent, and there are very few property developments, that could be commenced now, that could show that return.

In order to demonstrate how a development site is assembled and a decision taken whether to develop or not, there follows a working example structured along the lines of the earlier analysis. This is based on an actual scheme prepared by the author for a site early in 1973.

(a) *Need for Redevelopment*

The site which is some 3317 sq. m in area, is located in a south London borough, with good access to rail and road facilities, and although across the river from the City of London, in time–distance terms the site is very accessible. The site is occupied by a printing works and offices, warehousing, and a row of shops fronting the major road. Part of the island site is now derelict, whilst the remainder of the site is composed of buildings which in the main are not suitable for renovation. The most serious problem concerns the printing works, whose building is nearly 100 years old. Difficulties encountered with the present building include weak floors that mean that only certain areas can be used for machinery or storage. This creates an uneconomical factory layout. The office premises are a rabbit-warren constructed from three old buildings and approximately one-third of the space is corridors.

(b) *Acquisition*

A large part of the site is already owned by the printing company, who have had negotiations with a property company already owning part of the remainder of the site and interested in purchasing the other sites.

(c) *Town Planning Policies*

The site is zoned on the Development Plan for light industry purposes, but does not form part of a large industrial area. Land-use zoning around the site is for railway purposes, waterside commerce and residential. The Plan, however, was last reviewed in 1961 and has been overtaken by events, particularly the movement downstream of waterside commerce. Conscious of the problems caused by a Development Plan very much out of date, the London borough produced in advance of a new Borough Structure Plan a Draft Strategy Plan. Although not a statutory document, the main aim of the document was to give guidance to developers on the Council's objectives for the area. The important feature of the strategy was the inclusion of the whole of the island site in a broad category of central area uses, including offices.

(d) *Marketing*

From a marketing point of view the site is ideal, with good access to the City of London; a major railway terminus is close by, to which a pedestrian access is planned.

(e) *The Application of Detailed Planning Factors*

(i) The proximity of a railway terminus to the site is an important planning aspect, particularly in view of the major redevelopment of the station complex being carried out by British Rail. The redevelopment proposed for the office site is to incorporate a pedestrian footbridge which would link directly to the new platform concourse proposed by the rail authorities.

(ii) There is also the possible widening to a dual carriageway standard of the road which borders the site to the north. The road is part of the important link between the West End and the eastern riverside areas and is included in the Greater London Council's secondary roads network. The GLC for their part therefore would insist as a condition of planning permission that a road alignment for this purpose is safeguarded, and this has been incorporated into the scheme and the developable plot ratio transferred to the remainder of the site.

(iii) The other planning factor that has been of influence is that of the Council's high building policy. In the Draft Strategy it is recommended that a distinct grouping of high buildings should be established in relation to the railway terminus, and an area including this site in which high buildings will be permitted is indicated in the strategy.

(iv) In addition to their other planning policies, both the GLC and the London borough call for the provision of social facilities in any redevelopment that relies on an element of office space, to ensure its financial viability. The Borough has indicated that substantial shopping or residential development on the site is not appropriate and in order, therefore, to determine the most suitable form of social provision on the site, groups representing community interests in the area were consulted. The most welcome type of provision appeared to be a meeting place which could be used by various groups in the community, including preschool play groups and old people's clubs. This suggestion is incorporated into the scheme.

On the basis of this planning appraisal, the following development is proposed:

Site area		3,317	sq. m
Permitted plot ratio	3.5	11,608	sq. m
Of which, offices		7070	sq. m
Rebuilt printing works and ancillary offices		2657	sq. m
Community space including residential facilities for old people		1881	sq. m
Car-parking provision		22 spaces	

The development would permit 13 storeys of office space with a net floor area of 465 sq. m at each storey, together with a mezzanine level. Overall the ratio of net space to gross space is 85 per cent, taking account of the servicing arrangements which include air-conditioning.

(f) *Office Development Policies*

The Department of the Environment recognize the need to provide more office floorspace in central London, especially for City-based activities, and an application is to be made for an ODP that in part will be replacement and in part speculative. The Greater London Council is also concerned with office development in that, under the Greater London Plan regulations, the Council must indicate for each of the London boroughs the amount of new office floorspace that it will permit. The Council also operate locational criteria which determine where new office development should occur. In addition to these restrictions, the GLC also expect all proposed developments which incorporate new office use to attain certain planning advantages.

(g) *Financial Appraisal*

In order to carry out a financial appraisal of the development, certain basic assumptions have been taken into account, including:

(i) A three-year development and letting period;

(ii) A social contribution to be included in the form of old persons' bedsitters with a meeting and social room, the cost of which will be covered in the overall redevelopment costs and that no revenue will accrue in respect of this;

(iii) The estimated office rental element of the total revenue figures has been taken at present levels and no assessment has been made of likely future inflation;

(iv) That the office accommodation within the office tower, connected by a pedestrian walkway to the station, is of a high-quality finish and standard and is sufficiently flexible in layout to allow for letting off in floors.

The financial appraisal initially consists of an estimate of rental income and the potential investment value. The latter is the price that an investor would be prepared to pay for the completed development when fully let. At this point the investor would receive a stream of income that, in the market conditions prevailing, would produce a profit against the cost of the money needed to acquire the development.

Rental Income and Investment Value

  Printing Works

    Storage and printing 2258 sq. m gross say 1914 sq. m
    @ £21.50 pms   £41,200 pa
    Ancillary offices 399 sq. m gross, say 339 sq. m net @
    £43 pms   £14,600 pa
                                                                             ───────────
                                                                              £55,800 pa
    Year's purchase (8% in perp.), 12.5. Estimated Phase 1
    investment value   £697,500
  Offices and Shops
    Offices 7070 sq. m gross, say 6002 sq. m net @ £70
    pms   £419,900 pa
    Shops 9 units @ 47 sq. m each, say £1500 pa per unit   £13,500 pa
                                                                             ───────────
                                                                             £433,400 pa

Year's purchase ($6\frac{1}{8}\%$in perp.), 16.34. Estimated Phase
2 investment value   £7,081,500

                                                                         £7,779,000
                                                      Say   £7,780,000

The estimated cost of demolition and redevelopment, which has been assumed over a period of three years, is approximately £2.6 million, including site clearance, construction fees and finance, but not site acquisition and costs. The estimated capital investment value of the completed and fully let development is approximately £7.78 million, as shown in the preceding table, and therefore a figure of approximately £5 million is available for site acquisition and costs and capital profit. On this basis the developer decided to go ahead and assemble the site and seek the necessary statutory planning consent and ODP. These were obtained but the process took so long that by the time they were received, market conditions had changed and in 1976 institutional finance was not available for an office project of this character. The final development is likely to be a refurbishment of the existing office premises.

Conclusion

Inevitably we are now discussing the role of the developer in retrospect, for very little speculative office space is under construction or planned. Figures collected by the Location of Offices Bureau and quoted in the *Estates Times* of 25 February 1977 show that about 0.318 million sq. m of offices were being built for letting in Britain (excluding central London), which is under half the total of January 1974. The combination of high interest rates and low rents has ensured that, in general, it is no longer viable to build new office blocks. For the future, it does appear that the refurbishment of office space will be a more promising prospect, particularly as such development is *excepted* from the provisions of the Community Land Act. This, however, requires very different skills from those normally associated with the private developer. Several commentators have predicted the demise of the developer and the traditional development company. Their rationale is that in recent years the developer has not been fully taking the risks associated with speculative development. These have had to be borne by the financial institutions themselves, who have lent heavily to the development companies. In a depressed market, when development companies have crashed, the institutions have been unable to sell properties with which they have been associated and have had to bear the costs themselves and written off huge debts. In this situation the developer cannot justify a unique position for himself, and his role could become more akin to that of a professional property manager, associated with the financial institutions. These agencies, because of inflation of salaries, and hence savings and pensions, now have enormous sums to invest at a time when little new development is being started. The question of whether the traditional developer's role is now redundant or only temporarily not in demand has still to be answered.

Acknowledgment

I would like to acknowledge the help of Michael S. M. Read, FRICS, with the valuation figures quoted in this chapter.

References

Abercrombie, P. (1945), *Greater London Plan, 1944*. London: HMSO.

Department of the Environment (1976), *Statistics for Town and Country Planning, Series II, No. 4, Floorspace*. London: HMSO.

Greater London Council (1972), *Greater London Council Plan for Office Development*. London: Greater London Council Press Office.

Greater London Council (1975), *Office Development Policy*. London: Greater London Council Press Office.

Greater London Council (1975), *Office Location Policy*. London: Greater London Council Planning Committee.

London County Council (1951), *Development Plan, 1951*. London: London County Council.

London County Council (1957), *A Plan to Combat Congestion in Central London*. London: London County Council.

London County Council (1960), *Development Plan Review*. London: London County Council.

Marriott, O. (1967), *The Property Boom*. London: Hamish Hamilton.

Ministry of Housing and Local Government (1963), *London, Employment: Housing: Land*. London: HMSO.

Ministry of Housing and Local Government (1964), *The South East Study*, London: HMSO.

9

The Office Pattern in New York City, 1960–75

GAIL GARFIELD SCHWARTZ

Introduction

The city of New York dominates office activities in the United States, despite the rapid growth of many smaller American cities. As the headquarters city *par excellence* of the nation, New York is home to 90 (18 per cent) of the country's 500 largest manufacturing firms. Of the 50 largest commercial banks, 20 per cent have their headquarters in New York; of the 50 leading life insurance companies, six or 12 per cent are headquartered in New York City. Of the 50 top diversified financial businesses, 28 per cent have their main offices in the city. Even among retailing establishments, one of the geographically most dispersed sectors, nine or 18 per cent of the top 50 corporations have their headquarters there.

The concentration of office activities is reflected in the fact that 50 per cent of all employment in New York City is in office-type white-collar occupations. White-collar jobs have been a steadily increasing proportion of city employment throughout the last 25 years, more than doubling as a portion of total jobs as compared to 1950. The period of greatest increase was the second half of the 1960s, when white-collar employment expanded by 171 per cent.

The office development cycle in New York during the last 15 years can be characterized as a boom–bust performance. Since most office construction is undertaken by private real estate developers and financed by banks and insurance companies, the development pattern is highly unpredictable. Inadequate information and long lead time for construction distort the relationship between supply and demand, which is uneven and often appears to verge on the irrational.

The spatial organization of offices within the central business district, as distinct from the total volume of space, is the result of the interaction of private market forces, and development controls and incentives imposed by the municipal government. These controls are exercised by the City Planning Commission through its jurisdiction over the zoning resolution and the official City Map. The controls regulate land use and building bulk. Much of the Manhattan CBD allows the highest-density commercial development, giving a total permitted floor area of 15 times the lot size. High-density commercial zones are also mapped in the downtowns of the four other boroughs of the city. In certain designated areas, up to 20 per cent additional floor area may be permitted in exchange for public amenities such as plazas, pedestrian ways or subway improvements. The potential for negotiating such zoning bonuses is a major influence on the real estate developer as he enters the first phase of development, the assemblage of a suitable parcel of land. But it is only one factor among several, which include proximity to transport nodes, proximity to existing prestige office structures, and other market considerations.

Both volume of space and distribution of offices are affected by long-term economic trends which have been acting to erode the strength of New York City, like other older American cities. Population has been moving west and south. Economic development, encouraged by an extensive trans-continental highway system which opened up new locations for cheap exploitation, has sought suburban locations within metropolitan areas. While the greatest impact of centrifugal movement has been registered in the manufacturing sector, the continued dominance of New York City as the office headquarters of the United States depends on its ability to compete with the lower costs and the park-like ambience of suburban settings, and on the City's superiority in certain highly specialized economic activities.

Within the New York Metropolitan Region, push and pull forces normally present in any regional economy are exacerbated by political boundaries. The economic region covers parts of three separate states, and includes more than a dozen counties (boroughs) as well as several cities (Fig. 9.1). Each of the three states has a different taxing system. While portions of all three states are dependent on highly developed mass transit ties to New York City, only New York State participates in the financing of the system (as does the national government). Therefore, it is physically possible and often economically beneficial for firms desiring a close relationship with New York City to be located, not only outside the city, but outside New York State, achieving a more favourable tax position and lowering net costs of land and labour. It is similarly possible for executives and other workers to hold jobs in the city, but live outside the taxing reach of both the city and the state, with the net result that the fiscal contribution of their earnings is diverted from the city's revenue base.

The government of the City of New York has considered techniques for counteracting some of the attractions of other portions of the metropolitan region. The city's ability to do so is very limited, owing to the fact that in the United States municipal powers are derived from the state government. All

Fig. 9.1. New York Metropolitan Region

taxing authority, and the authority to abate taxes as well, must be sought from the state legislature. Powers to implement incentive programmes, or set up government organizations for the purpose of easing financing of construction, are also derived from the state. Even though the City of New York accounts for half the economic activity in the State of New York, political differences often prohibit or deter efforts to acquire home-rule powers.

The question of the proper role of government in relation to economic growth in general, and to certain sectors of the economy in particular, is complex. The office sector, which fuses real estate speculation with major economic forces, is a sector least amenable to public regulation. As a secondary type of economic activity, many services which are housed in offices follow primary activity, such as manufacturing. The rate at which the secondary activities will grow or decline is difficult to assess. The private sector deals with the difficulty by taking risks, in the hope of high profits. Whether or not some of the risk–and hence, some of the profit potential–should be absorbed by government is a question which has only recently been posed.

Office Market Trends

One of the more astounding facts about office space in New York City is that 83 per cent of it is located in the Manhattan central business district. Of the estimated 280 million sq. ft in the inventory, 228 million sq. ft is in Manhattan and about 52 million sq. ft in the four outer boroughs. When it is realized that each of these outer boroughs houses a population larger than most other American cities, the intensity of concentration does appear remarkable. Despite the fact that each of the outer boroughs boasts a major downtown and at least one additional commercial hub, office market demand in the boroughs has been largely limited to local market activities, even in the face of a public strategy designed to encourage dispersion of regional office activities to the boroughs.

Articulated initially by the New York Regional Plan Association (1968) and later adopted by the City Planning Commission, the subcentre strategy aimed to strengthen the core areas of the boroughs through transportation improvements, zoning incentives, and city participation in land redevelopment. Not only commercial development, but also new housing and community and cultural facilities were to be encouraged, so as to introduce 24-hour vitality in formerly thriving downtowns which were beginning to reflect the negative consequences of age and suburbanization. Urban renewal areas were designated in the subcentres of Brooklyn, Queens, and the Bronx, and sponsors were sought for mixed-use redevelopment, including office space. The City of New York was prepared to acquire land through eminent domain, deliver it to a sponsor at a price below its acquisition cost, and budget funds for infrastructure. The city was even prepared to forego part of its real-estate taxes in order to encourage new development.

The subcentre strategy has produced only one new privately developed office building of any size in any of the four subcentres (in Brooklyn). The only other private office development outside Manhattan has been in an area of Queens county which is competitive with the county's designated subcentre.

The reasons for the failure of the subcentre strategy are several. Employment did not continue the upward trend that had been anticipated. The decentralization of back office space to the outer boroughs from Manhattan which had been predicted to continue along with increasing total employment did not take place. The population of the boroughs did not increase substantially, and therefore local market services did not grow dramatically. Most important, however, New York City's superior rail mass transit system allows workers to reach the Manhattan central business district from virtually any point within the city in no more than 45 minutes. This is the strongest possible influence in favour of locating office structures in the central business district. At the time of writing, while the subcentre policy remains in effect, there is little likelihood that any office structures of substantial size will be built in the outer boroughs in the near future.

The task of monitoring and predicting trends in office space markets in New York City is greatly impeded by the inadequacy of the existing data base. While this problem may exist in other cities as well, the city's tremendous inventory means that even a 1 per cent error accounts for a considerable amount of space. The problem in tracking trends adequately lies in the fact that no agency, public or private, keeps complete records on construction, demolition, or rentals; therefore it is difficult to estimate either net stock or vacant space.

The primary sources of estimates are realty firms, the Real Estate Board of New York, and the *New York Times*, which surveys several realty firms periodically. Other sources include the Dodge Reports, a private service reporting new construction plans, and the New York City Buildings Department, where permits for new construction and for demolition are registered. Unfortunately, the buildings department files are kept in several different locations in the city, and are kept by hand rather than stored in a computer. In addition to being difficult to access, the records are often not up-to-date. The most recent field survey of office space in the city was undertaken by the Tri-State Regional Planning Commission in 1963, and in addition to being outdated, was subsequently shown to have been inaccurate in substantial measure. Periodically, various agencies within the city and the regions undertake to reconcile different estimates, and, as often happens, feed on each other's misinformation, thus entrenching errors in the base estimates.

Recently the City Planning Department staff reviewed all the trend lines on office building completions published within the last 15 years. While there was rough agreement among two of the three sources as to volume of completion during nine of the years recorded, there was only one year in which all three sources reported substantially the same magnitude of completions. Averaging the data over three-and five-year periods minimizes the disparity accounted for by differences in the recorded year of completion for particular buildings. Nevertheless, judgment is necessary. For the purposes of this chapter, we have averaged the estimates of the most reliable sources, occasionally weighting one source more heavily for a given year if there is evident reason to do so.

Supply

Between 1960 and 1975, total office space in the Manhattan CBD increased by about 84 per cent, from 124 million sq. ft to 228 million sq. ft (numbers are net rentable square feet) (Fig. 9.2). The 104 million sq. ft increase represented the net of an erratic construction cycle and a volatile speculative real-estate market, assisted by fairly radical changes in local regulations affecting office construction.

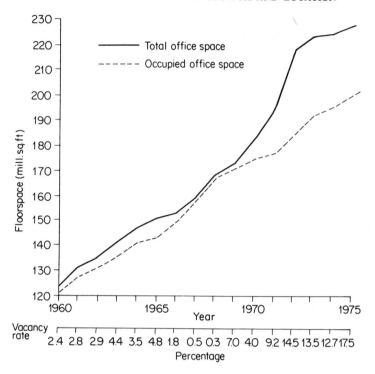

Fig. 9.2. Growth of total and occupied office space in
Manhattan CBD, 1960–75

The 15-year period with which we are concerned can be divided into three subsidiary periods: the years 1960–66, during which space was tight, and new construction was erratic; the boom period, 1967–72; and a down cycle, which the city is still in today.

In 1960, total office space on the market was at 124 million sq. ft and during 1961 alone close to 7 million sq. ft of new construction took place. In 1962 construction fell to 4 million sq. ft, but an upturn put more than 7 million sq. ft of new space on the market in 1963 and almost the same amount in 1964. But in 1965 only 4 million sq. ft were built and in 1966, the slowest year of the 15-year period, less than 2 million sq. ft were added to the supply.

During this period, on an annual average basis, about 4 per cent was added to total available space each year, and in 1966 there were 152 million sq. ft in the office inventory. But the vacancy rate was less than 2 per cent, and absorption of vacant space was high; 6 million sq. ft and 8 million sq. ft were absorbed in 1966 and 1967 respectively. By 1967, the beginning of the five-year boom in office construction, the vacancy rate had fallen to 0.5 per cent. Although Fig. 9.2 shows an uneven rise to the peak construction year in 1972, there was no year during

Table 9.1 Changes in Office Space, Manhattan, 1960–1975

	New construction*	Demolition	Total office space	Vacancy rate %	Vacant space	Occupied space	Absorption
1960	4559	665	123,861	2.4	2973	120,888	3888
1961	7703	770	130,794	2.8	3662	127,132	6244
1962	4773	1014	134,553	2.9	3902	130,651	3519
1963	7620	406	141,767	4.4	6238	135,529	4878
1964	5279	283	146,763	3.5	5137	141,626	6097
1965	4408	143	150,668	4.8	7232	143,436	1810
1966	1927	49	152,546	1.8	2746	149,800	6364
1967	6981	752	158,775	0.5	794	157,981	8181
1968	9869	483	168,161	0.5	841	167,320	9339
1969	6637	1710	173,088	1.0	1731	171,357	4037
1970	9645	280	182,453	4.0	7298	175,155	3798
1971	13,101	214	195,340	9.2	17,971	177,369	2214
1972	22,445	112	217,673	14.6	31,790	185,883	8514
1973	6333	175	223,831	13.5	30,120	193,711	7828
1974	1360	554	224,637	12.7	28,610	196,027	2316
1975	2790	82	227,345	11.5	26,261	201,084	5507

*Floorspace figures in million sq. ft (net).
Source. New York City Planning Department; Julian Studley, Inc.; Goy and Brown, Inc.; *The New York Times*.

this period when fewer than 6 million sq. ft were completed. During the three most active years of this upswing, at no time did the figure fall below 9 million sq. ft with 9.6 in 1970, 13.5 in 1971, and 22 million sq. ft in 1972. In total, between 1967 and 1972, 68.7 million sq. ft of new office space was built. This represented 55 per cent of the total space on the market in 1966. By 1972, there were 217 million sq. ft of space on the market, an increase over 1966 of 93 million sq. ft. (demolitions removed some 0.5 − 1.0 million sq. ft per year).

Office construction dropped in 1973 to 6 million sq. ft, with only seven new buildings added to the inventory. The downward trend continued, with 1.4 million sq. ft in five buildings completed in 1974 and less than 3 million sq. ft constructed in 1975. In 1975, as we have seen, the total was estimated at 227 million sq. ft (Table 9.1).

Geography of the CBD

As Fig. 9.3 illustrates, the Manhattan central business district stretches for some 80 blocks north to south, covering an area of about nine square miles. Within the CBD, there are two primary concentrations of office buildings: Midtown and Lower Manhattan. The core of the Midtown area extends between 3rd and 6th Avenues, 42nd and 57th Streets. Lower Manhattan south of Canal St, which houses the international and national finance sectors, is virtually saturated with office structures, and contains few non-office uses other than local retail facilities on ground and first floors and the printing and other service establishments which support the financial sector.

Between these two major concentrations office buildings are more scattered with very few being of major national importance such as the Metropolitan Life Insurance Building at 23rd Street. However, for the past 15 years new office construction has been concentrated in the core areas and, with few exceptions, offices in the interstices constitute a secondary market for regional and local-market firms. For the sake of clarity, the region between Canal Street and 42nd Street is incorporated in the summary statistics for Midtown.

The demand for office space in Midtown Manhattan is conditioned by headquarter firms, the headquarters of manufacturing firms in particular. In Lower Manhattan, the demand is centred on the components of the finance sector: bank headquarters, securities and exchange members, and the legal and accounting professionals serving them.

During the three periods which we are discussing, construction of new office space in Midtown outpaced construction in Lower Manhattan, although planned construction in Lower Manhattan far exceeded the amount eventually built. About 65 per cent of new construction over the entire 15-year period took place in Midtown and about 35 per cent in Lower Manhattan (Table 9.2). On a square foot basis there were about 77 million sq. ft constructed in Midtown and about 38 million sq. ft in Lower Manhattan during 1960–1975.

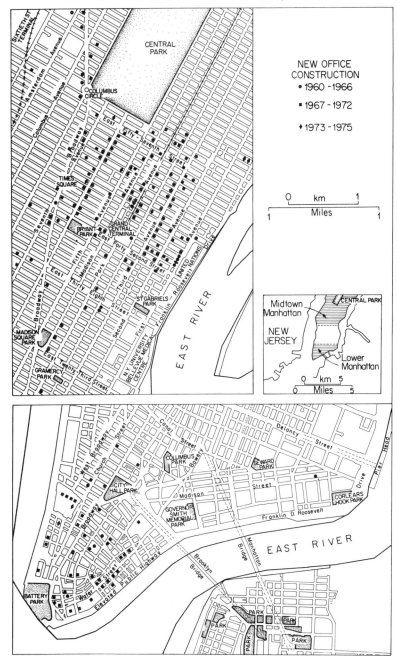

Fig. 9.3. Office construction 1960–75, Midtown
and Lower Manhattan

Table 9.2. Geographical Distribution of New Offices in Manhattan, 1960–1975

Year	No. of buildings Midtown	No. of buildings Downtown	No. square feet built Midtown (000's)	No. square feet built Downtown (000's)	Buildings Total	Total square feet (000's)
1960–1966	71	16	32,706	8381	87	36,000
1967–1972	55	30	36,671	26,830	85	69,000
1973–1975	14	2	7583	2900	16	10,500
Total	140	48	76,960	38,111	188	115,500

Source. New York City Planning Department.

In Midtown, the prime areas are those accessible to the two railroad stations which service commuters from the suburbs. On Fig. 9.3 the high-density corridor is clear, extending from Third Avenue on the east to Avenue of the Americas on the west, and from 38th Street on the south to 61st Street on the north. Virtually all of the building along the Avenue of the Americas took place in the 1966–72 boom, as did most of the Third Avenue construction.

In Lower Manhattan, a considerably smaller and more densely developed area, the distinction between prime sites and less prime sites is not easily made. The area is so well served by subways that few sites are more than one-quarter mile from a subway station. The most notable development in recent years has been the extension of offices from the core of the financial district, represented by the intersection of Wall Street and Broad St, to the periphery. Governmental action has spurred this centrifugal expansion, with construction of the 10 million sq. ft World Trade Centre on land fill by the Port Authority of New York and New Jersey, a quasi-public agency. In the very short period of 1968–73, 22 private buildings, in addition to the twin towers of the World Trade Center, were completed, for a total of 8 million sq. ft and the total space available in Lower Manhattan nearly doubled in a four-year period.

Boom–Bust

The boom–bust cycle in office building in New York City was conditioned by several factors: overestimation of the depth and extent of probable growth in employment; overextension of credit; two national recessions at close intervals; and the fiscal uncertainty of the city. Government participation encouraged the boom, thus exacerbating the bust.

The office market was relatively tight at the beginning of the 1960s, with a 2.4 per cent vacancy rate. The city's economy was strong, reflecting the generally prosperous nationwide economic scene. Beginning about the middle of the decade, substantial increases in white-collar employment were registered in office-type activities, particularly in firms beginning to computerize their routine functions. The banking and securities industries were leading contributors to the expansion of demand for clerical and technical personnel. More than 175,000 white-collar jobs were added in New York City in the period 1965–70.

The burgeoning number of employees increased the overcrowding of existing office space. Furthermore, standards of floorspace per worker were raised, partly as a response to prosperity and partly as a reflection of an increase in the volume of machinery per office worker. Rents in existing space rose rapidly in response to the tightness of the market. Given the prospects of quick lease-up under very favourable terms, developers rushed to complete plans for new structures.

Most of these plans were for sites which had long been assembled in anticipation of the proper conditions for development. As mentioned earlier, the assemblage process can be a long and costly one. Most of the offices replaced existing structures on sites formerly occupied by several buildings. Frequently, the ownership of the land under the larger parcel was divided, and years of negotiation were required to buy out the previous owners. The new office buildings on Avenue of the Americas almost universally occupied the entire 200-ft Avenue frontage with a depth of 300 sq. ft; on Park Avenue, several buildings filled the 200 ft × 400 ft blocks. Since the typical lot in these blocks is 25 × 100 ft, as many as six or more owners could easily be involved in one assemblage. Whenever an assemblage is known to be taking place, of course, owners demand top dollar for their property.

Anticipating a long-term bull market for new space, institutional lenders willingly agreed to finance office construction. For the first time since the Depression, conservative requirements were relaxed for both interim and permanent financing. The 'three-quarters' rule, which means that a developer had to present firm leases for 75 per cent of his planned space before a mortgage commitment would be given, was ignored. Banks, the primary lending source for construction financing, advanced loans without the security of a permanent financing commitment. In the absence of restraint traditionally imposed by conservative lenders, developers rushed to be the first to complete the new structures, despite high interest rates.

A final contributor to the overbuilding of the 1960s was the City itself. A new zoning ordinance, passed in 1961, permitted a floor area ratio (FAR) of 15 in high-density commercial zones. C–5 and C–6 zones were mapped along all the major avenues of Midtown Manhattan, and over most of Lower Manhattan. In these zones, 'as of right' bulk on a typical 200 × 200 ft parcel would be 0.6 million sq. ft. Thus only five parcels would have had to be developed to add 3 million sq. ft to the office inventory. On the Avenue of the Americas, where assemblages had depths of 300 sq. ft, a single 'as of right' building would have added 0.9 million sq. ft to the supply.

However, this was a base amount which could be increased by as much as 20 per cent in exchange for the development of amenities defined by the zoning ordinance as being in the public interest. Such amenities include plazas for public use, which require extra setbacks from street lines; pedestrian links with other buildings or with the subway system; aesthetic improvements to subway entrances and corridors. The additional bulk allowed for the provision of amenities is worth (in revenue potential) substantially more than the cost of providing the amenities. The trade-offs permitted were negotiated for each building where additional floor area ratio was sought by the developer.[1] This system, known as incentive zoning, is intended to prevent the crowded street levels which result from 'straight' application of the zoning and to provide a varied, functional, pedestrian-oriented configuration of structures.

In Lower Manhattan, the Greenwich Street Special Zoning District covers about 20 blocks, so that many of the new buildings constructed within the district have taken advantage of incentive options. On the Avenue of the Americas, all of the buildings constructed in 1966–72 took advantage of the increase in FAR in exchange for plazas in front of the structure.

There is evidence that incentive zoning contributed substantially to overbuilding. A study (Kayden, 1976) of all offices constructed from 1960 to 1974 showed that 91 took advantage of one of the five possible types of zoning incentive. Most buildings took advantage of the plaza bonus, since it was the simplest to administer and the most advantageous economically. In the aggregate, it was estimated that about 12 million sq. ft of space was provided through utilization of the incentives. This was equal to roughly half of the amount vacant in 1975.

Were the incentives utilized simply because they were there, or did they themselves induce the construction of space that otherwise would not have been built? Without incentives, would the same amount of construction have taken place on different sites? The answer to the second question is no, for two reasons: the cost and difficulty of assemblage acts as a brake on real-estate activity; and the marginal cost of one foot of 'incented' space is less than the marginal cost of one foot of base space. The answer to the first question is most likely that the buildings would have been built in the absence of zoning incentives because 15 FAR offered sufficient potential revenues to take out any building on a parcel that had earlier been assembled. Later during the boom, when speculation had driven land prices up, zoning incentives might have contributed to the increase.

It can be noted that the development industry in the United States is not characterized by restraint. Profits can be very respectable, and risks are readily taken to try for them. A complex of tax laws makes equity participation in real-estate development highly desirable for individuals in the higher tax brackets. These laws allow individuals to participate as limited partners in development projects while having no operational liability. Advantages accrue during the construction period, when construction loan interest is deductible along with real property tax, ground rent, and brokerage fees. During ownership, permanent loan expenses, operating deficits, and accelerated depreciation create deductions. Upon sale of the equity, profits can be treated as capital gains which are assessed at half the rate of income. In New York City's office market of the 1960s, it was therefore easy to attract equity through syndication of the tax shelter.

Even had market studies pointed out that to maintain a reasonable 5 per cent vacancy rate only a few million square feet net needed to be added to the existing space, the development community might not have behaved much more conservatively. Each developer sees an opportunity to offer the best space, in the preferred location, at the earliest date, and tends to err on the side of optimism. Had the World Trade Center not been constructed by the bi-state Port Authority of New York and New Jersey with the backing of the governor of the State of New York, the city's vacancy rate would have been several points lower. On the other hand, the plans for the World Trade Center were announced years in advance of its construction, and the private market took a knowing rise in planning and building the square footage it was responsible for.

By the time the national economy faltered in 1970 causing a precipitous loss in white-collar jobs in the city, overbuilding was too far advanced to be reversed. Had employment continued to expand at the average annual rate of the late 1960s of 3 per cent, an additional 35 million sq. ft could have been absorbed by 1975, assuming a generous 200 sq. ft per worker. Instead, a total of nearly 46 million sq. ft for which construction began in 1968–71 came on the market during 1971–75. The city's job base never rebounded from the 1970–71 recession; in the 1974 recession, 74,800 more jobs were lost in the securities industry and in administrative offices of manufacturing, helping to send the office vacancy rate to 13 per cent.

Supply Related to Demand: Anomalies of the Market

Office markets in large urban centres are characterized by differentiation which tends to keep them in constant disequilibrium. The supply of office space is differentiated on the basis of location and on the basis of age and design. Office space is not a unitary product, like steel ingots, but a series of quasi-distinct products, whose degree of substitutability varies according to fluctuations in demand. These fluctuations are in turn conditioned by general economic conditions, and more accurately, by economic conditions in particular industries. When there is a large amount of space on the market, and rents are relatively soft, a firm may seek to upgrade its space by moving into larger or newer or more centrally located quarters, but it will do so only if the short- to medium-range prognosis for profitability is fairly good. No matter how cheap or how available space may be, in general, firms will not plan new expenditures, or even incur the expense of relocating, in times of recession or anticipated recession. This is clear from the statistics of net absorption in New York City. As Fig. 9.4 shows, the amount of space absorbed on lease or sublease in the local recession in years 1970–74 fell drastically, although the available supply was increasing constantly over the total period.

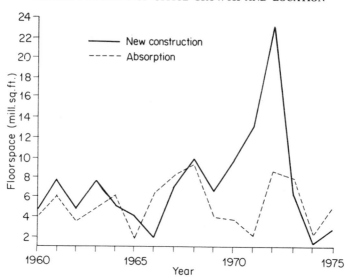

Fig. 9.4. New office construction in relation to the absorption rate
in New York City, 1960–75

Another characteristic of the office space market is asymmetrical price elasticity. Price will vary in a lagged manner to meet demand conditions and does not fall as rapidly to meet slack demand as, in the contrasting situation of tight supply, it rises to meet excess demand. Since price varies according to term of lease, fixtures, and lease basis, it is virtually impossible to calculate a median rent, or even a mean which is a useful statistic. Nevertheless, rough indicators of price sensitivity show that when the office vacancy rate was at its low point in 1962, the price of prime space offered for lease was $10.00–15.00 per sq. ft; when the vacancy rate rose to 12 per cent, the price fell to $6.00–9.00 per sq. ft, a substantial real decrease considering inflation.

In addition to absolute and relative economic advantage and price, demand for office space is also influenced by economic linkages, and by activity mix within a firm and within the industry of which it is a part. The ready availability of a large variety of services, especially advertising, public relations, legal and accounting, and of printing and graphic arts, has always dictated the attraction of New York City for headquarters and front offices. In addition, the market-making function of the city is a strong inducement to firms to locate there. For this reason, the garment-manufacturing industry is still heavily represented with showrooms in New York City, even though production has been largely moved out of the city. International banks are heavily concentrated in New York City for market-making purposes.

The externalities offered by a large urban area tend to maximize its attraction to international and national market firms of a size too small to encourage internalization of these services. This does not preclude their attractiveness for middle-market and even local-market firms, however. As technology improves communication, by transporting persons and transmitting information rapidly, some of the need for clustering to achieve communication between these external activities and the firm is reduced. Improved communication also makes it easier for different divisions of a corporation to be physically separated. Electronic communication and computer technology have been the chief conditioners of the spin-off back offices now found in the suburbs and even at rural locations far distant from the city. The processing of insurance forms, the automated mailings of publications, and record-keeping of all kinds can be performed by machines in areas remote from the transactions which make the record-keeping necessary. What has been witnessed is a process of constantly increasing centrifugal movement. Initial spreads were but a few miles, with back offices of Manhattan headquarters located in Queens, Brooklyn and other portions of the core of the New York Metropolitan Region, but recent moves have stretched ties northwards 50 miles to areas of the region where land is cheap, taxes are lower, and a potential labour pool of relatively well-educated females can be tapped.

New York City's office market is affected negatively by the fact that the city is the centre of an economic region which incorporates parts of three states each with different tax systems. This means that a firm can be located in the city and draw workers from Connecticut and New Jersey; it also means, of course, that a firm can be located in either of the two neighbouring states and still have access to the services and markets of New York City. Because both the State of New York and the City during the past 25 years have imposed a heavier tax burden on residents than have the neighbouring states, which do not tax personal income, there has been an incentive for higher-income persons to move to the other states (New Jersey passed a personal income tax law in 1976). The southern edge of the State of Connecticut has attracted many high-income executives who cluster in the elite residential suburbs. A critical mass of executives resident in these suburban areas has influenced the location decision of the firms they manage (White, 1976). Combined with the other advantages of cheap land, permitting an office park setting, easy access to the regional super-highway system and a highly educated Caucasian labour pool, southern Connecticut has increasingly attracted headquarter relocation from New York City.

Analyses of locational shifts among the *Fortune* 500—the nation's 500 largest manufacturing firms—and the 'Second 500' indicate that when NYC headquarters are relocated, about one-third relocate outside the Metropolitan Region, while the great majority remain within a 75-mile radius of New York City (Table 9.3.). However, since 1970, there has been a marked cessation of regional attraction. None of the *Fortune* 500 which left NYC before 1970 left the tri-state metropolitan region, and only one of the Second 500 left. After 1970, 50 per cent of the 500 and about 44 per cent of the Second 500 still responded to the attraction of the region.

Table 9.3. Destination of Headquarters Firms Moving out of New York City, Before and After 1970

Type	Total 1960–75	Before 1970 Total	Before 1970 Tri-state metro.	Before 1970 Out of region	After 1970 Total	After 1970 Tri-state metro.	After 1970 Out of region
1–500	54	15	15	0	39	21	18
500–1000	30	6	5	1	24	10	14
Total	84	21	20	1	63	31	32

Source. *Fortune* Magazine, 1960–1975.

Space occupied by the *Fortune* 500 and the Second 500, as well as the other major institutions, constitutes a large proportion of the prime ('class A') space occupied in New York City. Moreover, the 500 serve as a magnet to the thousands of accountants, law firms, public relations, advertising firms and other services which make the city the nation's most sophisticated service centre. In turn, the agglomeration of these skills makes the city attractive to top corporations. Hence, retention of a critical mass of headquarters firms is essential. Since major corporations confront many economically viable options in selecting their headquarters location, their choice is not always a profit-maximizing decision (Gerard, 1976). The power of the corporate image, and the weight of intangibles such as location near a golf links or a mother-in-law, are considerable. Hence, it is very difficult to predict office space demand on the basis either of broad economic trends, or of trends within an industry.

Among the tangible factors influencing New York City office location, as clearly evidenced in 1974 and 1975, is the fiscal condition of the local government. In the late spring of 1975 it became clear to the public that the City of New York was in serious fiscal condition, with a huge budget deficit and an inability to borrow further to meet upcoming expenses. The installation of a three-year financial plan put the city into semi-receivership. The city's budget is now largely controlled by the Emergency Financial Control Board which monitors expenditures and revenues and the Municipal Assistance Corporation which provided for the refinancing of the outstanding debt.

The fiscal crisis, even though it proved not to be unique to New York City, is sufficient to make many businessmen consider relocation. Uncertainty about the future revenue base is a situation which leaves few firms sanguine. Emergency measures to increase revenues are often detrimental to business interests. A further exodus of the *Fortune* 500 in 1976 will probably occur.

Summary

It can be argued that every potential office site constitutes a unique and discrete market, with the developer's decision to construct based on probability estimates that only he can assess. A developer, according to this paradigm, seeks either to maximize his minimum return on investment, or to minimize his maximum loss. In good times, he will decide to build on the maxi–min rule; but he will not necessarily decide not to build in bad times, because he will use the mini–max rule. He may well build even in face of substantial existing vacancy rates, if the only alternative is to hold vacant land on which he gets no income but must pay taxes or else sell the land at a large loss. Tax laws which allow him to write off losses encourage construction even under negative conditions.

The total amount of office space constructed in any given time period is the net result of many individual decisions, which do not, it appears, take into account very heavily the other similar decisions which are being made. They are conditioned by a general assessment of the business climate, local and national, but the tendency is towards an optimistic expectation of being able to rent up a particular building, rather than a pessimistic or even realistic expectation of capturing a total market share.

Public Policy

The boom-bust experience in New York City is not unique in the United States. While the vacancy rate in New York City registered about 13 per cent in 1975, the fast-growing sunbelt city of Atlanta had a 23 per cent vacancy rate; Dallas had 18 per cent; Los Angeles had a rate equal to New York's. Since real-estate investment requires entrepreneurial boldness, overestimation of demand is common.

Nevertheless, from the point of the public interest, extremes in the office market cycle can create negative consequences. One is the premature demolition of existing buildings to make room for new offices. A New York City Planning Department study in 1973 estimated that some 400 dwellings and many industrial buildings had been unnecessarily demolished. A second negative is the image of a city with vacant offices as one that is on the way down.

On the other hand, there are benefits to be gained by short-term surpluses of office space. Within limits, a surplus tends to keep rents in the central city competitive with rents in suburban areas, thus having a centralizing effect which from the point of view of city government officials is desirable. A surplus of new space by depressing rents permits some firms to upgrade. The general tendency is for firms in class C to move to class B more readily than class B space is exchanged for class A. Thirdly, a surplus can induce longer terms and more favourable lease conditions for tenants, thus tying them to the city for a longer period of time than they would be able to commit for in a seller's market.

In 1973, perceiving that realtors and investors were being hard hit by the slump in demand, the New York City Planning Commission put before the public the policy issue of governmental intervention in the market. The question was posed, should municipal government intervene to smooth the peaks and troughs in the construction cycle, and if so, how? The general consensus of the private sector was that, while on the downside intervention in the form of tax concessions and other measures to lower rents to tenants while retaining profits for investors might be acceptable, intervention of the public sector on the upside, which would mean limiting entrepreneurial activity when too much space appeared to be planned, would not be desirable.

Given the private sector's domination of the real-estate sector in the United States, this view was not surprising. Even from the point of view of a public official, there are serious doubts whether government, especially local government, should intervene in the office market. These doubts arise from the nature of the beast we are trying to control, and the difficulty in assessing its potential behaviour. They are compounded by the cumbersome possible control mechanisms, none of which could be automatic or self-enforcing.

With respect to the nature of the beast, a policy of government intervention assumes that government will somehow be better at predicting demand for office space than is the private sector. Is a truly objective tracing of total demand to be expected if it emanates from a source that has no interest in development?

The efforts which have been made to date to predict both total demand and distribution of new construction have universally failed to hit the mark. In 1972, the Regional Plan Association (Armstrong, 1972) forecast that CBD office employment would reach 1.3 million by 1985; instead, the trend was in the opposite direction. Current estimates are for a 10 per cent decline between 1975 and 1985. The City Planning Department (1971) forecast an absorption rate which, combined with growing employment levels, would have brought supply and demand into equilibrium with a 4.5 per cent vacancy rate by 1977, and possibly by 1975. A 1973 consultant's report for the city (Booz-Allen & Hamilton, 1975) predicted that another 8 million sq. ft will be needed in Lower Manhattan by 1980 to accommodate new workers; but new workers must be added to the employment rolls to bring the total up to its 1973 levels.

In fact, since many public investment decisions and even the flow of public funds from higher levels of government to the city (as for mass transit) are dependent upon optimistic growth projections, one can argue that government cannot in fact be an objective forecaster of demand. Further, the private sector asks, with some justification, why should government care if its forecasts are wrong, since it is the private developer, not the government, who will suffer?

Perhaps, then, if local government had a monetary stake in the market projections, government could be a more accurate predictor. But public enterprise is not part of the American economic system, and in New York City government cannot afford to be a joint venturer in new construction. Where state government has been a partner in some developments, as the World Trade Centre, the consequences for the private sector were negative (A not-for-profit quasi-governmental corporation issued tax-exempt bonds to finance development and the project is exempt from real property taxes although it makes a fixed payment in lieu of taxes).

Even if local government could forecast more accurately, how might it intervene? If development is proceeding too quickly, it would be possible to slow the issue of building permits. But the result might be that the first applicant to get a permit is the only one to build, and the building is in the least desirable location.

It might be possible for all builders seeking permits to submit their plans to the Planning Commission, which would then decide which structures were most in the public interest. However, there exists no statutory definition of the public interest against which the projects could be measured. To move in this direction would constitute a very radical limitation of property rights. New legislation would be required, extending the concept of zoning to include a timing element. It would be challenged in the courts, as have been similar measures designed to control the residential subdivision of vacant land. The issue would be more problematic because the public interest is not at all clear or measurable.

Can there be a more judicious application of incentive options? If such application were to be based on projections of supply, problems of inadequate information, which are also conditioned by the fundamental secrecy of the real-estate sector, would obtain. Adding market considerations to zoning review would involve many disputes among interested parties and would expand the opportunities for favouritism.

Another possible mechanism would be the tax system. Under present local tax laws, vacant land is taxed at a uniform rate on the basis of an assessment that takes into consideration its existing and potential use under the zoning law. If the tax system were to be more flexible, allowing the Tax Commission and/or the Planning Commission to raise or lower the assessments on vacant land depending on whether or not development was desired, the pace and location of development would become more completely controllable. This, too, is a very radical proposal; the likelihood of a legislature passing such a law is virtually zero. Nor is it clear that, given the sometimes questionable dealings between public bodies and real-estate interests, such a mechanism would be benign.

The most effective control mechanism is the financial community. If the lenders are strict in their demands for lease commitments, then overbuilding cannot readily occur. Since lenders are a competitive system, it is in their interests to act independently of one another and of political considerations. Since the overbuilding in New York, lenders, many holding title to foreclosed buildings, have returned to their traditional conservatism. The interaction of two profit-seeking components of the private sector would appear in the long run to provide the best self-regulation of the market. While it would be possible for the city to exercise the same sort of review before granting a building permit, any city agency would be suspect to the community at large.

The Future

A study prepared by the Regional Plan Association in 1972 projected the distribution of office employment in the New York region in 1985 (Table 9.4).

Table 9.4. Distribution of Office Employment in Premises Classified as Office Buildings, New York Region and City, 1959–85

	1959 Number	Per cent of total	1967 Number	Per cent of total	1985 Number	Per cent of total
New York Region	1,417,520	100.0	1,669,220	100.0	2,506,790	100.0
New York City	1,011,630	71.0	1,125,400	67.0	1,513,400	60.0
Manhattan	792,080	56.0	889,490	53.0	1,203,450	48.0
Bronx	42,220	2.9	45,160	2.7	55,180	2.0
Kings (Brooklyn)	99,900	7.0	104,090	6.0	130,550	5.0
Queens	66,410	4.4	74,070	4.5	107,500	4.3
Staten Island	11,020	0.7	12,590	0.8	16,720	0.7

Source: R. B. Armstrong (1972), p. 131. Reproduced by permission of Regional Plan Association, *The Office Industry*, The MIT Press, 1972.

The total number of jobs in the region was projected to increase by 1,086,283 jobs, or 43 per cent. New York City's share would fall by 11 per cent but total jobs would increase by roughly 0.5 million. Most of the new jobs were projected to be in Manhattan, although Manhattan's share would be less than half the region's total. Outside Manhattan, borough shares of the total were also projected to decline, although absolute increases requiring some new building were forecast for all the boroughs (Table 9.5).

Behind these projections were assumptions of continued population growth in the region. Trends since 1970 suggest that, on the contrary, the region's population will remain constant or even decline slightly. Current birthrates are barely sufficient to replace the population lost through death and out-migration, and in-migration has slowed markedly. Relative to the rest of the nation, the New York region is not expanding its local-market or middle-market activities. 1974/75 has shown office-sector jobs to be more vulnerable than expected. Some of the largest employers in the region, and especially New York City, face long-range price constraints which will force curtailment of labour costs. Among these are the power companies and the telephone company, which is constantly seeking to improve productivity through capital investment. Thus, by 1985, it is conceivable that the region's total job count in office-sector jobs will be lower than in 1975.

Whether total jobs remain stable or decrease slightly, all evidence points to a declining share of office-type jobs to be located in the central city. Thus, it is not realistic to anticipate dramatic new growth in office-space needs arising from space needs of new employees. However, many of the structures in the current office stock are outmoded, especially the 4 per cent of total space which was constructed before World War II. It is reasonable to expect new construction to replace this space. Additionally, new buildings will be put into construction as a result of prestige requirements or other individual needs of major corporations. Signs of serious planning for new buildings will be revealed as soon as large amounts of contiguous space become difficult to find. When this occurs, the upward pressure on rents and lease terms will begin. It is likely that, by 1980,

Table 9.5. Projected Demand for Office Space, New York City, 1985

	New employees	New square footage
Manhattan	411,370	82,274,000
Kings	30,650	6,130,000
Bronx	12,960	2,592,000
Queens	41,090	8,218,200
Staten Island	46,790	9,358,000

Source. R. B. Armstrong (1972), p. 130. Reproduced by permission of Regional Plan Association, *The Office Industry*, the MIT Press, 1972.

three or more major buildings will be in construction, probably in Midtown. These buildings are signs of confidence in the city's continued future as one of the world capitals, in which major corporations and institutions must have a presence.

The actual pace of construction can be encouraged or retarded by other public actions, particularly the beginning of a new convention centre which has long been in planning but for which a satisfactory financing arrangement has yet to be arranged. The latter, in turn, depends in large degree upon the city's fiscal status, which promises to be precarious far beyond the 1978 final date of the current Financial Plan.

While the location and design of new office buildings are considered a legitimate concern of the public sector, the timing of new construction is not considered legitimately subject to public regulation. If it were so considered, complex statutory changes would be required and would surely be challenged in the courts. Public financial assistance to office development is severely limited by the New York State Constitution, which prohibits the State from using its credit to assist the private sector. Recent laws aimed at economic development in New York City which give tax incentives to non-residential development and renovation require findings that qualified offices are needed and would not be developed without tax abatement. Given the current glut of space on the market, this is a sound prohibition.

Acknowledgment

I am grateful to Richard Satkin and John Wang of the Division of Economic Planning and Development, New York City Planning Department, who prepared the data for this analysis. Mr Wang prepared the maps and charts.

Notes

1. The basic zoning ordinance, written by the City Planning Department, and subsequent modifications, are adopted by the seven-member City Planning Commission and the local governing body, the Board of Estimate. (The Board of Estimate consists of the Mayor, the President of the City Council, the Comptroller, and the presidents of the city's five boroughs.) Zoning changes in response to conflict situations or development opportunities are frequent. They may be introduced by the City Planning Department staff or by the staff of the mayoral area development offices, of which there are five: in Midtown and Lower and Upper Manhattan; in Brooklyn; and in Jamaica, Queens. (Reduced in 1976 to one office, owing to fiscal crisis and slowdown in development.)

Negotiations between developers wishing to take advantage of incentive zoning and the city involve the particular development office and the planning department; final approval is granted by the Board of Estimate following approval by the City Planning Commission. In cases where an owner can demonstrate that the ordinance presents an unusual economic hardship, he has recourse to the Board of Standards and Appeals, which may grant a variance.

References

Armstrong, R. B. (1972), *The Office Industry: Patterns of Growth and Location.* Cambridge, Mass.: MIT. Press.

Baer, John, and Friebourg, Anne (1971), *The Demand for Office Space in Manhattan.* New York: City Planning Department, Economic Development Section Technical Memorandum.

Booz-Allen & Hamilton (1975), *Lower Manhattan Market Analysis Report 1975–1990.* New York: Booz-Allen & Hamilton.

Carruth, Eleanor (1969), Manhattan's office building binge, *Fortune,* **80,** 114–25.

Carruth, Eleanor (1971), New York hangs out for-rent sign, *Fortune,* **83,** 86 *et seq.*

Cross and Brown, Inc. Periodic reports on leasing in New York.

Cushman and Wakefield, Inc. Periodic maps of new office construction.

Fisher, Robert (1967), *The Boom in Office Buildings.* Washington DC: US Federal Reserve System.

Fortune Directory of the 500 Largest Industrial Corporations, *Fortune,* May, 1974; May, 1975.

Gerard, Karen (1976), Headquarters firms in New York City, New York. Unpublished paper, Chase Manhattan Bank.

Julian Studley, Inc. Periodic reports on leasing activity.

Kayden, Jerold S. (1976), Incentive zoning in New York City. Unpublished Master's Thesis, Harvard University.

New York City Planning Department (1971), *The Demand for Office Space in Manhattan.* New York: New York City Planning Commission, Unpublished Technical Report.

New York City Planning Commission (1973), *Manhattan Office Development.* New York: City Planning Commission.

The New York Times. Manhattan office building completion, (Carter Horsley), various years to Feb. 15, 1976.

The Real Estate Board of New York, Inc. (1968), *Office Vacancy in Manhattan 1967.* New York: The Real Estate Board.

The Real Estate Board of New York, Inc. (1972), *Rebuilding Manhattan: A Study of New Office Construction.* New York: The Real Estate Board.

Rubenstein, Albert I. (1974), Secrets of the office building developer, *Real Estate Review,* **4.**

Schultz, Harvey (1971), *Regulating Office Construction.* New York: City Planning Department, Technical Memorandum.

White, William H. (1976), End of the exodus: the logic of headquarters city, *New York,* Sept. 20.

10

Office Location: The Role of Communications and Technology

ROGER PYE

Introduction

People who work in offices spend much of their time communicating–talking to others who work in that office or in other offices, making telephone calls, writing letters, memoranda or reports, completing forms or entering data. Since office occupations are concerned with the administration and direction of physical processes or with the provision of information services to those so employed, *most* office activity is communication. Indeed it is difficult to identify many office activities which do not entail communication. Even reflection, thinking and planning, when conducted by an isolated individual, have little value until their results are either communicated in order to change the physical activity of the organization or sold to a client.

Communication often involves physical movement. People must walk or travel to meet each other; letters and other written records must be transported physically from sender to recipient. Hence the ability of administrative and executive staff to communicate is influenced by the location of their workplace. In order to facilitate easy communication between the executives and administrators of an enterprise, they have been concentrated together in single establishments, which we now call offices. Furthermore these offices are conventionally located near each other in the centres of cities in order to ease communication with offices performing similar administration and control either for other organizations or for the region or state itself.

Communication and administration have always been central to the development of cities. The first cities developed in Mesopotamia, soon after 4000 BC, around religious temples, whose priests acted as public and economic administrators. Urbanization was followed within 500 years by the invention of writing, itself first used for administrative and legal records (Adams, 1960; Kramer, 1957). The functions of religion, public administration and trade rapidly became differentiated, at least to a considerable degree, as civilization advanced. As trading became more or less *laissez faire*, and as the strength of the nation, city and their related public administrations grew or lessened, the balance between the administrative functions changed. In Medieval Europe, for example, most cities were predominantly centres of trade. Then the industrial revolution resulted in larger and more specialized units of manufacturing production. The larger units needed specialist managers to control them. Product specialization resulted in more interaction between organizations, leading in turn to more communication between their managers. The managerial control staff were increasingly concentrated in offices, which were in turn located in city centres. With improvements in long-distance transportation—notably the railway—many of these offices were located in the capital city, in order to be close to government. Only in countries where nationhood developed late (Italy, Germany), where national government was initially weak (USA) or the seat of government was deliberately located elsewhere from major trading centres (USA, Netherlands, Australia) is the majority of office employment not concentrated in or around the capital city.

Many city centres grew to such an extent that, although they contained a large number of office employees, and so offered a wide potential for communication, their size and related congestion made the maintenance of routine communications more difficult. The further development of modern cities, with central business districts, would have been impossible without the telephone, telegraph and regular postal service to facilitate more easily that routine communication. Other technologies have of course also influenced the development of cities. Better local transport—trains, buses and automobiles—has enabled the large office workforce to be assembled daily in the centre. Subsequently, especially as car ownership has become widespread, better transportation has led to lower-density housing patterns and suburbanization. The development of office centres has also been influenced by transportation systems. In cities such as those of the western and southern USA which have grown up since automobile ownership became virtually universal, there is often no single major office centre—employees can drive to places of employment anywhere in the city and later use their car again to travel to meetings if necessary. Even in conventional cities these effects are visible. The City of London is a long-established finance and trading centre in which similar organizations tend to concentrate together in city blocks. Office areas in west central London have developed more rapidly and recently, are more dispersed and less specialized. When he compared the rates at which the areas generated taxi journeys, Goddard (1970) found that the City generated far fewer. Arguably the development of office areas in west central London was influenced by the availability of the taxi, without which offices would have found it necessary to be more concentrated and specialized. In turn, that might have prevented their rapid development in a period of less than 20 years. Recently, especially since the rapid growth in the volume of office employment in the 1960s, offices have left city centres and followed their employees to the suburbs, relying primarily on automobiles for transportation. Often they have located at the intersections of motorways/freeways in order to achieve access to good road facilities.

The importance of communication in office activities, and the strong and visible influence of technology on the development of cities, have led many to speculate how advances in telecommunications technology could influence the pattern of office development and so the nature of cities. Since telecommunication services—the telephone, telegraph, telex and data-communication services—are available everywhere in advanced countries at tariffs which are relatively independent of location, telecommunications is not now an important factor in decisions concerning office location. Even though advanced services are usually offered first in major cities (especially in North America, where competition between telecommunication carriers results in specialist services being offered on a limited geographical basis), it is not expected that many organizations will choose an office site in order to obtain access to services in the same way that they now do for access to transportation. Instead, it is anticipated that telecommunication could *reduce* the spatial constraints by providing alternatives to face-to-face meetings, to physical transportation of documents and to physical accession of records. If the staff of an organization could use teleconferencing systems instead of travelling to meetings then perhaps their office need no longer be near those of other organizations. If they could communicate with each other via teleconference systems and send each other memoranda rapidly and access files remotely *via* office automation systems, then perhaps they need no longer be concentrated in a single office. They could work in a large number of neighbourhood centres or possibly even at home. These futuristic ideas were first suggested as science fiction: by E. M. Forster in *The Machine Stops*, published in 1928 but written before 1914, and by Isaac Asimov in *Mother Earth* (1975—originally published 1949) and *The Naked Sun* (1971—originally published 1956). However, they are no longer possibilities for the remote future. A number of successful audiovisual and audio-only teleconference systems are already operating (see Hough, 1976 for a review) and office automation systems—which provide all text services—are under rapid development (see *Business Week*, 1975). Much of the renewed speculation about the effect of telecommunications on office location was by technologists (Healy, 1968; Wise, 1971; Cassidy, 1969; Cherry, 1970; Young, 1971; Libby, 1969) in response to the Bell System's plans to launch a video-telephone service (Picturephone (R)). Two-way video is not itself new—it was demonstrated at about the same time as television and operated as a service to businessmen in Nazi Germany. However, the cost of providing coaxial cables for transmission (video cannot be carried on standard telephone lines without considerable modification) had made the overall cost prohibitive for anything but very specialized services; the American Telephone and Telegraph Company (AT & T) had devised techniques for modifying telephone lines in order to provide a somewhat cheaper and more widespread service. The launch of a Picturephone (R) service in Chicago was unsuccessful—very few organizations wishing to subscribe—but work continues on other applications and to reduce cost. Moreover, substantial research (which will be discussed further below) has shown that moving picture video may not be necessary and that audio systems enhanced by still graphics should be adequate for many current meetings; audiographic systems are relatively cheap. Office automation technology is also in trial use and is developing rapidly.

The *broad possibility* that telecommunication could influence office location can quite reasonably be deduced from the obvious importance of communication to office work. However, the feasibility of change and its possible extent cannot be assessed without some detailed knowledge of the interaction between location and communication and of the ability of telecommunications systems to effectively replace traditional modes of communication.

Research on the Role of Communications in Office Location Decisions

The importance of communication to offices and its significance in location decisions was recognized in 1926 by Haig, who cited the opportunity for extensive contact with other organizations to be an important externality available in city centres. However, no more *detailed* research was conducted until the late 1960s, spurred by the very considerable increase in the amount of office employment and by the realization by such writers as Greer (1962), Hall (1963), Meier (1962) and Webber (1964) that easy communication was still a major benefit obtainable in cities.

Initial work concentrated on confirming that the importance assigned by researchers to communication was shared by managers in organizations. The Location of Offices Bureau (LOB) sponsored interviews with executives in offices in London and that had relocated from London. 78 per cent of 1234 organizations interviewed by the Economist Intelligence Unit (EIU/LOB, 1964) cited the need to maintain contacts with others in central London as the reason for being within 30 miles of central London; 38 per cent also mentioned London's superior national travel facilities. When Interscan interviewed managers in offices in central London and managers in offices which had relocated from central London, both groups quoted 'communications with London' as the principal disadvantage to relocation (Interscan/LOB, 1967; 1970). In particular, managers in offices which had given up the idea of moving out gave communication as the principal reason behind their decision (Interscan/LOB, 1967). Similar results were obtained by Cowan et al. (1969).Of the firms which decided against relocation after contacting LOB during the period 1963–1975, only 30 per cent gave a reason. Of those reasons, 33 per cent were that 'reorganization/economic climate' had removed the need to relocate; the reason mentioned next most often was 'loss of contacts', accounting for 12 per cent of the total; while another 4 per cent of reasons were 'communications problems'. Subsequent work may be divided into two streams, both heavily quantitative, dealing with the effect of relocation on either the nature of communication or the associated costs.

In addition to being a valuable externality, communication may be regarded as the input and output of an office. An office is concerned with one or more of the following:

1.   The *control* of manufacturing or other physical processes of the organization;

2.   The *administration* associated with those processes—issuing of invoices, making payments, etc.;

3.   The provision of information or advice as *consultation* to other parts of the same organization or to other organizations which themselves control and administer.

The inputs to and outputs from each of these activities are information, and the means of conducting that information is a communication act, with associated costs. One possible approach to the theory of office location would be directly analogous to that of factory location—minimizing the costs of inputs and outputs (communication). Unfortunately, this approach has a major shortcoming: much of the control activity, especially the more creative aspects concerned with handling unexpected events or with identifying new opportunities, is not conducted in a way which is wholly planned, itself controlled or properly understood. As a result, a change in location is likely to result in a quite different pattern of communication with different costs and *different benefits* to the organization. Moreover, because of the lack of detailed understanding of the contribution to the organization's overall productivity resulting from any single communication or even from a relationship between organizations, it is impossible to value changes in contact patterns.

As a result of this problem, most researchers have made one of two partial approaches. Some have ignored virtually entirely the qualitative changes in the nature of communication patterns resulting from relocation. Instead they set out to minimize increases in travel resulting from relocation either as a goal in itself (Persson, 1974) or as a surrogate for all forms of communication damage—increased travel, reduced communication and transfer of relationships to different organizations. The last approach was used for the Location of Government Review, which recommended dispersal of over thirty thousand civil servants from central London (Elton *et al.*, 1970; UK Civil Service Department, 1973). The second partial approach has largely ignored costs and investigated the effect of location on the *pattern* of communication. It has been used to select organizations suitable for relocation on the basis that their communication patterns make it appropriate for them to be outside the capital city. For example, Thorngren (1973) used it to select civil service departments suitable for relocation from Stockholm. Ideally, of course, the two approaches should be combined, at least for micro-economic decisions concerning single organizations: for example, minimizing costs subject to constraints on the types of change in communication pattern that are permitted; or alternatively selecting departments for relocation subject to constraints on cost.

The Qualitative Approach: Thorngren's Theoretical Classification

The approach which concentrates on the effect of relocation on the quality of an organization's communications has been most extensively used by Thorngren. It has been used by several others, notably Goddard (Goddard, 1973; Goddard and Morris, 1976), who has contrasted the contact patterns of organizations in different UK locations, and also by Bannon and Murphy (1975) for Dublin and Movold (1976) for Oslo. The conceptual framework, described in Thorngren (1970), relies on the earlier schemes of Jantsch (1967) and Ehrlemark (1964).

Jantsch saw the process of technological innovation as one of combining knowledge of technological potential with assessments of social values. The more innovative a product, the more likely it would be to employ technology utilizing advances in basic science and the more necessary would be an accurate assessment of basic ideologies. Minor variations on existing products would by comparison most likely use small advances on existing technology and require only cursory reexamination of contemporary social values in order to check against the possibility of recent changes. The set of all technological and value information was called by Jantsch the *development space* within which technological advances could be classified.

Thorngren (1970) summarized Ehrlemark's concepts in terms of key phrases used regularly in his own work:

He (Ehrlemark) distinguishes between programme processes related to routine transitions and transactions with the environment, and planning processes related to changes of programme processes. A third type consists of orientation processes aimed at directing the planning processes by extensive scanning of the environment.

Thorngren then proceeded to combine these two sets of concepts to obtain a framework describing both the processes and their associated information flows in terms of the development space. Programme processes, involving the *utilization* of existing production alternatives, require only information from those elements of the development space adjacent to those already employed or assumed by current activities, that is, information about other existing technologies or about the actions of others in the current socio-economic environment. Planning processes involve the *development and choice* of new alternatives and so require knowledge of potential technology, that is, products and processes presently under development, and of potential social values. Orientation is concerned with the identification of *new alternatives* and requires knowledge of research into basic science and of basic ideologies. Of the three types of process, only the first is concerned with existing production activity and so is the only one strongly associated with flows of money and transaction-oriented communications such as orders and invoices.

Thorngren's classification is extremely attractive and intuitively sensible. All organizations and people clearly have processes and contacts of these types. A chemical plant varies its product mix according to the quality of its raw materials and the prices of its products; a computer manufacturer assembles a set of modular components to meet the needs of its clients; an individual dresses according to the weather forecast. All these are programmed activities, associated with routine communication. Similarly, planning contacts might involve the selection of process equipment for the chemical plant, the design of new modules for the computer, and the purchase of new clothes. Orientation activities might require searching for entirely new chemical processes following a major disaster and legislation preventing use of the previous ones; incorporating the use of wholly new technology (such as silicone chips) in computer design; or the choice of clothing style to reflect the individual's personality and social outlook.

The framework is also universally applicable, despite being formulated in terms of technology which is more readily associated with manufacturing. Consultants, insurance companies and bankers all have their technologies, although they are less physically immediate than those of shipbuilding and coalmining organizations. Similarly, although government and public administration use technology only indirectly, they are almost exclusively concerned with the socio-economic environment—the actions and aspirations of individuals and groups within society. The framework applies to divisions of an organization as well as to the organization itself, since the socio-economic environment of one division includes the plans and objectives of others of the same organization.

Another strength of the classification is that it is broadly compatible with the work of other organizational theorists—although no-one else has developed classifications based conceptually on the type of information being sought or its importance to the organization. Ansoff (1965) also identifies three types of decision: operating decisions, such as budgeting, scheduling of production, pricing, setting output levels and making marketing and R & D policies; administrative decisions concerning the structure of the organization and procedures for finance, acquisition, supply and recruitment; and strategic decisions concerning objectives and goals, the choice of market areas and broad philosophies towards methods of finance and other administrative matters.

Simon (1965) similarly emphasizes the difference between *programmed* and *non-programmed* decisions. He also subdivides the decision-making process into three stages, called intelligence, design and choice (Simon, 1960). Intelligence is searching the environment for conditions requiring decisions; design is the process of inventing, developing and analysing possible courses of action; choice is the process of selecting between those possible courses of action.

Thorngren's orienting processes correspond closely to Ansoff's strategic decisions and to Simon's intelligence processes; his planning processes to Ansoff's administrative and operating decisions and to Simon's design and choice processes. Indeed, intelligence, design and choice are words that were used in the description of Thorngren's classification.

Yet there are some major differences between Thorngren's and the other typologies. Ansoff argued that an organization *should* be constantly monitoring the environment and modifying its strategies; however, he recognized that in practice it would first seek solutions to problems at the operating level, then at the administrative level, and only finally, if all else failed, at the strategic level. Simon also believed that the basic drive for the identification phase was dissatisfaction with current performance. Simon and Ansoff saw organizations as *reacting* to problems; Thorngren saw them as *proactively* searching for new opportunities.

Another major difference concerns the interaction between the various processes. Simon saw corporation decision-making as a nest of identification–design–choice sequences, each of which would lead to a subproblem also requiring solution; implementation of a decision was treated as a new problem in itself rather than as a final phase of the old one. Ansoff (1965) also saw a complex pattern: 'while distinct, the decisions are interdependent and complementary'. By contrast, Thorngren treated the processes as rather more separate, as will be seen from the way in which he applied the concept to select Swedish government agencies for dispersal from Stockholm.

Swedish Government Dispersal

Thorngren surveyed the communications of all Swedish government agencies and associated them with the three processes; then he examined the contact patterns of each government agency, and identified the process with which contacts were primarily associated and the types of organization with which it was in contact. Agencies with a high proportion of orienting contacts or with a high proportion of contacts with central government were considered unsuitable for dispersal. (The Swedish Civil Service is organized unusually, with a small central policy-making core and agencies which administer established policy relatively independently of policy-makers day-to-day control—see Vinde (1971) for details). Agencies with a high proportion of routine, programming activities were also rejected as unsuitable since they 'would not give rise to the desired level of regional spread effects, and the demand for labour in routine office operations can be expected to decline in the long run. . . Emphasis was placed on relocating offices characterized by planning processes—agencies with highly qualified and well-paid staff having rather narrowly defined areas of work. Often these agencies had specific contacts with other agencies outside the government sector. Insofar as possible, agencies were relocated to centres which provided services and facilities matching their particular requirements' (Thorngren, 1973). The approach was therefore to strike a balance between stimulating regional development and not disrupting public administration too severely.

Three aspects of Thorngren's analysis deserve comment and discussion: the processes are treated as relatively independent; more emphasis is given to contacts with non-government organizations than those with government agencies; the conclusions rely heavily on the method of making operational the orienting/planning/programming concept and identifying contacts with one of those processes. The first two aspects are interrelated and are a consequence of the level at which the orienting/planning/programming concept was applied in order to meet the objectives of the relocation study. Thorngren was attempting to choose agencies suitable for dispersal by consideration of the process they conducted for the public administration as a whole. He therefore applied the concept—which focuses on communications with the environment—to national public administration as a whole with the result that communication between agencies is given relatively little emphasis. Had the concept been applied to an individual agency, then other agencies would be part of its environment and their actions would be socio-economic information; communication between agencies would then be explicitly included. Inter-agency contacts, together with contacts within agencies, coordinate the three types (orienting, etc.) of process. Unfortunately, the essential comparison between agencies would not then have been possible. A disadvantageous side-effect of this approach was the relative lack of emphasis given to contacts between agencies. His earlier work (which will be discussed later) has shown that the pattern of such contacts is less affected by relocation and the main effect is one of higher costs. A second objective—either minimizing the cost of inter-agency contacts or some similar measure—would have been desirable in order to give more emphasis to inter-agency contacts.

Differences in scale of analysis also explain the greater emphases given by Simon to interaction between different stages of decision-making and by Ansoff to different types of decision-making. Clearly the stages of a decision are interrelated and any single organization (or indeed person) must have strategic, administrative and operating decisions, which must also be interrelated. However, when an organization is segmented and its parts are considered separately, any individual part is very likely to be more concerned with one type of decision than with another, although it must coordinate those decisions with other types conducted by other parts. The importance of clearly specifying the level at which the orienting/planning/programming concept is applied has been discussed. For contacts with organizations outside the national public sector, it is also essential that that concept be made operational in a way consistent with the conceptual scale—in other words, that the identification of contacts be conducted to ensure that a contact is only called 'orienting' if it is concerned with the identification of new, long-term opportunities of the government as a whole.

Thorngren's Empirical Classification

Thorngren used the same method of classifying contacts in each of his two major surveys—KOMM 68 and KOMM 71. KOMM 68 concerned about 3000 executives in 100 private-sector organizations in four city regions (Stockholm, Gothenburg, Sundsvall and Umea), and KOMM 71 concerned 18,500 civil servants in 34 public agencies that were candidates for dispersal from Stockholm. In each survey respondents were asked to record all meetings and telephone calls involving someone from outside their own company/agency that took place during a three-day period. Respondents were asked to record, for each contact: its duration; the number of participants; the length of time ahead that the contact had been prearranged; the range of subjects discussed; the frequency with which contact was made with this group of people; the extent to which the discussion concerned research and development; the nature of the contact (giving information, receiving an order, giving advice, exchanging information, negotiation, general discussion, etc.). The last was then recoded into a simple variable called feedback reflecting the extent to which the communication was one-way (giving/receiving orders/information/advice) or two-way (exchanging information, general discussion, negotiation). The above seven scalar variables, together with the mode of the contact (meeting, telephone call), were then used to allocate the contacts between types; analysis was conducted using a multivariate statistical procedure called latent profile analysis.

Latent profile analysis (LPA) is an unusual method of clustering observations into groups. (For a full description of the technique see Gibson (1959) or Isaksson (1972), and Goddard (1973) gives a brief mathematical statement as Appendix D.) Most other methods begin with as many groups as observations and progressively combine the most similar groups until the desired number of groups is obtained; the more sophisticated methods then reconsider the allocation of cases to clusters and relocate those which appear to be anomalous. These approaches require the algorithm to make a large number of comparisons between observations and so can only handle a relatively small number of cases, certainly not as many as the fourteen thousand data points of the KOMM 68 survey. Another problem concerning the application of common cluster algorithms is that they become more difficult to apply when the variables are correlated. The simplest approach is to use as the measure of similarity the distance between observations or between an observation and the mean of a group. When the variables are orthogonal then the standard measure of distance between observations $\mathbf{x} = (x_1, x_2, \ldots x_n)$ and $\mathbf{y} = (y_1, y_2, \ldots y_n)$ is:

$$|\mathbf{x} - \mathbf{y}| = \sum_{i=1}^{n} (x_i - y_i)^2$$

If this simple approach is taken when the variables are correlated then errors will arise. Suppose, as an extreme case, that two variables have a correlation of 0.99, and effectively measure the same dimension in two different ways, and that all other variables are independent of each other and of those two. Then the dimension that is measured in two ways will receive twice the weight in the analysis as do the others and will dominate the classification. Two approaches are normally adopted: using the above standard metric but weighting the data to reduce the effects of correlations; using a different measure of similarity between cases, for example the 'correlation' between them.

Latent profile analysis has a different objective and proceeds by different steps. Instead of using distance minimization or similarity maximization as the objective, it attempts to find clusters such that, within each cluster, correlation between the surveyed variables (dimensions) is as small as possible. Algorithms proceed in two stages. First the matrices of first- and higher-order correlations between the variables are analysed in order to identify the latent classes—those classes in the data set which minimize the within-class correlation between variables. Latent classes are described by the class mean of each of the variables. The set of means for a class is called its profile. At this stage of the analysis the classes and profiles have been derived from calculations based on the correlation matrix; they are called theoretical or expected. The next stage is to allocate observations to the theoretical classes; the resulting sets of observations are called observed classes and their profiles are called observed profiles. Allocation is made by calculating the distance (using a suitable metric) of each observation from each theoretical profile and allocating it to the class associated with the nearest. In order to reduce computation it is often assumed that reduction of correlations within clusters has been successful. The simple distance metric may then be used. LPA has two major advantages over other methods of cluster analysis: it may be applied to very large data sets; being based *primarily* on correlation rather than on distance, it may be used with ordinal data and is easier to operate with correlated variables, although care must be taken, when allocating observations to clusters, to ensure that correlated variables do not dominate the allocation.

Thorngren applied LPA to the fourteen thousand contacts recorded during the KOMM 68 survey in order to obtain three groups. The first group, accounting for 14 per cent of the total, consisted virtually entirely of meetings, and he identified its members as orienting contacts; the members of the second group, 63 per cent of the total, were both meetings and telephone calls and they were identified as programming contacts, probably because they were the simplest in terms of 'range of subjects' and 'feedback'; the final group were identified as planning contacts, because they had more connection with R & D, although 95 per cent of them were telephone calls. Thorngren summarized the analysis in Fig. 10.1, which shows the observed profiles in standard deviations above or below the population mean.

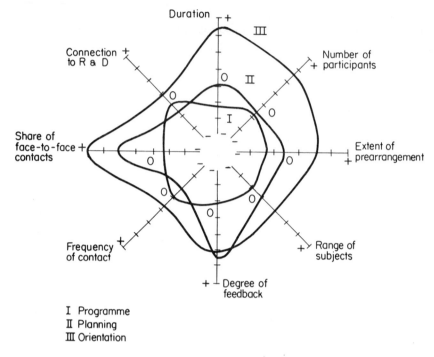

I Programme
II Planning
III Orientation

Fig. 10.1. Observed latent profiles for KOMM 68 contact data. Reproduced from Thorngren (1970) by permission of Pion Ltd

Further Analysis of the KOMM 68 Data

The disadvantage of LPA is that it does not generate statistics which indicate the success of the fit. It is therefore difficult to decide whether a smaller or larger number of groups would be preferable. Thus one of the fundamentals of Thorngren's conceptual model—the number of types of communication—remains quite untested. However, it is possible to investigate the degree to which the objective of reducing within-group correlation has been achieved. Bertil Thorngren has kindly made available his data base after contacts had been allocated to classes. Table 10.1 shows the Pearson correlation coefficients for the whole data set; Tables 10.2, 10.3 and 10.4 show those coefficients for observations in the orienting, planning and programming classes respectively. Comparison of the tables shows that although correlation has been substantially reduced, some variables, such as 'medium', 'duration' and 'number of participants', are still quite strongly correlated. Admittedly Pearson's product moment coefficient should only be used for cardinal data, but the computation of rank-order coefficients is impossible for such a large data set. Nevertheless, the

Table 10.1. Pearson Correlation Coefficients for Entire KOMM 68 Data Base

	Medium	Duration	No. of participants	Extent of prearrangement	Frequency of contact	Feedback	Range of subjects
Duration	0.67						
No. of participants	0.55	0.63					
Extent of prearrangement	0.52	0.63	0.52				
Frequency of contact	-0.02	-0.04	-0.05	-0.07			
Feedback	0.22	0.27	0.22	0.20	0.12		
Range of subjects	0.22	0.27	0.21	0.19	0.08	0.31	
Connection to R & D	-0.10	-0.12	-0.04	-0.10	-0.01	-0.01	-0.02

Table 10.2. Pearson Correlation Coefficients for KOMM 68 Orienting Contacts

	Medium	Duration	No. of participants	Extent of prearrangement	Frequency of contact	Feedback	Range of subjects
Duration	0.10						
No. of participants	0.04	0.37					
Extent of prearrangement	0.05	0.43	0.33				
Frequency of contact	-0.04	-0.04	-0.87	-0.15			
Feedback	0.00	0.01	-0.05	-0.03	0.19		
Range of subjects	0.00	-0.03	0.01	-0.05	0.02	0.02	
Connection to R&D	-0.01	-0.12	-0.05	-0.11	-0.08	-0.05	-0.05

Table 10.3. Pearson Correlation Coefficients for KOMM 68 Planning Contacts

	Medium	Duration	No. of participants	Extent of prearrangement	Frequency of contact	Feedback	Range of subjects
Duration	0.11						
No. of participants	0.08	0.13					
Extent of prearrangement	0.03	0.08	0.09				
Frequency of contact	0.13	0.08	0.04	0.05			
Feedback	0.07	0.16	0.09	0.04	0.05		
Range of subjects	0.02	0.16	0.03	0.04	0.07	0.28	
Connection to R&D	−0.04	−0.04	0.05	0.01	−0.11	−0.18	−0.17

Table 10.4. Pearson Correlation Coefficients for KOMM 68 Programming Contacts

	Medium	Duration	No. of participants	Extent of prearrangement	Frequency of contact	Feedback	Range of subjects
Duration	0.36						
No. of participants	0.24	0.19					
Extent of prearrangement	0.12	0.18	0.07				
Frequency of contact	0.02	0.02	0.01	0.00			
Feedback	−0.02	0.07	0.07	0.04	0.11		
Range of subjects	−0.01	0.09	0.05	0.02	0.09	0.24	
Connection to R&D	−0.03	−0.07	0.07	0.00	−0.09	−0.03	−0.03

results are illuminating and suggest that the classification may be dominated by factors other than those desired.

In order to further understand the structure of the KOMM 68 data base, other multivariate statistical techniques were used. Latent profile analysis is a generalization of latent structure analysis, the latter only being applicable to dichotomous data.

Fielding (1972) describes latent structure analysis in the following way: it is 'a method of differentiating groups of people. . ., with respect to some underlying characteristics which can neither be observed or measured. . . . In many ways a parallel can be drawn between the Latent Structure Model and the Factor Analysis model for quantitative indicators, with one factor. . .'. (For a standard text on factor analysis, see Harman, 1967.) Given the existence of this parallel, a factor analysis of Thorngren's data set should assist in understanding the nature of the underlying characteristic by which the variables have been classified. If a one-factor model explains a substantial percentage of the variance in the data then it seems very likely that the same underlying characteristic will have been implicitly used in the latent profile analysis. Admittedly the objectives of the methods—namely the explanation of variance and the identification of groups within which the observed variables are independent—are quite different; but if the results of the methods are completely dissimilar then they are valueless algebraic exercises, for their results are excessively dependent on the techniques. In view of this conceptual similarity between LPA and factor analysis, factor analysis of Thorngren's KOMM 68 contacts was carried out. A substantial criticism can be made of the use of this technique on data of this kind: product moment correlation coefficients are not applicable to the ordinal scales present in the data; rank-order correlations should be used; unfortunately, computation of these is extremely time-consuming—for data sets the size of KOMM 68's their computation is in practice impossible, even using a large computer. The technique of latent profile analysis is undoubtedly more suited technically to the data, but it is a less well-developed and less well-understood technique than factor analysis and its results are harder to interpret.

Factor analysis of the variables used by Thorngren to classify the KOMM 68 data revealed only one factor with an eigenvalue of greater than 1.0; that factor explained 33 per cent of the variance. Details are shown in Table 10.5. The factor *loaded* very highly on the variables 'medium', 'duration', 'number of participants' and 'extent of prearrangement', showing that the factor explains much of the variance in those dimensions. When the factor is expressed as a linear multiple of the variables (the coefficients being called the factor score coefficients), it is most strongly related to 'duration'. The factor will therefore be called the duration factor.

Essentially the factor results from the propensity of a larger group of people to talk longer, to need to meet face-to-face (given the present availability of teleconference equipment) and to need to arrange their meetings longer in

Table 10.5. Factor Analysis of KOMM 68 Data

	Mean	Stan. dev.	Factor loadings	Communality	Factor scores
Medium	1.230	0.421	0.749	0.749	0.191
Duration	1.558	1.001	0.897	0.804	0.522
No. of participants	1.175	0.472	0.729	0.531	0.173
Extent of prearrangement	1.550	1.059	0.704	0.496	0.153
Frequency of contact	2.994	1.224	−0.019	0.000	0.010
Feedback	1.282	0.450	0.341	0.117	0.051
Range of subjects	1.450	0.671	0.331	0.109	0.051
Connection to R&D	2.556	0.700	−0.222	0.049	−0.028

Table 10.6. Factor Scores for Contact Types

Cluster	Duration factor Mean	S.d.
Orienting	1.94	0.88
Planning	−0.41	0.29
Programming	−0.29	0.44

advance. The complexity of the meeting, as measured by the amount of feedback and the range of subject material, was significantly but comparatively weakly related to the duration factor, while the frequency of contact and extent to which the discussions involved R & D were almost independent of it.

The means and standard deviations of the duration factor for the orienting/planning/programming clusters are shown in Table 10.6. Assuming that factor scores are normally distributed, the duration factor discriminates between orienting and planning contacts—but does not discriminate programming contacts from either of the other types.

In order to identify which of the variables used to form the orienting, planning and programming classes did distinguish between them, discriminant analysis was conducted. The objective of discriminant analysis is to identify a linear multiple of a set of variables which discriminates well between a pair of groups of observations; each observation has a score on the discriminant function, and ideally all cases in one group have a score higher than a critical value while all those in the other group have a lower score. (See, for example, Anderson, 1958.) As for most multivariate techniques, the analysis assumes that the data are cardinal, and the same criticisms apply to its use on ordinal data, such as those of KOMM 68, as were cited above for factor analysis. Nevertheless, the results are illuminating and similar assumptions were made by the second stage of LPA when observations were allocated to groups.

Wilks' method of stepwise discriminant analysis was used: the variables are entered into the three discriminating functions (one of each pair of classes) in turn, those with highest F-ratio for the test of differences among the discriminant scores of the observed profiles (class means) being entered first. The variable which maximizes the F-ratio also minimizes Wilks' U-statistic, a measure of group discrimination. Table 10.7 summarizes the stepwise procedure.

All the variables entered the discriminant functions with large F-ratios, as expected with such a large data set. However, after the first three variables did so the reduction in U is small. The first two variables to enter were also the two loading most highly on the duration factor: duration and medium. The next to enter is the extent to which the contact involved discussion of R & D.

The U-statistic remains quite large, showing that the power of the variable to discriminate between the clusters is poor. Since those variables were used as the basis of the classification, this confirms the results of the analysis of within-group correlation: the classification is only partially successful.

Table 10.8 shows the coefficients of the three functions which discriminate

Table 10.7. Summary of Stepwise Discriminant Analysis for KOMM 68 Observed Classes.

Step	Variable entered	F-ratio to enter variable	Wilks' U-statistic
1	Duration	10,202.50	0.409
2	Medium	2031.55	0.317
3	Connection to R&D	723.88	0.288
4	Extent of Prearrangement	577.40	0.266
5	Feedback	504.41	0.248
6	No. of participants	320.30	0.237
7	Frequency of contact	307.04	0.227
8	Range of subjects	177.35	0.222

Table 10.8. Coefficients of Functions to Discriminate Between Pairs of Groups of Contacts

Variable	Orienting/ planning	Orienting/ programming	Planning/ programming
Medium	8.11	8.85	0.74
Duration	3.26	3.36	0.10
No. of participants	3.08	3.06	− 0.01
Extent of prearrangement	1.54	1.83	0.29
Frequency of contact	− 0.13	− 0.57	− 0.43
Feedback	0.95	0.45	− 0.50
Range of subjects	1.12	0.74	− 0.38
Connection to R&D	0.29	− 0.68	− 0.98
Constant	− 32.19	− 28.28	3.91

between each pair of groups. Orienting contacts are distinguished from both planning and programming contacts by variables that load highly on the duration factor: by 'medium', by 'duration', and by 'number of participants'. Planning and programming contacts are discriminated primarily by 'connection to R & D' and secondarily by 'medium', again. Thus of the variables used by Thorngren to classify the KOMM 68 contacts, those with the most influence on the classification are the ones which load on the duration factor; the connection to R & D has an important, but secondary effect and the frequency of contact, which was independent both of the duration factor and of the connection to R & D, has little influence on the classification system. The overall dominance of the duration factor may be caused by the LPA programme used by Thorngren, which is described by Isaksson (1972). The second major stage, which allocates observations to groups, assumes that the first has been successful and has minimized within-group correlation and that the Euclidean measure of distance may be used. Since the first stage appears to be somewhat unsuccessful—Tables 10.2 to 10.4 show that considerable correlation remains—it is not surprising that the classification is dominated by highly correlated variables loading on the duration factor.

The classification of the KOMM 68 contacts depends first on variables which are, at best, only indirectly related to the concept—the extent to which contacts involve the identification of new product alternatives, the development and choice of new alternatives or the utilization of existing alternatives. Only one variable—extent to which the discussion was related to R & D—having secondary influence on the classification concerns the content of the meeting in a way which is related to the conceptual framework. Even then it only refers to the technological side of the development space—not to the socio-economic side.

Multivariate statistical methods are often referred to disdainfully and critically as sausage machines—implying that they are mechanical, in ways that are poorly understood by the researchers who use them, and 'chop up' the input data until they are no longer recognizable. The criticisms have some validity, but ignore the value of such techniques for understanding complex data with many interrelated variables. The analogy may however be usefully extended: if meat is put into a sausage machine, then it is reasonable to call the output a sausage; if bread is put in, then it is not. The question then is, are the variables that were used by Thorngren for the empirical classification adequately related to the underlying concepts? It has already been argued that with one exception they are not *directly* related. Their use, despite this lack of direct relation, has been argued by Goddard and Morris, who have conducted in the UK very similar work to that of Thorngren. Factor analysis of contact data collected by Goddard (1973) in central London has also identified a single factor within the variables used for classification, which were identical to those used by Thorngren with the one exception that 'the extent to which the contact was connected with a sale or purchase' replaced 'the extent to which the contact involved discussion of R & D.

That factor was a duration factor, which was found yet again as a result of factor analysis of data collected by the Communications Studies Group in the British Civil Service. For further details of these supplementary factor analyses see Pye (1972). Goddard and Morris (1976) argued as follows:

> The model of contact activity that has been postulated assumes that there is an underlying or *latent* dimension to contacts relating to the time horizon, and that the three classes or orientation, planning and programmed contacts refer to specific sections of this continuum. The object of any classification of the contact data should be to assign each contact event to a position along this continuum and more specifically to one of the three basic classes. The individual contacts can only be related to these latent classes by way of their scores on the observed or manifest indicators such as length and number of people involved which have been assumed to be relevant to the latent continuum. Although a large number of characteristics might be appropriate for identifying which contacts are concerned with orientation, planning and programme processes, it has been postulated that on average orientation processes are most likely to occur in long contacts involving a large number of people and arranged a long time in advance in which wide ranging discussion with a lot of feedback occurs. In complete contrast, programmed processes are most likely to occur between two people who are in fairly regular and unarranged contact in order to discuss specific matters which involved few two-way exchanges. Like programmed processes, planning processes involve familiar individuals in short but more wide ranging discussions. The scores of each contact on the various diary questions can be used to test for the existence of the three hypothesized latent classes using a multivariate classification procedure known as latent profile analysis. (Reproduced by permission of Pergamon Press Ltd).

They, like Thorngren, *assumed* that the surveyed variables were related to the theoretical concept, classified the observations on the basis of those variables and then identified the observed profiles with the theoretical concept. This is a dangerously circular argument, relying entirely on the assumed relationship. Latent profile analysis can only find dimensions which are *latent* within the *observed* data which should consist of variables all of which are directly related, on theoretical grounds, to some aspect of the underlying concept even though none of them completely coincide with that concept. The analysis will then identify the latent dimension in the form of clusters. It cannot enrich the data with dimensions that were not originally present.

Most of the observed variables have an intuitive connection to the dimension underlying the orienting/planning/programming concept *when that concept is applied to an individual manager* and his/her decision-making responsibilities and their related communications. It is likely that the contacts which involve the most fundamental change to a manager's role will have long duration, involve many people and take place in meetings. Conversely, changes that are routine to that job are likely to be short, two-person telephone calls. However, contacts which are orienting from the perspective of the individual may not be orienting for the organization as a whole or even for a more senior employee. A minor change in detail for a senior manager may completely alter every aspect of one of his/her subordinate's jobs. Thus it is unlikely that a classification system based on the duration factor will be related to the orientation/planning/programming activities of the Swedish Civil Service (as was intended in KOMM 71) or of a representative sample of all private-sector organizations in Sweden (KOMM 68). Instead the classification should be based entirely on such variables as the extent to which the contact involved discussion of R & D or transactions or the timespan over which discussed decisions would take effect. The last variable was included in the KOMM 71 survey but not used in the classification, presumably to maintain comparability with KOMM 68.

In summary, the orienting/planning/programming concept is extremely attractive in itself but as yet does not seem to have been adequately operationalized. Attempts to do so have relied too heavily on variables which have little theoretical connection with the underlying dimension and on computer analysis which makes questionable assumptions as to the success of its earlier stages.

A Simple Mixed Approach

On relocation, an office does not retain the same communications that it had before, simply requiring more effort and cost to maintain them. Only one study of the communications of an office both before and after relocation has been conducted. In 1965, the Swedish National Defense Industries Corporation moved from Stockholm to Eskilstuna, 120 km to the west; communications were surveyed by Thorngren, who in 1973 reported the results as follows:

> The total volume of communication was rather unaffected by the move; the use of face-to-face contacts compared to telephone calls also remained stable. There was little or no substitution of telephone calls for face-to-face contacts; instead the organization found new commercial contacts in its new location to replace some of its Stockholm sources. Similarly, there was a large increase in the number of internal contacts with one of the plants in Eskilstuna, where a new R & D department was created. Contacts with the thirteen other plants all over Sweden were largely unaffected. Thus, with respect to internal and commercial contacts the organization adapted rather rapidly to the new location.
>
> However, different parts of the communications system reacted markedly differently to the change. In contrast to the radical change taking place in the internal and commercial sub-systems, communications with outside sources like Government, research organizations and other uncontrollable sources were markedly stable, in spite of a travel time of two hours to Stockholm.

Supporting findings have been obtained by Goddard and Morris (1976), although their major results are at first somewhat contradictory. They found that offices which had relocated from London had fewer contacts than those in London and that a higher proportion of contacts were made by telephone. However, when the contacts of people in offices in London that were to be relocated were compared with those of people in offices whose executives had decided against relocation, it was found that the former had contact patterns fairly typical of staff in relocated offices while the latter's were similar to other central London office workers. It appears that offices are selected for relocation on the basis of the type of work conducted and the associated communication activity. This selection is presumably intuitive and relies heavily on imitation of other successful relocations in the same economic sector.

Since contact patterns change considerably on relocation, the standard transport-cost-minimizing approach cannot be taken. Yet the very considerable attempts to base an approach primarily on the nature of the effects of relocation on the qualitative nature of contacts have not been entirely successful. This chapter has included a detailed criticism of those approaches, without which departure from such a well-known and often repeated method would not be justified. An alternative approach will be advocated here which makes use of Thorngren's and Goddard and Morris' findings concerning the effect of relocation on communication patterns, and integrates those findings into a cost model. The approach is therefore a simple combination of elements of the quantitative cost-minimizing approach and the qualitative approach. It will only be described here in outline. Full details are given in Pye (1977).

Suppose an organization is considering moving some office staff to town A, where its operating costs (in pounds per week) would be lower than in central London, but where the return travel from A to central London costs f, in fares and expenses, and takes t hours. Then, assuming that the number of employees is unchanged, the total saving resulting from moving n jobs to town A is ns, where s is the weekly saving per person. If m of these n jobs involve people who travel to face-to-face meetings in London on average x times each week, then the cost of maintaining contact may be estimated to be $mx(f + ct)$, where c is the average cost or value of communicators' time. The move to town A results in a net saving if

$$ns \geq mx(f + ct),$$

that is,

$$\frac{mx}{n} \leq \frac{s}{f + ct}$$

The organization may feel that it cannot adapt to more than a certain amount of travel by those staff who have communications with outside organizations. Suppose that it wished to limit to d the number of hours an average communicator could spend each week travelling to meetings in London. Then the move would only be feasible in terms of time if

$$xt \leq d, \quad x \leq K = \frac{d}{t}$$

Generally, the further an office moves from London the greater the financial savings it receives, but the greater are its communication costs. Consider town A which, although offering greater rent, rate, and salary savings than town B, is further from London. A move to town A results in greater net saving if

$$ns_A - mx(f_A + ct_A) \geq ns_B - mx(f_B + ct_B),$$

or

$$\frac{mx}{n} \leq L = \frac{s_A - s_B}{(f_A - f_B) + c(t_A - t_B)},$$

where the suffixes refer to towns A and B respectively.

Rhodes and Kan (1971) showed that the components of s are: rent for office floorspace; rates (local taxes) for office floorspace; wage and salary costs. In addition, government grants are available to offices moving to the Assisted Areas—generally the remoter parts of Scotland, Wales and Northern England. the model was therefore calibrated using rent and rate data provided by the Location of Offices Bureau and the Department of the Environment and statistics on wage rates provided by the Alfred Marks Bureau. Travel times and costs were based on the assumption that travel would be by inter-city rail, except for moves to office centres in the Greater London area for which it was assumed that travel would be by suburban or underground railway.

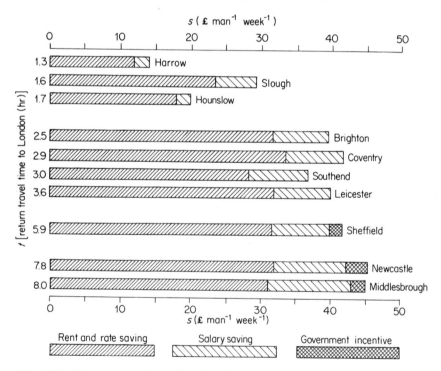

Fig. 10.2. Components of total savings for selected locations outside central London. Reproduced from Pye (1977) by permission of Pion Ltd

It was found that financial saving(s) did not increase proportionately to distance from London (Fig.10.2). In particular, the government incentives add little to the total saving. The values of x and mx/n were estimated from contact frequency statics obtained from six communication surveys:

1. Goddard's (1973) survey of 72 central London offices

2. Goddard and Morris' (1976) survey of 20 relocated offices

3. The 1973 Office Communications Survey, conducted by the Communications Studies Group in 145 offices in three regions of England (see Connell, 1974a; 1974b and Tyler et al., 1976 for details)

4. A pilot study, for the last, of an engineering consultancy (Connell, 1972)

5. The contact survey conducted by the Civil Service Department for the relocation of government review (see Collins, 1971; 1973)

6. Thorngren's KOMM 71 survey of the Swedish Civil Service (see Thorngren, 1972).

A number of assumptions were necessary to obtain the estimates. The key assumption—as observed by Thorngren in his Swedish before-and-after study—is that after relocation each employee will still have 30 per cent of the number of meetings in London that (s)he had before. This assumption is also consistent with the contact patterns observed by Goddard and Morris in relocated offices.

The estimates of x and m/n^x were compared with the limits K and L respectively. It was found that for each 'typical' office representing the results of a survey, for most values of travellers' time in the range £10 to £20 per hour, maximum net savings would be obtained by moving to a town (Brighton) in the economic subregion called the Outer South East of England. Only if time were valued at zero was a move to the Assisted Areas optimal. Only if time were valued at £20 per hour were the central London offices (surveyed by Goddard and Morris, 1976) justified in remaining there.

For the Civil Service data it was possible to derive a statistical distribution for the test statistic m/n^x. Comparing a distribution with L is preferable to use of a mean value associated with a supposedly 'typical' office which may truly represent only those offices which have a test statistic in a fairly small range about the mean. The analysis (Fig. 10.3) assumes that the blocks-of-work (pragmatically defined organizational units considered too small by the Civil Service Department to permit further subdivision—their average size was 19 people) would behave, on relocation, like the agency studied by Thorngren and the firms studied by Goddard and Morris. The findings cannot therefore be taken as direct criticisms of the recommendations made by the Hardman Committee (UK Civil Service Department, 1973). They apply to hypothetical commercial organizations whose distributions of contact frequency before relocation are similar to those observed in the Civil Service: the before-relocation average frequencies observed in the UK Civil Service and by Goddard were comparable. A fairly constant proportion of the blocks-of-work (around 20 per cent, depending on the

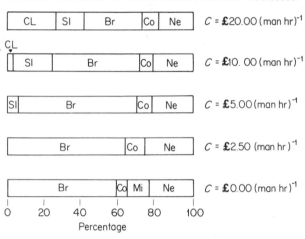

Fig. 10.3. Percentage of blocks of work, from three Departments of State, which should remain in London or be relocated to each town for values of time of 0.00, 2.50, 5.00, 10.00, 20.00 £ (man hr)$^{-1}$. CL, central London; Br, Brighton; Co, Coventry; Mi, Middlesbrough; Ne, Newcastle; Sl, Slough. Reproduced from Pye (1977) by permission of Pion Ltd

value of travellers' time) should be relocated to the Assisted Areas. The remainder should be relocated to a town in the Outer South East (Brighton) or in the Midlands (Coventry) except for the higher values of time when a large number should remain in or near London. When similar calculations were based on the distribution of m/n^x observed in the KOMM 71 survey of the Swedish Civil Service broadly comparable results were obtained. However, the dispersal was rather less widespread; rather fewer blocks-of-work should either remain in London or be moved to the assisted regions. The resulting greater concentration on the Outer South East and the Midlands may be because the blocks-of-work were much larger, containing on average 319 people. Splitting up of departments of commercial organizations might therefore permit the dispersal of more work to the Assisted Areas.

The results of the analysis may be favourably compared with actual dispersals. During the period 1963–1975 most moves monitored by the Location of Offices Bureau were to areas within the South East and very few were to the Assisted Areas (LOB, 1975a; 1975b). Most organizations had not moved as far within the South East as recommended by the model, but that area was receiving more interest in 1974–5, the period to which the calibration is really applicable. Other reasons, within the framework of the model, may explain the occurrence of shorter-distance moves. The additional savings obtained in the Outer South East are fairly marginal and may not be worth the risk of a more uncertain move;

moves are often imitative of those of similar organizations and are made with only an intuitive estimate of the organizations' contact pattern, which is itself constantly changing. The distribution of m/n^x for commercial UK offices may be more like that of the Swedish than the UK Civil Service, especially if large units are considered for relocation. Finally, organizations may not wish to place such a heavy burden on their senior staff and may set a limit for d, the number of hours per week each can spend travelling, which constrains the organization to moves fairly close to London. The loss in net saving would be comparatively small compared with the saving in communicators' time.

Finally, of course, other factors—such as the availabilities of office accommodation and staff—may have influenced decisions. Nevertheless, the results of the analysis are sufficiently close to reality for the model to be useful as a method of assessing the effect of variations in financial savings and communications costs.

The model has only been calibrated for the UK. However, it would be very unlikely to apply to the USA, where the forces for dispersal are very different. Of the reasons for decentralization given by organizations which approached the Location of Offices Bureau during the period 1963–1975, including organizations which subsequently decided against relocation, the most frequently given reason was the need for economy, which accounted for 31 per cent of responses. Among firms which relocated it accounted for 29 per cent of the reasons cited (LOB, 1975b).

In the USA, there have been two strong recent trends in office relocation. Many offices have moved from the centres of cities in the North East of the country to those cities' suburbs. More recently, many others have moved from the North East to the South and West. Although small savings in staff salaries may be obtained by suburban moves, suburban costs of physical office space are often as high if not higher than in the central areas of cities. Moves to the suburbs are instead being motivated by the desire to recruit from the suburban population and by personal, especially tax and education, advantages to employees. Moves to the South and West of the country do result in financial benefits to the organization, but the savings are not as great as those obtained by moving from London to the provinces. In view of the much greater travel distances involved, it is unlikely that the net benefit, as measured by the model, would be positive, unless the amount of travel back to the old location is small. The economy of the United States is very much less concentrated than that of either the UK or Sweden. It may therefore be possible to replace a much higher proportion of contacts on relocation. Unfortunately, little research on communication patterns has been conducted in North America, so accurate assessment of the applicability of the model is impossible. For further discussion of the motivation of office relocation in the USA and the associated benefits and costs see Harkness *et al.* (1977).

The *policy implications* of the model, calibrated for the UK, concern ways in which the trade-off between communication costs and financial savings may be altered. The methods, some of which are probably totally unacceptable because of their side-effects, are:

1. Increasing government grants to offices moving to the Assisted Areas;

2. Increasing rent or salary costs in the South East, through economic pressure, by awarding greater cost-of-living allowances, or by floorspace and employee taxes;

3. Subsidizing business travel;

4. Increasing local contact autonomy, that is, increasing the number of contacts that a relocating office can transfer to local sources, for example by devolving more decision-making in the public sector or by encouraging the development of specialization of major regional office centres;

5. Reducing the need for travel by providing telecommunications alternatives.

It would be necessary to increase the government incentives very considerably in order to make the Assisted Areas attractive to an office typical of the relocated ones studied by Goddard and Morris (1976). Such an office should now relocate to Brighton. Table 10.9 shows the value of government incentives required to make Sheffield, Newcastle and Glasgow equally attractive. In 1974–1975, these incentives were worth about £2–£3 per person per week.

The Replacement of Meetings by Teleconferences

The possibility that meetings might be replaced by teleconferences has been the subject of considerable research, especially at the Communications Studies Group, University College London. The work will only be summarized here—for a more thorough review see Pye and Williams (1977); for more psychologically oriented discussion see Short et al. (1976).

Three approaches were used to assess the potential for replacing meetings by teleconferences:

1. whether the tasks occurring in business meetings would have different outcomes if they were conducted by teleconference media

Table 10.9. Value of Government Incentive Necessary (£ man^{-1} week^{-1}) for Moves to Sheffield, Newcastle and Glasgow to Result in the Same Net Savings as a Move to Brighton, Assuming $mx/n = 0.4$.

| | Value of time (£ man^{-1} hr^{-1}) | | | | |
	0.00	2.50	5.00	10.00	20.00
Sheffield	3.10	6.60	10.00	16.80	30.40
Newcastle	4.40	9.80	15.10	25.70	46.90
Glasgow	7.30	15.90	24.40	41.40	75.40

Source. R. Pye (1977).Reproduced from Pye (1977) by permission of Pion Ltd.

2. whether users would perceive teleconferencing as an effective or acceptable replacement for a meeting

3. whether use of teleconferencing was cheaper or more expensive than travelling to a meeting.

Assessment of the effect of use of teleconference systems on the tasks of business meetings was based on psychological experiments. Civil servants and commercial managers conducted, *via* different modes of communication (face-to-face, audiovisual and audio only), various types of meeting-tasks in a controlled laboratory setting. The outcome of the tasks was measured and the average outcomes *via* different modes compared. For some types of task, such as transmission of information or cooperative problems-solving, similar solutions were obtained whichever mode of communication was used. For other types, notably those involving a greater amount of interpersonal interaction, differences in outcome were found. It was, for example, found that it was possible to change someone's opinion *more* using an audio-only channel than using either an audiovisual channel or face-to-face contact. Similarly, it was found that in a negotiation, the side with the objectively stronger case did better when using an audio-only mode than when using either of the other modes. So effects of mode on outcome were found, although it was by no means clear that use of an audio-only medium was overall inferior to use of an audiovisual medium or face-to-face communication. Moreover, when differences in outcome occurred, audiovisual teleconferencing usually resulted in an outcome more similar to that obtained *via* audio-only teleconferencing than that obtained face-to-face.

When users of real (not laboratory) teleconference systems were asked their opinions of the systems, their perceptions of effectiveness were slightly different from the laboratory results. They perceived both audiovisual and audio-only systems to be effective for the more impersonal tasks. However, they perceived both media to be somewhat unsatisfactory for tasks requiring more interpersonal interaction; although audiovisual systems were seen as somewhat superior to audio-only, they were still regarded as rather unsatisfactory. Similarly, although users had a preference for audiovisual systems over audio-only, in a hypothetical situation, requiring choice between teleconferencing and travel, choices were more strongly influenced by other factors such as the tasks of the meeting, the familiarity with other participants and the length of travel involved.

Having confirmed both that users and potential users perceive the importance of task-type in choices between travel and teleconferencing and that their perceptions as to effectiveness for tasks are broadly comparable with the experimental findings, then it was important to know how often various meeting tasks occur. That knowledge made it possible to generalize from findings about meeting *tasks* to conclusions about the universe of present meetings. Two different approaches were used by CSG. The second approach is the more sound, but the first is also interesting, especially in that it was replicated by Goddard and Morris (1976) who obtained similar findings.

The first approach was used mainly in the UK Civil Service. Staff who were candidates for relocation were asked why a particular meeting could not have been conducted by telephone. They were offered a range of alternative reasons, including the need for a group to participate, for display of documents, for security, to assess other's reactions, to maintain courtesy and to persuade. Meetings were assessed as suitable for transfer to teleconference media on the basis of those reasons and the results of the psychological experiments. Two teleconference media were considered, both assumed to be completely secure and to enable groups of up to 12 people to participate. The first was an audiovisual system, with moving pictures of participants and visual aids, the second was an audiographic system, that is an audio system with facilities for showing still graphics. Table 10.10 shows the results of the Civil Service study and Goddard and Morris' (1976) use of the same question in their survey of relocated offices.

The second approach was based on a study called the Description and Classification of Meetings (DACOM) (see Pye et al. (1973) for further details). Managers were asked to describe the function of and activities at a recent meeting. A set of key phrases was extracted and a second group of managers were asked to rate the applicability of those phrases to a recent meeting. The ratings were then reduced by factor analysis to 12 independent functions of meeting function and activity, which were then assessed for their suitability, on the basis of the laboratory experiments, for conduct by teleconference media. The results are shown in Table 10.11.

The 12 descriptors were then incorporated in the 1973 Office Communications Survey (see Connell, 1974a; 1974b), conducted at 145 office establishments in three regions of England. Each subject person was asked to record up to 10 meetings involving someone from another department or organization. During a five-day period, 3160 meetings were recorded. As a result of this survey, Tyler et al. (1976) estimated that of the present business meetings held in the UK, 45 per cent were suitable for being conducted by either an audiographic system or an audiovisual system, 8 per cent were suitable for being conducted by an audiovisual system but not by an audiographic system and 47

Table 10.10. Results of Surveys Using the 'Contact Record Sheet' Methodology

	Civil service	Decentralized offices
Number of meetings	6397	344
Suitable for:		
Face-to-face	26–41%	22%
Video	7–40%	27%
Audiographics	31–49%	38%
Telephone	3%	13%

Source. Communications Studies Group, Interim Report, May 1972. Report B/72145/RD.
J. B. Goddard and D. Morris, *The Communications Factor in Office Decentralization*, 1976.

Table 10.11. Effect of Medium on Meeting Tasks

Outcome of meetings is:	Fairly definite decision	Tentative decision
Different by audio or video from that face-to-face	Inspection of fixed objects	Conflict; negotiation; disciplinary interview; (presentation of report)*
The same by video and face-to-face, different by audio	Forming impressions of others	Giving information to keep people in the picture
The same by audio, video, and face-to-face	Problem-solving; information-seeking; policy decision-making	Discussion of ideas; (delegation of work)

*For the types of task in parentheses, evidence is more sparse, so the allocations are inevitably less reliable.
Source. E. Williams, 'A summary of the present state of knowledge regarding the effectiveness of the substitution of face-to-face meetings by telecommunicated meetings; type allocation revisited'. Communications Studies Group paper P/74294/WL, 1974.

per cent required face-to-face communication to ensure no change in the outcome of tasks.

When the costs of teleconferencing are compared to the costs of travelling, use of audiographic systems is almost always cheaper but use of audiovisual systems is usually more expensive. When Tyler *et al.* (1976) added cost factors to their previous behavioural assessment they found that, of present meetings: 22 per cent could be conducted more cheaply by audio-only systems without changing the outcomes of tasks; 17 per cent could be so conducted by audiographic systems; 2 per cent by audiovisual systems; 59 per cent would either be more expensive or would have their outcome changed if conducted by a teleconference system.

It must be emphasized that these estimates of the potential for replacement of meetings by teleconference are in no sense predictions of the level of replacement which *will* occur. Teleconferencing has advantages over meetings which have not been included in the above analysis, which is very conservative. A meeting is only considered suitable for replacement if its outcome would be unaffected. From the perspective of some participants, the outcome of a meeting would sometimes be preferable if it were conducted as a teleconference. However, since most users and potential users perceive teleconferencing to be inferior for such meetings, they have been considered only suitable for being conducted face-to-face. Nevertheless, in practice users would often accept a change in the outcome of tasks in order to gain some of the advantages of teleconferencing. Such trade-offs can only be predicted through complex studies of model choice aimed at assessing the weighting of different factors in the decision. As yet there is insufficient use of teleconferencing for this type of research to be possible. Instead the simpler approach, outlined here, has been used to provide a quantified estimate of the proportion of existing meetings which could be conducted as teleconferences without changing their outcome.

It is also true that teleconferencing could receive much use that does not directly replace currently existing meetings. It could be used for additional communication with those who are already met and might make feasible new long-distance relationships. Thus it is possible that in some circumstances, teleconferencing might increase rather than reduce travel. Examples certainly exist of situations where teleconferencing has been successfully introduced in order to reduce travel and where it has been successfully introduced in order to increase communication. The outcome is dependent on the manner of introduction, the constraints imposed and instructions given by management, and the amount of prior communication. Teleconferencing can be employed either to reduce travel or to increase communication, and policy-makers, either at an organizational or national level, can influence which of those alternative effects will predominate.

Implications of Teleconferencing for Relocation

Having established that communication is an important factor in office location decisions and that teleconferencing could economically replace many meetings, it remains to assess the extent of the effect on patterns of relocation. Suppose audiographic teleconferencing replaces at negligible cost 34 per cent of all travel to meetings at the old location. That percentage, somewhat less than the potential stated in the previous section, was the result of an earlier, more conservative estimation process. However, the difference is so small it is unlikely to affect substantially the results. If teleconferencing replaced 34 per cent of meetings, then travel would, using the above notation, be $0.66x$ and relocation to a town would be feasible in terms of travel time if:

$$x \le K/0.66$$

and be optimal if:

$$\frac{mx}{n} \le L/0.66$$

When the comparisons of frequencies observed in the various surveys are compared with $L/0.66$, the results are very similar to when they were compared to L. That is, the replacement of 34 per cent of meetings requiring travel back to the old location does not greatly alter the trade-off between financial savings on relocation and increased communication costs. Most relocations would still be to towns in the South East or Midlands. However, it must be remembered that most moves are not now to the outer parts of that area, even though many would already be cost-effective, and it is very possible that relaxation of the time constraint would make these moves more attractive.

Introduction of telecommunications would not alone make moves to the remote Assisted Areas cost-effective. The financial advantages of moving to those areas are still outweighed by increases in communications costs for most offices. Nevertheless, use of teleconferencing would assist other measures aimed at making those areas more attractive; for example, smaller increases in government grants would be required to persuade organizations to relocate there.

Conclusion

Communication is clearly an important factor in decisions concerning office location. Early theoretical insights and the attitudes of executives have been supported by studies showing that, after relocation, an organization's pattern of communication will change substantially and that considerable contact with organizations near the old site will be required. When the costs of maintaining that contact are compared with the financial benefits resulting from dispersal, for many organizations the communication costs are the greater. If all organizations were optimizing the trade-off between communication costs and savings then the resulting pattern of dispersal would be similar to that observed. Since other factors—notably the supply of office space and availability of office staff—also influence the decision, the comparison is really very close.

Few organizations move to the UK's Assisted Areas, because the increase in benefits—including government grants—is small compared with increased communication costs. Government grants would need to be increased very substantially in order to encourage relocation to those areas.

Substantial research shows that teleconferencing could replace many meetings more cheaply and without changing the outcomes of tasks. Most substitution could be achieved through use of audio-only systems; although audiovisual systems would be preferred by users, they are more expensive and offer fewer advantages in terms of more nearly matching the task performance of face-to-face meetings. Only when their costs can be substantially reduced will audiovisual systems be an important alternative to face-to-face communication.

Despite the apparent feasibility of replacing around 40 per cent of current meetings by teleconferences, that replacement alone would not alter drastically the trade-off between communication costs and other savings. The increase in the number of moves to the Assisted Areas would not be large. The disadvantages of those areas are considerable and could only be overcome by coordinating a number of very different policies—increasing grants, improving travel and communication facilities, restricting or making more expensive office development in the presently more popular areas, and increasing the contact autonomy of provincial centres by devolving more public-sector decision-making or by encouraging the development and specialization of regional contact centres.

The most crucial limitation of the research on which this chapter is based is the shortage of studies of an office's communications both before and after relocation. Only one such study has been completed and although its conclusions have been supported by observation of offices after they have relocated, direct replication is desirable. Replication would confirm or modify current findings; the results of such studies would also help explain the patterns of communication which have been observed and would assist in identifying ways in which telecommunications could help ameliorate damage to communication.

Another limitation of existing research is that most surveys have been conducted in countries where office employment is heavily concentrated around the capital city. A very different pattern of contacts could be expected in countries—such as the USA or the Federal Republic of Germany—with more decentralized economies.

Organizations relocating between major office centres in such countries may be expected to be able to replace locally a much higher proportion of previous contacts; the costs of maintaining contact would, as a result, be much lower. Knowledge of communication patterns in such countries would clearly assist in the overall comprehension of organizational communication, which is at present rather partial and fragmented, both overall and specifically when examining spatial effects. Despite the criticisms that have been made of the 'orienting/planning/programming' concept, it is one of the few attempts to develop a conceptual model of inter-organizational communication.

Future research on teleconferencing systems needs a different orientation from that now complete. Controlled experiments and cost studies are unlikely to make further practical contributions, although the former could contribute much to psychological theories of inter-personal interaction and to an understanding of the processes giving rise to existing findings about the effect of medium on the outcome of tasks. One limitation of present research is that surveys of existing meetings are fairly representative (of present meetings) and so do not include many entailing long-distance travel. This limitation will, however, be removed to a considerable extent by a survey of London–Newcastle travel which will be further described below (see also Ch. 2). However, the greatest need is to understand the reasons behind the success and failure of teleconference systems and the reasons for individuals choosing between travel and teleconferencing when systems are available to them. Although some installations have been successful, many others have failed. No systematic studies of the patterns of travel before and after installation have been conducted and little is known of the detailed effects of the manner in which systems are introduced, even though such effects have been shown to be very important for other office technologies. Such research could also indicate how teleconferencing can be implemented so as to either increase communication or reduce travel, as desired.

The London–Newcastle travel survey is part of a comprehensive project to understand better the communications of office workers in the Newcastle area.

Although use of teleconferencing alone could not make the UK's Assisted Areas attractive to most offices relocating from London, it could benefit the development of office employment indigenous to those areas. That employment is at present hampered by the same lack of external economies of scale in the form of a rich variety of contact opportunities, which require staff in relocated offices to travel often back to London. In order to identify the manner in which telecommunications could aid the communications of staff in offices indigenous to the Newcastle area, a project is being conducted jointly with Professor John Goddard, now at the University of Newcastle-upon-Tyne. The project involves the following studies:

1. A survey of business travel between the North East and the South East of England providing information on the characteristics of business travellers (e.g. their job functions), their workplaces (industry, organizational status), together with similar information for the persons/organization whom they have travelled to meet, and the characteristics of their meetings.

2. Business travel information is being related to data on the characteristics of office employment, manufacturing firms and commercial organizations in the Northern Region as indicated by census and other sources as a means of deriving an aggregate picture of the demand for business communications.

3. A more detailed picture of the factors influencing the communications needs of firms in the Northern Region is being obtained by an interview survey of a sample of 120 Northern Region firms addressed to principal decision-makers in each sampled establishment. A questionnaire schedule has been devised to quantitatively assess these factors. In turn, they will be related to data on communications behaviour obtained from a selection of personnel within each establishment.

4. The communication data obtained in modules 1 to 3 will give only a crude cross-sectional picture of information needs. Statistical analysis will indicate the *association* between organizational variables and communications behaviour. The final module will examine communication processes in large dispersed organizations and will concentrate on how business communication patterns develop over time.

Finally, most work has concentrated on the extent to which verbal telecommunications systems could aid remote offices. The usefulness of office automation systems—which provide fast transmission of messages and retrieval of files—has been relatively neglected. This priority has been understandable: verbal contact is more heavily dependent on proximity and teleconference systems developed more rapidly. However, with the current rapid development of office automation systems, their usefulness to relocating and other remote offices should be thoroughly investigated. It is unlikely that this assessment can be conducted in a laboratory or other artificial environment, other than for specific aspects of ergonomic design. Proper evaluation will require the trial of a system in an organization, preferably one which is intending to or has already relocated or one which has some other special requirements not easily met by conventional technology.

Note on Further Reading

The relocation of offices from city centres to the suburbs or to other regions would have a wide range of impacts on cities and on transport systems. Such impacts were the subject of a major technology assessment of the Telecommunications/Transportation Interactions, conducted by Stanford Research Institute and funded by the US National Science Foundation (NSF). The interested reader is referred to the final report of that study (Harkness *et al.*, 1977) for further information. That report contains discussion of the feasibility of remote working—working in neighbourhood centres or at home—as well as the feasibility of relocating offices and replacing travel by teleconferencing, which have been the subject of this chapter. At present too little is known about the patterns of communication within offices to assess thoroughly the feasibility of remote working, which would require major changes in the supervision of staff and seriously alter job satisfaction. Such issues are of course primarily of interest to students of organizational rather than geographic studies. Another, earlier and less wide-ranging, technology assessment, also funded by NSF, discussed remote working and showed that it would have been cost-effective for an insurance company office (Nilles *et al.*, 1976). However, the case-study may well be atypical and it would be dangerous to generalize too extensively from it. For the author's further comments on that study see his book review (*Environment and Planning A*, Vol. 9 (1977), pp. 1202–1203).

References

Adams, R. M. (1960), The origin of cities, *Scientific American*, September.
Anderson, T. W. (1958), *Introduction to Multivariate Statistical Analysis*. London: Wiley.
Ansoff, H. I. (1965), *Corporate Strategy: An Analytic Approach to Business Policy for Growth and Expansion*. New York: McGraw-Hill.
Asimov, I. (1971), *The Naked Sun*. London: Fawcett Crest.
Asimov, I. (1975), Mother Earth, in *The Early Asimov*, Vol 3. London: Panther.
Bannon, M., and Murphy, B. (1975), *A Study of Person-to-Person Communications in the Department of Health*. Dublin: An Foras Forbartha.
Business Week (1975). The Office of the Future (special issue), June 30th.
Cassidy, W. D. (1969), Substitutes for transportation, *Transportation Research Forum*, 141–150.
Cherry, C. (1970), Eletronic communications: a force for dispersal, *Official Architecture and Planning*, **33**, 773–776.
Collins, H. A. (1971), *The Telecommunications Impact Model, Stages I and II, September 1971*. London: University College, Joint Unit for Planning Research (CSG Report P/71275/CL).
Collins, H. A. (1973), *Analysis of Face-to-Face and Telephone Contact Generation in the*

Public and Private Sectors. London: University College, Joint Unit for Planning Research (CSG Report P/73200/CL).

Connell, S. (1972), *Report on the Pilot Office Communications Survey Contract, Volume 4; the Findings of Pilot Surveys and General Conclusions.* London: University College, Joint Unit for Planning Research (CSG Report P/72293/CN).

Connell, S. (1974a), *The 1973 Office Communications Survey.* London: University College, Joint Unit for Planning Research (CSG Report P/74067/CN).

Connell, S. (1974b), *The 1973 Office Communications Survey: Additional Analysis.* London: University College, Joint Unit for Planning Research (CSG Report P/74225/CN).

Cowan, P. D., Fine, D., Ireland, J., Jordan, C., Mercer, D., and Sears, A. (1969), *The Office: A Facet of Urban Growth.* London: Heinemann.

Ehrlemark, G. (1964), *Proceedings of International Labour Organization Advanced Management Seminar,* Ootacamund.

EIU/LOB (1964), *A Survey of Factors Governing the Location of Offices in the London Area.* London: Report by Economist Intelligence Unit for Location of Offices Bureau (mimeo).

Elton, M., *et al.* (1970), *An Approach to the Location of Government,* London: Institute of Management Science (mimeo).

Fielding, A. (1972), Latent Structure Analysis. London: London School of Economics (unpublished mimeograph).

Forster, E. M. (1928), The machine stops, in *The Eternal Moment and Other Stories.* New York: Harvest Books, Harcourt Brace Johanovich.

Gibson, W. A. (1959), Three multivariate models: factor analysis, latent structure analysis and latent profile analysis, *Psychometrika,* **24**, 54–77.

Goddard, J. B. (1970), Functional regions within the city centre: a study by factor analysis of taxi flows in Central London, *Transactions and Papers, Institute of British Geographers,* **49**, 161–82.

Goddard, J. B. (1973), *Office Linkages and Location.* Oxford: Pergamon.

Goddard, J. B., and Morris, D. M., (1976), *The Communications Factor in Office Decentralization.* Oxford: Pergamon.

Greer, S. (1962), *The Emerging City.* Glencoe: Free Press.

Haig, R. M. (1926), Toward an understanding of the metropolis, *The Quarterly Journal of Economics,* **40**, 402–34.

Hall, P. (1963), *London 2000.* London: Faber and Faber.

Harkness, R. C., *et al.* (1977), *Technology Assessment of Telecommunications/Transportation Interactions.* Menlo Park, California: Stanford Research Institute.

Harman, H. H. (1967), *Modern Factor Analysis.* Chicago: University of Chicago Press.

Healy, T. J. (1968), Transportation or communications: some broad considerations, *IEEE Transactions on Communication Technology,* COM-16, 195–198.

Hough, R. W. (1976). *Teleconferencing Systems: A State of the Art Survey and Preliminary Analysis.* Menlo Park, California: Stanford Research Institute.

Interscan/Location of Offices Bureau (1967), *Report on the Survey of Non-Movers.* London: Report by Interscan for the Location of Offices Bureau.

Interscan/Location of Offices Bureau (1970), *A Survey of Offices in the Central Area.* London: Report by Interscan for the Location of Offices Bureau.

Isaksson, A. (1972), *Latent Profile Analysis—A Brief Description.* Sweden: Telecommunication Theory/Electrical Engineering, Royal Institute of Technology, Technical Report No. 54.

Jantsch, E. (1967), *Technological Forecasting in Perspective.* Paris: Organization for Economic Co-operation and Development.

Kramer, S. N. (1957), The Sumerians, *Scientific American*, October 1957.
Libby, W. L. (1969), *The End of the Trip to Work*. The Ohio State University, (mimeograph).
Location of Offices Bureau (1975a), *Office Relocation Facts and Figures: LOB Statistical Handbook 1975*. London: Location of Offices Bureau.
Location of Offices Bureau (1975b), *Annual Report 1974–5*. London: Location of Offices Bureau.
Meier, R. (1962), *A Communication Theory of Urban Growth*. Cambridge, Mass.: MIT Press.
Movold, K. (1976), *Kontatundersøkelse i Offentlige Institusjoner I Oslo*: Oslo: Norwegian Institute of Urban and Regional Research (Nork Institutt for By-Og Regionsforskning).
Nilles, J. M., Carlson, F. R., Gray, P., and Heinemann, G. J. (1976), *The Telecommunications Transportation Tradeoff*. New York: Wiley Interscience.
Parkinson, C. N. (1958), *Parkinson's Law*, London: John Murray.
Persson, C. (1974), *Kontaktarbete och Framtida Iokaliseringsförändringar: Modellstudier med tillämpning på statling forvaltning*. Lund.
Pye, R. (1972), *The Telecommunications Impact Model Stage II: October, 1972*. London: University College Joint Unit for Planning Research (CSG Report P/72319/PY).
Pye, R., et al. (1973), *The Description and Classification of Meetings*. London: University College, Joint Unit for Planning Research (CSG Report P/73/60/PY).
Pye, R. (1976), Commucnications effectiveness and efficiency, in *Technology Assessment of Telecommunication/Transportation Interactions: Volume II, Detailed Impact Analyses*, Menlo Park, California: Stanford Research Institute.
Pye, R. (1977), Office location and the cost of maintaining contact, *Environment and Planning A*, **9**, 149–168.
Pye, R., and Williams, E. (1977), Teleconferencing: is video valuable or is audio adequate?, *Telecommunications Policy*, **1**, 230–241.
Rhodes, J, and Kan, A. (1971), *Office Dispersal and Regional Policy*. London: Cambridge University Press.
Short, J., Williams, E., and Christie, B. (1976), *The Social Psychology of Telecommunications*. London: Wiley.
Simon, H. A. (1960), *The Shape of Automation for Men and Management*. New York: Harper and Row.
Simon, H. A. (1965), The new science of management decision, in *The Shape of Automation for Men and Management*. New York: Harper and Row.
Thorngren, B. (1970), How do contact systems affect regional development?, *Environment and Planning*, **2**, 409–427.
Thorngren, B. (1972), *A Communication Study of Government Relocation in Sweden*. Stockholm: Stockholm School of Economics.
Thorngren, B. (1973), Swedish office dispersal, in M. Bannon (Ed.), *Office Location and Regional Development*. Dublin: An Foras Forbartha.
Tyler, R. M., Cartwright, B., and Collins, H. A., (1976), *Interaction Between Telecommunications and Face-to-Face Contact: Prospects for Teleconference Systems*. London: Telecommunications Systems Strategy Department, British Post Office, Long Range Intelligence Bulletin No. 9.
UK Civil Service Department (1973), *The Dispersal of Government Work from London*. Cmnd 5322. London: HMSO.
Vinde, P. (1971), *Swedish Government Administration*. Stockholm: Bokforlaget Prisma/The Swedish Institute.

Webber, M. (Ed.) (1964), *Explorations into Urban Structure*. Philadelphia: University of Pennsylvania Press.

Wise, A. (1971) The impact of electronic communications on metropolitan form, *Ekistics*, No. 188, 22–31.

Young, G. A. (1971), Commuters—Stay House, Paper No. 71–490 presented to Urban Technology Conference, New York Coliseum, NYC, May 24–26,

11

Face-to-Face Linkages and Office Decentralization Potentials: A Study of Toronto

GUNTER H. K. GAD

This chapter has two aims: firstly, to acquaint the reader with the issues surrounding vigorous office expansion in the central area of a fast growing metropolis, and secondly, to introduce what is perhaps the only North American large-scale study of face-to-face linkages. Consideration is given not only to findings but also to methodological issues in surveying inter-establishment face-to-face communication. In discussing the Toronto face-to-face study, particular attention is paid to the implications of the findings for office decentralization policies at the metropolitan or intra-urban scale.[1]

Office Growth and Office Development Policies

Questions concerning office location in Toronto are linked to its expanding role as a centre of national importance and the tensions imposed on the urban fabric of the metropolis by population and employment growth. A brief statement about the national importance of Toronto's office complex will precede a short report on the intra-urban adjustment processes necessitated by growth and an outline of policies for office development in Metropolitan Toronto.

Toronto as National Management and Control Centre

Employment in the Toronto Census Metropolitan Area[2] climbed from about 527,000 in 1951 to about 790,000 in 1961 and to more than 1.2 million in 1971

(Canada, Dominion Bureau of Statistics, 1953; 1963; Canada, Statistics Canada, 1975b). Undoubtedly some of this increase is due to boundary expansions of the Census Metropolitan Area but, as special surveys indicate, employment within the municipality of Metropolitan Toronto (See Fig. 11.1) has also increased vigorously. Between 1960 and 1970 the number of jobs grew from about 675,000 to about 920,000 (Toronto, Metropolitan Planning Board, n.d.).

Toronto's role as a national business centre becomes apparent when its share of the nation's employment in economic sectors or divisions characterized by office employment is considered. According to the 1971 *Census*, 22.0 per cent of the Canadian labour force in the finance–insurance–real estate division and 22.6 per cent of the Canadian labour force in business services worked in Metropolitan Toronto, whereas the city's overall share of the national labour force was only 11.2 per cent (Canada, Statistics Canada, 1974; 1975a). Toronto also performs an obviously important regional function as seat of Ontario's provincial government, although this did not inflate Metropolitan Toronto's share (9.0 per cent) of all Canadian employment in public administration at the time of the 1971 *Census*.

The categories used in the Canadian *Census* are not entirely adequate to judge Toronto's role as a management centre. Measures regarding financial transactions or the control of business assets may be better indicators of 'metropolitan dominance' (Kerr, 1968). At present, Toronto is the focal point of the second largest stock market in North America after New York. The value of stock market transactions started to outpace the combined transactions of the two Montreal exchanges at the beginning of the 1950s and the gap has since widened continuously (Kerr, 1973, p. 69). Together, Toronto and Montreal clearly dominate capital markets in Canada, and decisions concerning the deployment of the vast majority of assets owned by Canadian corporations are made in Toronto and Montreal offices. While Montreal still holds a small lead with regard to control over bank, trust company and 'industrial' assets, Toronto leads in the administration of assets belonging to consumer and business finance, life insurance and mining companies (Kerr, 1973, pp. 67–77).

Toronto's role as an international, rather than national, control and management centre has been very little explored. There are indications that Toronto is the main secondary centre (after London, UK) in the Euro-dollar market, probably the chief medium for international money transfer and speculation (Chodos, 1975). Canadian banking and life insurance companies are heavily involved abroad (Gad, 1976, p. 115). Little has been published concerning the role of multinational corporations not belonging to the banking and life insurance industries which have headquarters in Toronto, although there are interesting examples of 'empires' involved in mining, utilities, publishing, farm and construction machinery and brewing which are administered from Toronto head offices.

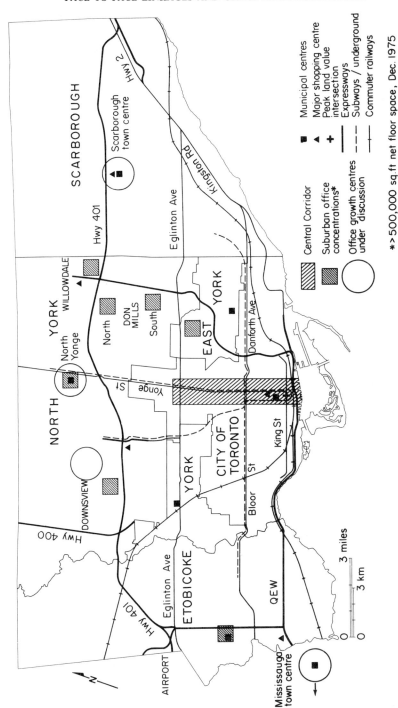

Fig. 11.1. Reference map: Metropolitan Toronto

Toronto's importance as a centre of control is tempered, however, by the domination of Canadian manufacturing by United States interests. It is in New York, Detroit, Chicago and many lesser known places, such as Neenah (Wisconsin), that the strings of control are manipulated. Foreign control is not restricted to the secondary sector. There are many insurance companies, advertising, employment and insurance agencies, or computer leasing and engineering branches which are part of organizations owned by foreigners. In the conceptualization of the Canadian urban system suggested by Simmons (1974), Toronto is the contact point between the primary control centre of the continental economy, New York, and the Candaian hinterland.

In spite of these aspects of foreign control, this examination of labour force and other data, together with an admittedly casual investigation of Canadian business, does show that Toronto functions not only as a provincial capital but also as a national business centre and to a moderate degree even as an international banking and insurance centre. Toronto's control and adminis-trative functions were undoubtedly major factors stimulating growth through-out most of the 1950s and 1960s. The expansion of business and government is due, on the one hand, to general growth of the Canadian economy and, on the other hand, to growth differentials in the urban system. In terms of the latter, Toronto may have gained additional office employment at the expense of other cities, with Montreal in the seemingly difficult situation of losing some ground in a long struggle for dominance.

Recent Office Growth in Toronto

The rapid growth of employment and population (the latter climbing from 1.1 million in 1951 to 2.1 million in 1971) in Metropolitan Toronto, together with changes in public policy, technology, private tastes and the ageing of the preexisting physical plant have resulted in dramatic changes in the landscape of the Toronto area. Hand in hand with the expansion of the residential areas at the fringe came new industrial districts and factories, shopping centres, universities and community colleges, hospitals and the transportation infra-structure to link these areas and nodes to each other and with the traditional core or 'downtown area' of the metropolis (Bourne and Doucet, 1973). It is important to keep in mind that these changes have not resulted in a significant polarization of central city and suburbs as far as social class, ethnicity or race are concerned, although sentiments and interests of central city and suburban dwellers might sometimes conflict strongly. At least during the 1951–61 decade the pattern of sectors or 'wedges of social class' has shown a remarkable stability, with the thrust of change leading to a radial extension of these sectors from the inner city to the suburbs (Murdie, 1969).

Apart from the extension of older patterns into new territory (although often in the form of new physical shapes, e.g. shopping plazas rather than retail strips), another striking change has taken place in the central part of the metropolis. Apartments and offices have dramatically transformed the strip of land along Yonge Street from the 'waterfront' to Eglinton Avenue (see Central Corridor, Fig. 11.1). Although construction of new offices and especially apartments has not been restricted to the central part of Toronto (Bourne, 1968), the impact is seen more strongly here because change in this area comes in the form of redevelopment. During the last two or three decades a large number of brick and stone buildings, many of only three or four storeys, were replaced by tall towers of concrete, steel and glass. Some of the larger office structures of earlier periods were also demolished to make way for even bigger buildings. It is this highly visible change in the appearance of the central part of Toronto, documented in precise studies (Bourne, 1967; Toronto, Core Area Task Force, 1974) and mourned in a number of critical essays or photo albums (e.g. Filey, 1972), which provided the fuel for the opponents of the growth policies of the 1950s and 1960s.

A clear spatial pattern of employment increases and decreases between 1956 and 1970 accompanied these physical changes (Fig. 11.2). Peripheral employment increase is very marked in districts stretching along expressways in northern Toronto (Highway 401) and south-west Toronto (Queen Elizabeth Way). Inner area increase coincides strongly with the Yonge Street corridor from Front Street to Eglinton Avenue, the area which has experienced the major share of office development. Inner area employment decline coincides largely with older manufacturing areas in the City of Toronto and the inner suburban municipalities.

The changing location of workplaces is undoubtedly due to the shift of manufacturing activities from the older industrial districts to new plants within easy reach of the expressways (see Kerr and Spelt, 1961; Toronto, City Planning Board, 1971, pp. 33–48), and to the increase of office employment in the Yonge Street corridor. The City of Toronto lost about 53,000 jobs in manufacturing industries between 1951 and 1971, while the suburban boroughs altogether gained about 127,000 new manufacturing jobs in the same two decades (Gad, 1976, pp. 127–128).

To comment further on these changes in office employment, it is estimated that employment in the four square kilometre Inner Core Area,[3] the southern part of the Yonge Street corridor, increased from about 160,000 in 1956 to about 192,000 in 1970 (Gad, 1976, p. 121). Similar to the dispute about employment increase in central London during the 1950s (Evans, 1967), there is considerable argument about the figures for Toronto. It has been pointed out that earlier employment surveys by the Metropolitan Toronto Planning Board could rely on the expertise of Statistics Canada, whereas the 1970 figures were indirectly derived from real-estate taxation data and could be considered 'somewhat shaky' (Nowlan, 1974, pp. 15–17). While the City's pro-decentralization planning staff seem to be convinced that employment has grown strongly in the Inner Core Area, others, including the opponents of growth controls, emphasize the stability

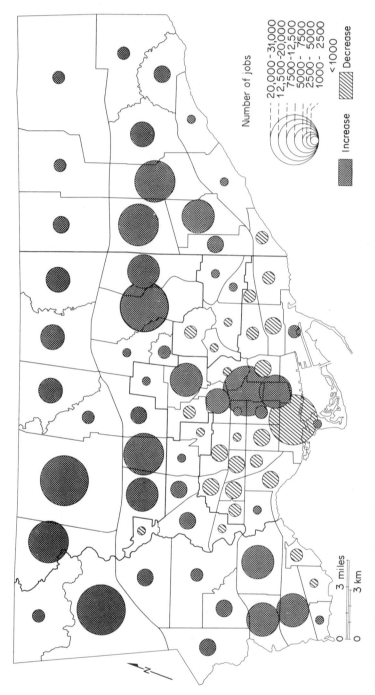

Fig. 11.2. Employment change 1956–70, Metropolitan Toronto Minor Planning Districts (data source: Metropolitan Toronto Planning Department)

of traffic inflow into the Inner Core Area over the last two decades (e.g. Code, 1975, p. 99). It is difficult to reconcile these two views in the light of available information.

The dramatic increase of net rental office floorspace in the Yonge Street corridor from 8 million sq. ft in 1953 to 27 million sq. ft in 1971 and nearly 43 million sq. ft at the end of 1976 (A. E. LePage, 1969; 1972; 1977) may be evidence of substantial office employment increase. Even if one assumes that office floorspace consumption per employee has nearly doubled from about 100 to 185 sq. ft per employee, one is still left with an increase of about 65,000 office workers in the Yonge Street corridor between 1953 and 1971. The 1951 and 1971 *Census* figures for the City as a whole can be used to support this argument (Gad, 1976, pp. 147–152). Although it is certain that office employment has increased in central Toronto, one could still argue that the total employment level may have shown relative stability because of the decline in manufacturing. (It is an intriguing thought, however, that the replacement of factories and warehouses by 20– to 80–storey office towers has not led to higher employment densities.)

As implied above, offices are highly concentrated along the Yonge Street axis between the 'waterfront' in the south and Eglinton Avenue in the north. It can be argued that the Central Corridor (see also Note 3 and Figs. 11.1 and 11.3), determined by detailed mapping of office floorspace, is the most appropriate area for the analysis of Toronto's central office complex. Special tabulations by the Metropolitan Toronto Planning Board based on the 1970 employment survey suggest that about 160,000 persons worked in office buildings in the Central Corridor (Gad, 1976, pp. 136–44). According to detailed data collected by A. E. LePage Limited, a real-estate firm conducting annual surveys, there were 25.6 million sq. ft of rentable floorspace in office buildings with over 20,000 sq. ft of floorspace in the Central Corridor in 1971 (Gad, 1976, pp. 136–44). This central agglomeration, comprising only 2.6 per cent of Metropolitan Toronto's area, accounted for 68 per cent of the employment in offices and about 77 per cent of the net rentable floorspace in office buildings over 20,000 sq. ft at the beginning of the 1970s.

Non-central office locations received very little attention from office developers and tenants until the mid-1960s. In 1965 the share of all non-central locations was 10.1 per cent of the total net rentable floorspace. By 1970 this had risen to 18.2 per cent and by 1976 to 21.1 per cent (A. E. LePage, 1966; 1971; 1977). Since the early 1970s the increase in the proportion of non-central offices has slowed down, and it is important to note that more recently there has no longer been a tendency for suburban locations to gain a larger share of Toronto's office space. Between 1975 and 1976 the non-central share actually decreased from 21.5 per cent to 21.1 per cent (A. E. LePage, 1977). Although no clearly identifiable subcentres have appeared on the suburban scene so far, there are trends which may eventually lead to the establishment of non-central agglomerations at strategic nodes in the expressway and public transit network (see Fig.

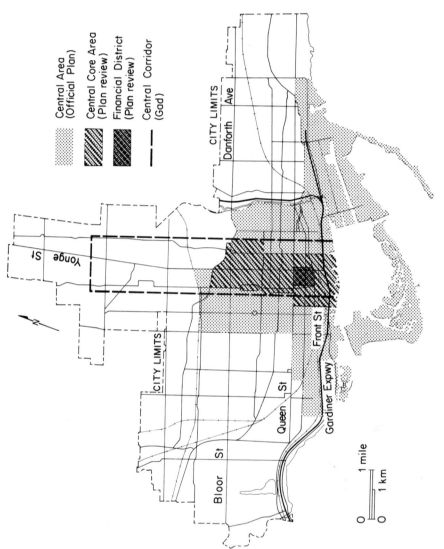

Fig. 11.3. Reference map: Central Area definitions

11.1). Recent debates concerning development policies for Metropolitan Toronto include vigorous discussion about the possibility of deliberately channelling office growth into some of these emerging office subcentres.

Office Development Policies

Office employment increases at the centre and recent growth in some suburban locations are not entirely spontaneous occurrences but, to some extent at least, the result of direct and indirect government policies. So far only very few and partial reviews of government action concerning office location in Toronto have been carried out (e.g. Toronto, City Planning Board, 1974; Code, 1975; Bourne, 1975). Thorough and comprehensive inquiry must come to terms with many complexities: the tangled relationships of different levels of government; uncertainty as to whether ideas and initiatives originate with politicians or with 'planners' and other local or provincial government staff; the lack of political parties and explicit political programmes at the municipal government level; uncertainty about the composition and representativeness of residents' groups; and the uncertain impact of indirect measures such as investment in transportation and other infrastructure facilities. The best that can be offered here, given the lack of an in-depth study and the limitation of space, is a broad outline and some generalizations.

During the post-war decades, up to about 1970, there were few explicit policy statements concerning offices as a specific land use but many actions taken by the City Metropolitan and Provincial (Ontario) governments which helped to facilitate the concentration of office employment in central Toronto. Most of these actions involved the improvement of transportation facilities: subways (undergrounds), commuter trains and buses, expressways and improvements to the arterial road network. Very often the improvements in the transportation system increased access to central Toronto. The importance of the Central Area (see Note 3 and Fig. 11.3) as a focus for activities which serve 'the entire region or a larger area' was acknowledged in the Official Plan of 1969, and the concentration of commercial office buildings in parts of the Central Area was explicitly 'encouraged' (Toronto, City Planning Board, 1969). Before the final approval of the Official Plan, the city had already stimulated Central Area redevelopment and growth through investment in a showcase city hall, the coordinating hand of the Buildings and Development Commissioner, and liaison with the business-dominated Downtown Redevelopment Council.

Sustained by the critical mood of the late 1960s, vocal citizens of Toronto first rebelled against the expansion of the expressway network and then against further redevelopment of low-rise residential districts and commercial areas for high-rise apartments and offices. The 1972 civic election was a critical turning point, when a loose grouping of 'reformers' defeated the pro-development 'old guard'. Under the influential leadership of a 'reform' mayor, Toronto City

Council initiated a number of moves which eventually culminated in a curb on office development through revisions of the 1969 Official Plan and the zoning bylaw.

A stepping-stone in the Official Plan review was the Core Area Task Force, which was formed early in 1973 to look initially into the possibilities of improving traffic conditions in central Toronto. The Task Force quickly realized the futility of increasing the level of transportation services according to the demands of land-use intensification and began to articulate strong opposition to the whole trajectory along which the rebuilding of central Toronto moved (Toronto, Core Area Task Force, 1974). Reaching similar conclusions, the City Council of 1972 decreed a virtual halt to development in 1973 through the so-called '45 Foot Height By-Law', which was conceived as a holding measure until studies could be carried out and the Official Plan could be revised. (The Ontario Municipal Board, a provincial body arbitrating in planning matters, declared this bylaw invalid in 1975.)

In October 1975 the City's planning staff published the proposals for the revision of the Official Plan (Toronto, City Planning Board, 1975). These proposals were based on the following six concerns and critical reckonings about development trends (Toronto, City Planning Board, 1975, pp. A33–A38):

Declining Diversity in the Role of the Central Area. Concern was expressed that the function of the Central Area as a 'city residence area, as an industrial area and as a focus for community life for City and Metro residents is in danger of being overshadowed by its function as a centre for specialized service activity serving larger area interests' (Toronto, City Planning Board, 1975, p. A35). Rapid expansion of non-residential activity and marked increase in Central Area employment was felt to be a threat to diversity.

Inadequacy of Transportation Facilities. Doubts were expressed about the ability of the transport system to cope with the shift towards, and increase in, high-density office employment. Also, an increase in the use of the private automobile gave rise to the demand that alternative forms of transportation and a pedestrian system be developed.

Narrowing Employment Opportunities. It was argued that employment opportunities were lost for industrial workers and low-income people in the City. Blame was seen to lie with the loss of industrial jobs and increases in service employment reflected in the number of office jobs.

Declining Housing Opportunities. It was claimed that family and low-to moderate-income households had been displaced from inner city neighbourhoods. Concern was expressed that, by virtue of proximity to the centres of business and other activity, inner city neighbourhoods might be negatively affected and put under development pressure. The future of housing in the Central Area was felt to be in jeopardy in general, because of the competition for land by users such as offices, shops and institutions.

Inadequacy of Public Amenities. Concern was expressed over inadequate public amenities such as parks and recreation areas to meet the needs of residents, workers and visitors. Also, social services for inner city residents were judged as inadequate.

Deteriorating Quality of the Urban Environment. Concern was voiced over the deterioration of the built environment, caused by unpleasant micro-climatic effects (wind, shadow) associated with large-scale buildings, the demolition of buildings of architectural or historic merit and the loss of vistas and views.

The dominant theme in the criticism sketched above is the loss of diversity through the growth of offices and large institutions. The sentiments of the critics are expressed by the following passage from the Core Area Housing Study in the context of commenting on the role of the Central Area as regional and national business centre:

> In strengthening its role on the larger scale, the Core Area loses strength on its domestic scale; in becoming more highly specialized, it loses the colour and excitement which is derived from its great diversity of functions and variety of people. And in losing these, the City loses some of the richness of experience and complexity of texture which have always been among the most attractive qualities of urban life. (Klein *et al.*, 1974, p. 14.)

At the root of 'rapid redevelopment and phenomenal growth, in particular, of office space' (Toronto, City Planning Board, p. A7) the City's planning staff saw the Official Plan of 1969 with its aim of stimulating further concentration of regionally-oriented services, explicit encouragement of office growth, and liberal zoning provisions, which allowed a building intensity of up to 12 times coverage in large parts of the Central Area (Toronto, City Planning Board, 1975, pp. A39–55).

The overriding goal of the proposals put forward by the planners in 1975 is the strengthening of diversity in the Central Area in the context of advocating a multicentred distribution of office employment in the Toronto region. The multiple role of the Central Area, combining business, the focus of community life and housing, and the goal to improve the quality of the urban environment demand a number of measures:

Curb of Office and Institutional Growth in the Central Area and the Creation of Suburban Office Centres. Office growth is to be restrained in the Central Area and redirected towards other parts of the metropolitan region. Redirection is to be achieved by controlling office employment growth indirectly through 'down-zoning' in the Central Area and by encouraging particularly the Metropolitan

Boroughs and the Metropolitan and Provincial levels of government to facilitate the establishment of office subcentres outside of the City of Toronto. Large institutions like the University of Toronto, hospitals and museums are also to be subject to strict growth controls.

Encouragement of an Increase in the Central Area Housing Stock. Parallel to the reduction in maximum permissible office floorspace, the planners' proposals aim to encourage the development of new housing in the Central Area. The production of 30,000 new housing units, half suitable for low-and moderate-income households and one-sixth suitable for families with children, is to be encouraged. Generally, these units are to be built in a manner compatible with low-rise neighbourhoods and in the form of mixed commercial–residential developments in the core of the Central Area.

Improvement of Amenities in the Central Area. Other suggestions by planners concern provisions for more recreation space, retention of historic buildings, and improvements in the visual form of the Central Area, and transportation. With regard to the latter, it is interesting to note that the planners purposely did not recommend an expansion of peak-hour transportation capacity, a move which is consistent with the thrust to decentralize office development.

Since the control of office growth is crucial to the policy proposals, this point deserved further comment. An increase in *office* employment from about 165,000 in 1975 to a maximum of between 259,000 and 307,500 by 1985 is permissible under the new policies. This seems a staggering increase, but it has to be measured against what would have been possible under the 1969 Official Plan or the zoning bylaw. Whereas *total* employment in the core of the Central Area was 250,000 in 1975, the Official Plan of 1969 and the zoning bylaw would have allowed approximately 1.1 million persons to be concentrated in this small area.

Although the planners are primarily interested in restricting office employment, existing planning legislation makes no provision for regulating employment and the City has to resort to conventional land-use and building intensity controls as tools of implementation. Within the Central Core Area (see Note 3 and Fig. 11.3) a total office gross floorspace of 80 million sq. ft is to be permitted. This compares to 44 million sq. ft which existed in the same area in 1975.

In order to allow for the expansion of finance, legal and mining activities, which are strongly interrelated by face-to-face contacts (see the discussion following), the traditional 'financial district' south of Queen Street is designated as an 'office priority area', where new maximum densities of eight times lot coverage, compared with 12 previously, are to be allowed. Even in this 'office priority area' the policy proposals call for the introduction of housing. So-called 'high-density mixed commercial–residential areas' are secondary office expansion districts. Here, however, offices may only be built to a maximum intensity of 4.5 times lot coverage. In some parts of the Central Area, especially along the

Yonge and Bay axis, this means a reduction in the floorspace–lot ratio from 12.0, as specified in the Official Plan of 1969, to 4.5.

The planners' proposals were by and large accepted by Toronto's City Council in January 1976 through amendments to the Official Plan and through zoning bylaw changes. Before these new policies and measures are effective, they will have to be approved by the Ontario Municipal Board, a body appointed by the Provincial cabinet of Ontario and entrusted with a supervisory function over municipalities.

At all stages in the revision of the Official Plan conflicts surfaced both within the City Council and at public hearings. After the 1972 election Toronto City Council was basically split into a 'reform' group, advocating growth controls, and a 'pro-development' group. After the 1974 election, however, new alignments emerged. Some members of the 'reform' group formed a more or less left-wing populist caucus. Toronto's mayor dissociated himself from the left-wing caucus and surrounded himself with a 'moderate' group, and on the right the old 'pro-development' faction continued to maintain a pro-growth stance. The proposals put forward by the planners were bitterly fought by the left-wing caucus, because they were seen as a 'sell-out' to real-estate interests. The left-wing caucus demanded a further reduction of commercial densities. The pro-development group was initially critical of what by now had become known as the 'mayor's plan', but eventually enough aldermen of this group supported the 'moderate' group. Interest groups in the city were strongly polarized. On the one side ratepayers' and residents' groups in unison with the left-wing caucus demanded stronger protection of existing low-rise residential neighbourhoods, whereas business associations, various organizations of the real-estate development industry and individual development companies consistently opposed growth controls.

Among the arguments the City had to contend with was one which concerned its powers in the attempt to stimulate growth in suburban office centres. As mentioned above, the City's planning powers consist by and large of land-use controls—and these do not extent beyond the political boundaries of the City. The City could argue, however, that its attempts to de-emphasize the office function of the Central Area could be seen as part of a more general search for a new metropolitan form. Parallel to policy formation by the City of Toronto, the Metropolitan Toronto Transportation Plan Review (1975), prepared by a joint Provincial–Metropolitan task force, discussed the possibilities of a multicentred metropolitan area in great depth. The City could also argue that it would find direct or indirect cooperation amongst other municipalities, and the Metropolitan and Provincial governments (Toronto, City Planning Board, 1975, pp. B1/34–44). Two of the Metropolitan boroughs (North York and Scarborough and Mississauga, a municipality to the west of Toronto) had expressed their intention to encourage the growth of suburban office concentrations. Also, the proposed plan for Metropolitan Toronto stresses a multicentred urban structure with office growth poles outside the Central Area as a fundamental goal (Toronto, Metropolitan Planning Department, 1976, p. 4). Further, the Ontario government is committed to decentralization. While some stated intentions of the Province still await action, particularly the development of a 'new town' with special emphasis on office and research employment, the Ontario government in the spring of 1977 announced the decentralization of several of its own offices to municipalities east of Metropolitan Toronto. Other actions by the Provincial government, however, such as further investment in commuter facilities focused on central Toronto, tend to counteract Provincial government office decentralization.

Compared with some European cities (e.g. London, Paris, Stockholm, Hamburg), direct office location policies are relatively new in Canadian cities. As in other places, much of the current debate in Toronto has its origin in the belief that beyond a certain level highly concentrated employment is difficult to service even by mass transportation. Increasing hostility towards the architectural expression of the modern office has certainly provided another source of emotional opposition to Toronto's office boom of the last two decades.

Toronto's office control policies are surrounded by many questions, some of which concern their origin, others their implementation and effects. Both aspects provide ample scope for research. As far as the origin of office location policies is concerned, there is a special question about the role which research has played in its formation. In order to revise the Official Plan for the Central Area, the City of Toronto, mainly through an advisory body, the City of Toronto Planning Board, had commissioned a number of research reports. These research reports, published in 1974 and 1975, cover a number of aspects: buildings and streetscape design (Design Guidelines Study Group, 1974: Baird, 1975), the real-estate development process (Peat Marwick and Partners, 1975), the economic impact of development controls (Buckley et al., 1975; Clayton Research Associates, 1975; Dewees, 1975; Nowlan, 1975), housing in the Central Area (Klein et al., 1974), and transportation capacities (Parkinson, 1975). Several studies are directly concerned with different facets of offices: office space demand forecast by means of the Delphi procedure (Price Waterhouse and Associates, 1974), trends in office floorspace consumption (Peat Marwick and Partners and IBI Group, 1975a), a review of the literature on agglomeration economics (Peat Marwick and Partners and IBI Group, 1975b), and empirical observations on face-to-face contacts (Gad, 1975). The latter study, already begun in 1971, is outlined below.

Toronto's Central Office Complex

The detailed study of Toronto's offices located in the Central Corridor was based on the hypothesis that central office agglomerations are internally differentiated in terms of functions, spatial organization, and communication patterns. Some indication of the heterogeneity of central office agglomerations can be found in numerous publications, and substantial evidence is provided by several detailed studies on office location and linkages (e.g. Morgan, 1961; Facey and Smith, 1968; Croft, 1969; Goddard, 1967; 1968; 1973; Gad, 1968; Bannon, 1973). It is this heterogeneity which provides the basis for advocating the decentralization of some offices. This argument is made eloquently by Goddard (1973, p. 115) and Manners (1974).

Economic and Spatial Structure

The enumeration of offices in the Central Corridor of Toronto reveals a total of 4852 establishments with about 140,000 employees (Fig. 11.4).[4] Table 11.1 shows some significant features of the structure of Toronto's central office agglomeration. For instance, only eight of 68 industry classes account for 54 per cent of the employment. Five of these industry classes are shown separately in the table (Manufacturing, Banks, Investment Dealers, Life Insurance, Law Firms), while three others are 'hidden' as a result of aggregation (Utilities, Federal Government, Provincial Government). Although they have large numbers of employees, most of these eight industry classes are characterized by small numbers of establishments, whereas other industry classes with relatively few employees consist of large numbers of small establishments (e.g. Insurance Agencies, Accountants, Architects). Law firms constitute an exceptional industry class: the high level of employment is a reflection of a very large number of establishments. Table 11.1 is only a pale reflection of the heterogeneity of a central office agglomeration, and the myriad of highly specialized financial business, media and technical or engineering services present great problems in establishing linkage characteristics and communication networks.

The complexity of economic structure is also reflected in the spatial structure of Toronto's central office agglomeration. A comparison of 68 maps and spatial indices (gravity centres, standard distances, Gini coefficients) reveals a wide range of location patterns. Two extreme examples of these are shown in Fig. 11.5, where the distribution of employment in Banks (excluding branch employment) provides an example of a highly concentrated location pattern, while the distribution of employment in Advertising Agencies presents an example of a highly dispersed pattern. Only very few of the 68 industry classes, namely Trust Companies, Investment Dealers, Mining Companies, Mining Services and Law Firms, display a concentration of employment south of Queen Street similar to that shown in the map for Banks. Other industries may be clustered, in the sense that employment is concentrated at several nodes within the Central Corridor, but it is important to note that these nodes occur always in *several* places within this area.

Further investigation of these spatial patterns by means of factor analysis and cluster analysis does confirm the pattern visible through the interpretation of the mapped data. Both factor analysis and cluster analysis were carried out at

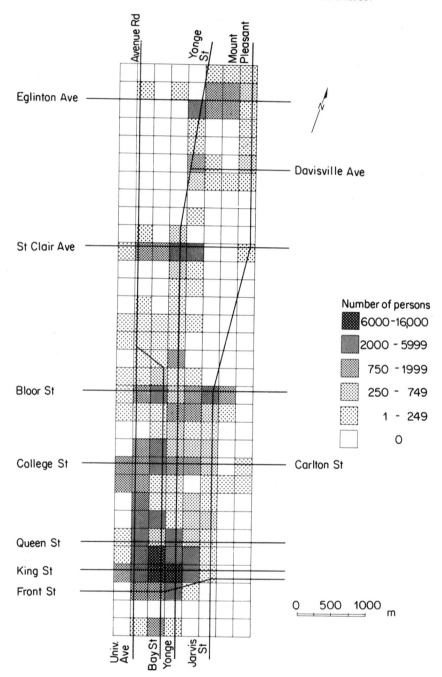

Fig. 11.4.   Distribution of office employment, all industries, Central Corridor

Table 11.1. Office Establishments and Employment by Major Industry Division and Selected Industry Classes, Central Corridor

	Establishments		Employment	
	No.	%	No.	%
Mining, manufacturing, transportation, utilities	624	12.9	27,077	19.6
111 Mining	163	3.4	2293	1.7
121 Integrated Oil Companies	9	0.2	3230	2.3
122 Manufacturing	237	4.9	8006	5.8
Other	215	4.4	13,548	9.8
Finance, insurance, real estate	1107	22.8	42,977	31.2
211 Banks	34	0.7	8557	6.2
213 Trust Companies	16	0.3	2802	2.0
221 Investment Dealers	136	2.8	6721	4.9
231 Consumer and Business Finance	8	0.2	788	0.6
233 Business Finance	46	1.0	445	0.3
241 Life Insurance	117	2.4	10,254	7.4
242 General Insurance	65	1.3	4540	3.3
244 Insurance Agencies	215	4.4	2458	1.8
251 Real Estate Developers	61	1.3	794	0.6
Other	409	8.4	14,698	10.7
Business services	1732	35.7	17,856	13.0
311 Law Firms	816	16.8	6492	4.7
321 Accountants	195	4.0	3761	2.7
333 Management Cons., Personnel Services	48	1.0	363	0.3
334 Management Cons., Actuaries	19	0.4	289	0.2
336 Management Cons., Market Research	24	0.5	312	0.2
341 Advertising Agencies	136	2.8	2989	2.2
342 Public Relations Consultants	66	1.4	374	0.3
Other	428	8.8	3276	2.4
Technical services	290	6.0	3842	2.8
411 Architects	102	2.1	1022	0.7
413 Town Planners	12	0.2	69	0.1
421 Diversified Engineering	14	0.3	1174	0.8
422 Construction Engineering	60	1.2	943	0.7
426 Mining Services	53	1.1	292	0.2
Other	49	1.0	342	0.2
Communication and media	265	5.5	8519	6.2
Associations	435	9.0	4918	3.6
611 General Civic Associations	169	3.5	2441	1.8
612 Business Associations	144	3.0	1422	1.0
Other	122	2.5	1065	0.8
Government	128	2.6	30,081	21.8
Other offices	271	5.6	2470	1.8
Total	4852	100.0	137,740	100.0

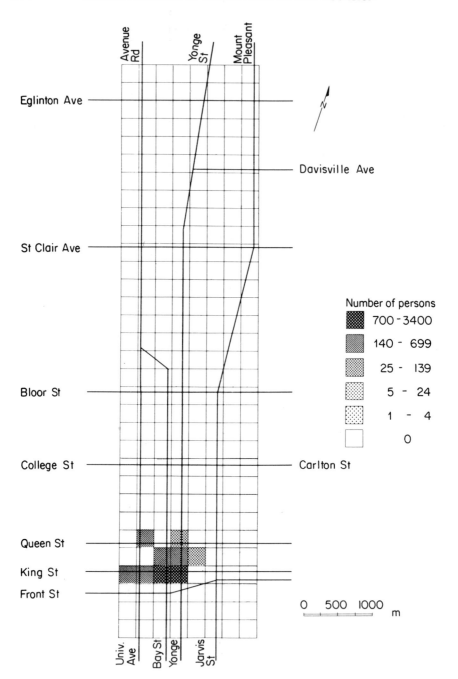

Fig. 11.5. Employment in Banks (excluding branches)

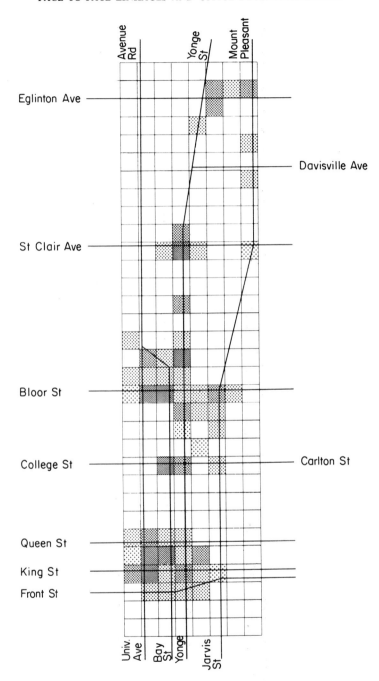

Advertising Agencies, Central Corridor

varying levels of spatial and industrial aggregation. The results shown here are for spatial units of 500 by 500 metres (i.e. four times the size of the units shown in Fig. 11.5) and 68 industry classes.

The factor analysis is based on logarithmically transformed percentage data. Only a small number of large correlation coefficients are apparent: of 3273 possible correlation coefficients, a mere 65 are equal to or larger than 0.5. Generally low correlation coefficients are reflected in a small percentage of explained variance: the first five factors account only for 37 per cent and the first 10 factors for 57 per cent.

The factor structure (Table 11.2) is complicated and not easy to interpret. Mapping of factor scores, however, aids greatly in the interpretation. Factors 1 and 10 stand out with low to high factor scores concentrated in a small area south of Queen Street. Variable loadings suggest that these two factors capture a cluster consisting of mining, financial and some transportation activities. The factor score maps for all the other factors show no particularly striking distribution patterns. Medium to high factor scores appear in various locations throughout the central area and resemble the many shades of the distribution patterns portrayed in the single-variable maps.

Cluster analysis, used to identify grid cells with similar employment composition, does not offer any further insight into the spatial structure of Toronto's central office complex. The procedure used identifies three groups of spatial units: those with relatively high proportions of employment in mining and financial activities, all contiguous and spatially concentrated in the area south of Queen Street; a large number of units, which can be found at most nodes in the study area, with a very broad mix of employment; and a small number of highly specialized units, mostly showing low office employment densities and occurring in locations peripheral to the major office employment nodes.

Analyses at lower levels of spatial aggregation (e.g. using the 250 × 250 metre grid cells) do not significantly alter the picture. The cluster of activities located south of Queen Street stands out as remarkably stable, whereas other variable or spatial unit groupings change moderately to considerably. The choice of the level of spatial aggregation is obviously important. It seems that the 250 by 250 metre grid is too finely-grained, whereas at the 500 by 500 metre level spatial variations might already be evened out. More analysis with filters between those two levels and with different grid alignments might be worthwhile. A more finely-grained locational pattern of industries in the high-density core south of Queen Street and a coarser texture in the other parts of the Central Corridor could complicate such analysis.

The outstanding spatial cluster south of Queen Street is generally known as the 'financial district' and coincides with the high-density core between Queen and Front Streets. Although employment in most financial activities is concentrated in this area, there are a number of industries not belonging to the financial sector which also show a strong degree of concentration: Mining, Mining Services, Law Firms, Accountants, as well as some of the industries belonging to the media and

Table 11.2. Factor Loadings: Industry Divisions and 500 by 500 Metre Grid*

Factor no.	Factor loadings†	Industry code	Industry division	% variance expl. Each Factor	Cumulative
1	0.90	11	Mining	14.7	14.7
	(0.49	13	Transportation)		
	0.93	21	Banks & Trust Co's		
	0.92	22	Investment Services		
	(0.49	32	Accounting)		
2	0.56	13	Transportation	12.7	27.4
	0.52	36	Personnel Agencies		
	0.56	39	Other Business Services		
	0.85	74	Foreign Government		
3	0.75	29	Misc. Fin., Insur., R.E.	7.8	35.2
	0.75	42	Engineering Consultants		
	0.72	81	Construction, Trade, Personal Services		
4	0.90	33	Management Consultants	6.3	41.5
	0.83	52	Publishers		
5	0.75	12	Manufacturing	5.8	47.3
	0.56	35	Industrial Designers		
	−0.50	73	Municipal Government		
6	0.50	14	Utilities	5.6	52.9
	0.55	36	Personnel Agencies		
	0.58	39	Other Business Services		
	0.74	51	Radio, TV & Motion Pict.		
7	0.84	23	Financing	5.0	57.9
	0.59	24	Insurance		
8	0.77	61	Associations	4.7	62.6
	−0.77	72	Provincial Government		
9	0.65	31	Law Firms	4.3	66.9
10	0.58	25	Real Estate	4.0	70.9
	(0.49	41	Architects & Town Pl.)		
	−0.65	71	Federal Government		

*Logarithmically transformed percentage data (employment). 28 variables (industry divisions) and 48 observations (500 by 500 metre grid cells). Orthogonal rotation of 10 factors with eigenvalues ≥1.0.
†Only variables with loadings ≥0.50 or ≤ − 0.50 included.

transportation divisions. Other industries, which are distributed throughout the Central Corridor are also represented to varying degrees in the so-called 'financial district' contributing to make it the most complex office area in Toronto.

The absence of specialized office clusters in central Toronto does not conform to the often expressed belief that a series of activity clusters may be found in the central area of large cities. The observations made in Toronto, however, are supported by empirical studies carried out elsewhere. Particularly important are Goddard's findings based on a thorough analysis of central London office employment data. His conclusions concerning activity clusters suggest that discrete, or clearly recognizable, complexes of offices are restricted to the City of London, and that outside the City the spatial arrangement of office activities appears to be far less structured (Goddard, 1973, pp. 138, 152).

The findings described here obviously have implications for decentralization policies. It could be suggested that the majority of office activities are able to 'survive', in economic terms, within a relatively wide range of locations. The argument can be made that it does not matter where in the central area a certain office locates as long as the office is somewhere within the central area. This argument loses some of its power when offices outside the central area are considered. In the case of Toronto no systematic inventory of various office activities in 'suburban' areas exists, but impressions gained in this study point to the fact that locational flexibility stretches beyond the confines of the central office agglomeration. For instance, 23 per cent of Metropolitan Toronto's Law Firms, about 50 per cent of all Accountants, 15 per cent of the 'elite' Advertising Agencies and 62 per cent of Engineering Consultants were located outside the Central Corridor in 1971. Moreover, head and large regional offices of manufacturing and insurance companies can be found in suburban locations along with the data centres of a wide range of industries. Again, the locational flexibility of certain kinds of offices is well documented and not unique to Toronto (Foley, 1957; Riquet, 1966; Goddard, 1967; Merriman, 1967; Gad, 1968; Armstrong, 1972; Lichtenberger, 1972; Bannon, 1973; Manners, 1974).

Face-to-Face Linkages

The web of information linkages is one of the most intriguing aspects of office location, irrespective of whether the questions are asked by researchers preoccupied with explaining existing location patterns or by planners in search of prescriptions. Several key ideas have aroused and kept alive interest in the nature and role of communication links: 'transportation of intelligence' (Haig, 1926, p. 427), 'knowledge in a hurry' (Robins and Terleckyj, 1960, p. 33), the central business district as a 'highly specialized machine for producing, processing and trading specialized intelligence' (Hall, 1966, p. 239), or 'the interweaving of quaternary activities' (Gottman, 1970, p. 322). Regrettably, in the heat of debate over the possibility of decentralizing offices, the discussion of linkages has often been reduced to the simple question of which offices 'need' face-to-face contacts and which ones do not. That this approach is simplistic has become more than apparent in the research of the past 10–15 years, and a more complicated differentiation of offices according to several facets of information flows has been recognized (see particularly Thorngren, 1970, p. 415, and Goddard, 1973, pp. 183–199). There are many questions concerning empirically observable linkages at any particular point in time, the stability of linkages under conditions of locational, technological or economic change, and the relationship between communication linkages and other location factors. Although the importance of all these questions is recognized, the following discussion is restricted to existing face-to-face linkages between different types of businesses or industries, ignoring other modes of communication, the question of substitutability of communication modes, or other broader questions.

The examination of communication linkages is an immense task, particularly when answers are sought through empirical approaches. A special problem arises when the emphasis is on inter-industry or sectoral contacts. While the interest is focused on establishments or organizational units, it is the individual who is the communicator and often the sole person fully knowledgeable about the various aspects of a business contact. Thus, in order to acquire reliable data, communication events have to be recorded by individuals (Goddard, 1973, pp. 154–157). Methods have then to be found by which the communication behaviour of individuals can be summed in order to arrive at the aggregate communication pattern of an organizational unit.

Two routes towards this aim can be considered: either the whole staff of several establishments of the same industry are monitored and the contact patterns of these several establishments are averaged, or the linkage patterns of individuals are synthesized into linkage patterns of establishments. The second approach was adopted in the central Toronto study. The organizational units for which these synthetic patterns of face-to-face linkages have been constructed are termed 'model establishments', each of which is representative of an industry. The six steps used to arrive at the linkages of model establishments involved:

1.   Collecting information about the employment composition (job types) for samples of establishments from sampled industries;

2.   Construction of model employment compositions, one each for 30 industries, using averages and particularly well-structured organization charts;

3.   Collecting information about the face-to-face linkages of a sample of persons by means of diaries or questionnaires;

4.   Forming average interaction patterns for the various job types and occupations within each of the surveyed industries;

5.   Weighting the average interaction patterns described under (4) by the frequency of occurrence of a certain job type determined as described under (2);

6.   Adding the weighted average interaction patterns.

This approach is methodologically not very elegant. It violates the principle that statements based on one unit of analysis (here the individual person) should not be used to make statements about another unit of analysis (here the establishment). It makes it impossible to adhere to strict random or stratified random sampling and makes the use of inferential statistics extremely hazardous if not irrelevant. It is difficult, however, to think of other practical ways which permit the monitoring of face-to-face contacts originating from organizational units.

It is impossible to present here a detailed account of the myriad of procedural details and dozens of qualifications concerning the collected data.[5] Diaries, covering a one-week period, were used as principal monitoring instruments. These diaries were brief, covering only *external* face-to-face meetings and information about the meeting partner's business associations (industry) and location of normal place of work. External face-to-face meetings include those between locationally separate parts of the same firm or organization (e.g. meetings between head and branch office staff).

The alternative to the diary, a recall questionnaire of the programmed type, consisted of a list of activities constructed with the aid of the Standard Industrial Classification and the semifinished inventory of central Toronto offices. An accompanying explanatory letter requested the respondent to estimate the total number of meetings he may have had with all the representatives of establishments under a certain industry category within a time-span he felt to be appropriate for reporting.

Sampling involved a three-tiered approach. First, from the large number of office activities or industries a few had to be selected for study. Secondly, within each of these industries establishments had to be selected; and thirdly, in cooperation with the management of participating establishments, diaries or questionnaires had to be channelled to selected individuals. The survey was started in July of 1971 and with some exceptions the material used was received by April 1972. Altogether 1060 persons returned diaries and 541 filled in questionnaires.

The linkage patterns discussed below are for 30 model establishments. The industries they represent and the status and size characteristics of the model establishments are shown in Table 11.3 along with the number of establishments which have supplied useful employment composition data, the number of diaries and questionnaires available for the construction of each model establishment, and an indication of whether the linkage intensities and inter-industry linkages discussed below are based on diaries or questionnaires.

Since the job classification used for the construction of model establishments is based on a hierarchial system, it is possible to arrive at the interaction pattern at various levels of aggregation. It has been assumed that certain jobs do not vary strongly between industries belonging to the same broad area of activity. If diaries for certain job types were not available or only available in very small numbers, the 'borrowing' of interaction patterns was used. In this way one arrives not at one linkage pattern for a model establishment, but a series of them. Further discussion below is based on a relatively high level of job aggregation and a minimal amount of 'borrowing'.

Only selected aspects of the face-to-face linkages recorded in the context of this

Table 11.3. Characteristics of Model Establishments and Data Base

Industry	Establishment status	Size class	Employment composition (no. of establishments)	Diaries (no. of persons)	Questionnaires (no. of persons)
111 Mining	Head	21–50	5	25*	11
121 Integrated Oil Companies	Head	400+	1	56*	—
122 Manufacturing	Head	51–150	7	187*	42
122 Manufacturing	Branch	1–20	4	15*	—
1341 Shipping Agencies	Branch	1–20	6	8*	10
1343 Customs Brokers	All	21–50	3	1	7*
211 Banks	Head	400+	1	—	112*
213 Trust Companies	Head	151–400	3	60*	58
2211 Investment Dealers	All	51–150	7	20	28*
231 Consumer and Business Finance	Head	51–150	3	15*	—
233 Business Finance	Branch	1–20	5	15*	—
241 Life Insurance	Head	400+	4	180*	87
242 General Insurance	Head	51–150	3	15*	23
244 Insurance Agencies	All	51–150	3	15*	3
251 Real Estate Developers	All	21–50	5	51*	12
311 Law Firms	All	21–50	4	15	21*
3211 Accountants	All	1–20	6	12*	15
3212 Accountants/Management Consultants	All	21–50	4	43*	5
3331 Executive Search Consultants	All	1–20	4	6*	—
334 Actuaries/Employee Benefits Consult.	All	21–50	2	12*	—
336 Market Research	All	21–50	4	16	20*
3411 Advertising Agencies	All	21–50	4	59*	13
342 Public Relations Consultants	All	1–20	5	10*	6
411 Architects	All	21–50	4	43*	23
413 Town Planners	All	1–20	5	14*	10
421 Diversified Engineering Consultants	All	51–150	2	24*	9
422 Construction Engineering Consultants	All	21–50	6	40*	20
426 Mining Services	All	1–20	5	6*	6
611 Civic Associations	Unilocational	51–150	1	10*	—
612 Business Associations	Head	51–150	1	11*	—
Other	N.A.	N.A.	96	63	—
All industries	N.A.	N.A.	213	1047	541

*Indicates whether diaries or questionnaires were used in calculating linkage intensities and inter-industry linkages discussed below.

central Toronto study can be discussed here. The linkage facets emphasized will be those which are important in the debate about intra-metropolitan decentralization. These are linkage intensity, the geographic location of meeting or contact partners and some aspects of the inter-industry or sectoral relationships.

The terms linkage partners, meeting partners and contact partners are used interchangeably; they refer to the persons met by the survey respondents or model establishment representatives. The industry categories used to classify the meeting partners are referred to collectively as the meeting partner industries. The linkages or interactions between the model establishments and the meeting partner industries are measured in links per week. Links are different from meetings in that they indicate the number of establishments involved in meetings. When the survey respondent or diary-keeper meets with one or several representatives of one other establishment, the meeting and link would be identical. In many instances, however, more than one establishment, other than the diary-keeper's, is involved in a meeting. The ratio of links to meetings varies slightly between model establishments or from occupation to occupation; the overall average is about 1.1 links per meeting. The terms interaction pattern or linkage pattern refer to the list or array of meeting partners with which the respondents and the model establishments interact.

The magnitude and intensity of linkages for the 30 model establishments is shown in Table 11.4 (see also Fig. 11.6). The total number of links per model establishment is, to a large extent, a function of establishment size. For instance, the three model establishments with more than 500 links per week (Banks, Integrated Oil Companies and Life Insurance) also belong to the largest establishment size class considered (over 400 employees).

In order to remove the effect of establishment size, the total number of links can be divided, either by the total number of employees constituting a model establishment, or by the number of 'communicators'. A communicator is defined as someone who might have external face-to-face contacts at least occasionally. For most model establishments the communicators are identical with the non-clerical staff.

Both the link/employee and link/communicator ratio are measures of linkage intensity. Both have implications for deconcentration. The link/communicator ratio may be a more important, though somewhat conservative measure. It indicates the intensity of face-to-face contacts of specialists, managers and executives, who must meet schedules regardless of whether a large or small number of non-communicators (who have a considerable weight when link/employment ratios are calculated) support them. Because of this the link/communicator ratio is used in further discussion.

The linkage intensities show a remarkably wide range of values from a low of 2.9 to a high of 13.5 links per communicator per week (mean 6.9, median 6.4). Generalizations about the distribution of industries across this range are difficult. There seems to be a slight trend which puts some of the business services

Table 11.4. Linkage Characteristics of Model Establishments*

Model establishments (industries)	Total no. of links†	Links/ emp.‡	Links/ com.**	Links in central Toronto§
				%
111 Mining	136	3.4	7.2	58.3
121 Integrated Oil Companies	1271	2.4	4.0	33.1
122 Manufacturing, Head Offices	263	2.4	4.2	32.7
122 Manufacturing, Branch Offices	31	1.9	5.2	21.7
1341 Shipping Agencies	66	9.4	13.2	42.5
1343 Customs Brokers	98	3.9	8.9	42.5
211 Banks	1729	2.1	7.6	70.0
213 Trust Companies	452	1.7	6.4	75.4
2211 Investment Dealers	199	2.5	4.7	78.5
231 Consumer and Business Finance	118	1.9	5.6	23.8
233 Business Finance	38	4.2	6.3	30.8
241 Life Insurance	567	0.7	2.9	53.5
242 General Insurance	226	3.2	7.8	32.1
244 Insurance Agencies	253	2.5	5.9	64.7
251 Real Estate Developers	161	4.5	9.5	46.1
311 Law Firms	270	6.8	13.5	84.0
3211 Accountants	66	3.7	5.5	34.4
3212 Accountants/Management Consultants	216	4.7	6.2	51.0
3331 Executive Search Consultants	86	7.2	9.6	61.4
334 Actuaries/Employee Benefits Consult.	162	2.9	6.5	31.9
336 Market Research	61	2.0	4.4	47.9
3411 Advertising Agencies	206	5.4	7.6	59.1
342 Public Relations Consultants	121	8.1	12.1	69.3
411 Architects	145	3.6	6.3	35.3
413 Town Planners	43	2.7	4.3	30.5
421 Diversified Engineering Consultants	134	1.5	4.5	32.3
422 Construction Engineering Consultants	161	4.2	8.1	37.4
426 Mining Services	35	5.0	7.0	70.4
611 Civic Associations	198	3.0	7.3	65.4
612 Business Associations	175	2.6	5.6	38.5

*The figures in this table are subject to several qualifications. See Note 5.
†Total number of links per week. For definition of 'link' see text, p. 302.
‡Number of links per employee per week.
**Number of links per communicator per week. For definition of communicator see text, p. 302.
§Percentage of all meeting partner (establishment) locations in Central Corridor. For location and extent of Central Corridor see Figs. 11.1 and 11.3.

and smaller model establishments at the upper end of the range, and some of the big head offices and small research-oriented model establishments at the lower end. Amongst big head office model establishments, Banks and Trust Companies are an exception: with 7.6 links per communicator, they are close to the mean value and are sharply differentiated from some of the other head offices (e.g.

Manufacturing 4.2, Integrated Oil Companies 4.0, and Life Insurance 2.9 links per communicator).

Financial activities, very often believed to be at the communication-intensive core of the central office agglomerations, demonstrate considerable variation in linkage intensities: Banks lead with 7.6 links per communicator per week, followed by Trust Companies (6.4), Business Finance branches (6.3), Consumer–Business Finance head offices (5.6), and Investment Dealers (4.7). If these figures reflect 'reality' with a reasonable degree of accuracy, then the relatively low linkage intensity for Investment Dealers is remarkable, although not entirely unexpected. Investment Dealers or stockbrokers are among the oldest office functions, which may have led to a high degree of standardization of business procedures. They are also the type of business into which electronic communication technology of almost every kind has made deep inroads.

The geographic distribution of the establishments represented by the meeting partners recorded in the diaries is complex. In the case of some industries the proportion of the meeting partners' workplace locations declines regularly with distance from the central area. There are examples, however, where the Central Corridor accounts for an extremely large share of the meeting partners' locations or where locations outside the *Census* Metropolitan Area are strongly over-represented. Of major interest in the discussion of office decentralization at the intra-metropolitan scale is the proportion of links that exist between the model establishments and other establishments in the Central Corridor. Table 11.4 gives a detailed account of the percentage of meeting partner establishments located in the Central Corridor and Fig. 11.6 conveys these proportions in graphic form. The proportion of meeting partner locations in the Central Corridor ranges from about 22 per cent for the sales branches of Manufacturing companies to 84 per cent for Law Firms. The mean within this range lies at 48.5 per cent, the median at 46.1 per cent.

Among the model establishments with higher percentages (about 60–84 per cent) of meeting partners in the Central Corridor are some business services and some of the financial activities. Although the linkage intensities of these model establishments range from low to high, there is a clear trend towards the higher linkage intensities. With the exception of Public Relations Consultants, the model establishments involved are themselves strongly concentrated within the Central Corridor and there are many inter-industry linkages between these activities. The strong concentration of meeting partners in the Central Corridor can be interpreted as being the result of spatial and functional clustering.

A variety of model establishments can be found at the other end of the spectrum (22–38 per cent of meeting partners in the Central Corridor). These include technical services which are part of the urban development industry, business services, some financial activities, and manufacturing company offices. Most of these are characterized by low to medium linkage intensities and dispersion within the Central Corridor. They have inter-industry linkage

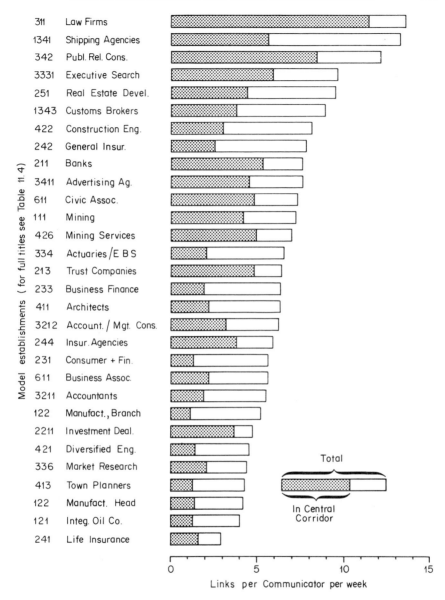

Fig. 11.6. Linkage characteristics of model establishments

patterns which indicate that interaction within the model establishments' own organizations and interaction with manufacturing and with other generally dispersed economic and administrative units play a great role.

The inter-industry or sectoral communication patterns are complex and defy

easy generalizations. The interrelationships between the 30 industries represented by model establishments and 40 potential kinds of meeting partners are
illustrated in Fig. 11.7 (an explanation of the mnemonics used in the figure is given
in Table 11.5). This interaction matrix, which indicates the strength of linkages by
the link/communicator ratio, is not symmetrical: the model establishments along
the vertical axis represent highly specific industries, whereas the meeting partners
along the horizontal axis are grouped into more general industry divisions. The
reason for the higher level of aggregation of the meeting partners lies partially in
the technical problem of handling over 100 variables and partially in the hazards
of allocating the establishments named or described in the diaries correctly to
rather specific categories of businesses. While it is impossible to comment
extensively on the information provided in Fig. 11.7, a few general points may be
kept in mind on inspection of the matrix.

The model establishments vary greatly with regard to the concentration of
linkages: for instance, in the case of Real Estate Developers 12 different kinds of
meeting partners account for 75 per cent of all links, whereas in the case of
Executive Search Consultants only five industry divisions account for 75 per cent
of all links. Over 42 per cent of the links of the Executive Search Consultants are
with one type of meeting partner, namely individuals.

When the model establishments are compared with regard to the mix of
meeting partners, some stand out by having a unique mix while others display
features common to a number of model establishments. For example, Real
Estate Developers, Law Firms or Advertising Agencies each have very distinct
patterns of industries they interact with. Others such as the head offices of
Mining, Integrated Oil Companies, Manufacturing, Consumer/Business
Finance, or Life Insurance have similar patterns. Intra-organization links, i.e.
links with establishments of their own firm, are the most important in percentage
terms; intra-industry links and links with the 'Other Business Services' category
including Data Processing are also prominent.

An interesting picture is gained by examining which of the meeting partner
industries are in relatively strong demand by many model establishments and
which ones by only a few. A look at the columns in Fig. 11.7, for instance, reveals
that Manufacturing (as a meeting partner) is outstanding: every model
establishment interacts with Manufacturing. For 18 of the 30 model establishments Manufacturing is either the first or second most important linkage partner
in quantitative terms. Little can be said about the quality of these links, but the
impression gained during diary coding indicates that many of these are the result
of field salesmen from manufacturing companies visiting the surveyed establishments.

'Individuals', i.e. persons interacting with the surveyed establishments in their
capacity as private citizens rather than representatives of a business, appear as
important meeting partners for a number of model establishments. Job-seekers
partially account for the interaction between 'individuals' and some of the model

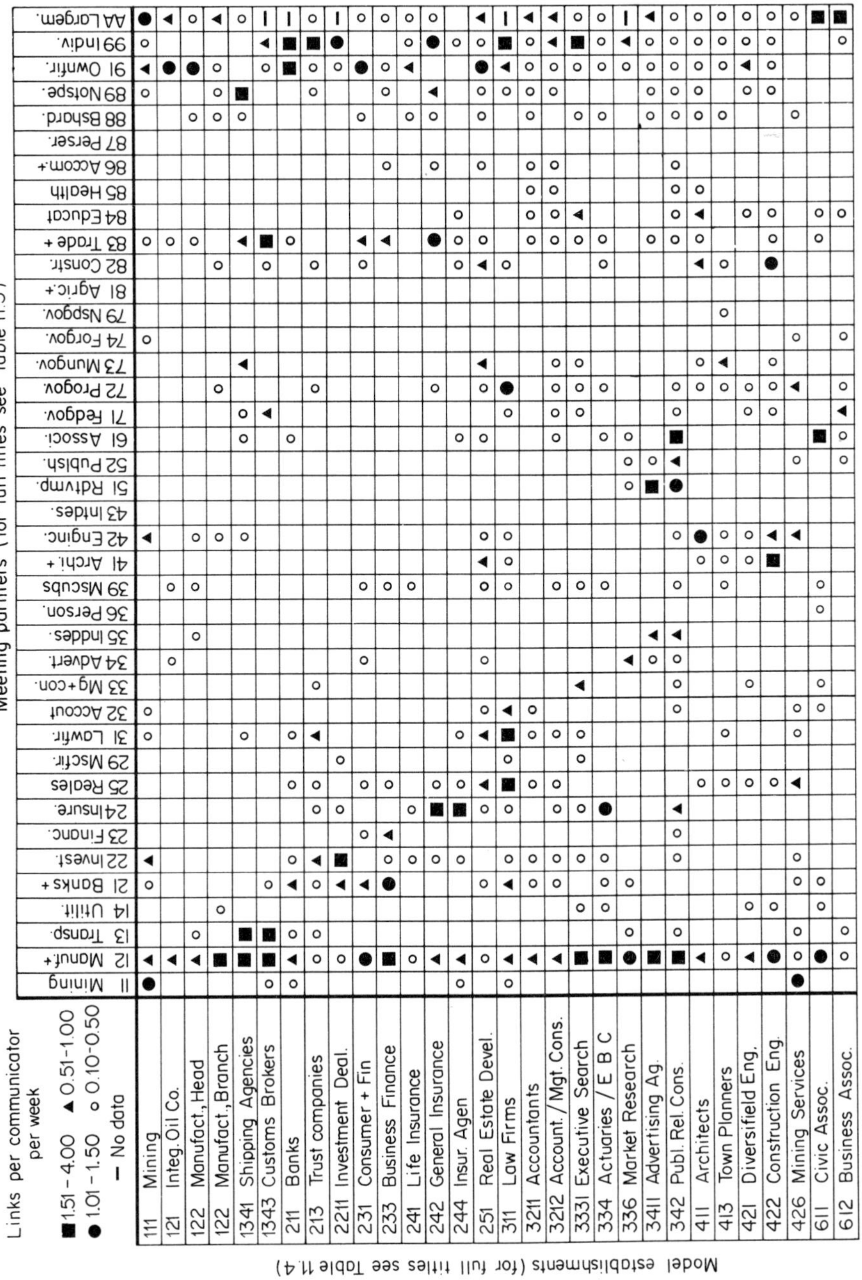

Meeting partners (for full titles see Table 11.5)

Links per communicator per week

■ 1.51 - 4.00   ◄ 0.51-1.00
● 1.01 - 1.50   o 0.10-0.50
— No data

Model establishments (for full titles see Table 11.4)

Fig. 11.7. Inter-industry linkage matrix (links per communicator per week)

Table 11.5. Classification of Meeting Partners (Industries) and Abbreviations

Ind. code	Abbreviations	Full title and remarks
11	Mining	Mining
12	Manuf+	Manufacturing a. Integrated Oil Companies
13	Transp	Transportation
14	Utilit	Utilities (including Ontario Hydro)
21	Banks+	Banks and Trust Companies
22	Invest	Investment Services
23	Financ	Financing
24	Insure	Insurance
25	Reales	Real Estate
29	Mscfir	Miscellaneous Finance, Insurance a. Real Estate
31	Lawfir	Law Firms
32	Accout	Accountants
33	Mgtcon	Management Consultants
34 ·	Advert	Advertising and Promotional Services
35	Inddes	Industrial Designers (Packaging Designers)
36	Person	Personnel Agencies
39	Mscbus	Other Business Services (incl. Data Processing a. Investigation Services)
41	Archi+	Architects and Town Planners
42	Enginc	Engineering Consultants
43	Intdes	Interior Designers
51	Rdtvmp	Radio, TV and Motion Pictures
52	Publsh	Publishers
61	Associ	Associations
71	Fedgov	Federal Government
72	Progov	Provincial Government (incl. Courts)
73	Mungov	Municipal Government (incl. Toronto Harbour Comm.)
74	Forgov	Foreign Government (incl. Tourist Information Office a. Trade Commissions)
79	Nspgov	Government, not further specified
81	Agric+	Agriculture, Fishing, Forestry
82	Constr	Construction
83	Trade+	Trade (incl. Retail, Wholesale, Manufacturers' Agents, Service Stations)
84	Educat	Education (incl. Libraries a. Museums)
85	Health	Health and Welfare Services (except Government Departments and Associations)
86	Accom+	Accommodation, Food and Recreation
87	Perser	Personal Services
88	Bshard	Business Services (Hardware)
89	Nospec	Other and Not Specified
91	Ownfir	Establishments of own firm with a different location from that of reporting establishment
99	Indivi	Individual consumers, clients, employees, prospective employees, etc.
AA	Largmm	Meetings with representatives from more than six establishments present

establishments. On the other hand, the diaries show that in the case of Trust Companies, Investment Dealers, Law Firms and General Insurance, 'individuals' form a substantial proportion of meeting partners. This indicates that the central office complex may still be a place of high-order consumer services, rather than a pure business management complex.

The identification of functional clusters has serious limitations, chiefly because of the asymmetry of the interaction matrix. It is only possible to sketch the rough outlines of the network of linkages at present, and Fig. 11.8 illustrates the emerging network of interaction when linkages with more than 0.5 links/communicator/week are considered. Since Manufacturing shares links with 23 of the 30 model establishments at this level of intensity, it has been omitted from the discussion of functional clusters. It can be argued that three functional clusters are identifiable, with fairly strong links between two of these clusters. One of these clusters consists of financial activities (Banks and Trust Companies, Consumer/Business Finance and Business Finance, Investment Dealers and Mining). The other one, related to the first, consists of Real Estate Developers, Architects and Town Planners, Engineering Consultants, and Construction, as well as Municipal Government and Education as peripheral network members. These two clusters are joined by Law Firms and Engineering Consultants. While the link formed by Engineering Consultants is very weak, the one formed by Law Firms is extraordinarily strong and begs the question where, if at all, these two clusters should be separated. However, when all links have been considered, including those at a very low level, the balance tips slightly in favour of allocating Law Firms to the 'finance-mining' cluster.

Another functional cluster revolves around Advertising, Public Relations and the media. Although media establishments were not sampled, the Radio, Television and Motion Picture category turns out to contain the most important meeting partners for both Public Relations Consultants and Advertising Agencies. These two activities also interact with Industrial Designers. Other links of Public Relations Consultants involve Associations and Publishing, and Advertising Agencies have links with Market Research. If Publishing, Radio/TV/Motion Pictures and Industrial Designers had been among the model establishments studied, a denser network may have been visible.

On the basis of Fig. 11.8 one may be tempted to identify a further functional cluster centred on Trade, with strong links between Trade and Shipping Agencies and Customs Brokers on the one hand, and General Insurance and Insurance Agencies on the other. Although there are precedents for the functional and spatial clustering of shipping, wholesale and transportation insurance activities, it is highly doubtful whether the linkages shown in Fig. 11.8 reflect this historic association. The complete interaction matrix (see Fig. 11.7) shows Trade to be a fairly ubiquitous meeting partner for the model establishments studied, albeit at a fairly low level of linkage intensity.

It is interesting to note the relationship between functional and spatial clusters.

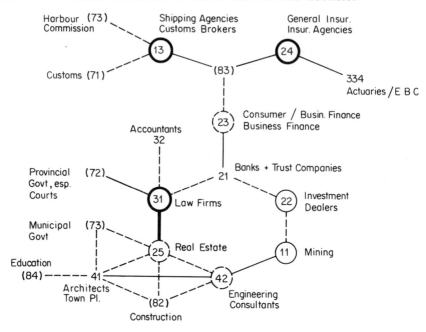

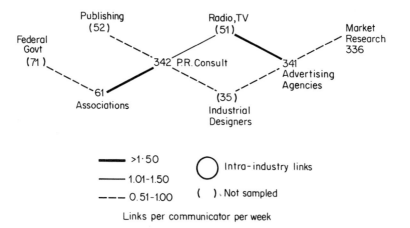

Fig. 11.8. Generalized linkage network (based on links per communicator ratio). For full industry titles see Tables 11.4 and 11.5

Most of the model establishments belonging to the 'finance–mining–law' clusters are spatially very concentrated in the area south of Queen Street, whereas the activities belonging to the functional cluster 'urban development industry' are all highly dispersed within the Central Corridor. Functional and spatial clustering explains, of course, why Law Firms, Banks, Trust Companies, Investment Dealers, Mining Companies and Mining Services have a large to very large proportion of meeting partners within the Central Corridor. With the exception of Real Estate Developers, the 'urban development industries' covered in the survey have only relatively few of their meeting partners in the Central Corridor (37.4 per cent or fewer). This observation indicates that the functional cluster formed by the 'urban development industries' does not coincide with a spatial cluster. There is the possibility that spatial clustering at the scale of the Central Corridor as a whole, however, may apply to Advertising Agencies, Public Relations Consultants and the media. According to the standard distance measures discussed earlier, Public Relations Consultants are dispersed within the Central Corridor and Advertising Agencies are highly dispersed. Since the meeting partners of these two industries are predominantly located within the Central Corridor (59.1 per cent for Advertising Agencies and 69.3 per cent for Public Relations Consultants), one could argue that they are part of a functional–spatial cluster with a network of links diffused throughout the Central Corridor.

Decentralization Potentials

Although the data on face-to-face linkages are more indicative than conclusive (due to small sample sizes and the inferential problems associated with the aggregation of individuals into organizations), some conclusions can be drawn about which industries would find it possible to decentralize without incurring grave 'communication damage'. There are two major criteria which should be used to make judgments about locational flexibility: linkage intensity and the spatial concentration of meeting partners. Low linkage intensity and a small proportion of meeting partners in the central area would result in relatively small direct and indirect increases in travel cost after decentralization. In order to combine these two criteria into a single measure, the percentage indicating the concentration of a model establishment's meeting partners in the Central Corridor has been applied to the 'links per communicator' measure. For example, Law Firms show 13.5 links per communicator and it has been estimated that 84 per cent of Law Firms' meeting partners are located in the Central Corridor; 80 per cent of the links or 11.3 links per communicator would be strongly affected by deconcentration. The resulting ratio, i.e. the number of links per communicator with meeting partners in the Central Corridor, has been labelled here as the 'communication damage index'.

The model establishments are ranked according to their communicator damage indices in Table 11.6. The indices range from 1.1 to 11.3 (mean 3.5; median 3.2). Although there are some natural breaks in this range, particularly at the upper end, it shows remarkable continuity. This continuity poses a dilemma, since it is obviously impossible to arrive at a simple dichotomy of industries

Table 11.6. Communication Damage Index and Measure of Dispersion
(Model Establishments Ranked by Communication Damage Index)

Model Establishments (industries)	Communication damage index*	Standard distance (km)	Concentration within Central Corridor % employment North of Queen St	Concentration within Metropolitan Toronto†
311 Law Firms	11.3	0.9	8.7	3
342 Public Relations Consultants	8.4	1.8	50.5	2
3331 Executive Search Consultants	5.9	2.8††	60.7	1
1341 Shipping Agencies	5.6	0.6††	6.9	1
211 Banks	5.3	0.2	0.0	1/P
426 Mining Services	4.9	0.6	4.1	2
213 Trust Companies	4.8	0.2	0.0	1
611 Civic Associations	4.8	2.0	83.7	2
3411 Advertising Agencies	4.5	2.0††	68.3	3
251 Real Estate Developers	4.4	2.8	49.2	2
111 Mining	4.2	0.9	1.9	1
1343 Customs Brokers	3.8	0.6††	0.4	1
244 Insurance Agencies	3.8	1.8	19.1	3
2211 Investment Dealers	3.7	20.3††	0.0	1
3212 Accountants/Management Consultants	3.2	1.5††	5.5	1
422 Construction Engineering Consultants	3.0	2.1	79.2	3
242 General Insurance	2.5	1.5	30.8	3
411 Architects	2.2	2.2	72.0	3
612 Business Associations	2.2	2.2	44.4	2
334 Actuaries/Employee Benefit Consult.	2.1	1.9	38.4	2
336 Market Research	2.1	2.3	94.9	2
233 Business Finance	1.9	2.6	38.0	2
3211 Accountants	1.9	1.5††	32.2	3
241 Life Insurance	1.6	1.7	69.2	2
122 Manufacturing, Head Offices	1.4	2.4	59.2	2
421 Diversified Engineering Consultants	1.4	2.8	41.3	3
121 Integrated Oil Companies	1.3	2.0	100.0	2/P
231 Consumer and Business Finance	1.3	1.6	100.0	3
413 Town Planners	1.3	2.1	84.1	3
122 Manufacturing, Branch Offices	1.1	2.3	59.2	3

* Defined as number of links per communicator per week with meeting partner in Central Corridor (for further explanation see text).

† Estimate of concentration: 1, all establishments in Central Corridor, only very few exceptions outside; 2, several establishments known to be outside Central Corridor; 3, more than 20 per cent of establishments outside Central Corridor; P indicates the occurrence of 'partial' deconcentration.

†† Standard distance only available for three-digit industry classes.

which 'need' and those which 'don't need' face-to-face linkages; and there are no theoretical or empirical grounds on the basis of which judgments could be made about the possibilities for decentralization. Given the comparative approach chosen for the study discussed here, and the difficulty of bringing other research to bear on the continuum of communication damage indices, the points at which cuts can be made have to be determined on the basis of what benefits various levels of decentralization yield. These benefits are difficult to calculate and may affect various interest groups in different ways. Conceivably, benefits could be compared to the increased communication costs incurred through de-centralization. Even this task faces enormous practical obstacles, since the linkages observed and measured are based on a spatial structure which would change through the relocation.

It can be argued that the present location patterns of various kinds of offices and particularly the dynamics of locational change may be of value in interpreting the communication damage indices and in making decisions about decentralization possibilities. If it can be observed that establishments belonging to a certain industry 'survive' in one or several locations outside the central area over a reasonable length of time, then one could conclude that all, or at least most, establishments of this industry could 'survive' in non-central locations. If location patterns are fluid with a clear trend towards a relative increase of those establishments in non-central locations, then the argument gains particular strength. This does not imply, of course, that industries which do not display such locational behaviour cannot also be urged to decentralize. This argument, which is basically a very conservative one, gives credence to those activities which demonstrate persistent spatial concentration. The argument suggested above has not been fully explored here, mainly because of the lack of reasonably detailed and accurate data on office activities outside the central agglomeration. Thus the following paragraphs provide only tentative suggestions.

In Table 11.6 an attempt was made to juxtapose communication characteristics, expressed through the communication damage index, with several measures of spatial distribution. Two of these measures, relating to the distribution of various industries within the Central Corridor (standard distance, and the percentage of employment located north of Queen Street, i.e. outside the 'financial' district) can be stated in precise numerical terms. The other one; indicating the balance of distribution between Central Corridor and other areas of Toronto, can only be stated in the form of a very crude index.

There is a moderate inverse relationship between the communication damage index and geographic dispersion. In general, those model establishments which are dispersed or highly dispersed within the Central Corridor have relatively low communication damage indices, whereas those which are highly concentrated in the area south of Queen Street nearly all have above-average communication damage indices.

The model establishments representing Advertising Agencies and Real Estate

Developers are particularly interesting. Both have a communication damage index above average, and yet these activities are dispersed within the Central Corridor. Moreover, a recent study indicates that Advertising Agencies display a great deal of locational mobility (Handzink, 1977). For instance, of the 36 agencies existing in 1941 the vast majority (93 per cent) were located in the area south of Queen Street, whereas of the 130 agencies in 1976 only 21 per cent were found in that area. Only 6.7 per cent of the advertising agencies were located outside the Central Corridor in 1941, but by 1976 various 'suburban' locations outside the Central Corridor had attracted 25 per cent. Most of the advertising agencies now located in the 'suburbs' had moved from the Central Corridor. There are no indications of reverse moves from the 'suburbs' to the Central Corridor. This example demonstrates that even activities with high linkage frequencies (7.6 links per communicator) and a strong concentration of meeting partners in the central area (59.1 per cent in the Central Corridor) may be locationally more flexible than previously assumed.

In Table 11.7 the model establishments are grouped according to the degree of decentralization potential. Although the communication damage index has been used as a major criterion for the grouping, other factors have been taken into account, particularly present spatial distribution patterns, functional clustering, and linkages other than those conducted *via* face-to-face contacts. The last-mentioned are messenger linkages between financial activities such as Banks, Trust Companies, Investment Dealers, and perhaps Law Firms and Mining Companies to facilitate the exchange of financial documents.

The group of model establishments judged as showing considerable decentralization potential consists of quite varied industries. The head offices of Integrated Oil Companies, Manufacturing, Consumer and Business Finance, Life Insurance, and General Insurance account for a large amount of the employment that could be decentralized. The prominence of head offices may justify the speculation that head offices of industries not surveyed may also show considerable decentralization potential. Smaller model establishments which fall into this category are sales offices (Manufacturing, Business Finance) and certain 'business services' (e.g. Accountants, Architects). It is remarkable that among the 'business services' with considerable decentralization potential are several whose operations involve a fair amount of research (e.g. Market Research, Actuaries, Town Planners, diversified Engineering Consultants). It may be worthwhile in future investigations to determine whether relatively infrequent meetings associated with research are of the 'orientation' type (Thorngren, 1970), i.e. fairly long, prearranged meetings involving several persons and a wide range of discussion topics.

An additional factor, which supports the judgment that a number of industries have considerable decentralization potential, is the pattern of locational change of these industries. With the exception of Integrated Oil Companies and Actuaries, the offices of all other industries represented by the model establish-

Table 11.7. Decentralization Potential*

(a) *Considerable decentralization potential*
(Communication damage index: 1.1–2.5; percentage of employment north of Queen Street: 31–100%; standard distance: 1.5–2.8 km)

121	Integrated Oil Companies	3211	Accountants
122	Manufacturing, Head Offices	334	Actuaries/Employee Benefits Consult.
122	Manufacturing, Branch Offices		
231	Consumer and Business Finance	336	Market Research
		411	Architects
241	Life Insurance	413	Town Planners
242	General Insurance	421	Diversified Engineering Consultants

(b) *Some decentralization potential or uncertain*
(Communication damage index: 3.2–8.4; percentage of employment north of Queen Street: 5–80%; standard distance: 1.5–2.8 km)

244	Insurance Agencies	3411	Advertising Agencies
251	Real Estate Developers	342	Public Relations Consultants
3212	Accountants/Management Consultants	422	Construction Engineering Consultants
3331	Executive Search Consultants		

(c) *Restricted decentralization potential*
(Communication damage index: 3.7–11.3; percentage of employment north of Queen Street: 0–9%; standard distance: 0.2–0.9 km)

111	Mining	213	Trust Companies
1341	Shipping Agencies	2211	Investment Dealers
1343	Customs Brokers	311	Law Firms
211	Banks	426	Mining Services

*All model establishments except 611 Civic Associations and 612 Business Associations are included.

ments described as having considerable decentralization potential can now be found outside the Central Corridor in Toronto. Many have moved from the Central Corridor to other locations in Metropolitan Toronto over the last 10 years, while others have been newly established outside the Central Corridor. As far as Integrated Oil Companies are concerned, however, only regional offices and data centres have moved from the Central Corridor to 'suburban' locations.

It may be worthwhile to draw passing attention to the model establishments which have been judged as having 'restricted decentralization' potential. Amongst these are Banks and Investment Dealers (stockbrokers), which are invariably upheld as the prime members of spatial and functional clusters. Impressions gained from a variety of sources, however, point to the fact that communication linkages as important location factors may weaken in the future. For instance, there is a slight trend to partial decentralization in the case of banking. Of the big five Canadian chartered banks, all of which either have their head office or other very large and important regional offices in the Central Corridor, one bank has its data centre in suburban Don Mills, another has recently announced the relocation of its data centre from the heart of the financial district to a 'midtown' location (Yonge and College Streets), another one has its data centre at the periphery of the financial district, and two of the five have their data centres in-house or across the street. Financial markets seem to rely more and more on electronic communication modes and security depositories rather than the physical-spatial transfer of financial instruments such as share certificates or bonds. The further development of communication technology and practices in the financial markets may lead to a considerable weakening of the bonds which tie banks and stockbrokers to the traditional financial districts. It has been stressed above that the face-to-face linkage intensity displayed by investment dealers is already very low.

The findings concerning decentralization potentials should not be applied mechanically, since several reservations have to be made. First, the data base varies strongly from one model establishment to the other and, as explained before, it is possible to calculate several interaction frequency and meeting partner concentration figures for most establishments. Second, a change in location patterns most probably means a change in interaction patterns. Even after an incomplete decentralization of two or three industries, linkage patterns may have changed and this may necessitate not only a rethinking of decentralization policies, but a second survey to capture the new linkage pattern. Third, it should not be concluded that activities listed under 'considerable decentralization potential' are geographically 'footloose'. Clearly, all offices rely on some face-to-face contacts and need accessibility. What can be argued here is that many office activities do not need locations in small spatial clusters which are characterized by a high degree of complementary activities. Locations at nodal points within the metropolitan transportation network, however, must be given great consideration.

While accessibility is important for the maintenance of linkages, it is appropriate to remember that there are other important location factors and that accessibility may be even more important for the daily assembly of office workers. Offices are probably the most intensive land use in terms of employees per unit of ground or floor space. These high densities are facilitated by a production technology which allows a great degree of substitution of labour for capital. Under these conditions transportation between home and work assumes utmost importance. Office agglomerations may well be explained by a circular, cumulative growth process: offices locate at strategic points of the transportation network, congestion leads to demands for improved transportation facilities, increased facilities attract new offices, and so on.

The importance of accessibility does not imply that central office agglomerations should be given licence to grow indefinitely nor should they be continually reinforced by public investment in transportation facilities. It should be possible to create a multicentred office distribution pattern in which travel between home and work can be adequately provided for. As suggested in the discussion above, there are many types of offices which would appear to be able to locate at strategic points outside the central area of the metropolis.

Outlook for Future Development

The future of office development in Toronto is wide open to speculation. First of all, final decisions have to be made about the City's revised plan and the Metropolitan plan. It will be interesting to see whether the Ontario Municipal Board approves of the City's control measures or leans towards the influential real-estate lobby opposing the City's constraint on office construction. Whatever the outcome of decisions taken in Toronto, the powers of the contesting parties pale against larger macro-economic forces, such as national and worldwide economic fluctuations, international differentials in productivity, wage rates, returns on capital, etc., availability of capital for major infrastructure improvements, and long-term trends in the structure of the Canadian economy.

At the time of writing there seems to be little demand for additional office space in Toronto. The worldwide recession of the mid-seventies, coupled with high inflation rates, has left its mark. In the last half decade formerly buoyant population growth in Metropolitan Toronto has faded to a mere trickle. Major development companies hitherto strongly interested in building offices in the city have shifted some of their capital and activity to New York and half a dozen other large cities in the United States. Meanwhile unemployment in the construction industry, including white-collar construction services such as architectural and engineering firms, has reached record levels. Whether these conditions are of a cyclical and short-term nature or of longer duration is difficult to predict. There are indications that the secular trend towards an increase in office jobs is slowing down.

Predictions for Toronto are further complicated by uncertainty over the future of Quebec. Since the autumn of 1976 the political separation of Quebec has become a possibility to be reckoned with. Separation of Quebec most probably would mean a move of several if not many head offices from Montreal to other Canadian cities. Although Toronto will not get the undivided attention of firms leaving Montreal, since some of them may prefer Ottawa, Edmonton or Calgary, it can safely be assumed that an exodus from Montreal will stimulate demand for office space in Toronto considerably.

While a prolonged recession may suspend the effects of the City of Toronto's decentralization policy, renewed demand for office space would clearly put this policy to the test. Again, what exactly would happen is not easy to predict. Will the reduced development densities, together with measures that may be taken by other municipalities and the Metropolitan government, lead to the desired decentralization and a new, more equitable distribution of employment visualized by the City's planners? Will rents soar and keep new office employment completely away from central Toronto? The City's policy relies heavily on a moderate rent increase which, it is hoped, would initiate some movement of office employment to the suburbs and also direct some of the new establishments to suburban office centres. Research discussed earlier in this chapter clearly establishes that there are a number of activities that should not be seriously impaired in their functioning at suburban locations. It is not clear, however, whether the rent mechanisms will have an impact on those activities.

The following scenario is quite possible. Some of the smaller and some of the marginal firms will be hardest hit and may put pressure on residential and industrial areas to find office space. Larger establishments, particularly head offices which can draw on diverse company resources to finance a central head office location, will either not respond at all to moderate rent increases or will resort to partial decentralization. Partial deconcentration will, of course, consist of relocating 'routine' departments with infrequent face-to-face contacts and a very high proportion of clerical employees, while executives stay behind in central area offices.

Partial office decentralization coupled with the attempts by City planners, politicians and citizen groups to enhance central area amenities, 'richness of experience' and 'complexity of texture' may well lead to a high-quality executive enclave. Given the trend to higher energy costs and particularly the growing inability of governments to finance major improvements to the metropolitan transportation network, resulting in further congestion, more of the executives may wish to live closer to work by upgrading inner city residential neighbourhoods. The net result: the 'executive city'.

No doubt the increased quality of the inner city areas will please many city fathers. The picture is incomplete, however, without considering what may happen at the suburban office centres. Partial decentralization may lead to office clusters with primarily clerical employment and a strong reliance on telecommunication rather than face-to-face contacts. Many of the facets of central area business life may not be available for these suburban office workers. Also, it remains to be seen whether suburban residents will put up with increased development and traffic intensification.

This scenario is based on speculation, but then the introduction of far-reaching policies is open to uncertainties. It could be argued, as indeed it has been (Bourne, 1975, p. 2), that the City of Toronto's attempts to control growth should have awaited further research and discussion. This, of course, is a traditional academic war-cry, which planners and policy-makers, due to the urgency of certain situations, cannot always follow. There remains, however, the rather intractable question about the redistributive effects of Toronto's decentralization efforts. Which geographic and social population groups will be positively or negatively affected? Which kinds of business, finance and real-estate interests will lose or gain in the process of employment decentralization? Research on these 'income'-

redistributive effects of an office decentralization policy is clearly appropriate.

There are other research questions, the answers to which may have played further into the hands of the decentralization advocates. Throughout this chapter it has been assumed that communication patterns and the nature of office work in general will stay fairly constant. These, of course, are unrealistic assumptions. For instance, there is every reason to believe that linkage patterns are location-dependent. In new suburban locations the level of face-to-face linkages would most probably be lower than in central locations. Some contacts may be abandoned altogether, some may occur in the form of face-to-face contacts with businesses in the new suburban office centres (transfer) and still others may be switched from face-to-face encounters to telecommunication (substitution). On a more fundamental level, more research is also needed about the changing nature of offices in the context of economic and social change. There is no reason to believe that, for instance, the rate of office employment growth will continue unabated or that office workers will perform the same functions in the same ways with the passing of time. Future research will have to consider the changing nature of office work and its implications for location and the use of urban land.

Notes

1. Shortage of space does not allow a full documentation of all arguments and data sources. Special problems acknowledging sources occur when data refer to change, since statistics are often based on several published and unpublished sources. For a thorough documentation of the establishment, employment and face-to-face contact surveys of central Toronto offices see Gad (1975). The background to many of the ideas presented here is documented in a Ph.D. Thesis (Gad, 1976). The sections on 'Office Development Policies' and 'Decentralization Potentials', however, have not been presented in this form before.

2. The Toronto Census Metropolitan Area, as defined by Statistics Canada for purposes of the *Census*, is an area housing about 2.6 million persons in 1971. This area is contained within a semicircle of approximately 40 kilometres radius, centred on the intersection of Yonge and King Streets. (For the location of this intersection in the core of Toronto see Fig. 11.1) Metropolitan Toronto is a local government area consisting of six member municipalities, i.e. the City of Toronto and five Metropolitan Boroughs (see Fig. 11.1).

3. Several 'central areas' have been defined by various authors. Central Area refers to a part of the City of Toronto defined in the Official Plan (Toronto, City Planning Board, 1969). It includes office, retail and institutional complexes as well as substantial residential and industrial districts. The Central Core Area, which is characterized by office, retail and institutional land use, was defined in the context of the Official Plan review (Toronto, City Planning Board, 1975). The extent of the Inner Core Area as defined by an earlier report (Toronto, Core Area Task Force, 1974) is almost identical with the Central Core Area. The Central Corridor, suggested by Gad (1975) as a useful area for the study of offices, comprises the Central Core Area and extension of this area northward along the Yonge Street underground line. Especially in its northern parts, it includes substantial residential districts. Central Area, Central Core Area and Central Corridor are shown in Fig. 11.3. (For the location and extent of office development in the Central Corridor see

also Figs. 11.1 and 11.4.) Central area (in lower case) is used in a less specific sense than the planners' Central Area. Inner areas (in lower case) refer to the densely developed nineteenth-century parts of Metropolitan Toronto, involving substantial areas of the City of Toronto to the east, north and west of the Central Area.

4. Office establishments for the purpose of this study are defined as organizational units of firms which are physically separated from plants, warehouses or shops, etc. (see also Goddard, 1975, p. 4). Office establishments and employment were enumerated by the author in 1971 using a variety of published and unpublished directories, association lists, business files and government reports as well as direct inquiries by letter and telephone (for details see Gad, 1975).

5. Procedural details for the face-to-face linkage study may be found in Gad (1975). Figures on linkage intensity are identical with those reported in Gad (1975; 1976), but figures on meeting partner concentration in the Central Corridor differ, due to general recalculation and allocation of meeting partners for which no location was provided in the diaries according to the proportion of Central Corridor outside Central Corridor meeting partner locations reported in the diaries. The allocation of non-reported meeting partner locations follows a suggestion by Code (1977, pp. 53–54). Some qualifications have to be made concerning the use of diaries and questionnaires. The data base for calculating linkage intensity and meeting partner locations of the following model establishments must be considered as weak: Shipping Agencies, Customs Brokers, Executive Search Consultants, Civic Associations, and Business Associations. In the case of the model establishments, Mining, Banks, and Market Research, the data base for estimating meeting partner concentration in the Central Corridor is weak. for Banks an estimate was derived from the data on Trust Companies. The model establishment Insurance Agencies cannot be considered representative, since data are from a few commercially oriented insurance brokers rather than the innumerable household oriented insurance agencies. Most civic and business associations have very individual constituencies, and the model establishments Civic Associations and Business Associations cannot be regarded as representative of these heterogeneous industries.

References

A. E. LePage Limited (1966), *Annual Real Estate Market Surveys. Metropolitan Toronto.* Toronto: A. E. LePage Limited. (Issues for 1969, 1971 and 1977 published under the same title.)

Armstrong, R. B. (1972), *The Office Industry: Patterns of Growth and Location.* Cambridge, Mass.: MIT Press.

Bannon, M. J. (1973), *Office Location in Ireland: The Role of Central Dublin.* Dublin: An Foras Forbartha.

Baird, G. (1975), *Built Form Analysis.* Toronto: City of Toronto Planning Board.

Bourne, L. S. (1967), *Private Redevelopment of the Central City. Spatial Processes of Structural Change in the City of Toronto.* Chicago: University of Chicago, Department of Geography, Research Paper No. 112.

Bourne, L. S. (1968), Market, location and site selection in apartment construction, *Canadian Geographer,* **12**, 211–226.

Bourne, L. S. (1975), *Limits to Urban Growth: Who Benefits, Who Pays, Who Decides? A Commentary on the Current Planning Climate in Toronto.* Toronto: University of Toronto, Centre for Urban and Community Studies, Research Paper No. 68.

Bourne, L. S., and Doucet M. J. (1973), Components of urban land use change and physical growth, in L. S. Bourne *et al.* (Eds.), *The Form of Cities in Central Canada. Selected Papers.* Toronto: University of Toronto Press, pp. 83–103.

Buckley, M., *et al.* (1975), *The Land Market and the Core of Toronto. Theory, Analysis and Policy Alternatives.* Toronto: City of Toronto Planning Board.

Canada, Dominion Bureau of Statistics (1953), *Ninth Census of Canada, 1951. Volume IV, Labour Force Occupations and Industries.*

Canada, Dominion Bureau of Statistics (1963), *1961 Census of Canada Industries by Sex, Metropolitan Areas.* Vol. III—Part 2. (Bulletin 3.2–2).

Canada, Statistics Canada (1974), *1971 Census of Canada, Industries. Industries by Sex for Canada, Regions and Provinces.* Vol. III—Part 4. (Bulletin 3.4–3).

Canada, Statistics Canada (1975a), *1971 Census of Canada. Industries. Industries by Sex for Municipal Subdivisions of 30,000 and over, Place of Residence and Place of Work.* Vol. III—Part 4. (Bulletin 3.4–7).

Canada, Statistics Canada (1975b), *1971 Census of Canada. Industries by Sex for Census Metropolitan Areas (Regina–Winnipeg).* Voll. III—Part 5. (Bulletin 3.5–9).

Chodos, R. (1975), The gnomes of Nassau, *Last Post,* August, 20–26.

Clayton Research Associates Limited (1975), *Municipal Finances and the City of Toronto's Inner Core Area.* Toronto: City of Toronto Planning Board.

Code, W. R. (1975), *Controlling the Physical Growth of the Urban Core. A Study of the Implications of Restrictive Zoning in the Central Business District of Toronto.* Toronto: The Mayor's Industry and Labour Advisory Committee.

Code, W. R. (1977), *The Containment of an Office Community. An Analysis of the Structural and Economic Effects of Restricting the Growth of Office Space in Toronto's Core.* London, Ontario: University of Western Ontario.

Croft, M. J. (1969), *Offices in a Regional Centre: Follow-Up Studies on Infrastructure and Linkage.* London: Location of Offices Bureau, Research Paper No. 3.

Design Guidelines Study Group (1974). *On Building Downtown.* Toronto: City of Toronto Planning Board.

Dewees, D. N. (1975), *The Economic Effects of Changes in Land Use Control in the Central City.* Toronto: City of Toronto Planning Board.

Evans, A. W. (1967), Myths about employment in Central London, *Journal of Transport Economics and Policy,* 1, 214–225.

Facey, M. V., and Smith, G. B. (1968), *Offices in a Regional Centre: A Study of Office Location in Leeds.* London: Location of Offices Bureau, Research Paper No. 2.

Filey, M. (1972), *Toronto: Reflections of the Past.* Toronto: Nelson, Foster and Scott.

Foley, D. L. (1957), *The Suburbanization of Administrative Offices in the San Francisco Bay Area.* Berkeley, Calif.: University of California, Bureau of Business and Economic Research, Real Estate Research Programme, Research Report No. 10.

Fray, L. A. (1975), *Office Districts in Central Toronto: a Multivariate Analysis.* Unpublished MA Research Paper, University of Toronto, Department of Geography.

Gad, G. H. K. (1968), *Büros im Stadtzentrum von Nürnberg, Ein Beitrag zur City-Forschung.* Erlangen: Erlanger Geographische Arbeiten, Heft 23.

Gad, G. H. K. (1975), *Central Toronto Offices: Observations on Location Patterns and Linkages.* Toronto: City of Toronto Planning Board.

Gad, G. H. K. (1976), *Toronto's Central Office Complex: Growth, Structure and Linkages.* Unpublished Ph.D. Thesis, University of Toronto.

Goddard, J. B. (1967), Changing office location patterns within Central London, *Urban Studies,* 4, 276–285.

Goddard, J. B. (1968), Multivariate analysis of office location patterns in the city centre: a London example, *Regional Studies,* 2, 69–85.

Goddard, J. B. (1973), Office Linkages and Location. A Study of Communications and Spatial Patterns in Central London. *Progress in Planning.* Vol. 1, Part 2, Oxford: Pergamon.

Goddard, J. B. (1975), *Office Location in Urban and Regional Development*. London: Oxford University Press.

Gottmann, J. (1970), Urban centrality and the interweaving of quaternary activities, *Ekistics*, **29**, 322–331.

Haig, R. M. (1926), Towards an understanding of the metropolis, *Quarterly Journal of Economics*, **40**, 179–208, 402–434.

Hall, P. (1966), *The World Cities*. London: Weidenfeld and Nicolson.

Handzink, W. (1977), *The Media Industry in Metropolitan Toronto. A Study of Locational Change*, Unpublished BA Thesis, University of Toronto, Erindale College, Department of Geography.

Kerr, D. P. (1968), Metropolitan dominance in Canada, in J. Warkentin (Ed.), *Canada. A Geographical Interpretation*. Toronto: Methuen.

Kerr, D. P. (1973), The economic structure of Toronto, in J. Spelt, *Toronto*. Toronto: Collier-MacMillan Canada.

Kerr, D., and Spelt, J. (1961), *Industry and Warehousing in Toronto*. Toronto: City of Toronto Planning Board.

Klein, Sears, Damas and Smith (1974), *Core Area Housing Study*. Toronto: City of Toronto Planning Board.

Lichtenberger, E. (1972), Okonomische und Nichtokonomische Variablen Kontinentaleuropaischer Citybildung, *Die Erde*, **103**, 216–62.

Manners, G. (1974), The office in metropolis: an opportunity for shaping metropolitan America, *Economic Geography*, **50**. 93–110.

Merriman, R. H. (1967), Office Movement in Central Christchurch 1955–65, *New Zealand Geographer*, Vol. 23, pp. 117–131.

Morgan, W. T. W. (1961), A functional approach to the study of office distributions: internal structures in London's central business district, *Tijdschrift voor Economische en Sociale Geografie*, **52**, 207–210.

Murdie, R. A. (1969), *Factorial Ecology of Metropolitan Toronto, 1951–1961: an Essay on the Social Geography of the City*. Chicago: University of Chicago, Department of Geography, Research Paper No. 116.

Nader, G. A. (1975), The city centre, in G. A. Nader, *Cities of Canada. Volume 1: Theoretical, Historical and Planning Perspectives*. Toronto: MacMillan of Canada, pp. 89–126.

Nader, G. A. (1976), Toronto, in G. A. Nader, *Cities of Canada. Volume II: Profiles of Fifteen Metropolitan Centres*. Toronto: MacMillan of Canada, pp. 190–242.

Nowlan, D. M. (1974), Land policy in the central city: a Toronto perspective (final draft prepared for 'The Management of Land for Urban Development', a conference sponsored by the Canadian Council on Urban and Regional Research, Toronto, April, 1974).

Nowlan, D. M. (1975), *Development Control Policies: Their Purpose and Economic Implications*. Toronto: City of Toronto Planning Board.

Parkinson, T. E. (1975), *An Examination of the Capacity of the Existing and Committed Transportation System Serving Central Toronto*. Toronto: City of Toronto Planning Board.

Peat Marwick and Partners (1975), *Development Process; Private Sector Decision Making*. Toronto: City of Toronto Planning Board.

Peat Marwick and Partners and IBI Group (1975a), *Trends and Influences on Floor Area Ratios for Downtown Office Workers*. Toronto: City of Toronto Planning Board.

Peat Marwick and Partners and IBI Group (1975b), *The Economics of Agglomeration*. Toronto: City of Toronto Planning Board.

Price, Waterhouse and Associates (1974), *Core Area Office Space Forecast to the Year 2000*. Toronto: City of Toronto Planning Board.

Riquet, P. (1966), Le Quartier de L'Opera et l'evolution du Centre d'Affaires de Paris, in M. van Hulten (Ed.), *Urban Core and Inner City*. Leiden: Brill.

Robbins, S. M., and N. E. Terleckyj (1960), *Money Metropolis. A Locational Study of Financial Activities in the New York Region*. Cambridge, Mass.: Harvard University Press.

Simmons, J. W. (1974), *The Canadian Urban System: A Conceptual Framework*. Toronto: University of Toronto, Centre for Urban and Community Studies, Research Paper No. 62.

Simmons, J. W., and Bourne, L. S. (1972), Toronto: focus of growth and change, in L. Gentilcore (Ed.), *Studies in Canadian Geography. Ontario*. Toronto: University of Toronto Press, pp. 83–106.

Thorngren, B. (1970), How do contact systems affect regional development?, *Environment and Planning*, **2**, 409–427.

Toronto, City Planning Board (1969), *Official Plan for the City of Toronto Planning Area*. Toronto: City of Toronto Planning Board.

Toronto, City Planning Board (1971), *Report on Industry 2. Survey of the Central Area*.Toronto: City of Toronto Planning Board.

Toronto, City Planning Board (1974), *Core Area Task Force. Technical Appendix*. Toronto: City of Toronto Planning Board.

Toronto, City Planning Board (1975), *Proposals. Central Area Plan Review. Part 1: General Plan*. Toronto: City of Toronto Planning Board.

Toronto, Core Area Task Force (1974), *Report and Recommendations*. Toronto: City of Toronto.

Toronto, Metropolitan Planning Board (n.d.), *Statistical Tables. Table E 1.1.1.: Employment by Place of Work—1956, 1960, 1964, 1970*. Toronto: Metropolitan Toronto Planning Board.

Toronto, Metropolitan Planning Department (1976), *Metroplan. Concept and Objectives. A Report for Public Discussion*. Toronto: Metropolitan Toronto Planning Department.

Toronto, Metropolitan Transportation Plan Review (1975), *Choices for the Future: Summary Report*. Toronto: Metropolitan Toronto Transportation Plan Review, Report 64.

12

The Social Effects of
Office Decentralization

M. BATEMAN AND D. BURTENSHAW

Introduction

The literature concerning office dispersal has concentrated initially on many of the economic benefits to the large corporations and the social effects of relocation[1] have taken second place because the major beneficiaries and instigators of policy have had to be persuaded first. However, research monographs and projects completed during the last decade by both academics and company personnel sections have stressed the diversity of attendant social issues that arise when a company relocates beyond a large city.

Studies of the social effects of office location policies have gained in importance as employers have realized that new locations and new lifestyles have to be 'sold' to employees. Early advertisements on the social effects of decentralization were euphoric and made claims that were frequently based on impressions rather than empirical evidence. The research that is outlined in this chapter has provided the empirical evidence that has both confirmed some of the original impressions and posed some questions about our basic assumptions. It has also revealed problems that the migrating families faced that were not regarded as the concern of employers. The cooperation of firms in allowing employees to answer questionnaires, invariably in company time and therefore at company expense, is appreciated by all researchers. One must assume that they agree to assist in such exercises because they do gain tangible evidence on the success or, rarely, failure of their relocation decision from the social point of view. In fact, the authors can point to changes in company policy which might be attributable to the answers that they received.

On the broader front many of the results documented here are of interest to anyone concerned with the impact of migration on the nuclear family. The surveys cited all concern families who had to move and, therefore, the social costs and benefits that have been measured could be of use to other companies and institutions who regularly shift employees between locations. The major British banks and building societies move middle management regularly and, to our knowledge, they are not aware of the effects of this on social life. At the other end of the scale, one company used in this report moved several hundred families from New York to Paris and is obviously well versed in the social issues arising from migration and how to allay the fears of employees.

Typologies of Social Problems

There have now been at least five independent surveys of various social aspects of office relocation and it is becoming clear that one can see typologies of problems. Sidwell (1974a) in her early work was able to point to four main fields of concern. First, there were the problems for the individual households concerned with the decision to move. This particular topic can be difficult for the individual researcher to investigate objectively for a variety of reasons. To really prepare an objective assessment of the social life of an employee and his family prior to a move being announced is almost impossible. How can a family be asked to subject themselves to investigation if the main purpose of the investigation is not declared to the individual? Companies have only permitted researchers to begin work once a move has been announced and then there are already alterations in the employees' attitudes to a move and consequently their behaviour. Therefore, it would appear that no one will be able to make a completely objective assessment of the pre-move social patterns.

Sidwell saw the second major field of concern as the problems of adjusting to the new environment. This has been the field of greatest interest and includes a whole variety of studies that concentrate on both the social patterns of the relocators and more quasi-economic aspects of their lifestyle. The studies by Hammond (1968), Carey (1969), Bateman *et al.* (1971; 1975) and Daniels (1972) have all been concerned to a greater or lesser extent with these aspects.

Third in the typology came the problems of the employment prospects of wives and other dependants first discussed by Burtenshaw (1974), although most would recognize that there are a whole set of problems that overlap with those in the previous paragraph. Not only are there problems of employment for some wives and for the children, but there are also a whole range of new domestic problems that might face the mother in any move of house.

Finally, there are the problems of those who decide not to move or who are not relocated. This problem, like the first, is more difficult to study because many firms are reluctant to discuss how they arrived at the list of staff to be relocated, or, in a few cases, staff willing to move. Some companies do take advantage of the relocation to leave 'dead wood' behind or to prematurely retire employees and these policies are very difficult to discuss openly. Sidwell was able to interview those who chose not to move, but for many employees decentralization was little more than a Hobson's choice. In one company newspaper in reply to the simple question, 'Will my promotion chances be affected if I refuse to move to X?' the simple but effective answer from a personnel section renowned for its reasoned replies was, 'Yes'!

While the typology above suits the problem-solving role of the social science researcher, it does not enable us to do more than offer a broad grouping of the studies. On the other hand, it has been left to individual researchers to identify further potential problems. Therefore, an examination of the topics covered by individual projects does give a better indication of the breadth of research. A look at the methods of data collection and the research hypotheses also enables us to classify the approaches and to be aware of the problems and pitfalls facing the researcher.

Two major research themes stand out because of their simplicity and because the data are more amenable to statistical processing. Studies of the journey to work patterns of decentralized employees have been undertaken almost entirely by Daniels (1972; 1975) since the initial Location of Offices Bureau survey (National Opinion Polls, 1967), although Carey (1969), Bateman et al. (1971; 1975), and Poyner and McCowen (1973) have also considered the journey to work within the framework of broader studies. Housing is the other topic that has received much attention throughout all the studies. Hammond (1968) devoted much of his study to the problems of rehousing, while Poyner and McCowen (1973) have considered potential housing problems. Bateman et al. (1974) have broadened the scope of the housing studies to an analysis of the changed conditions in the new location and an assessment of the factors influencing the way employees were viewing the new environment while selecting houses.

The third theme which has received increased attention is the post-move employment of wives and dependants. This particular theme has concerned Burtenshaw and Sidwell, and involves a more costly research design because of the scattered distribution of the respondents and problems of establishing contact while maintaining the anonymity of the employees.

There are a whole group of other themes that have been discussed in various reports. Carey (1969) has examined changes in the cost of living, social amenities and job attitudes. Hammond also investigated the nature of the information concerning the new location, the reasons for volunteering (in the move which he studied, volunteers were called for) and new recruits.

Hypotheses and Methodologies

Another way of overviewing the studies undertaken to date is to look more closely at their hypotheses and methodology. On the whole, most surveys have been based on the premise that office relocation brings social gains for employees as well as economic gains for the employer. Therefore, much of the literature is a product of attempts to test this hypothesis. Shortcomings of varying magnitude have been highlighted by almost all the workers. However, there is a danger when some of the published findings are produced by a governmental agency such as the LOB that only those which best serve the interest of that agency see the light of day. On the other hand, it is true to say that most findings have been published in several forms. Sponsorship of research programmes can face the researcher with the problem of humouring the company while still striving to produce results appropriate to the standards of objective research. In some cases the companies under scrutiny only agreed to cooperate if they had approved the questionnaires and had had the opportunity to modify the questions to suit their images of the move. Thus the number of questions or the level of detail demanded in responses could be altered, so affecting both the interpretation of results and the statistical manipulation of the data. While the investigators are all willing to admit the imperfections of their researches, it would be folly to negate the findings. The time constraints on employees and their wives necessitate that brevity is a paramount consideration in designing questionnaires.

Most researchers have recognized the value of longitudinal studies. It was soon realized that the 'one-off' study does produce results which reflect the timing of a study relative to a relocation and the individual policies of the companies organizing the relocation. In the pilot study undertaken by Bateman and Burtenshaw (Bateman *et al.*, 1971) of a major insurance company move to Portsmouth, the authors realized that face-to-face interviewing of employees took time. In fact they were acutely aware in the final stages of interviewing relocated employees that the respondents already knew the questions and had more time to formulate answers. More importantly, the later respondents did depend very heavily on images built up by some of the earliest movers. Attitudes can harden or relax with time, and for this reason Carey (1970) followed up her initial study of the move to Ashford with an attempt to assess the changes in attitude over two years later. The survey of employees moved to Portsmouth over the period 1972–76 by Bateman *et al.* (1974) has also made the assumption that knowledge of the housing environment in the receiving area will be filtered back to employees yet to be decentralized. Daniels has also taken another look at his original offices some seven years later (see Ch. 14).

The majority of the studies have used questionnaires which contain many of the faults that are familiar to the social scientist. It is worthwhile examining how they were administered as this can obviously affect the findings. All the work of Hammond (1968), Daniels (1972), Bateman *et al.* (1971) and Carey (1969) was retrospective, with the results being based on assessments made concerning the period prior to, during and immediately after the move. Sidwell (1974a) rightly observed that this 'brings with it all the dangers of bias and inaccuracy when individuals are required to recall their situations and feelings during various stages of the dispersal'. Recall is full of pitfalls, but there is rarely a substitute in this field.

The questionnaires have been administered by post, by company distribution, by assembling relevant employees at work and by personal interview both at home and in the office. The personal interview is expensive on time in particular and only suitable when the population is small, while postal and company distributed questionnaires suffer from lower response rates and poorer standards of completion. In the authors' opinion the assembly of relevant employees at work, while costly to the company, does provide the best atmosphere for the most conscientious completion of a questionnaire. This particular conclusion is based on the authors' experience of attempting several methods of questionnaire administration. The changed format for administering the questionnaire illustrates the point made earlier about company intervention. Initially, we were able to gather the employees section by section in the cafeteria, and have the questionnaire explained and completed along with another circulated internally. The advantages were a high response rate and the identification of the researchers to the population under investigation. Subsequently, the company issued a second block of questionnaires through the management hierarchy with the predictable outcome of a lower response rate and garbled information on the purpose and authenticity of the survey. The final batch of questionnaires were distributed and collected by internal mail and contained not only the authors' letter of introduction but also an explanation letter from the company. Even then enthusiastic secretaries removed the latter, resulting in queries regarding company approval. The response rate was slightly improved.

Other Considerations

It is also essential when assessing the social effects of decentralization to bear in mind two other variables. There is firstly the all-important consideration of scale. The scale of the decentralization obviously affects the social problems that might be faced by employees. Large-scale relocations can lack the personal touch that reassures individuals, and rumours are more prevalent in larger moves unless the exercise is handled with the utmost delicacy. The rumours can be internal to an organization, in particular if it is a partial decentralization with some departments or sections remaining behind. When a move is phased and the final stages are in the distant future and not fully planned, then there will inevitably be rumours and counter-rumours about which sections or departments are to be moved. Facts, opinions and rumours regarding housing, social life and other facilities at the new location are fed back to the old location from early relocators. One compnay even withdrew a local newspaper from the London office on the days when a murder hunt was featured in its columns in order to prevent the media distorting the image purveyed by the compnay. On the other hand, the smaller-scale relocations, of 100 or fewer individuals and their families, are more manageable. The large-scale move obviously demands that the receiving location is sufficiently large to absorb the incoming families without detriment to either the receiving town's citizens or the migrant population. Publicity has been given frequently to the inability of local housing markets, in all but the largest provincial centres, to absorb the relocators. Certainly IBM in their move to South Hampshire and the Midland Bank in their move to Sheffield (Kinloch, 1977) have found that pressure is put on certain sectors of the housing market which is blamed solely on the company, despite other national and local trends affecting the supply of housing. Thus the choice of receiving location is important if the company wishes to avoid some strain on employees.

The distance moved from London obviously affects the social lives of the employees. Relocations to major office nodes in the London suburbs, such as Croydon or Sutton, will disrupt the social life of a smaller proportion of employees because it is probable that some will end up living closer to their work. Poyner and McCowen (1973) noted this in the pre-move study of the International Publishing Corporation employees decentralizing to Sutton. The greater the distance from Sutton the greater were the problems of the move for the employees, the exception being those who lived in the outer south west suburbs and the inner south-western Metropolitan Area.

Likewise, relocations to the centres in the Outer Metropolitan Area and just beyond do enable the employees to keep easier contact with their old neighbourhoods and friends. In these cases, the economic arguments for remaining in the south-eastern quadrant of the country have aided the solution of the problems of keeping contact with the home area. Therefore, it is possible for a lucky few to reverse commute to Reading or Portsmouth and stay in their former homes, or for others to be within two hours' journey time of relatives in the London suburbs.

The problem of distance has highlighted another potential social problem and that is the divide between the public and private reactions to decentralization. The government has seen the decentralization of the civil service as part and parcel of its regional policy and has placed office decentralization in the private sector on a par with industry since 1973 by granting aid for relocations to the development regions. However, the governmental aims embodied in the Hardman Report (Civil Service Department, 1973) and the *Office Location Review* (DOE, 1976) have been to view the distribution of the civil service as an instrument of regional policy. Dispersal to Glasgow, 'which always sounds on the telly like a victorian slum' (*Guardian* 16.8.76, report on National Savings Bank's move to Glasgow), is, for the man living south of Potters Bar, an unspeakable punishment. Other centres have also been seen in a similar light by civil servants, including Durham (Hammond, 1968) and Southport.

It is very noticeable that most civil servants have been decentralized further than their private sector acquaintances. Dispersed employees in the private sector are moved to Ipswich (Guardian Royal Exchange), Cheltenham (Eagle

Star Insurance), Bristol (National Westminster Bank Insurance Services), Worthing (Excess Insurance), Knutsford, Cheshire, and Poole, Dorset (both Barclay's Bank). Is a policy that moves state employees to the development regions and the private sector employees intra-regionally, socially divisive? If it is, is there a policy solution that will satisfy the civil servant and the insurance manager, destined to leave Surbiton for Glasgow and Reading respectively? The policies for any future dispersal must be seen to be aware both of the overall national need for the dispersal of employment opportunities and of the wishes of employees. It might be more satisfactory if the long-distance moves by the civil service relied more heavily on volunteers rather than involuntary migration. In addition, it is easier to create new or reorganized units in the development regions, such as the Family Benefits Office at Washington, rather than to transfer existing bodies of work. In this way the size of the London-based civil service might be reduced over a longer time period as a result of governmental reorganization of departments, voluntary relocation, promotion to new units and the creation of new bodies of work. In many senses, these questions must remain unanswered in the context of this chapter, but we are able to look at some of the social effects of relocation policies.

The major areas of investigation concern housing changes, changes in patterns of social activity, changes in employment prospects for dependants and journey to work changes. The latter is the subject of a separate analysis elsewhere, but some passing reference will be made to it in this chapter. Employees' attitudes to relocation may be a profitable starting-point since these do inform us of both the expectations and misgivings in contemplating a move which can be studied in the post-move enquiries.

There is little doubt that the initial reactions to a move are understandably hostile because of the uncertainty created by a somewhat limited knowledge of the new environment. Dutch civil servants presented with a move to Enschede, in the eastern Netherlands, were concerned by the 'away from it all' image of the town. In their opposition to many of the recommendations of the Hardman Report, current attitudes of the unions representing the civil servants in Britain are a collective institutionalized response which reflects the attitudes of many individuals in the past. The reactions of the Post Office Savings Certificate Division workers likely to be involved in the proposed move to Durham, eventually to begin in 1963, are recorded by Hammond (1968). Petitions were organized against the move and MPs were lobbied and, 'Of the two unions involved, the Civil Service Clerical Association was the more strident. Its SCD (Savings Certificate Division) *Bulletin* for April/May 1962 stated, "It is common knowledge that practically no one wants to move to Durham", and used phrases such as 'bleak prospect', 'double-dealing' and 'infamous treatment'. There is no doubt that the union representatives had many of the staff breathing fiercely down their neck' (Hammond, 1968, p. 12). In fact, the number who actually refused to move varied with the grading of the post held by each individual. The

Table 12.1. Employment Grade and Refusal Rates for the SCD Move to Durham

Grade	Comple-ment	Refusals	Refusals as % of complement
Higher Executive Officer	32	21	66
Executive Officer	137	85	62
Higher Clerical Officer	49	35	71
Clerical Officer	844	600	71
Temporary Clerical Officer	106	43	41
Clerical Assistant	321	268	83
Temporary Clerical Assistant	409	339	83
Sorting Assistant	118	113	96
Typist	30	29	97
Total	2046	1533	75

Source. E. Hammond, *London to Durham* (1968), p. 28.

higher grades had a lower refusal rate than the lower grades, which is the pattern to be expected (Table 12.1).

In this case volunteers to move were called for and the relocation was both over a considerable distance and to a Development Area. It may well be that the refusal rates were higher than anticipated, but the feeling against moving from London obviously ran high. Movement over shorter distances and in the private sector, cushioned sometimes by salary reviews and often by favourable mortgage schemes together with extremely generous assistance with legal fees and even refurnishing, may be expected to meet with less opposition. In an analysis of post-move attitudes carried out by the authors after the move of one group to Portsmouth, it was found that the major aspects of London and its facilities which were missed by migrants were its shops and entertainment, and access to friends and relatives. Whilst these responses may be balanced against a reaction to be well rid of noise, dirt and congestion, they do give an indication of the features of London which may make potential migrants reluctant to undertake a move.

Changes in Housing

Undoubtedly one of the employee expectations of a move from London is the opportunity either to buy their own property for the first time, by moving to an area where housing is relatively inexpensive compared to London, or to improve on their own property by being able to buy a larger or better equipped house as a result of selling in the London area and buying elsewhere. Obviously the ability to do either of these does depend on the extent of the discrepancy in price between London and the reception area. A detailed study of housing changes was carried out by the authors on a company moving to Portsmouth. The area of residential search for the migrants was principally South Hampshire and the extension of the urban region into neighbouring West Sussex. It is somewhat difficult to make informed comment concerning the nature of property prices in the area, since the period under study, the early 1970s, was one of deceleration in the nationwide property boom. In addition, South Hampshire itself had seen considerable population growth during the 1960s, bringing with it pressure on the housing markets. Nevertheless, for most people, the move did present a number of opportunities. It would have been possible to realize some capital by purchasing a house similar to that owned in the London area, but at a lower price, or to buy a larger house in the reception area. Alternatively, the opportunity to make a move up the housing scale which was greater than could have been made in London was possible, with a subsequent increase in mortgage outgoings. Finally, for those who did not own, or were not buying their own property in London, a move from the highly-priced property market of London presented the opportunity to enter the housing market for the first time.

The results of the authors' survey of a move to Portsmouth in 1972 suggested a number of trends in housing tenancy changes (Table 12.2). As these results show, there was a significant increase in the number of owner-occupiers, rising from 36 per cent (65/175) in the London area to 73 per cent (128/175) in Portsmouth. The corresponding decrease in rented properties, from 46 per cent in London to only 23 per cent in Portsmouth, is partly accounted for by differences in the available property in the two locations. Certainly it was noted that many younger employees found some difficulty in obtaining a flat or apartment in the new location, simply because there was not a supply on the scale of that available in London. This experience is obviously found in every provincial centre. In these circumstances, it is not surprising that many turned to buying their own property. Of the 24 in the sample who previously lived in the parental home, 10

Table 12.2. Housing Tenancy Changes in London and Portsmouth

London type of housing tenancy		I	II	III	IV	V	VI	VII	VIII	IX	Total
		Portsmouth type of housing tenancy									
I	Own house*	52	3	–	–	–	–	–	–	1	56
II	Own flat*	8	1	–	–	–	–	–	–	–	9
III	LA rented	–	–	–	–	–	–	–	–	–	–
IV	Rented house (furnished)	–	–	–	3	–	2	–	–	–	5
V	Rented house (unfurnished)	2	1	–	–	–	–	1	–	–	4
VI	Rented flat (furnished)	16	1	–	7	–	9	1	2	1	37
VII	Rented flat (unfurnished)	24	7	–	1	1	1	1	–	–	35
VIII	Parental home	8	2	1	8	–	3	–	–	2	24
IX	Others/No data	3	–	–	–	–	1	–	–	1	5
Totals		113	15	1	19	1	16	3	2	5	175

*These categories include those purchasing their own property.

entered the property market on moving to Portsmouth. It may be concluded that for these new entrants into the housing market the move was probably beneficial, at least in the long term, since it coincided with a period of rising property prices. We may reinforce these conclusions by an analysis of housing change by age group of migrants. It was principally the younger age groups that benefited most from these changes. An example is in the 20–24 year age group, of which only 13 per cent (9/67) owned or were buying their own property in London, whereas the proportion had risen to 66 per cent (44/67) in Portsmouth. On the other hand, for those over 35 years, there was little change found in this respect, but many of these employees, who already generally owned or were buying their own property, stood to gain in other ways.

One way in which they were able to benefit was by moving up the housing scale. A guide measure of this is to assess the type of house owned in each location. Although it is true that a Georgian terraced house in unlikely to be at the bottom of the housing scale, such houses are somewhat unusual and we may assume in a general sense that a move from a terraced to a semi-detached house, or from a semi-detached to a detached house is an upward movement on the housing scale. In fact, it was found that a much larger proportion lived in detached houses in Portsmouth than in London (35 per cent compared with 11 per cent), whilst there was a smaller proportion living in flats or maisonettes (19 per cent in Portsmouth compared with 43 per cent in London).

Price comparisons have to be treated with caution, since the time lapse between sale and purchase may be affected by an interim rise in property prices. However, we are able to show that only a relatively small number of the sample actually saved money by moving from London. Of the 55 who were involved in both selling property in London and buying property in the Portsmouth area, only 14 sold their property in London at a higher price than that which they paid for their new property in Portsmouth. On the other hand, 37 bought at a higher price, probably taking the opportunity to improve on the property owned previously, whilst three bought and sold at identical prices.

The move brought a noticeable transfer to newer property. For instance, of the 60 who lived in property built between 1900 and 1945, two-thirds moved to properties built since 1960. Whilst this may in part be a reflection of the differences in the housing stock in the two locations, there is a positive trend which can be identified. Perhaps more significant were the changes in accommodation and facilities. Obviously in buying a house for the first time, having previously tenanted a flat, one would expect an increase in the number of rooms in the accommodation, but of those who had two-bedroomed properties previously, 33 moved to three/four-bedroomed property, whilst 23 moved from three-bedroomed properties to four- or five-bedroomed accommodation. Similarly, there were additions in the spheres of garaging and garden space. Seventy-eight migrants who had no garaging in London moved into properties in Portsmouth with garage space. Of those who had a single garage space in London, 21 had double garages in Portsmouth.

Similar housing improvements were found in the investigation of a move to Ipswich by Hall (Bateman *et al.*, 1971). The responses listed in Table 12.3 indicate the changes in housing standard experienced by the migrants. Certainly the gain of a more modern house with a larger number of rooms, more spacious accommodation, and a garage was regarded as being more important than the prospect of buying a cheaper house of the same size. In this instance, some migrants were able to reduce their financial outlay. In the example of the move to Portsmouth cited earlier, however, this was rarely the case. In fact, it was found that the average monthly payments for rent or mortgage payments had risen for a larger proportion of the migrants, presumably as they took the opportunity to trade upwards in the housing market, or to enter the market for the first time.

Although generalizations are difficult to make in a situation involving so many individual domestic variations, it would appear that for the vast majority of the migrants, the move has been beneficial in the context of their accommodation changes. Admittedly, the lure of cheaper housing and possibly tangible financial gain, if it ever existed, proved to be a false one. Intangible financial gains are undoubtedly made, however, as people are presented with the opportunity of entering the housing market for the first time or of trading up in the market. This may possibly take place prematurely, but in a situation of rising property prices and progressively wider price differentials between the various stages in the housing scale, and sectors of the housing market, there is no doubt a long-term financial benefit to be had by buying a larger or better equipped house slightly earlier than might otherwise have been the case.

A side issue, and a contentious one, is the effect that a large move has on the local housing market. This is somewhat difficult to assess, but there is no doubt

Table 12.3. Alterations in Housing Standards

Type of alteration	Number of respondents
A garden for the first time	7
A larger garden	42
A garage for the first time	19
A larger garage than before	31
More rooms than before	52
Larger rooms than before	50
More modern house in terms of amenities and conveniences	62
Similar standard at a lower cost	11
Better standard at a similar cost	30
Much better standard at a small extra cost	27

Sample total = 90.
Source. Adapted from Bateman *et al.*, *Office Staff on the Move*, 1971, Table 2.18, p. 38.

that a relocation by a large company, particularly to a relatively small centre, such as Cheltenham, or rural locations, such as the Barclays Bank headquarters near Knutsford in Cheshire, does put pressure on the local housing market, which may push up the price of certain kinds of property. The local population, benefiting if they are the sellers, but having to compete if they have the role of buyers, may find that they have to pay a price for having a new office employer in the area. In a free market situation, however, there is little that can be done to negate this side-effect. It would seem that pre-location publicity does lead to false hopes which can be dashed so easily by local housing market conditions and inflation.

A move into an area with relatively low property prices may have the worst consequences in this respect. Since, as we have shown, there is an obvious tendency to trade upwards in the market, increased pressure may be felt in a relatively restricted area of it. If all the sellers of London area houses are buying in the £20,000–£30,000 price bracket, the relatively small supply of such houses in a Development Area is bound to be restricted, with a resultant upward move in the price of such houses. The implementation of the Hardman proposals in Britain may well bring such problems to certain areas. An example which can already be cited is the relocation of 650 staff of the Midland Bank to Sheffield. The Bank had concluded that there were enough properties in and around the city, but with almost all purchasers looking for properties in the £20,000–£40,000 band, prices began to rise rapidly in a period of little national change in prices. Due to the small number of properties reaching the sellers' market and the fact that this figure was even smaller in the more desirable south-western suburbs, staff found themselves competing against one another and paying more than they anticipated from the pre-move publicity (Kinloch, 1977).

The particular study undertaken by the authors illustrates several of the problems that face the researcher. Were the questions that we asked really those that produced the answers we wanted to hear or did they test the hypotheses that were under examination? We were constantly aware of the retrospective nature of the investigation and the fact that, for logistic and financial reasons, the interval between learning of the move, moving and answering the questionnaire varied by up to six months. The need to reassess the opinions of migrants is obvious but the nature of the data collection makes it impossible to compare the results with a new survey. Many have already been moved again; three company contacts, for example, have come and gone as a result of job relocation during a five-year research period.

Social Activities

One area of investigation into the social effects of a move has been concerned with the changes which have been effected in the social activities of migrants. Certainly the responses cited earlier about the loss of contact with friends and relatives suggests that this may be an area of some concerns to some migrants. It can be suggested that this may affect different age groups in different ways. For instance, the young migrant, used to the facilities of London, may find his new social milieu somewhat restricted in comparison. In these instances, there may be some temptation to retain, as far as possible, social links with London and there is some evidence to suggest that this does happen. For older migrants, there may be some misgivings at the possibility of having to make new social contacts or to join new social activities. Conversely, many may welcome the move and even see it as a pre-retirement move. In the case of one move to Portsmouth in 1969, some of the migrants chose to live on the Isle of Wight and commute to Portsmouth, giving as their reason that they wished to retire to the island. However, such cases are, in the nature of things, rare and many migrants may be less satisfied.

The social impact of the move must vary from one company to the next and between one set of migrants and the next. For some, perhaps grown accustomed to some degree of mobility, the move can be easily undertaken, but for others the move may be more traumatic. The stage of the migrant in the life-cycle will be important here, the older generally finding moving more difficult. Indeed, as Hall found in his study of the move of an insurance company to Ipswich, 'it is clear that the move to a completely new location was an unusual experience for the majority and a unique experience for some' (Bateman *et al.*, 1971, p. 31).

There are a series of decisions concerning moving which are underpinned by both social and spatial inputs. These in turn have a set of obvious social consequences. Fig. 12.1 is a tentative exploration of these relationships based on the responses of migrants to Portsmouth.

The initial reactions of an individual to a move may well be based on an assessment of likely social upheaval. Indeed, it is possible to suggest a series of stages (T_1, T_2 and T_3 in Fig. 12.1) in any relocation process, linked to employees' attitudes to the information about the move, the new location, and propensity to migrate. The initial announcement (T_1) of a relocation may often be received with a fear of such a move, and such fear may well be based on social considerations such as breaks with friends, neighbours and relations as well as the domestic upheaval of moving house. In the period immediately after the move (T_3) there may well be a preoccupation with settling into the new working environment. At that time, it may not be possible to begin to take on new social activities, which may be delayed until the immediate domestic upheaval has been sorted out and there is less pressure in the working environment. This phase may well be followed by a period of consolidation in the new location, bringing with it new social contacts, and perhaps new social activities. The degree of social integration into the new area is going to depend to a large extent on family circumstances. Those migrants with wives not working, but bringing up children in the new home environment, may find that new social contacts are more easily made.

Table 12.4 is an attempt to give a tentative structure to the social adjustment

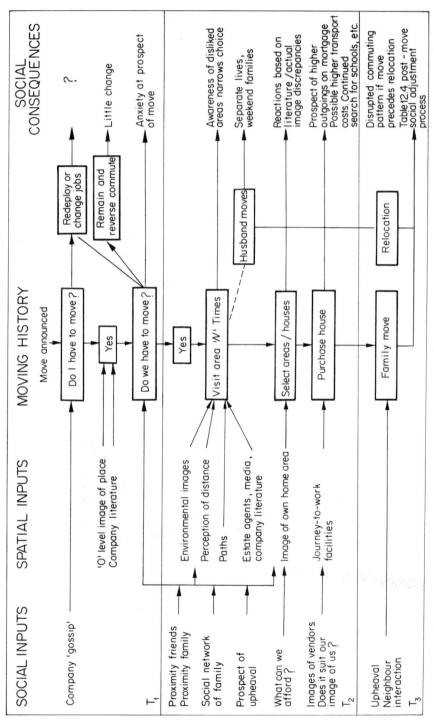

Fig. 12.1. Stages in the employee relocation process

Table 12.4. The Post-Move Social Adjustment Process

Individual	T_1	T_2	T_3	T_4
Husband	Absorbed in new working environment	Social life geared to work New work schedule established	Increased neighbourhood contact, school contact New social activities	Involvement in committees
Working wife	(a) No job	Contact pattern low Nest-building	Advent of family	
	(b) No job (c) Job in another firm	Part-time work Low contact with neighbours	Full-time work Social life geared to own/husband's work	Social life geared to own/ husband's work Increasing neighbourhood contact
	(d) Job in husband's firm	Social life geared to work	Secondary association beyond work/neighbourhood	
Mother and children	Post-move involvement in home creation	Integration with neighbours, babysitting	Integration with husband's social life	
Mother and schoolchildren	Post-move involvement in home creation	Integration via other parents/neighbours	New social activities Integration with husband's social life	
Children	School (initial integration depends on timing of move)	Integration in neighbourhood Formal non-school social life (Scouts)	Visiting	Complete integration
Time	T_1	T_2	T_3	T_4

process as it affects the various members of the nuclear family. No attempt is made here to include single persons or those few families where the relocated employee was the wife. It must be stressed that the time phases are not as coincidental as the table suggests. On the contrary, they are very flexible and the speed with which the individuals will adjust will depend on their own propensity to adjust, their stage in the life-cycle, and the nature of the working and residential environment. Whilst much of this process can only be conjecture, it does underline the importance of the timing of interviews in studies of the social effects of relocation. Ideally, a series of interviews spaced in time from the period before the move to several years after it has taken place would provide a complete portrayal of the changes in social linkages and activities. Few researchers have had these opportunities, although Carey was able to carry out a 'follow-up' survey of one move, some three years after it had taken place (Carey, 1970).

Once the move has taken place, it is possible to assess how far initial impressions are confirmed and how far there are distinct changes in social activities. One expectation of living in the new location may well be the possibility of having more free time since commuting times will be less. Studies of moves to Portsmouth have shown that indeed commuting journeys to Portsmouth are shorter in terms of time than those in London, although it is worth pointing out that there is a positive correlation between the journey times in London and those in Portsmouth, with those undertaking long journeys in London making the longest in Portsmouth. While the gains are obviously economic, there are also social side-effects. The use of additional free time was investigated in the case of the move of an insurance company to Portsmouth (Table 12.5).

An alteration in work time to give a longer lunch break affected these responses, but in addition, many were working longer hours to train new recruits or to make up for time lost in the transfer of the business to the new location. One can expect these extra hours to be a short-term expedient. The responses do reflect again the phase referred to above involving a preoccupation with the new working environment.

The type of changes in social life are illustrated by Hall's Ipswich study. Table

Table 12.5. Use of Additional Free Time by In-Migrants

	Number	%
No extra time/more work/greater travel time	36	48.8
Sport and recreation	9	12.8
Do-it-yourself/garden/car/housework	14	17.9
Domestic life generally	15	19.2
Social activities outside the home	3	3.8
Other activities	1	1.3

Source. Adapted from Bateman et al., 1971, Table 3.8, p. 61

Table 12.6. People Seen Most Often Socially by Respondents

	In London	In Ipswich
Relations	59	30
Other employees of firm	1	33
Friends living in London area	59	13
Friends living in Ipswich area	–	32
Total mentions	119	138

Source. Bateman *et al.*, Table 2.24, p. 42.

12.6 lists the responses given to a question enquiring into the frequency of social contact in London and Ipswich.

It is clear from this and other studies that social contact with other employees of the relocating company increases after the move. There are a number of reasons for this. In the new area, the migrants will often know initially only those with whom they work. There is often a tendency for migrants to live in the same sort of areas, which reflect the kind of housing which they are seeking. Some companies have found it necessary to provide some social facilities in the reception area for the benefit of their employees and such facilities would encourage social contact within the company.

Amongst the studies which have examined social contact patterns after a relocation, Carey's study of a move to Ashford is important in that there was a follow-up survey. In her first survey she makes reference to 'a drastic curtailment of social activities' (Carey, 1969, p. 25). The percentage of respondents seeing relatives at least once a week fell from 52 per cent to 23 per cent, whilst the frequency of meeting with friends in the London area fell from 52 per cent to 4 per cent. These findings are hardly surprising and Carey is able to report optimistically on the replacing of lost social contacts, reporting that 44 per cent of respondents had visited friends within one week of her survey. Indeed, in her follow-up survey (Carey, 1970), she found that the relocated employees were visiting London less often than at the time of her initial survey and that they were staying in the Ashford area for their social activities. This does suggest that any immediate problems in this sphere may be overcome with time.

In Hammond's (1968) study, he was able to examine some of the problems associated with integrating into the new environment. In this case, the migrants were volunteers and many were not native Londoners. Many went to Durham ready to mix socially and wanting to make a success of the move in this respect. He states that, 'a lot of the adult migrants originated in Northern England, Scotland or Wales, in areas with a way of life not very different from that of Durham. For them, it was "more like home" than London. The same applied to those from Ireland, who came from country areas or small towns. But those not in this category also came prepared to be more sociable, realising that this would be expected. Those most adaptable in this respect seemed to be the ones deriving most benefit, who could say, "I've made more friends in three months than in twelve years in London"; who got introductions to the local Workingmen's Club'. However, he does go on to point out that this degree of social integration was unusual and there were some problems for some people, at least initially, in making social contact.

Some of the social problems that are encountered are the result of heightened expectations of the new environment somewhat distorted by available infor- mation. On the one hand, the half-remembered facts of school geography may give an outdated impression of an area and its facilities. Hammond's entertaining analysis of the move to Durham makes the point that, 'school geography books were a source mentioned by young as well as older migrants . . . . There seems however to be a decided time lag in the revision of school geographies and this applies to some of the publications to which adults might turn for information. There appear to be few recent guides to County Durham . . . . Some migrants searching in their public libraries in London had fallen back on books published in the 1930's, the effects of which seem to have been discouraging' (Hammond, 1968, p. 78). Similarly the role of the Royal Navy in Portsmouth can be exaggerated to good or ill, as the following example illustrates. A relocation of an office involving many ex-servicemen from the Second World War to the naval port of Portsmouth was seen partly as a return to old haunts and the move was masterminded under the title 'Operation Victory'. In contrast, Portsmouth was viewed by many young employees of this and another relocating company as a cultural mono-industrial backwater being dominated by the relatively low wages paid by the Admiralty.

Environmental information can also be prepared by the relocating firm in its publicity material and in its initial links with the new location. In the most recent relocation to Portsmouth of the employees of one large organization it was also possible to look at the influence of the feedback of information from earlier phases of the decentralization process. One must not underestimate the influence that estate agents have over the impressionable relocators. Their information on areas, contained in such phrases as 'in the desirable', 'close to village centre', 'short distance to local schools', or the total absence of such comments does reinforce images that have been established by the company literature. The local newspaper and its reporting procedures also focus the migrants' attentions on the areas to avoid. These two sources were used extensively by the migrating staff.

The third source that is used by many is the company itself, either through house advertisements in the house newspaper which give the migrant the locations that colleagues have chosen in previous years, or by asking colleagues who have lived and worked in the area previously or who have been moved earlier. This latter source does provide a highly personalized set of data for the relocator on schooling, 'places to avoid', travel times and distances, shopping facilities and the location of public housing. Company literature is inevitably biased and raises expectations for those who are less familiar with the problems of moving. Maps showing the prewar built-up area, instead of that in 1970, raise hopes of village life, while photographs of the most desirable housing again increase expectations and bring an over-reaction to the new area's faults (Fig. 12.1).

Generally one can conclude that a move away from the immediate London region into the outer metropolitan region does bring with it a need to change one's social activities and patterns. There are a few people who are still able to maintain contact with London and who perhaps have no need to move house, but can reverse their commuting journey outwards from London to the reception town. One example is those people who lived in Guildford prior to a move of an office from London to Portsmouth, who merely catch the train from a different platform after the move. But this is the exception and whole families do have to adapt and change. A consistent problem which is cited after a relocation is the local shopping facilities, which compare unfavourably with those in London. As is often generally supposed, however, at least one survey shows that the use made of the major features of London, such as its theatres, galleries and major buildings, was really rather limited and consequently they are unlikely to be missed very much. Allegiance to football teams may be more ingrained and the foreseeing of London clubs for less spectacular attractions has often found a place in general comments on disadvantages of the move!

It does appear that on balance, and at least in the long term, there are more advantages to be had in social terms than disadvantages. However, the big disadvantage of post-move studies is that they are going to unearth all the immediate problems. Much more research needs to be undertaken on the longer-term effects which will restore balance to the social problems that appear in graphic form in the press (Laurence, 1977). It would be interesting to face the same employees with the original questions at intervals up to three years after a move. Alternatively, time budgets taken at intervals might produce more accurate findings.

Employment problems

In one area, that of employment prospects for dependants, there are more serious problems to be faced. The only detailed survey of the employment prospects of wives and dependants was carried out by the authors between 1970 and 1976. The results of the surveys undertaken over this long period are difficult to compare because of the changing composition of the relocating population and the declining economic fortunes of the country after 1973 which lowered the standard of life for many families.

In our initial survey (Burtenshaw, 1973) it was found that 45 per cent of wives were working prior to a relocation, whereas the proportion was 46 per cent in 1975–6. Concern was expressed that only 37 per cent had found work following decentralization. A more recent survey found that there was a 50/50 split among the wives doing full- and part-time work in London and that the percentage who had found a post in the new location was almost identical (36 per cent) despite the changed economic circumstances. Only 21 per cent had full-time posts and 15 per cent part-time jobs. Of those who were working in the London area 30 per cent were still seeking a job three to six months after their move. Twenty-five per cent did not intend to return to employment in the foreseeable future. There is little way of establishing whether these stopped working because of pregnancy, higher husband's income, a desire to be at home or the lack of employment prospects.

In the initial surveys great concern was expressed over the fact that 25 per cent of the working wives took a post with lower salary. This fact was confirmed emphatically in 1975–6, when 29 per cent found themselves working for less remuneration once they had moved. The figures would have been higher no doubt if it were not for the 13 per cent who kept or increased their salaries because they were working for the same company as their husbands. In fact the company even offered to employ suitably qualified wives.

It was difficult to analyse the responses concerning employment prospects for other dependants because of the youthful age structure of the population. However, those with children in employment or approaching employment were concerned by the suddenly restricted range of opportunities for school leavers. The son who had set his sights on the Metropolitan Police is less likely to find Suffolk constabulary as exciting a prospect. For those with children on examination syllabi there were further problems of being able to continue the courses, so much so that there are a few isolated cases where the family is split or the husband is commuting vast distances until the crucial examinations are completed. There were also a few isolated cases of wives being relocated and husbands having to find jobs or be transferred within the organization. In these cases the husband invariably worked for the Civil Service or the Post Office and was transferred.

In the earlier survey 20 per cent of the wives had lost status in their new posts compared with their old. By 1975–6 this figure had dropped to 15 per cent, although the presence of wives in the same company, noted above, obviously affected the results.

Concern about employment prospects for dependants varies according to whether any are seeking employment. Table 12.7 shows the feelings about job prospects for dependants in one city region. Obviously the concern was less among those without working dependants, but in both cases the strongest feelings were that the prospects were worse. 'There seem to be very few jobs for married women, either part or full time. What there are, are very badly paid and not worth the time wasted' (Burtenshaw, 1973). The difficulty of finding work that was suitably rewarded and the much diminished range of opportunity were frequent comments in the authors' studies. When so many migrants' wives have good secretarial qualifications there is unlikely to be the demand in Cheltenham

Table 12.7. Employment Prospects in South Hampshire

	Better than London	Worse than London	The same	Don't know Not applicable
	%	%	%	%
Employees with working dependants	8	78	4	12
Employees without working dependants	3	28	7	62

or Sheffield; cardiac technicians used to working in London teaching hospitals with their unique equipment, specialized cartographic draughtswomen, indentured journalists, *cardon bleu* directors' dining-room cooks, heads of science departments in schools, and Bond Street hairdressers can only find limited openings in the provinces. Although these wives were qualified and could expect to compete for most posts in their fields, there are fewer openings even at lower salaries and, in the conditions of recession existing since 1973, no openings.

Even among those whose wives or dependants were not working the same basic reactions to employment were expressed. Many of the wives who are at home at present might conceivably wish to return to their chosen careers in the future. Only 12 per cent of the sample in Gavron's study of wives did not intend to return to work after rearing a family (Gavron, 1968). It is interesting to note that the main groups of wives' qualifications in the recent moves to Portsmouth were education, nursing and secretarial. Given the current demographic and economic trends, it does seem unlikely that those who wish to return to the labour market will obtain jobs unless they are prepared to work unsociable hours, to take a less demanding job or to lose status.

Conclusions

In the 10 years of research into office decentralization there have been several major studies of its social impact and the results have been utilized in writing this chapter. The findings are far from conclusive due to the nature of the subject-matter, the timing of the relocations, the distance relocated and the scale of the relocations. Changing national economic fortunes, the changing policies towards decentralization and the increasing opposition to decentralization in many towns and cities, due to the adverse publicity given to property development, will obviously change the patterns of relocation and the consequent social problems.

Most local authorities in the South East have implemented very rigid policies regarding office development. Increasingly, towns such as Guildford, Sevenoaks, Reading and Bristol are banning further office development that might attract decentralizing companies. In contrast, it is towns such as

Sunderland in the less favoured parts of a Development Area that still hope to attract decentralizing companies. However, given that the changes in policy announced in May 1977 might help areas such as Sunderland and the inner suburbs of London, one could now ask whether the retention of the middle echelons of management in inner London will bring social benefits either to the inner suburbs or to the employees, as is one of the declared aims of the policy shift?

Given that 'memories are fallible. If one is asked to reconstruct the features of an event that has occurred even moments before, it is to be expected that the reconstruction be partial and modified' (Rossi, 1955), there are a series of observable social problems that the decentralizing office and its employees are bound to face. These problems can be exaggerated in the heat of the moment, but despite Rossi's salutary reminder they do represent real problems for individuals. Decentralization, like any move, is a major event in any family's life and it is surprising that many firms leave the social aspects to look after themselves, having cared for the more tangible aspects of the employees' lives beyond work. It was and is easy to assist home purchase and moving and the evidence is that, judging by the yardsticks used in this study, most relocated employees have gained.

It is in the more personal aspects of the quality of life where official company policies find it harder to cope with the range of circumstances facing employees during a move. In the short term, research has shown how there is a major upheaval in the domestic routine which begins to settle as the new environment becomes more familiar. However, first impressions can be lasting ones. Potential decentralizing companies ought to look at the physical and social environment of all locations, because the involuntary migration resulting from decentralization does not give the employee as much choice as a normal change of job when the employee chooses where to apply. Those companies with young workforces could give greater consideration to the total labour market beyond their immediate needs, as could the local authorities out to attract offices without consideration for the broader effects of relocation on journey to work patterns, hidden unemployment and education.

If research into this fascinating aspect of government policy is to continue there do seem to be several avenues that are worth pursuing. First, there is the reaction of the employed and home-based wives to relocation. An interesting contrast might be drawn with those organizations who regularly shift employees, such as the major banks. Second, there is still a need for follow-up surveys to assess the integration of migrants five years after a move. Third, the role of the employer in the social aspects of relocation could be investigated further. Fourth, to what extent are some environments better suited to absorb decentralization than others? Studies have concentrated on the field of contact environments in an economic sense, but is there not a case for examining the social contact environment in order to ascertain which cities and towns are best suited to absorb a migrating population which can be up to four times the number of relocating employees?

Notes

1. In this chapter 'relocation' refers to the company migration and 'move' to the migration of the individual employee and his/her family.

References

Ambrose, P., (1974), *The Quiet Revolution*. London: Chatto and Windus.

Bateman, M., and Burtenshaw, D. (1971), White-collar migrants, *Town and Country Planning*, **39**, 554–57.

Bateman, M., and Burtenshaw, D. (1976), *The Impact of Office Decentralization to a Provincial Centre*. London: Social Science Research Council Final Report.

Bateman, M., et al. (1971), *Office Staff on the Move*. London: Location of Offices Bureau, Research Paper No. 6.

Bateman M., Burtenshaw, D., and Duffett, A. (1974), Environmental perception and migration: a study of perception of residential areas in South Hampshire, in Canter, D., and Lee, T. (Eds.), *Psychology and the Built Environment*. London: Architectural Press, pp. 148–55.

Bateman, M., et al. (1975), Rehousing migrant office workers, *Giessener Geographische Schriften*, **35**, 55–62.

Burtenshaw, D. (1974), Relocated wives, *New Society*, **24**, No. 559, 680.

Carey, S. J. (1969), *Relocation of Office Staff*. London: Location of Offices Bureau, Research Paper No. 4.

Carey, S. J. (1970), *Relocation of Office Staff: A Follow-up Survey*. London: Location of Offices Bureau, Research Paper No. 4a.

Civil Service Department (1973), *The Dispersal of Government Work from London*. London: HMSO, Cmnd 5322.

Daniels, P. W. (1972), Transport changes generated by decentralized offices, *Regional Studies*, **6**, 273–89.

Daniels, P. W. (1975), *Office Location: An Urban and Regional Study*. London: Bell.

Gavron, H. (1968), *The Captive Wife*. Harmondsworth: Pelican.

Hammond, E. (1968), *London to Durham: A Study of the Transfer of the Post Office Savings Certificate Division*: Durham: Rowntree Research Unit.

Kinloch, B. (1977), Civil servants face problems on relocation, *Daily Telegraph*, 25th July.

Laurence, R. (1977), The rat race run at a cow's pace. *Sunday Times*, 9th January.

National Opinion Polls (1967), *White-Collar Commuters*. London: Location of Offices Bureau, Research Paper No. 1.

Poyner, B., and McCowen, P. (1973), *Survey of Staff Requirements for Sutton*. London: Tavistock Institute for Human Relations.

Rossi, P. H. (1955), *Why Families Move*. Glencoe: The Free Press.

Sidwell, E. (1974a), *The Problems for Employees in Office Dispersal: A Methodology*. London: London School of Economics, Graduate School of Geography Discussion Paper, No. 48.

Sidwell, E. (1974b), *The Attitudes of Firms and Local Authorities to Office Decentralization and Office Development*. London: London School of Economics, Graduate School of Geography Discussion Paper, No. 53.

13

London to Bristol: The Experience of a Major Office Organization and its Staff

ELIZABETH SIDWELL

Introduction

Micro-processes form the basis of any general picture, and so there is always a need for continuing empirical measurement at the micro-scale. The field of office decentralization is no exception. This particular study examines the effects of the policy of office decentralization on one office organization and its staff. It focuses on a 'partial' office move from London to Bristol, which is a major office reception centre in Britain. Partial moves, which account for 65 per cent of all jobs decentralized (LOB, 1975), include those firms who relocate sections of their operations from central London, but leave an office in the central area.

Bristol is the fastest growing office centre in Britain apart from London, and probably has a better long-term outlook than any other centre of its type. The main growth of offices has been in the central area of the city. In June 1973 there were 1,419,400 sq. ft of office floor space under construction in the central area, whilst a further 1,853,370 sq. ft had received planning permission. By 1980, 10.5 million sq. ft of office space is planned for this central area alone. The survey office is one of 13 major firms which had relocated to the central area of the city by 1972. It occupies 113,000 sq. ft of office space out of a total for the 13 of 968,000 sq. ft.

Bristol's popularity may be attributed to a number of factors. It is the nearest town of any significant size to London where Office Development Permits are not required. Rents are favourable in comparison with the London area. It is accessible: the M4 and M5 place the city at a major crossroads in the national road network. Rail services to and from Bristol are excellent. There are two main-line stations serving the city. Bristol Airport is situated seven miles from the city and London Heathrow can be reached in less than two hours *via* the M4. A good telecommunications service with the rest of the country is also offered. Among the remaining advantages of Bristol can be numbered the presence of a good shopping centre, large areas of accessible countryside, and a wide variety of educational opportunities. The city has extensive provision of hospital services, recreational and cultural facilities and a variety of hotel accommodation in the central area.

The precise aims of this study are firstly to provide an information feedback for the policy of office decentralization, and secondly to illustrate the potential contribution of a 'before-and-after' longitudinal survey to office dispersal research.

It is contended that the latter approach provides the study with its fundamental strength. Such a method involves surveys before and after the dispersal in order to collect data as events occur. This avoids the reliance on respondents' memories which is typical of the single post-move survey, and therefore renders the data more accurate. Previous research has relied largely on cross-sectional surveys undertaken in the reception environment (e.g. Hammond, 1968) and so far there has been limited use of the longitudinal approach. There are two studies which partially conform to this approach. Firstly, Bateman and Burtenshaw (1976) have conducted an extensive survey of each new department of an organization as it transfers to the reception centre rather than a survey of the same group of individuals at different time-intervals. Theirs is therefore a series of cross-sectional surveys at different points in time. Secondly, Carey (1969; 1970) has monitored an office move involving the same group of decentralized employees at two periods in time but with both surveys undertaken after relocation had been accomplished. In neither instance therefore is any information collected before the move actually begins.

Murray *et al.* (1972) have illustrated the type and variety of problems that do occur in the pre-move stage. Firstly, inherent prejudices about moving and about particular areas can seriously hinder the decentralization process. Secondly, there are external factors that might affect an employee's dispersal intentions. In the third place, there are the problems of special categories of staff and their associated needs. Fourthly, there are the problems associated with the arrangements for the move made by the decentralizing firm. Lastly, housing emerged as the topic about which concern was greatest in dispersal. When such pre-move data are collected, they ensure that problems are recognized and catered for in advance, thus smoothing the path of decentralization.

So far any data that are required about this first stage have been collected retrospectively and therefore necessarily rely on respondents' ability to recall the past. In addition, there is the strong likelihood of the situation after the move influencing the way the pre-move data are perceived. Only a before-and-after survey method can avoid such difficulties; not simply because it enables as objective an assessment as possible to be made of the effect of relocation, since the data are collected at the time, but also because it ensures that the non-migrant group is included. The latter group has been almost consistently ignored in the past through the absence of an adequate survey method, despite the obvious effect of dispersal policy upon them. Hammond (1968) did complete a very brief analysis of the characteristics of those who elected not to move to Durham.

There is one isolated instance of a before-and-after longitudinal survey of dispersal, but this belongs to the field of industrial rather than office dispersal research. Mann (1973) has monitored the decentralization of a factory from Birmingham to Banbury.

While the chief merit of the longitudinal methodology is its suitability for monitoring a continuing process such as office decentralization, its problems are those common to all survey work, but in a more acute form, since the series of surveys involves exponential increases in the degree of difficulty. For instance, the validity of the measurement techniques may come into question during the duration of the study. It is difficult to maintain the size and interest of the respondent group throughout the survey, and to prevent them from becoming less representative through the knowledge they acquire from repeated questioning. There is the danger that the vast quantities of data obtained will not be adequately analysed. Control groups are necessary because over the duration of the survey events will occur which are unrelated to the variable under investigation and which therefore cannot be attributed to its effects (Social Science Research Council, 1975). Unfortunately, very limited attention has been given so far to the improvement and refinement of longitudinal techniques.

One particular aspect of the relocation of offices is considered below, namely the social and related effect on the staff involved. This effect is at the outset an important influence on the type of relocation centre chosen, and this choice determines the ultimate pattern of office location. The reactions of staff are crucial in determining a move's degree of success.

The Social Effects of Office Dispersal

These involve the repercussions of decentralization on the individuals and families concerned, both migrant and non-migrant, and are exemplified by the changes in their behaviour patterns as a result of the move. In order to understand the social effects of office dispersal it is necessary to compare life-styles before and after the move, taking into consideration the influence of differing and changing attitudes and perceptions. The types of problem faced during the relocation process, and as a result of it, are included.

Research and policy has until recently focused primarily on the economic implications of dispersal and has established that decentralized firms make an important financial saving on office rents and staff costs (Rhodes and Kan, 1971). It is clear, however, that the policy also has a wide range of social repercussions which might not always be desirable from a community and individual point of view. Research on this aspect of dispersal is expanding but is still inadequate: 'there is little of a systematic and comprehensive character available about the experience of the individual from the moment he encounters the possibility of dispersal' (Murray *et al.*, 1972, p. 118). It is the attitudes of the staff, their personal preferences and perceptions, that largely determine the locational possibilities for dispersing offices. Consideration of these factors therefore must inevitably lead to an increased comprehension of the pattern of office relocation.

The survey firm planned a phased process of decentralization from the City of London to central Bristol. The initial phase of the relocation was scheduled for autumn 1973 and comprised the movement of two departments. These became the focus of the study, which involved two survey stages, one three months prior to relocation and one six month after relocation. Initially, postal questionnaires were distributed to all employees involved in the relocation, both migrants and non-migrants. For the former, this derived background information such as age, job status, family size, length of residence in the London area, attitudes to migration and to the company, and details of journey to work. For the latter, it established reasons for not relocating and attitudes to migration, the firm, their home area and the relocation area. It was suspected that a group of characteristics might emerge that would distinguish the non-movers from the relocating staff.

Follow-up interviews were conducted with the migrants. Their purpose was to derive a measure of the individual's leisure and residential preferences, his attitudes to the present and proposed locations and to the idea of migrating, the extent to which he was aware of and made use of the opportunities available to him in his present local area and in London, and to measure his knowledge and expectations of the new location. At the interviews, space–time diaries were distributed for completion by the migrant wives. The purpose of these was to record how the local environment was used and to identify space–time constraints in order to compare the departure and reception environments. The response rate for these was low, partly due to the lack of personal contact with the wives, partly due to the distribution being so close to the relocation date when wives were busier than usual with removal preparations.

This concluded the pre-move dataset. For the second stage of the survey all that was necessary in Bristol was a personal interview with the migrant employees based on a similar format to those conducted in London. Space–time diaries were again distributed and achieved a better response, indicative of the interest felt by many wives at this post-move stage. Finally, a second postal questionnaire was circulated to the non-migrants, to ascertain any changes in their life-style and job situation since the relocation took place. Two control groups, one in London, one in Bristol, were used in order to isolate the changes due to the experimental variable, the move, from those due to other factors.

The Non-Migrant Employees

This group has largely been excluded from previous studies because of the inadequacies of the retrospective method. Bateman and Burtenshaw recognize this omission in that 'as yet there have been no studies of the employees who choose to remain in London or who have been made redundant at the time of relocation' (Bateman and Burtenshaw, 1974, p. 3). All too often, efforts by the firm focus on keeping the movers content at the expense of the non-movers, yet both are a part of the decentralization process and should be considered as such. Non-migrants are in general either high- or low-status employees. The former, because of their privileged position in the social and economic structure, neither face nor pose real problems. The latter, however, are not so fortunate. They tend to be semi- or unskilled and their job opportunities in the capital are shrinking (Donnison and Eversley, 1973). For them unemployment may be a very real prospect and as such poses a real problem for London as well.

While it is impossible to generalize from one case-study, trends are identifiable and the type of effects and changes resulting from the move can be isolated for further large-scale investigation. There were 59 non-migrants in this study. The group of respondents was generally young, 40 per cent (12/30) under 23 years of age, female, 60 per cent (18/30), and married, 40 per cent (12/30). They were young because it is cheaper to replace young clerical staff within the reception area than to relocate them. They were female because clerical jobs are most easily replaced and are more likely to be filled by female recruits. In addition, they seemed less motivated to move than the men and to regard movement itself as endangering their security. They were married because married women tend to be tied to their locations by their husband's job and are less free to move than single women, who summon the confidence to migrate by doing so in peer groups of two or three. It is such people who may be expected to increase in numbers in the London area while the policy of dispersal continues, and it is their needs and problems that must be seriously considered if London is to avoid increased unemployment levels. The speed with which they are reemployed, the nature of their new jobs and their post-move degree of satisfaction calls for investigation.

It was expected that the non-migrants would be less tied to their jobs and to a career structure within one firm than the migrants. Indeed the vast majority were either of low status within the firms or held clerical positions. None were of managerial status. Also a correlation might exist between length of service with a firm and the likelihood of accepting relocation: the shorter the former, the more inclined the employee might be to remain in London, because he is not yet well established within the firm. Forty-three per cent (13/30) had been with the company less than two years, which would seem to represent a reasonable cut-off period after which the employee becomes increasingly dependent on his firm. Of the remainder only two respondents had been with the company more than five years. The majority of non-migrants therefore had not been employed by the relocating firms for periods long enough to have become either very well established or committed to its objectives.

The firm, aware of the importance for the move to Bristol of maintaining non-migrant satisfaction in London, operated a policy of redeployment, that is, they undertook to find alternative employment for the non-migrants within the parent company. This policy minimizes the problems from every point of view. Individuals do not have to face the problem of redundancy and unemployment and hence the aggregate numbers of unemployed are not affected. The company also undertook to pay 'severance loyalty bonuses' to those non-migrants who had acceptable reasons for not wishing to do alternative work, provided they remained in their sections until the date of relocation. This was an attempt to minimize the problems faced by relocating firms as a result of non-migrants resigning immediately the relocation is made public, thus leaving the firm with short-term vacancies to fill from expensive temporary labour supplies.

Within the redeployment policy, it would seem to be a prerequisite that non-movers be transferred to jobs of at least equal and, where possible, higher status than their present positions, if their satisfaction and cooperation is to be guaranteed. These employees deserve some compensation for the inconvenience they are required to endure for the benefit of their employer. The offer of a post of decreased status is hardly any improvement on no job at all and thought to be in the nature of an insult by many employees.

At this stage of the move, a number of non-migrants were already dissatisfied with their treatment:

> I feel more consideration should be given to those not going to Bristol—particularly as regards choice of jobs for those who are not well up in the firm's grades, e.g. typists.

Through no fault of their own and with no benefit to themselves, the non-migrants do face considerable upheaval. Problems associated with their position are emphasized by comparison with the migrants (Fig. 13.1). The latter emerge clearly as the more satisfied group.

Six months after the move had been completed there neither was nor had been any unemployment amongst the non-migrant group, either voluntary or involuntary. However, some had chosen part-time rather than full-time posts. More important, a significant number had held more than one job, an unsettling position. There was a feeling that the latter could have been avoided if the firm had exercised greater care in finding suitable jobs for its non-migrants:

> I was not happy with the first position I was given, but was moved after one week. I feel I should have had an interview before-hand which would have saved this upset.

Only three of the non-migrant group had found jobs outside the firm, all without its assistance. Of the rest, seven had achieved a job of higher status and only two had suffered a decreased status, leaving the majority at the level they had held before the move.

There was a decrease in the number of satisfied non-migrants after the move and an increase in those who were actually dissatisfied. However, only two of the latter group regretted not having moved to Bristol, while a further two were

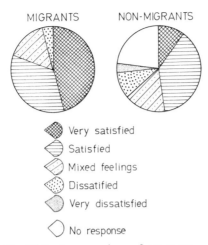

MIGRANTS   NON-MIGRANTS

◈ Very satisfied

⬡ Satisfied

◎ Mixed feelings

◉ Dissatified

◈ Very dissatisfied

◯ No response

Fig. 13.1. A comparison of pre-move
satisfaction over relocation terms

unsure. The reasons advanced for not regretting their decision to remain
emphasized community ties:

I did not wish to leave my friends and family.

I never felt that my job comes before my home and my family.

This last comment typifies the non-migrant. It is spoken by a woman whose
family are not dependent upon her job; it is, rather, a supplementary income. For
a man, the situation is different; his home and family depend on his job and
therefore he must maintain it at all costs, even the cost of migration. The
migrants may be differentiated from the non-migrants by the fact that they stand
to gain more from going than from staying.

The Migrant Employees

One hundred and two employees, accompanied by their families where
applicable, formed the migrant group. In general, they were male, between 20
and 40 years of age, and married. These employees have most to gain from
remaining in the career structure of one firm. The employment grades of the
migrants confirm their predominantly middle status. The vast majority were well
established within the firm, 79 per cent (64/82) for more than 10 years. There is a
clear contrast here with the non-migrant group, although the migrants had also
had little previous migratory experience.

Job Dependence

Employees have been divided into two basic types, characterized as 'locals'
and 'spiralists' in sociological literature (e.g. Pahl, 1970). The former may make

more than one housing move in their lifetime, but they tend to remain within the same locality, in this case London, and to achieve their desired career progression whilst remaining in this locality. The spiralists on the other hand are the managers or aspiring managers who move around geographically in order to move upwards socially. The non-work spheres of their lives are subordinated to the demands of their careers. Such a division, however, whilst contributing to an understanding of why employees move around in general, does assume that the choice lies with the individual, and therefore is not so helpful in the particular case of decentralization. It is suggested that dispersal policy provides a unique situation in that it largely disregards any distinction between locals and spiralists. Usually it involves the former, since it makes sense to decentralize the middle-status employees. High-status employees tend to remain behind to manage the smaller central office, while low-status employees are replaced in the new location. For the spiralists who do have to relocate, there is no reward at the end of the move in the form of promotion or pay increases such as they have been used to. The policy faces opposition on all fronts therefore: from spiralists because they are required to move without incentive, and from locals because they are unused to and ill-prepared for long-distance migration. Hence the urgent need for careful advance planning of office relocations.

Decentralized migrants exercise little real choice over the decision to move. Rather their decision is directed by their degree of job dependence. As soon as a relocation is announced, the employees must determine how easy it will be for them to find a comparable job, and the answer, if they are male, middle-aged and married, is that it will be very difficult. Mobility therefore becomes essential for the maintenance of security and present standard of living. Married men have their families to consider; they are obliged to ensure an acceptable income and can rarely afford to gamble with a new job. When they are middle-aged alternative job opportunities are very few and in those jobs which are available promotion prospects must be reduced by the job transfer. In the case-study, the possibility of redeployment within the firm seemed at first to offer a solution to this problem. However, in practice the higher the job, the less likely was the possibility of being transferred to a position of equivalent status. Secretarial staff stood to lose least from such exchanges, their jobs being fairly easily interchangeable, and hence they formed the majority of the non-migrant group. Johnson *et al.* (1974) note that it is the executive and, occasionally, skilled manual grades which are the groups encouraged to move with their jobs, as well as new recruits to management, while the manual and lower-paid clerical workers are rarely persuaded to relocate. The dominant reaction amongst migrant employees to the relocation was:

I must go to continue my career.

I have no practical alternative.

While the feeling of job dependence was universal within the migrant group, the degree of dependence varied considerably. Amongst the locals, the single employees indicated that, while they regarded their best opportunities as lying within the same firm, if their promotion prospects did not progress as they anticipated in Bristol, they would return to London in search of position which offered increased prospects. They were in a position to take such a gamble because they did not have dependent families. Their married counterparts did not see a return to London as feasible because of the upheaval it would necessitate for their families both socially and environmentally. This group were therefore more job-dependent than their unmarried counterparts. Similarly dependent were the older employees, married and single, who would not find alternative employment because of their age and who were loath to migrate at this advanced stage in their life-cycle:

I have worked in London (in the City) for twenty-two years and have a great affection for the place.

It is vital to ensure that such indiscriminate relocation does not have harmful social effects. Job satisfaction played only a minor role in the decision to migrate, it being at all stages subordinate to job dependence. This is shown clearly by the spiralists who were dissatisfied by the new situation, yet powerless to do anything about it:

My only reason for moving is the fact that I have been ordered to go.

Once the decision to move had been made, many employees appeared to rationalize the situation. One advantage they saw for moving was the opportunity to reside in a healthier environment:

I will be much happier to live and work in a more pleasant environment.

Most of the young migrants took the opportunity of moving to better their housing position and this provided them with an added incentive not applicable to the older employees who had already achieved what they regarded as a satisfactory standard of housing. Another popular reason was that advanced by young female employees who were using the opportunity to move as a means of testing their independence. They would be leaving their parental home for the first time, but the problems would be cushioned by the maintenance of a known work atmosphere:

To try and see if I'd enjoy living away from home.

Although, therefore, the migrants are said to be voluntarily moving, their choice is set against such formidable constraints that the word becomes of dubious value. The choice, in fact, is not concerned with moving, or to where, but whether or not to stay in the job.

Expectations of Bristol

It is on their working knowledge of Bristol at the pre-move stage that the migrants base their decision on where to buy a house, a factor which, because of the importance of accessibility, will have a significant effect on their quality of life. In fact, very few had first-hand experience of the area and even second-hand experience was minimal. Recognition of places in the city declined eastwards of the centre. This may be explained by the location of the most desirable residential areas to the west of the city. It is to these areas that the migrants will have been directed by estate agents. Bateman and Burtenshaw (1973) found in Portsmouth that it is from house-hunting that local area knowledge is largely derived. In view of the importance of the location of the migrants' homes in the reception area in relation to their quality of life, it is desirable that they be given more time to assess the situation. One weekend visit is inadequate and at best can only provide a superficial knowledge of the city centre and surrounding residential suburbs. By the time of the pre-move survey, 93 per cent (76/82) of the migrants had purchased their new houses in the Bristol area, their choice being made within their limited knowledge of the area. As in the South East, their new homes were widely scattered, the most popular location being villages on the outskirts of Bristol, 54 per cent (44/82). This choice satisfied their widely-held preference for rural access.

After Relocation

The problem of relocation are dealt with in order of the migrants' perception of their magnitude. The social isolation that resulted from moving away from family and friends was ranked first by the migrants. Thirty-five per cent (30/85) considered it to be their greatest problem. Comments such as these were common:

The loss of a wide circle of friends has led to boredom.

I am bored because we now live in the country.

The problem is felt acutely because of the flourishing friendship networks that have been lost. Friendship networks will probably take at least two years to redevelop properly, and therefore the only consolation is that the problem should eventually provide its own remedy. Meanwhile, migrants could be better prepared by the firm for the move and advised not to purchase homes in isolated positions. If the migrants do not have private transport of their own, they should be advised to locate within easy access of public transport. The firm could alleviate the situation somewhat by organizing social activities which bring the migrant families together both before and after the move, thus encouraging a closer bond between them and initiating friendship networks.

Employees' wives who do not have a job and single women are the chief sufferers from social isolation:

Being a female on her own restricts me from many social activities.

It is strange that the migrants did not realize how long it takes to replace friendship groups and how essential they are to quality of life.

The financial burden of relocation was also important. As many as 34 per cent (29/85) had spent over £500 of their private savings as a result of the move and 54 per cent (46/85) had spent over £200. These amounts represent significant sums when one considers that they had to be found at short notice. Sixty-nine per cent (59/85) had to draw on savings in order to finance the move, and as a result many were now having to economize on normal expenditure. It is difficult to anticipate all the expenses that migration involves and many employees found themselves in financial difficulties because of the 'unexpected costs involved'. The problem here is such that while migrants in general are prepared to undergo a measure of financial strain because they want to move, the dispersal migrant views it as a hardship he must endure for the benefit of the firm rather than himself. The situation is exacerbated by the loss of the London Allowance. Its replacement by a 'special allowance' of £201 for the first year after the move and the company's Large Town allowance of £51 per annum after that was considered inadequate. Dispersing firms should be wary of exaggerating the relative cheapness of decentralized living. The pre-move survey showed that the migrants expected Bristol to be a considerably cheaper place in which to live than London. Dispersing firms do make long-term financial gains from dispersal (Rhodes and Kan, 1971) and, in recognition of this face, should be prepared to be generous to the employees they relocate.

Problems resulting from the location and characteristics of the reception centre were felt acutely by 29 per cent of the migrants (25/85). In the case of Bristol, the chief complaint related to its transport facilities. Not only was private transport rendered almost impossible by congestion, particularly in peak periods, but public transport was totally unreliable:

The traffic is terrible and there is an awful parking problem.

Public transport is a farce.

Such problems are felt acutely because of the ramifications for every aspect of daily life: getting to work, to the shops, visiting, and so on. There were also complaints about poor shopping facilities and inadequate social provision particularly for youngsters.

These problems are exacerbated by a rapid increase in population which does not allow time for service provision to keep pace. The best way to prepare for such difficulties is to allow the migrants more time to assess the situation in the reception centre. Bearing in mind that they play no part in choosing their prospective residential area, there is a need to provide them with more and longer reconnaissance visits in order that they may make a realistic assessment of the services the town has to offer. Many migrants realized this need too late:

> Whilst it seemed at the time that we had been to Bristol enough to accept the move, on reflection from occasional weekend stays it is very difficult to obtain a clear picture of the place.

> The firm was rather ambiguous concerning details of the move. Various things such as rush hour are contrary to what we had been led to expect.

The sudden discovery of such discrepancies leads employees to conclude they have been purposely misled and hence brings dissatisfaction.

Twenty-eight per cent (24/85) considered housing to have been their chief headache. Not only were house prices higher in the Bristol area than they had been led to believe, but also they were unfortunately forced to sell in the South East in a buyer's market. Six months after relocation, at least 12 houses remained unsold in the South East and many others had finally been sold at lower prices than originally anticipated:

> I had to drop my price to find a buyer.

> It took nine months to sell even at reduced price.

Dispersal migrants are again at a disadvantage here compared with the individual migrant, who can at least choose the time of his migration to best suit his needs. It is essential for compensation in this field to be generous and speedy.

Complaints over education were minimal despite the firm showing little interest in this aspect. It would seem that in view of the general satisfaction with the education facilities, dispersing firms could use this to their advantage. It is likely that schools in the South East may be more crowded and offer fewer facilities than those in the provinces and therefore that the children will benefit from a move. Many employees found the Bristol education system better:

> The standard of education is higher.

> Greater interest in the child by the teacher.

If relocating firms could establish such facts before the move, they could be used to attract the employees to the new location, particularly since the employees most involved in dispersal are those with young families.

The final problem that emerged was that of finding employment for other members of the relocated employees' family, chiefly wives and adult children. Here the wives emerged as the chief victims. Firms have yet to realize the need to provide information on the job potential for dependants in the reception centre. The latter must provide an adequate range of job opportunities for dependants if

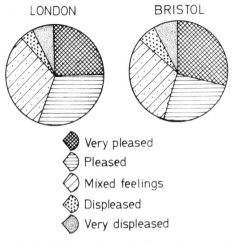

Fig. 13.2. Comparison of migrants' pre- and post-move attitudes to relocation

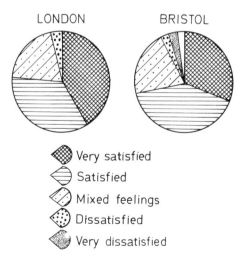

Fig. 13.3. Comparison of migrants' satisfaction with their treatment by the firm

careers are not to be curtailed simply as a result of decentralization.

Despite these problems, the majority of migrants remained pleased that they had relocated. No real shift of opinion had occurred since the pre-move stage (Fig. 13.2). Degree of satisfaction with the firm's treatment suffered only a slight decrease after the move (Fig. 13.3). A survey two years after relocation designed to identify the number of employees who actually did return to the South East would provide a long-term assessment of the success of dispersal schemes.

The Wives' Dilemma

The wives are affected most by relocation: they have to cope with a change of home, friends, and environment, while their husbands at least maintain a constant work atmosphere. Children too depend on their mother's ability to cope. A successful move therefore revolves in considerable measure around the wife. It is essential for the wives that relocation takes place to a centre with a variety of shopping, social, educational and employment potential. The problems vary depending on whether the wife is working or not. Working wives must find a new job, arrange transport to it, and find time for shopping and household chores, all in a foreign environment. There is some evidence that greater attention is finally being given to the problems of working wives (Bateman and Burtenshaw, 1976). Housewives' problems revolve around transporting children to new schools, shopping and generally operating in the strange environment. Their chief enemy will be boredom resulting from the sudden absence of friends. The problems for both types of migrant wife have often to be surmounted without access to private transport, because in the reception centre it is most usual for the family car to be used by the husband for work.

Seven wives completed space–time diaries both before and after moving (Table 13.1). These diaries ran for three days. Thursday, Friday and Saturday were chosen in order to obtain both weekday and weekend activities. All that was requested in the way of information was the nature, duration, and location of each activity throughout the three days and the type of transport used if any. Activities were broadly defined in categories such as household chores, shopping, work, leisure, and so on. This meant the wives were not required to be specific about the precise nature of their activities and would therefore be less likely to take offence. The general picture that emerged was one of increased dependence on the private car. Those wives who are both employed and do not have access to a car are the most severely constrained group. Wife A is an example (Table 13.1).

With regard to working wives, it was the professional jobs which caused the most severe problems. They do not fall vacant regularly and so few openings are created for newcomers and few opportunities presented for promotion. The situation in the South East is more fluid; people move from place to place creating waves of vacancies. This situation gave rise to comments such as:

Table 13.1. Comparison of Pre- and Post-Move Activities of Wives A to G

Wife	Location	Total time travelling	No. of leisure visits	No. of shopping visits	No. of work visits	No. of school visits	No. of other visits
A	London	2hr. 35min	3	3	2	–	–
	Bristol	6hr. 46min	3	2	2	–	–
B	London	1hr. 20min	1	2	–	–	–
	Bristol	1hr. 20min	2	1	–	–	–
C	London	1hr. 2min	1	3	–	12	–
	Bristol	1hr. 10min	3	1	–	–	–
D	London	2hr. 15min	3	5	–	–	–
	Bristol	6hr. 30min	3	3	–	–	–
E	London	2hr. 25min	3	4	–	–	–
	Bristol	2hr. 34min	2	3	–	–	–
F	London	2hr. 45min	–	4	4	–	–
	Bristol	30min	–	1	–	–	–
G	London	1hr. 40min	1	1	2	–	–
	Bristol	40min	2	1	–	–	1

My chief problem is the lack of job prospects in the immediate future. The surplus of teachers makes promotion for young people an impossibility in an area where the teachers stay in schools for years on end.

In contrast, office jobs in Bristol, while they did not compare favourably with the salaries received in London, were not in short supply and generally regarded as satisfactory.

Even once a job has been found, problems are not at an end. The migrant working wife must arrange transport to and from the job. While in the South East the majority had used public transport, in the dispersed location the majority used private transport, usually in conjunction with one or two forms or public transport:

My journey home *from* work is four miles and involves two buses, neither of which connects with the other. If I miss the second bus, I either wait one hour for the next one, or walk two miles to my home. I tend to opt for the latter! Fortunately, I have a lift *to* work in the morning (15 minutes). My return journey of four miles takes me between 40–80 minutes.

Not only is this an instance of the more complicated transport situation in the dispersed location, it is also an example of the considerable time constraint such a situation imposes. In this particular case, anything up to one hour is wasted daily on the journey home from work. In comparison with her pre-move situation, she has to leave half an hour earlier in the morning and, instead of arriving home at 4.30 pm, it is 5.30 pm (wife A). This was by no means an exceptional instance:

> Bristol traffic is very congested and it takes an excessive amount of time to reach home in the evening.

> I have to add 20 minutes to my 55-minute bus journey to work for my journey home from work because of traffic congestion.

It is essential that the planning authorities in reception centres ensure that such important services as public transport and road capacity are able to absorb the increased demands placed upon them by the influx of office migrant families. Service capacity must be increased in phase with population growth.

The chief problem of the non-working wives was boredom. This resulted from a combination of the loss of a wide circle of friends, isolated residential locations and the inadequate transport situation. Wives who do not have access to a private car are constrained to remain within a very restricted radius of their homes during the week (wife F). The chief mode of transport is walking, anything up to 20 minutes being common, for shopping, collecting children and socializing. Many wives were taking driving lessons with the intention of buying a second car. Such extra expense is unexpected and should not be so essential. There is a strong case for an improved bus service in Bristol.

Despite such problems, however, none of the wives admitted to being seriously disappointed with their move, although 46 per cent (10/22) did express mixed feelings.

Life-Style in Bristol—Work Access

An easier, shorter journey to and from work is one of the chief inducements for decentralization. Given that South East commuters are essentially long-distance travellers, it is anticipated that in the relocation centre savings will be made particularly in time, thus enhancing quality of life by reducing an unproductive pursuit and increasing family and leisure periods. In fact, the longest journeys undertaken in the South East were reduced, those over two hours per day from 39 per cent (32/82) to 7 per cent (6/85), and no one travelled for three hours each day as 7 per cent (6/82) had done in the pre-move environment. However, for the majority there was little saving in time. Seventy-four per cent (63/85) still travelled for more than one hour each day (Fig. 13.4). What savings there might have been were often eroded by employees having to leave home earlier than necessary and work later than necessary simply in order to avoid peak-hour congestion. A system of flexible hours might have eased this problem:

> I need to leave early in order to avoid the traffic at the morning peak hour.

Because the majority of employees used the train and/or tube for travelling to and from work in the South East (92.7 per cent), a change of mode was certain

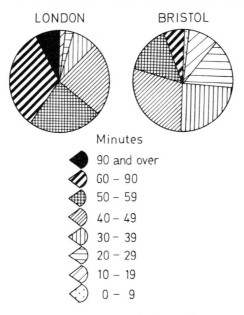

Fig. 13.4. Comparison of migrants' journey
to work : time

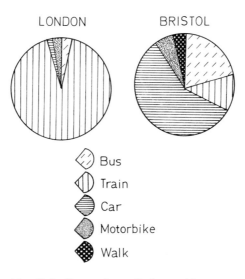

Fig. 13.5. Comparison of migrants' journey
to work : mode

after relocation. In Bristol, 57 per cent (48/85) used private cars, 21 per cent (18/85) the bus and only 12 per cent (10/85) were close enough to a station to use the train (Fig. 13.5). While most residents working in the central area of Bristol travel to work by bus, a sizeable majority do use the car as mode of transport (Bristol Planning Department, 1973). This change from public to private transport has serious ramifications for city centre congestion and parking in a city like Bristol, which is increasing office employment in its central area so rapidly. In view of the unprecedented rise in the price of petrol and the cost of city centre parking, this change of mode meant little financial saving was possible on the pre-move situation. However, for those still travelling by public transport costs were reduced after the move, with the majority paying between 20–40 pence per day instead of between 40–74 pence per day. In view of the individual and community gains if more use is made of public transport, it should be of high priority to increase the efficiency of the public transport service in reception towns.

Forty-one per cent (35/85) of the migrants complained about their journeys to and from work. Typical comments from the private motorists were:

Traffic is heavy and parking facilities are poor.

The volume of traffic entering and leaving Bristol city centre is very heavy.

The parking facilities provided at the office are very limited and only a few daily spaces are guaranteed. This gave rise to ill-feelings; the only alternatives available were the expensive multistorey car parks. Many considered the firm should provide a parking subsidy to offset such costs.

Complaints from public transport users took the following form:

The bus suits itself as to whether it turns up.

The bus crews have complete contempt for those they are employed to serve.

The problem of finding a bus to catch, added to that of road congestion, rendered this form of transport thoroughly unpopular. Because only a few employees had had the foresight to move within access of the railway, the latter played only a minor role despite its alleged efficiency by those who could use it:

It is shorter, less tiring and cheaper.

It is ironic that the journey to and from work about which so much is promised should prove so fraught with problems. As many as 27 per cent (23/85) felt that while it was not worse, it certainly did not represent an improvement. Some comments were:

I have the frustration of traffic jams and it takes the same time as previously.

Formerly I had a direct route, now it is bus/train/bus.

I am unable to be sure how long the journey will take, and therefore what time to leave for work in the morning.

The only solution is to improve the public transport system and lure as many as possible of the migrants at present using private transport on to public transport. New offices exacerbate the transport problem because they prefer city centre locations. This is in contrast with much of LOB decentralization propaganda, which emphasizes rural locations for relocated offices.

Service Access

The migrants experienced slight decreases in their levels of accessibility to shops, public transport, public open space and schools after relocation. Only public transport was poor enough to cause widespread dissatisfaction with the Bristol environment, however. Because public transport affects so much of daily life, any inadequacies are emphasized. Thus the migrants' perception of minor difficulties in other spheres of daily life is magnified. In Bristol, the general impression was one of a decreased level of accessibility to all services and facilities except the countryside. The migrants had been so well catered for in the South East that the services were taken for granted and their importance for quality of life only realized after many had moved to isolated residential locations in villages surrounding Bristol. While access to the countryside is pleasant, it is more essential to have access to less attractive services such as public transport, schools and a variety of shops. It is unwise of LOB to stress the advantages of decentralization in chiefly rural terms, thus encouraging migrants to relocate to isolated villages.

Leisure Access

There was a notable decrease in the migrants' social life after relocation. As anticipated, they visited friends less frequently, although the situation was relieved by increased interaction with colleagues and their families. Such contacts could be fostered by the firm through organized social events, since they form an important cushion for the harsh realities of social isolation that accompany relocation. Relatives were missed more than had been expected because of the scarcity of other social contacts. Social life is enhanced not only by personal interaction, but also by the individual's degree of involvement in the local community. In the South East, 39 per cent (29/74) of the migrants enjoyed being involved in community affairs and all the migrants led active social lives. There is no evidence that moving to Bristol constrained their leisure activities. Yet their degree of satisfaction with the recreational facilities at their disposal fell with the move from 68 per cent (50/74) regarding facilities as adequate in the South East

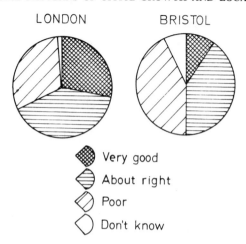

Fig. 13.6. Comparison of migrants' assessment of their local leisure provision

to 49 per cent (42/85) in the South West (Fig. 13.6). This drop in the level of satisfaction despite no actual fall-off in provision or participation may be explained by the fact that the migrants have a less satisfactory social life due to the absence of friends and they blame Bristol rather than the process of migration itself.

General Conclusion

This study has encompassed two objectives. The first was employee-oriented and considered the effects of decentralization on the life-styles of a group of relocated employees and their families. It is hoped that such information may help achieve a clearer understanding of the optimum location for offices and be of practical benefit both to putative relocating firms and their employees and to planning authorities likely to have to deal with the upheaval caused by such enforced migration. A second objective was to illustrate the potential of the before-and-after longitudinal survey technique for office decentralization research. There are therefore two areas in which conclusions may be drawn.

The Social Aspects

Naturally, the migrants were wise after the event. They regarded Bristol more realistically and recognized the importance of accessibility to essential urban goods and services for quality of life. It may well be that many of them will gradually move closer to Bristol than they are at present and in so doing reconcile their desire for urban and rural access. The relocating firm too should be wiser after the event and it is to be hoped that its experience, unlike so many others, will not be confined to itself. It is essential that prospective migrants be given realistic descriptions of their reception town and that aspects such as transport and employment for dependants be fully researched. The truth will not deter employees from migrating, because they are committed through job dependency; it would simply ensure that they were better prepared to cope with the migration situation. The migrants recognized this requirement after the event:

I trust that this survey will help management to avoid euphoria in their projected dispersals from London and in particular more note taken of public transport.

Although Bristol as a whole is a better environment than London, we were led to believe that all our worries would be over and the facilities were wonderful. From the point of view of variety of life especially entertainment, etc., this is not so and leaves a vague feeling of Bristol having been oversold.

The results show very little strong dissatisfaction amongst non-migrants, even though this is one of the greatest problem areas in the dispersal process. It does seem that the transition can be undertaken successfully. Ample warning of the move is essential to allow employees time to consider their situation and grow accustomed to what is involved, whether it be a new job in London or a new home in the reception area. The problem of unemployment did not materialize for the non-migrants in this particular study. Whether this is generally true for office employees, as opposed to factory employees, because jobs for the former are more plentiful in London, or whether it was due to the operation of the redeployment policy requires further investigation. In addition, contrary to any adverse effects as a result of relocation, some of the non-migrants even felt they had benefited from the enforced job transfer:

The change in work has given me a much broader outlook on employment which I feel I need.

Assessment of the extent to which such attitudes are general would provide strong justification for the future continuation of the office dispersal policy. Large-scale surveys are required into relocating firms who do not operate a redeployment policy. If the latter is found to be the real cause of diminished problems for the non-migrants as indicated, then either only large firms able to operate such a policy should be encouraged to decentralize or government aid should be made available. It has always been the excuse in the past that large groups of non-migrants are difficult to identify. This is no longer the case in view of the publicity which surrounds large office dispersals as soon as they are announced. The opportunities thus presented should be seized and the true costs and benefits of dispersal policy for the departure area and the non-migrant group established.

The experience of Bristol as a reception centre stresses the necessity for such centres to pre-plan carefully for large-scale dispersals. Services are likely to be subject to new pressures which must be catered for in order to prevent reducing quality of life, not only for the migrants but also for the established residents. But it was shown to be equally necessary that firms wishing to decentralize should take into account in their choice of location the infrastructure which each town can offer, and its relationship with the requirements of the employees it wishes to relocate.

A second consideration even more vital to the success of regional policy at the outset than the provision of an adequate infrastructure was the importance attached by the firm to the image of the reception area. Bristol has the image of an attractive, healthy and pleasant place in which to reside. The firm by their own admission realized that, while it would be more helpful in terms of regional development to decentralize in a northerly direction, their task in persuading key staff to move was likely to be facilitated by a move to a city like Bristol. Such a consideration was of prime importance to the company. Many people living in the South East remain unconvinced of the residential desirability of the towns in the Development Areas, which have a uniform image, despite their hetero-geneity. Until this image is corrected, firms will be the more reluctant to risk decentralizing to these areas.

The Methodology

The initial problem in this type of survey is to isolate a firm which is typical of the majority of decentralizers from London, both in its type of move and in its approach to the move. The latter presents the problem. It was found that only firms which had confidence in the success of their approach were willing to subject themselves to the scrutiny of a longitudinal survey. Thus, the study firm, while typical of many with respect to its move, was perhaps more inclined to be thorough in its pre-move preparations and more aware of the pitfalls than many firms which embark on decentralization.

There were two new features in the social framework of the survey. First, the survey comprised a before-and-after longitudinal study. The most convincing argument for the future adoption of this was that the method revealed significant changes in the migrants' attitudes to and perception of the situation during the process of the move. For instance, their perception of Bristol as a residential town was idealistic before relocation. And it was upon this pre-move idealism that they based their removal decisions, such as the location of their new homes. After the move the migrant families became more aware of the importance of access to urban services and particularly aware of the need for efficient public transport, matters which would materially affect the style and quality of their life in the new location, but which had generally played little part in the pre-move decisions.

A second innovation of the social study was the inclusion of all the groups of individuals affected by the move. Not only the migrant employees, but also their wives, and the non-migrant employees were involved. For the process of decentralization affects socially both those who leave and those who do not. Only the inclusion of all three ensures that every aspect of the implications of dispersal is considered as part of the complete process. Perhaps the greatest problem of the social survey lay in the initial attitude of the migrants. They were sensitive to identification and many objected to the request for addresses. Antagonism was reduced to a minimum by the personal interviews, where it was possible to offer detailed explanations.

Directions for Future Research

The study presented here is an isolated example. For its results to be verified and its conclusions to be substantiated, further studies along similar lines are required. The before-and-after longitudinal survey method for such research has proved comprehensive and effective and bears repetition in order to gain comparable results from other office dispersal exercises. The conclusions of the study indicate the areas where further research would prove fruitful. Using a similar approach, various sizes of office should be analysed, including both complete and partial moves, in order to establish whether the latter really are easier to effect. With the aim of facilitating the process of dispersal for firms which would in turn minimize the problems that arise, a framework could be constructed of the basic dispersal procedure using the experiences of successful case-study firms as a basis. Further research, so long as its results are made known and acted upon, can only make the lot of everyone involved in enforced migration a better one.

References

Bateman, M., and Burtenshaw, D. (1974), *Social Implications of Office Dispersal Policies*. Paper presented to the IBG Conference Symposium on Office Location Policy, Norwich, January.

Bateman, M., and Burtenshaw, D. (1976), *Office Decentralisation to a Provincial Centre*. London: Final Project Report to Social Science Research Council.

Bateman, M., Burtenshaw, D., and Duffett, A. (1973), *Re-Housing Migrant Office Workers*. Paper presented to the first Anglo-German Geographical Seminar, Giessen, Würzburg, München, April.

Bristol Planning Department (1973), *Offices in Bristol, 1945–1973*. Bristol: City Planning Department.

Carey, S. J. (1969), *Relocation of Office Staff: A Study of the Reactions of Office Staff Decentralized to Ashford*. London: Location of Offices Bureau, Research Paper No. 4.

Carey, S. J. (1970), *Relocation of Office Staff: A Follow-up Survey*, London: Location of Offices Bureau, Research Paper No. 4a.

Donnison, D., and Eversley, D. (Eds.) (1973), *London: Urban Patterns, Problems and Policies*. London: Heinemann.

Hammond, E. (1968), *London to Durham: A Study of the Transfer of the Post Office Savings Division*. Durham: Rowntree Research Unit.

Johnson, J. H., Salt, J., and Wood, P. A. (1974), *Housing and the Migration of Labour in England and Wales*. London: Saxon House.

Location of Offices Bureau (1975), *Statistical Handbook*. London: Location of Offices Bureau.

Mann, M. (1973), *Workers on the Move*. London: Cambridge University Press.

Murray, H., Spink, P. K., Welchman, R., Drake, R., and Griffiths, J. T. (1972), *The Location of Government Review: Human Aspects of Dispersal*. London: Tavistock Institute of Human Relations.

Pahl, R. E. (1970), *Whose City? And other Essays on Sociology and Planning*. London: Longmans.

Rhodes, J., and Kan, A. (1971), *Office Dispersal and Regional Policy*. London: Cambridge University Press.

Social Science Research Council (1975), *Longitudinal Studies*. London: Report of an SSRC Working Party.

14

Office Dispersal and The Journey to Work in Greater London: A Follow-Up Study

P. W. DANIELS

Introduction

Ever since the London Borough of Croydon showed in the late 1950s that it could successfully encourage suburban office development as a counterweight to the highly congested and expensive central area of London, there has been a steady outward movement of offices to suburban locations. Between 1963 and 1977 some 52,500 office jobs have left central London for destinations which are primarily in the outer suburbs and these statistics only refer to private sector companies (Location of Offices Bureau, 1976). Decentralization of this kind, although perhaps not at this scale, is now a well-established phenomenon in large metropolitan areas (Schwartz, Ch. 9; Armstrong, Ch. 3; Goddard, Ch. 2) and a growing number of them, including Greater London, are attempting to ensure that this restructuring process is carefully controlled and adequately meets strategic, as well as local, planning objectives (Greater London Council, 1976; Daniels, 1977). The need to decentralize office employment in London was encouraged during the 1960s by the ever-increasing length of journeys to work from the Metropolitan Region into the central area. The flight of office workers from inner London to residential areas within and beyond the Green Belt had, at least up to 1961, not been accompanied by equivalent changes in the distribution of employment, so that both journey to work costs to individual employees and congestion during the peak hours increased steadily during the decade as more and more people were affected by the deteriorating relationship between the location of residences and employment. Amongst the advantages mooted for dispersed patterns of urban office development have been the improvement in the journey to work both for those workers travelling to suburban rather than

373

central business district office buildings and for those who continue to travel to work under less congested conditions to the central city office complexes. Harkness (1973) has produced a good theoretical examination of the travel advantages of dispersed office development in cities, although unfortunately there is relatively little empirical work which lends support for one or other of the alternative models which are suggested.

Although intuitively attractive, support for dispersed suburban office development has not been universal in London or in other cities such as Toronto (Gad, Ch. 11), which is currently engaged in a careful examination of the issues involved. It has been argued that locating new office development in the suburbs and decentralizing some existing office employment so that more homes are nearer to workplaces does not bring about improvements in the journey to work. On the contrary, the journey to work will become more difficult, will jeopardize the future of public transport and will lead to excessive expenditure on redesigned suburban transport networks. With office workers continuing to move further and more rapidly out of London than their jobs in search of residential areas, it would be more advantageous to improve the conditions of existing journeys into the central area, including the staggering of work hours, than to attempt to move office employment out of the centre (Department of the Environment, 1972; Thorburn, 1970). Such views seem to ignore the realities revealed in *Census* data or by studies of the journey to work in large cities.

If the trends revealed by the 1966 and 1971 *Censuses* have been continuing, it would be difficult to escape the conclusion that proposals for locating office development in suburban London make sense. The number of office workers employed in Greater London increased from 1.53 million in 1966 to 1.56 million in 1971, and of these some 1.31 million were resident in the metropolitan area with the balance represented by in-commuters (Fig. 14.1). While the proportion of the total labour force employed in offices in each individual London borough increased in line with the overall increase from 36.1 to 38.3 per cent, these changes were not uniformly distributed. Almost all the inner boroughs, including the City of London, had a smaller share of total office employment in 1971 than in 1966, but the outer suburban boroughs increased their share or revealed no significant changes. Croydon, for example, had 2.9 per cent of London's office workers employed there in 1966, increasing to 3.6 per cent in 1971. The significance of this employment redistribution can also be demonstrated by comparing borough shares of total office jobs with their share of all jobs in Greater London. Outer boroughs such as Bromley, Bexley or Redbridge increased their share of office jobs while total employment remained static. Elsewhere in the outer boroughs where both values increased, the rate of change for office jobs was always higher, such as at Croydon, Hounslow or Kingston-upon-Thames. The converse occurred in the inner boroughs (which include part of the central area), where the share of office jobs fell more rapidly than total jobs between 1966 and 1971, particularly in the City of London and Westminster.

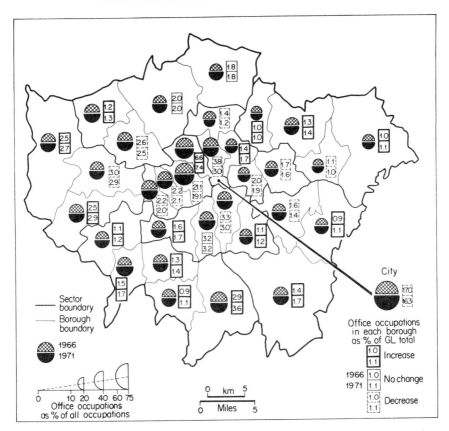

Fig. 14.1. Office occupations as a proportion of all occupations in the Greater London boroughs and changes in the share of Greater London office occupations in each borough, 1966–71. (Sources: General Register Office, *Sample Census 1966*, 1969; Office of Population Censuses and Surveys, *Census 1971*, 1975)

The corollary of these trends is that a growing proportion of Greater London's office workers now live and work in the same borough (Fig. 14.2). The number of clerical workers travelling into central London in 1971 declined by 7 per cent from 457,000 in 1966 to 425,000. Increased costs of commuting, and the changing location of office employment opportunities as well as changes in the market for office labour were all responsible for this decline. The high cost of office floorspace in central London is also likely to make organizations anxious to employ only those staff at that location who can give a high return in the form of more or larger contracts or high-quality market intelligence, for example, relative to the cost of the floorspace that they occupy. Although the number of clerical workers resident and working in Greater London increased by less than 1 per cent between 1966 and 1971, in the outer boroughs 2 to 4 per cent increases were

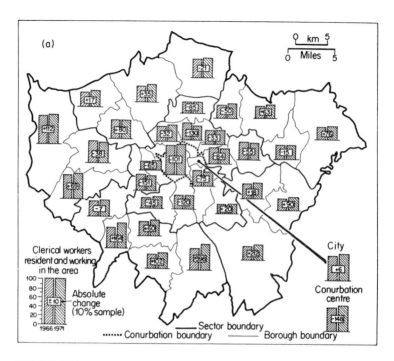

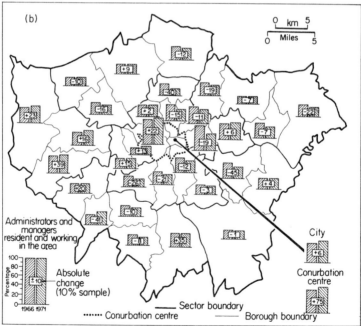

Fig. 14.2. Changes in the distribution of (a) clerical workers and (b) administrators and managers resident and working in the same London borough, 1966–71. (Sources: General Register Office, *Sample Census 1966*, 1969; Office of Population Censuses and Surveys, *Census 1971*, 1975)

common. Labour markets for clerical workers in the suburbs should therefore be tending towards greater self-containment as decentralized offices 'settle' into their new environment and as the related journey to work patterns become more stable. The changes between 1966 and 1971 for administrators and managers are less encouraging, however, since fewer were living and working in the same borough at the end of the period. At the same time, the number commuting into central London increased by 14.3 per cent (88,780 to 101, 510). To some extent this is a product of the character of office employment growth in the suburbs which has been dominated by routine clerical functions, and managerial and administrative functions become 'residual' activities in the central area. Further separation of the homes and workplaces of higher-order office workers, therefore, continued to be an important element of commuting in Greater London between 1966 and 1971.

Greater self-containment of suburban labour catchment areas may be partly due to the location behaviour of decentralized offices. More substantive evidence is still required but it appears that many office organizations which decentralize to the suburbs choose the same sectors as that from which a large proportion of their central London staff already travel (Townsley, 1973; Daniels, 1976; Orrom and Wright, 1976). Since the residential mobility of office workers in London relative to their workplace mobility is low compared to those affected by longer-distance office moves (Hammond, 1968; Bateman et al., 1971; Daniels, 1972a), coincidence between labour catchment areas prior to decentralization and subsequent location choices by relocating offices makes good sense if existing staff are to be retained. Certainly there are some commuters to suburban offices who accept the higher time and money costs of difficult work trips, but for the majority there is a marked improvement in the journey to work (White, 1976). More problematical is the 'cost' of these changes as a result of the lower levels of public transport utilization which seem to follow from dispersal of office jobs within cities (Wabe, 1967; Daniels, 1972b; 1973). To some extent the significance of this problem depends on whether the changes in the ratio of public to private transport revealed by cross-sectional surveys at suburban offices are in fact sustained as they become better integrated into decentralized locales. This issue will be very briefly examined in this chapter on the basis of a follow-up study of the journey to work to decentralized offices, which were first surveyed in 1969 and examined again in 1976, in suburban London.

The indications are that even though central area office workers reveal a city-wide distribution of residences every household is seeking to minimize the separation between home and workplace (Carroll, 1949; 1952). This is usually achieved by trading off the lower cost of a suburban residential area against the higher cost of travelling to the CBD. Accessibility to radial transport routes into the centre is important to these households and this factor may also promote further out-migration of CBD office worker households in the way which is taking place in Greater London for administrators and managers. But for off-centre or suburban workplaces these kinds of residential patterns no longer pertain (Carroll, 1952; Loewenstein, 1960) and the trade-off between housing and transport costs is likely to be less important. More employees will therefore live much closer to their places of work: a hypothesis supported by Carroll's figures and the statistics produced by Loewenstein, who demonstrates that the industry with the greatest number of off-centre workplaces in a selection of American cities, durable goods manufacturing, is characterized by a majority of work trips starting and finishing in the same out-of-town district. Taafe *et al.* (1963) have also demonstrated the higher degree of residential clustering by clerical workers around office centres in the West Suburban area of Chicago in comparison with the dispersed trip origins of clerical workers travelling to destinations in the Loop.

A number of studies have also examined the relationship between residential change and workplace location. In an analysis of residential movement in Philadelphia (Loewenstein, 1960) it was found that only 7 per cent of the moves were made in response to changes in job location but, in many cases, there was a concomitant reduction in the journey to work. Employees working in the suburbs were more prepared to change address than those working in the centre of the city and for workers already living in the suburbs, easing the stresses of work travel to off-centre and central area workplaces was more important than residential amenity of the kind which attracts households away from the central city. Burtt (1967) made similar observations in his study of the journey to work effects of industrial relocation in Boston, and Simmons (1968, p. 647) has noted that for the population as a whole the journey to work tends to increase with each move, reflecting the residential decentralization process. The only workers who consistently relocate closer to their jobs are those employed in the suburbs. There is an important distinction to be made here, however, between the short- and longer-term responses of workers affected by workplace relocation or who decide to move to workplaces nearer home. In the short term the initial residential location decision may appear adequate but complete residential adjustment may take rather longer. It has been shown (Roseman, 1971) that non-salaried workers at a manufacturing plant in East Moline, Illinois, increased journey to work distances when changing workplace location and although residential location changes certainly reduced travel distances, they did not return to the level of the original mean commuting distance. Similarly, the radical changes in travel conditions which usually follow office relocation produce an immediate modal choice response. While travel to the central area is a high-stress activity dictated by the concentration of offices and the need to rely on public transport, the subsequent transfer to private travel modes is not an unexpected reaction. But time and further expansion at suburban office concentrations may modify subsequent travel behaviour.

The Follow-Up Study in Greater London

One of the starting points for the project from which this chapter draws some material was the view that a single cross-sectional survey of a phenomenon leaves

Table 14.1. Comparison of Offices Participating in 1969 and 1976 Journey to Work Surveys for Greater London, New Malden and Gants Hill

	Greater London		New Malden		Gants Hill	
	1969	1976	1969	1976	1969	1976
Sample population	33	20				
No. of offices	20	14	1	1	1	1
Total employees	4225	3887	472	584	400	250
No. of respondents	1778	1012	239	206	260	53
Males	887	539	177	130	126	21
Females	891	463	62	76	134	32
Missing observations	—	27	3	8	6	4

Sources. Journey to Work Survey, 1969; Follow-Up Survey, 1976.

the researcher with an uneasy feeling about the medium- or long-term validity of the conclusions; say two or three years after the survey was undertaken. This concern seems particularly relevant to the volatile area of urban employment and travel behaviour, especially in view of the tendency towards more dispersed patterns of office development in most major metropolitan areas. A survey of the journey to work changes which are consequent upon office relocation was originally conducted by the author in 1969, when 20 offices which had moved to suburban London agreed to participate (Table 14.1) (Daniels, 1972a). In order to see whether some of the uneasiness about the results of that study were well founded a similar exercise, which involved approaching the same establishments, was again undertaken in 1976. Out of the original 20 offices, 14 agreed to assist again. The remainder had either ceased operations, had moved on to other office buildings at another location or refused to cooperate. In both surveys questionnaires eliciting information about occupation, previous place of employment, car-ownership, residential location, mode of travel and trip time for the journey to work, and other variables were distributed to all the office staff in post on the day of survey at each decentralized establishment. The response rates are given in Table 14.1 along with those for two case-study offices which will be considered later in this chapter after an examination of some of the methodological difficulties confronting follow-up studies of this kind.

Cross-Sectional Surveys

Cross-sectional surveys for examining changes in the journey to work and residential location behaviour of office workers have the advantage that they are a relatively cheap and effective way of obtaining data which permit description of respondent attributes as well as the establishment of some degree of association between continuously or discretely distributed characteristics. This is especially true of measurements related precisely to the particular point in time at which the survey was conducted but is rather less true of retrospective information which can also be gleaned in cross-sectional surveys. Both 1969 and 1976 surveys suffer from the latter; for example, it is necessary to ask office workers about their travel behaviour prior to taking up employment at the decentralized location in order that journey to work changes can be monitored. Here there is increasing dependence on accuracy of recall and this can vary widely between individuals even in relation to events which have taken place during the last 24 hours, let alone for journeys to work which may have been last undertaken several years ago. Repetition of a cross-sectional survey after an interval of time does not, of course, overcome this particular problem but it does allow the identification of trends which might otherwise be overlooked and which are relevant for policy-making to be monitored, provided that comparable survey methods are used and that similar populations are being sampled.

It is important to distinguish here between cross-sectional surveys, taken at time intervals which can vary in length from a few days to several years, and longitudinal surveys, which may be defined as studies which are based upon repeated measurements of the same individuals over time (Wall and Williams, 1970). The interest in a longitudinal study is very clearly focused on temporal change, which is also the objective of cross-sectional surveys repeated at time intervals, but there is extensive literature, much of it critical, on the value of time-consuming surveys which may be examining processes of human adaptation or anthropological change which take years or decades to express themselves as characteristic forms of human behaviour, human anatomy or human growth characteristics. In the context of the present study there are good administrative reasons for not adopting a longitudinal approach, even if it had been considered immediately after the original data collection exercise was completed in 1969. The basic task of retaining information, some of it personal, on a large sample of decentralized office workers would have been very complicated and probably unacceptable to a large proportion of the individuals involved. Longitudinal studies depend on more or less continuous access to the participants and this requires a great deal of mutual trust and cooperation. Given the wide scatter of respondents throughout Greater London and the South East, the task of maintaining contact would have been formidable and costly. There is also little doubt that over an extended period of time involving further questionnaire completion or regular interviews, the patience and enthusiasm of respondents would have quickly dissipated and the comparability of initial and subsequent responses made uncertain. Assuming that non-factual information was also gathered such as opinions about the impact of office dispersal on life-styles, the comfort of the journey to work or the advantages and disadvantages of the new residential environment, the effects of the changing values, aspirations, and goals of individuals would be difficult to take account of in the final analysis. Equally, repetitious completion of basic factual questions about journey times or changes in monetary expenditure on travel might also lead to disinterested and therefore increasingly unreliable respondents. Finally, the initial hypotheses upon which a longitudinal study is based may be modified through time or new hypotheses may emerge. There are therefore formidable administrative problems as well as methodological weaknesses in the longitudinal approach.

The present project is therefore clearly a follow-up cross-sectional study and involves, as far as possible, comparison of data sets derived from an identical sample of offices which have decentralized from central to suburban London and which have subsequently remained at the same location or have only moved a very short distance within the same suburb or urban centre.

The reasons for repeating the 1969 cross-sectional survey in 1976 may become clearer if some consideration is now given to the possible responses of office workers affected by the decision of an organization to decentralize some or all of its central Lodnon functions (see also Sidwell, Ch. 13; Bateman and Burtenshaw, Ch. 12). When a central London office announces to its staff that it intends to move to another location it triggers off a complex set of reactions from both office workers in the exporting location and, ultimately, at the importing or reception centre. Most of these responses are now widely documented (Burtt, 1967; Carey, 1969; Sidwell, 1974; Wabe, 1967; Yannopoulos, 1973; Bateman et al., 1971; Hammond, 1968) and need not be reiterated, but it does seem necessary to stress that they are unlikely to be confined to a relatively short period of one or two years either side of the actual change of location by the office; there may well be 'adjustments' some years after the relocation is completed. This can be illustrated for the journey to work and residential location decisions of different groups of office workers classified on the basis of the location of their place of employment prior to travelling to work at the decentralized office (Daniels, 1972b).

Some Employee Responses Triggered by Office Relocation

Consider first the case of those employees in post in a central London office at the time of the decision to decentralize to suburban London. Assuming that their department is to be moved, these employees must decide whether to stay with their present employer and, if the decision is affirmative, whether or not they should change their place of residence in relation to the new workplace location. If the dispersal does not involve all departments they could try to move to a department remaining in central London. The sequence of decisions is unlikely to exactly follow this pattern, however, since the basic facts about the destination of the relocating office and its accessibility from the present residential location may immediately resolve the problem for an employee of whether or not to remain with his employer. If the office moves to a location within the same sector of the metropolitan area for which the employee already commutes he will, all other things being equal, probably decide not to change address and risk family and other upheavals (Carey, 1969; Bateman et al., 1971; Hammond, 1968). An additional consideration in London is that labour catchment areas are generally well divided north and south of the Thames and any cross-river commuting would increase the probability of changing residence or, alternatively, changing job. Depending on how long it is since an office included in the 1969 survey has moved, an individual of this kind can be described as a 'central London non-mover', i.e. an individual who previously worked in central London but now travels to the decentralized office while remaining at his original address. However, it is possible that initial acceptance of the journey to work, possibly over a greater distance and at a higher cost, as a trade-off against residential immobility is eroded either by changes in accessibility of the decentralized offices caused by the withdrawal of a suitable suburban rail connection or increased tunnel tolls, for example, or by growing disillusionment with what initially seemed, by comparison with the journey to the central area, to be a less tiring journey to work. New personal circumstances such as those arising from promotion and improved income may also cause the 'central London non-mover' to reassess his residential location. Such a review could lead to one of three things: a change in method of travel to work since time may now be valued more highly, a decision to change address, or a decision to leave the company and to travel to another location. If either of the first two courses is chosen it will contribute to changes in the journey to work to the decentralized office some time after its establishment at the suburban location. If the latter course of action is chosen and it is assumed that a replacement is recruited, then it is also likely that this person will introduce new characteristics of origin, mode, trip time or distance. Viewed in aggregate for all 'central London non-movers' and those office workers brought in to replace them, these 'adjustments' or changes may possess some general characteristics which indicate that over an extended period of time, say 10 years, patterns and modal choice by this group of decentralized office employees are either likely to change in a certain direction or, alternatively, do not have any significant impact on the journey to work and residential location patterns which prevail shortly after an office has relocated. A cross-sectional survey taken some time after the first survey may help to answer some of these queries.

A second group whose medium- and long-term reactions to dispersal are worth monitoring are the 'central London movers' who, according to the previous study, have made a number of decisions about method of travel to their new place of work from an address selected shortly before or after (six months) their employer moved to the decentralized location. In 1969 some 60 per cent of the central London movers indicated that job location was a 'very important' factor in their decision to change address though, not surprisingly, only 30 per cent of the Greater London respondents in this group attributed this level of significance to this factor.

Depending on the distance moved by offices from central London, it is likely that the initial choice of residential location is based on imperfect knowledge of the housing market, on the quality of local schools, on the access to shopping, and various other criteria important to household when selecting a new address (Bateman *et al.*, 1974; Sidwell, Ch. 13). It therefore seems reasonable to hypothesize that these households will continue to scan local housing opportunities some time after the original move and will accumulate information and experience which could lead to a decision to change place of residence.

Such changes may also be encouraged by new circumstances relating to travel such as deterioration in bus or train frequencies on increased journey times as a result of traffic congestion at suburban centres. The 1969 survey showed that the initial reaction amongst car-owning migrants originally working in central London was to switch to private transport for their journey to work to decentralized locations. It was suggested that the predominant need at suburban locations was therefore to cater for the increased use of private transport for work journeys, especially by car, and that the demise of public transport, especially by rail, would continue.

But this initial wave of enthusiasm for private transport may also be modified as the employee adjusts to the new environment where traffic problems and parking may well be initially perceived as insignificant by comparison with central London but later become magnified as the central London experience recedes into the background. It is not suggested that this response will be widespread amongst the central London movers, but it is most likely at suburban locations in Greater London or in office concentrations in emerging 'office centres' such as Watford, Reading, Southend or Brighton. It is unlikely to be significant at offices which have moved to semi-rural locations 'isolated' from the transport systems of adjacent built-up areas. There are quite a few examples of office moves of this kind in the South East and a number were included in the 1969 study. But if the initial enthusiasm for car-based journeys to work does wane, then does it lead to more car-sharing or a new role for public transport? If this is happening it may also affect the pattern of any post-decentralization changes in residential location exhibited by office staff. Transport changes of this kind may also introduce stability into the modal split for journeys to work to decentralized offices rather than the continuing transfer to private transport which it has been assumed is occurring.

Finally, a similar sequence of decisions can be visualized for those employees who move to a decentralized location from jobs in suburban areas beyond what can be conveniently described as the 'local' recruitment area of each decentralized office. Such individuals may previously have been employed in other offices forming part of an organization's nationwide network or they may have been attracted to work for the decentralizing employer because of the possibility of higher wages. Given that these individuals are more likely to have travelled to work by private transport before changing jobs and are likely to have continued doing so subsequently, the main interest of the follow-up data will rest on any residential changes which have been made and, again, whether they reveal an underlying trend with reference to frequency, spatial configuration, or relationship with changes in travel mode choice for the journey to work.

The third group affected by the decentralization of office employment opportunities are local recruits, who are defined as those staff previously resident or employed in the same suburb as that to which an office has moved. In a metropolitan context this is an arbitrary definition since it is left to individual employees to decide, when they complete the questionnaire, whether they are local recruits or whether they were previously employed in another suburb. In Greater London this decision will depend a great deal on the perception of a particular suburb on the part of an employee; Gants Hill to one clerical worker may be Ilford to another even though both work in the same office building. When an office moves to its new premises local recruits are attracted from other employers, are recruited direct from school, by activating increases in the female activity rate, or by tapping the pool of unemployed labour. For most of the employees in this group a change of workplace location or a first job does not involve a change of residence but will necessitate decisions about mode of travel and trip time. The travel patterns generated depend on whether the decentralized office is located in existing business concentrations or whether an edge-of-suburb or equivalent low-density site is chosen. The latter may require a departure from reliance on the 'usual' mode of travel since edge-of-suburb sites, even in relatively small suburbs, are less well served by public transport than suburban centres. A follow-up cross-sectional survey also permits an assessment of the residential location behaviour of this group in that some employees may move further away from their place of work as their position within an organization crystallizes, including promotion or a better salary.

There is one further consideration relating to local recruits. At the time of the 1969 survey the offices which participated were often amongst the first to move into local labour markets, with one of the considerations in locational choice being the availability of young school-leavers or a female labour force with relatively low activity rates. Such recruits therefore travelled short distances and usually relied on public transport or travelled as car passengers. Since the 1969 survey, however, a number of centres have witnessed substantial growth of office employment and competition for suburban office labour has therefore also increased. This may lead to recruitment from much wider catchment areas and longer journeys to work which are above the average for local recruits as a whole and could be considered as a medium- or long-term disadvantage of dispersal.

Problems of Comparison

The problem of comparing journey to work and residential location patterns at two points in time should not be underestimated. It is easy enough to speculate about how three groups of staff are likely to be affected and about how aggregate travel and residential location patterns have changed between the two survey dates but it is more difficult to be confident about the accuracy of the actual comparisons. To begin with, like is not being compared with like even though the same office establishments are used in both surveys. While location may be a constant, transport and accessibility characteristics will have changed, perhaps following local road-widening, the opening of a motorway with an interchange near the office site, or as a result of changes in public transport timetables. The possibilities are numerous and include changes in local traffic conditions consequent upon other firms moving into an area and occupying office and other buildings which will generate additional journeys to work. There is not really any way in which all these new circumstances and their effects on trip times and mode choice can be fully measured in this follow-up study, particularly since no attempt was made to measure accessibility as objectively as possible for at least some of the offices in the earlier study. Emphasis, therefore, must be given to an analysis of the aggregate changes in travel and residential location behaviour where the effects of particular local circumstances of accessibility are overlooked. But their presence must be acknowledged and allowed for when interpreting the outline results presented later in this chapter.

A second qualification which is necessary when comparing the two data sets is that identical employees are not being sampled. There will have been considerable staff turnover between the surveys, as well as promotion of staff in post at the time of the 1969 study, and this does make direct comparison of the results difficult. It is possible to rectify this difficulty to some degree by identifying respondents employed at an office at or before the earlier survey and separating them from later recruits who could belong to any of three groups described above. The fact that individuals were employed by the company at the survey location at the time of the earlier study does not of course mean that those employees actually participated in that survey. In an effort to identify individuals common to both samples, it has therefore been necessary to ask respondents in the follow-up survey whether they can recall completing the earlier questionnaire. Pitfalls clearly abound in an exercise of this kind, but it is hoped that it will begin to provide some answers to the vexed question of whether there are any medium and long-term changes in the journey to work at decentralized offices of which planners and policy-makers should be aware.

Case-Studies in Greater London: Some Preliminary Findings

It is only possible to select a few themes for analysis here, since at the time of writing all the data available had not been analysed. Emphasis is given to a fairly general comparison between the data obtained in 1969 and 1976 from two offices, at New Malden in south-west London and Gants Hill in north-east London, and from all the respondent offices in Greater London (see Table 14.1). Both offices moved from central London to the suburbs during the late 1960s. The office building at New Malden is located adjacent to a Southern Region station approximately 15 km from Charing Cross. The company first occupied the premises in 1967, when it was estimated that 60 per cent of its former central London staff moved with their jobs to New Malden and approximately 40 per cent of these changed address in response to the decentralization decision. The office at Gants Hill moved to its present building in 1968 from the City of London some 13 km from its original location and has since expanded to accommodate an additional building in the centre of Ilford. A point of note concerning the response to the 1976 survey is the marked difference in the size of the sample at the Gants Hill office, although the ratio of male to female respondents is similar. The number of trips sampled at New Malden is about the same as in 1969 but with females comprising a larger share of the response.

The influence of occupation status on travel behaviour and the importance of

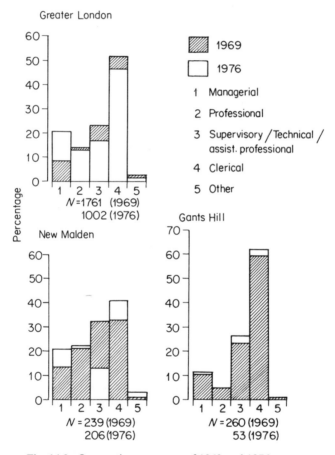

Fig. 14.3. Occupation structure of 1969 and 1976 survey respondents (sources: Office Dispersal Journey to Work Survey, 1969; Follow-Up Survey, 1976). Reproduced with the permission of the Controller of Her Majesty's Stationery Office

previous location of employment on the character of journey to work changes which follow office dispersal has already been stressed and the relevant details are illustrated in Figs. 14.3 and 14.4. The main contrast between the two offices is the predominance of clercial workers at Gants Hill in both years, when the proportion is consistently above the Greater London average. At New Malden, however, only 41 per cent of the 1976 respondents were clerical workers, which is higher than the proportion in 1969 but still below the equivalent value of 47.1 per cent for all the London offices. Managerial and professional occupations therefore represent less than 16 per cent of the respondents at Gants Hill and there is no respondent in the latter category in 1976. There are as many managerial and professional respondents as clerical respondents at New Malden and it can be anticipated that this will influence the structure of journey to work travel at each location.

Central London recruits represent a smaller proportion of the respondents in 1976, especially those who had previously worked for the decentralized employer in central London (Fig. 14.4). Both offices have continued to attract personnel from other central London employers, with the increase at New Malden reflecting the general trend. The central London recruits have been replaced, as

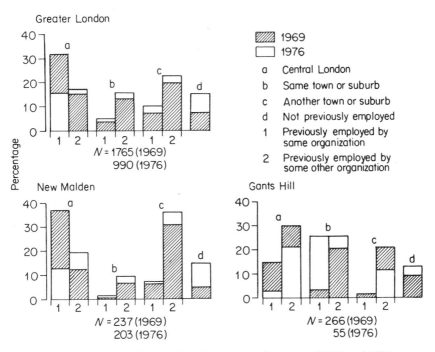

Fig. 14.4. Comparison of the previous places of employment of 1969 and 1976 survey respondents. (sources: General Register Office, *Sample Census 1966*, 1969; Office of Population Censuses and Surveys, *Census 1971*, 1975). Reproduced with the permission of the Controller of Her Majesty's Stationery Office

expected, by office staff recruited from the suburban area in which each office is located. Again, the case-study offices reveal divergent trends in that local recruits at New Malden comprise just 10.2 per cent of the respondents in 1976 compared with 20 per cent for Greater London as a whole and 51 per cent at Gants Hill. This represents a much slower growth in the number of local recruits since 1969 while the proportion at Gants Hill has more than doubled. It would be reasonable to expect therefore that the catchment area for Gants Hill office staff is even more compact and involves shorter journey times than in 1969 but at New Malden the changes are likely to be rather muted, especially as the proportion of staff from other suburbs and towns outside New Malden has increased to 36 per cent. An additional factor which will contribute to travel contrasts is the proportion of office staff who did not have previous jobs. These are usually the lower paid, often female, staff (sometimes employed on a part-time basis) who are largely from the local area. They now represent almost 15 per cent of the labour force in the offices which comprise the Greater London sample.

A continuation of the trend towards an increased share of private transport modes for the journey to work might also follow from higher levels of car ownership amongst suburban office workers. There have been some substantial changes since 1969 (Fig. 14.5), even though the proportion of lower paid office staff, especially the previously unemployed, form a larger part of the sample. For all Greater London offices the proportion of respondents from households without a car or van has declined from 25.5 to 14.1 per cent and this is replicated

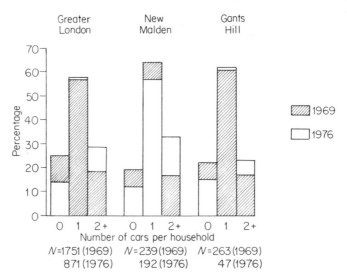

Fig. 14.5. Changes in household car ownership amongst de-centralized office workers, 1969 and 1976 (sources: Office Dispersal Journey to Work Survey, 1969; Follow-Up Survey, 1976). Reproduced with the permission of the Controller of Her Majesty's Stationery Office

at the sample offices. It also emerges that the proportion of households with one car or van has remained stable in Greater London as a whole (between 56 and 57 per cent) while at New Malden the figure has been reduced from 64 per cent to 55.2 per cent. The most significant changes have therefore occurred in the number of respondents from households with two or more cars/vans; even at the Gants Hill office where clerical occupations comprise a larger than average share of the sample respondents the proportion has increased from 12 to 23 per cent. At New Malden the proportion of two-car households has doubled; a characteristic which partly reflects the larger number of managerial staff who participated in the 1976 survey. Despite differences in the occupation structure of the 1976 respondents it is possible to conclude that in general there are more households with cars available for the journey to work to suburban office sites in 1976 than in 1969, and it may be anticipated that private transport as a whole will be used for a larger share of all trips than was revealed by the earlier survey.

Changes in Residential Distribution

Consolidation of labour catchment areas has taken place as, on average, decentralized office staff lived nearer to their places of work in 1976 than in 1969 (Fig. 14.6). The proportion resident within 10 km of their offices increased from 56.8 to 70.4 per cent at New Malden and 75.1 to 80.8 per cent at Gants Hill. Although there has been a corresponding reduction in the number of staff living more than 10 km from their offices, there has been an increase in the proportion travelling more than 48 km. This is mainly the result of the larger number of managerial and professional respondents in the sample. The net effect has been to increase average journey distances from 10.3 to 10.8 km for the total sample but to reduce trip distances by 1–3 km at New Malden and Gants Hill (Fig. 14.6). The increase in the proportion of local recruits has clearly reduced the extent of the catchment areas at most suburban locations. The reduction in the spatial distribution of office worker residences is also reflected in the time taken on the journey to work (Fig. 14.6). The proportion of journeys taking less than 35 minutes has increased from 56.1 per cent to 58.2 per cent for all 20 offices in Greater London although the average duration of each journey has increased from 33.8 to 36.8 minutes. At New Malden the reduction in these short journeys is even more marked, with a change from 54.9 per cent in 1969 to 69 per cent in 1976, and average times have also decreased as a result. The important feature about the change at New Malden is that almost all the improvement is accounted for by a large increase in the number of journeys which last for less than 15 minutes. There has only been a marginal change in the number of short journeys at Gants Hill and the proportion taking less than 15 minutes has actually been reduced from 24 to 21 per cent. Differences in the sample size in each survey may well explain this discrepancy but it is still the case that over 70 per cent of the trips to this office take less than 35 minutes. Trips in the intermediate category of 36 to 59 minutes have consistently declined at both levels of analysis but longer journey

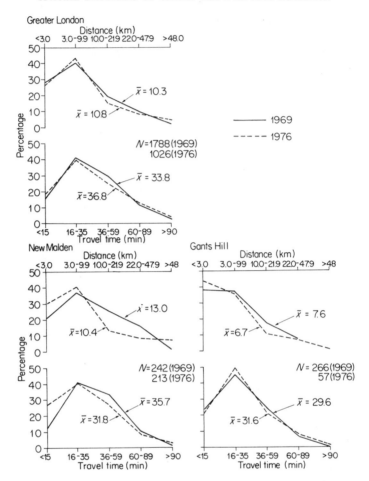

Fig. 14.6. Residential distribution (by airline distance from offices) and trip-time characteristics of 1969 and 1976 survey respondents (sources: Office Dispersal Journey to Work Survey, 1969; Follow-Up Survey, 1976). Reproduced with the permission of the Controller of Her Majesty's Stationery Office

times of one hour or more represent a larger proportion of all journeys in 1976. The wider distribution of some office worker residences explains the increase in the number of long journey times but this must be weighed against the clear improvement in the proportion of short journeys. Further analysis will be required, however, to isolate those changes which are attributable to differences in sample characteristics in 1969 and 1976 and those which represent a real difference in the journey to work characteristics of respondents. This preliminary evidence does suggest, however, that the general trend towards more compact labour catchments and therefore reduced journey distances is also helping to cut down the time taken for the journey to work in comparison with 1969.

This is corroborated by a comparison of the distribution of trip time gains and losses. In 1969, 24 per cent of the respondents who had previously travelled to work at some other office had journeys to work to decentralized offices which were at least 25 minutes shorter than before; the equivalent figure from the 1976 data is 36.5 per cent. The largest time savings have been made by office workers who now walk to work, with almost 50 per cent travelling for at least 25 minutes less than before. For the two-way trip this represents a saving of approximately one hour per day. Just over 17 per cent of the 1976 respondents for all the Greater London offices, however, had journeys to work which were more than 25 minutes longer than their previous journeys (compared with 10 per cent in 1969) and it is notable that train and bus users have above average proportions of users in this category.

This has coincided with some notable changes in the distances travelled by selected modes of transport (Table 14.2). In 1969 there was a basic dichotomy between short distance (less than 10 km) public transport trips, especially by bus, and a larger proportion of long (more than 22 km) and intermediate distance journeys by private transport (principally by car drivers). This divison has persisted through to 1976 except that there has been a tendency towards polarization of trips by both car and bus into the 3–9.9 km distance band. The proportion of journeys by bus which are less than 3 km in length has contracted while the proportion in the next distance zone has increased; for car drivers the proportion of all trips with origins less than 10 km from their offices shows a consistent increase at the case-study establishments and for all the offices in the Greater London sample. Although train journeys are numerically fewer than journeys using either of the other public transport modes, they are characteristically used for journeys in excess of 22 km. This distinction has become attenuated at New Malden where the proximity to a major commuter railway clearly seems to encourage long-distance commuting from the outer suburbs and beyond; there are more than twice as many trips by train as by bus, whereas at Gants Hill (which is also served by an underground branch line) the majority of public transport journeys are by bus over short distances.

A number of the contrasts between the 1969 and 1976 results will arise from differences in the occupation structure and car ownership characteristics of the respondents (see Figs. 14.3 and 14.5). In both 1969 and 1976 the majority of car-driver trips were undertaken by managerial or professional staff (Table 14.3). Car-driver trips by managerial staff increased from 20 per cent of the total in 1969 to almost 40 per cent in 1976 in both Greater London and the case-study offices. But clerical workers have also contributed to an increase in the level of car-driver trips at the expense of journeys to work by bus; 81 per cent of the latter were undertaken by clerical staff in 1966 but this figure has been reduced to approximately 70 per cent in 1976. This is also complemented by a reduction in

Table 14.2. Residential Location of Decentralized Office Workers by Distance and Principal Mode Used for the Journey to Work, 1969 and 1976

Residential location (distance from office)*	Travel mode†	Greater London offices		New Malden office		Gants Hill office	
		1969	1976	1969	1976	1969	1976
km							
<3	Car-driver‡	16.0	14.8	9.1	14.1	23.4	35.7
	Bus	40.3	24.6	35.0	27.3	41.8	39.1
	Train**	16.0	4.3	9.4	4.8	25.0	—
3–9.9	Car-driver	38.5	43.8	33.3	43.6	28.3	28.6
	Bus	56.6	68.2	60.0	72.7	52.7	56.5
	Train	48.9	33.3	49.0	42.9	50.0	33.3
10–21.9	Car-driver	31.9	23.0	38.3	20.5	34.5	28.6
	Bus	3.1	5.2	5.0	—	2.7	4.3
	Train	25.5	23.9	26.4	23.8	15.0	—
22–47.9	Car-driver	15.2	11.9	17.1	10.3	13.5	7.1
	Bus	0.8	0.9	—	—	2.7	—
	Train	9.0	23.9	13.2	14.3	10.0	66.7
>48	Car-driver	1.6	6.1	2.0	10.3	—	—
	Bus	—	—	—	—	—	—
	Train	0.5	14.5	1.8	14.3	—	—
Total trips	Car-driver	631 (100)	427 (100)	99 (100)	78 (100)	81 (100)	14 (100)
	Bus	402 (100)	211 (100)	19 (100)	22 (100)	74 (100)	23 (100)
	Train	188 (100)	117 (100)	53 (100)	42 (100)	20 (100)	3 (100)

*Airline distance calculated using O.S. grid reference of residence and workplace.
†Principal mode defined as longest journey stage in minutes.
‡Other categories are also used in the full tabulations: car passenger, walk, two-wheeled vehicle, ferry and private bus.
**Includes trips *via* underground trains.
Sources. Journey to Work Survey, 1969; Follow-Up Survey, 1976.

Table 14.3. Occupation and Principal Travel Mode for the Journey to Work of Decentralized Office Workers, 1969 and 1976

Occupation group	Travel Mode*	Greater London offices		New Malden office		Gants Hill office	
		1969	1976	1969	1976	1969	1976
Managerial	Car-driver§	15.7	36.6	20.2	35.5	21.5	38.5
	Bus	2.0	6.2	–	4.5	2.7	–
	Train‡	5.4	19.1	5.7	23.7	21.1	50.0
Professional	Car-driver	24.5	17.9	25.3	19.7	11.4	–
	Bus	3.3	2.9	–	4.5	–	–
	Train	10.9	13.6	20.8	21.1	–	–
Sup./tech.	Car-driver	33.6	13.2	39.4	11.8	34.2	23.1
	Bus	12.0	18.6	23.8	18.2	18.7	30.4
	Train	19.6	21.8	33.9	10.5	15.8	50.0
Clerical	Car-driver	24.5	29.9	14.1	27.6	31.6	38.5
	Bus	81.0	68.6	71.4	68.2	76.0	69.6
	Train	62.5	41.8	37.7	42.1	63.2	–
Other	Car-driver	1.8	2.4	1.0	5.3	1.3	–
	Bus	1.7	3.8	4.8	4.5	1.3	–
	Train	1.6	3.6	1.9	2.6	–	–
Total trips	Car-driver	625 (100)	418 (100)	99 (100)	76 (100)	79 (100)	13 (100)
	Bus	400 (100)	210 (100)	21 (100)	22 (100)	75 (100)	23 (100)
	Train	184 (100)	110 (100)	53 (100)	38 (100)	19 (100)	2 (100)

*Principal mode defined as longest journey stage in minutes.
†Other categories are also used in the full tabulations: Car passenger, walk, two-wheeled vehicle, ferry and private bus.
‡ Includes trips *via* underground trains.
Sources. Office Dispersal Journey to Work Survey, 1969; Follow-Up Survey, 1976.

the proportion of clerical workers who travel to work by train. Such changes are clearly important since this group are far and away the largest single category of occupations in office establishments and major changes in their travel behaviour could have important consequences for the demand for travel facilities at suburban office centres. Although less significant in absolute terms because there are fewer of them, there has been an increase in the proportion of public transport trips by office workers in the supervisory grades and above. The Gants Hill figures are not very helpful because of the limited size of the sample, but the New Malden data conform with the average for Greater London. Hence, whereas only 2 per cent of the managers travelled to work there by bus in 1969, this has increased to 6.2 per cent in 1976; the equivalent figures for train journeys are 5.4 and 19.1 per cent.

It is not immediately clear why these contradictory trends have occurred given that previous evidence clearly indicates that the most likely users of private transport, especially the car, are office workers in the professional and managerial groups and users of public transport are mainly from the clerical and other categories. There are two possible explanations. Firstly, the wider spatial distribution of managers and related staff in 1976 puts public transport in a better competitive position against the car, especially as the largest increases have been in train-based journeys to work. Secondly, even though clerical staff have much shorter distances to travel, local congestion is much more likely to manifest itself in the form of delays in bus journey times (buses are most commonly used for short trips) and, given the increases in car ownership in clerical worker households, the possibilities for transferring to more reliable and 'quicker' methods of travel, i.e. the car, are enhanced. It should also be noted that there has been an increase in the number of journeys to work on foot so that the reduced proportion of public transport trips by clerical workers does not imply a major transfer to private mechanically assisted modes.

While there may be some distinction between the degree of travel mode transfer exhibited by different occupation groups, the net effect of the changes has been to reduce the share of all journeys by public transport from 46.6 per cent in 1969 to 35.8 per cent in 1976 (Fig. 14.7). The proportion of journeys made by private transport has increased for all three categories identified in Fig. 14.7, with only the proportion of train journeys holding its own with the 1969 distribution. At the case-study offices the picture is again different at each location, with the proportion of bus journeys rising to 40 per cent at Gants Hill but increasing to just 10 per cent at New Malden where the proportion of journeys to work by train has remained constant at around 20 per cent. Location is clearly a critical determinant of mode choice for the journey to work as well as affecting the distances travelled and time taken. Trips on foot have increased at both locations along with car-passenger journeys, which have compensated for the reduction in car-driver trips at both locations.

In common with the situation in 1969, the majority of new car-driver journeys to decentralized offices originate from office workers who had previously

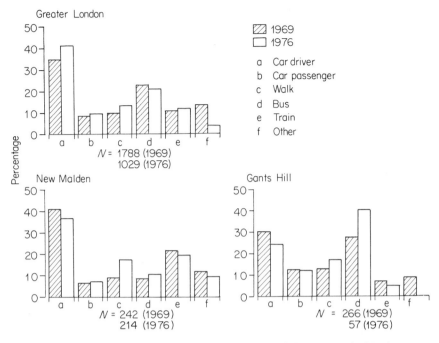

Fig. 14.7. Travel mode choice for the journey to work in 1969 and 1976 (sources: Office Dispersal Journey to Work Survey, 1969; Follow-Up Survey, 1976). Reproduced with the permission of the Controller of Her Majesty's Stationery Office

travelled to some other workplace by public transport (Fig. 14.8). This trend is particularly marked amongst previous bus users, less than half of whom continued to travel by bus after taking up their jobs at decentralized locations compared with approximately 60 per cent in 1969. Apart from those office workers who had previously travelled to work on foot and have continued to do so, the largest proportional increases in journeys on foot have been made by bus users in addition to the fact that they also now undertake more journeys by car. Office workers who previously travelled by train have also made large-scale switches to mechanically assisted modes, even at destinations such as New Malden where commuting by train is best served. The evidence suggests that amongst previous private transport users any transfer to other modes is most likely to affect other private transport modes rather than public transport. Amongst office workers who walk to work, for example, the 1976 results show that those who now travel some other way have added to the number of car journeys and have contributed to a further reduction in the number of public transport trips even though the short journeys which they are undertaking are more likely to be serviced by bus routes and in some cases the underground system. It also seems that in 1976 car drivers were more likely to walk to work or to obtain a lift from a colleague than they were to use public transport.

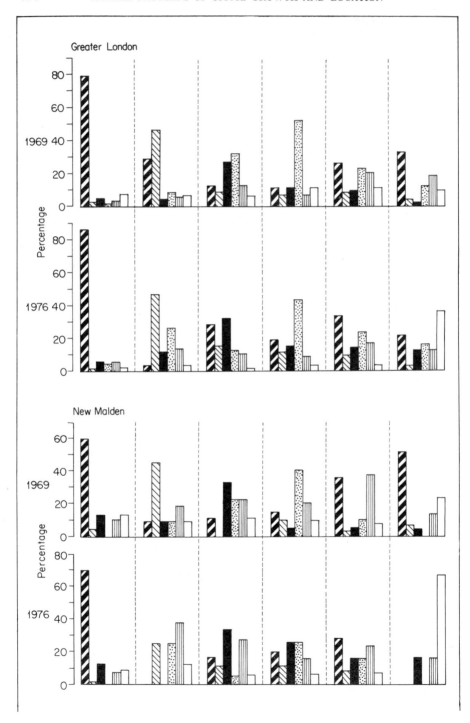

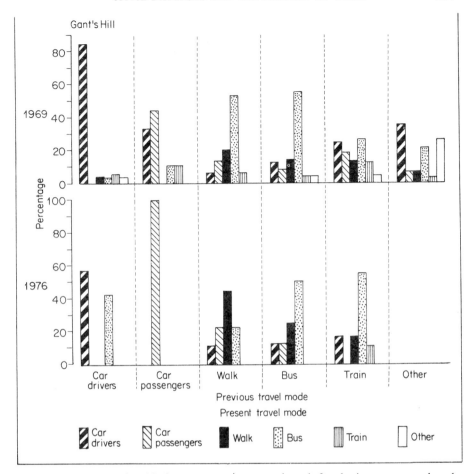

Fig. 14.8. Relationship between previous travel mode for the journey to work and present travel mode, 1969 and 1976 (sources: Office Dispersal Journey to Work Survey, 1969; Follow-Up Survey, 1976). Reproduced with the permission of the Controller of Her Majesty's Stationery Office

Flexible Hours and Car-Sharing

There are two variables which might have an important effect on the comparability of the two data sets used in this project. The first is a product of the trend towards the use of flexible working hours in offices; this system permits office employees to select their hours of work provided that they are at their desks during certain specified 'core periods' such as 10.00 hr to 12.00 hr. As far as the journey to work is concerned, the introduction of flexible hours during the last five years has permitted a growing number of office workers to undertake journeys which avoid the consequences of the traditional peak hours such as overcrowding on public transport or delays which create longer journey times. Preliminary data for the arrival times of staff at the 1976 sample of decentralized offices in Greater London indicate that the spread is much wider than would be expected from conventional starting times and it is likely that office workers participating in flexible hours schemes are responsible for this difference. Some 28 per cent (290) of the Greater London respondents were travelling to offices which operated flexible hours and 80 per cent of them participated in such schemes. Further analysis will be undertaken to establish whether these employees have trip times or travel mode characteristics which are significantly different from those of other office workers and which should therefore be taken into account when comparing the trends revealed in the two main data sets.

The second variable which has become an important feature of journey-to-work travel in recent years, especially since the effects of the energy crisis in 1973 on petrol prices, is the incidence of car-sharing (or car pools) for the journey to · work. Unfortunately, information pertaining to this phenomenon was not collected in 1969 but the level of this activity in 1976 may explain at least some of the changes in aggregate travel behaviour between the two surveys, particularly with reference to the modal split. The level of car-sharing is lower in Greater London than elsewhere according to the 1976 data, partly because of the diverse origins of journeys to decentralized offices, but 20.7 per cent (213) of the respondents who had travelled to work by car or van on the day of the survey had shared with at least one other person; this represented 35 per cent of the employees who had travelled to work as car-drivers or car passengers. Almost 50 per cent (103) of the car-sharing office workers shared with colleagues travelling to the same office and this represented 10 per cent of all the trips undertaken. Presumably, many of these journeys would otherwise have been completed by using public transport or, assuming that individuals had chosen to travel alone by private transport, would have generated more single-person journeys and therefore a larger number of vehicles on suburban roads.

Conclusion

It is not possible to present a carefully reasoned conclusion at this stage of the project since it would not be helpful to do so on the strength of the very general analysis which has been presented here. There are some grounds for commenting, however, that at least some of the results of the first study in 1969 have been endorsed, at least as far as the position in Greater London is concerned. There have undoubtedly been some changes in employee travel characteristics which can be tentatively attributed to contrasts in the socio-economic profile of respondents in each survey; to a general trend towards more compact labour catchment areas; and to the impact of two factors, flexible hours and car-sharing, which were not considered in 1969 because they were less important at that time. The minor role of public transport for travel to suburban offices compared with the journey to work to central area offices continues to be an important characteristic but this does not mean that suburban relocation of offices is undesirable; further scrutiny of the relationship between office location and travel behaviour of office workers which is possible with data from this project may indicate ways in which the level of transfer to private transport could be alleviated without compromising the case for a policy of office relocation based on a number of major suburban office centres.

Acknowledgments

The Office Dispersal Journey to Work Survey (1969) was partially funded by the Ministry of Transport and the Follow-Up Study (1976) is part of a three-year research project financed by the Department of the Environment. I would like to acknowledge the assistance of Mr A. W. Duffett, the project's Research Assistant, with the processing of data and preparation of the tabulations upon which the figures and tables in this paper are based.

References

Bateman, M., Burtenshaw, D., and Duffett, A. W. (1974), Environment, perception and migration: a study of perception of residential areas in South Hampshire, in D. Canter and T. Lee (Eds.), *Psychology and the Built Environment*. London: Architectural Press.

Bateman, M., Burtenshaw, D., and Hall, R. K. (1971), *Office Staff on the Move*. London: Location of Offices Bureau, Research Paper No. 6.

Burtt, E. J. (1967), *Plant Relocation and the Core City Worker*. Washington: United States Department of Housing and Development.

Carey, S. J. (1969), *Relocation of Office Staff: A Study of the Reactions of Staff Decentralized to Ashford*. London: Location of Offices Bureau, Research Paper No. 4.

Carroll, J. D. (1949), Some aspects of home-work relationships of industrial employees, *Land Economics*, **25**, 414–22.

Carroll, J. D. (1952), The relation of homes to workplaces and the spatial pattern of cities, *Social Forces*, **30**, 271–82.

Daniels, P. W. (1972a), Office Decentralization from London: The Journey to Work Consequences, Unpublished Ph.D. Thesis, University of London.

Daniels, P. W. (1972b), Transport changes generated by decentralized offices, *Regional Studies*, **6**, 273–89.

Daniels, P. W. (1973), Some changes in the journey to work of decentralized office workers, *Town Planning Review*, **44**, 167–88.

Daniels, P. W. (1976), Office relocation in Greater London: case studies of employee journey to work and residential changes, Supporting Paper for Experimental Poster Session, Institute of British Geographers, Lanchester Polytechnic, Conventry. January.

Daniels, P. W. (1977), Office policy problems in Greater London, *The Planner*, **63**, 102–5.

Department of the Environment (1972), *Greater London Development Plan, Report of the Panel of Inquiry, Vol. I*. London: HMSO.

Greater London Council (1976), *Greater London Development Plan*. London: Greater London Council.

Hammond, E. (1968), *London to Durham: A Study of the Transfer of the Post Office Savings Certificate Division*. Durham: Rowntree Research Unit.

Harkness, R. C. (1973), Telecommunications Substitutes for Travel: A Preliminary Assessment of Their Potential for Reducing Urban Transportation Costs by Altering Office Location Pattern, Unpublished Ph.D. Thesis, University of Washington.

Loewenstein, L. K. (1960), *The Journey to Work in Philadelphia: Its Patterns and Perspectives*. Philadelphia: University of Philadelphia.

Location of Offices Bureau (1976), *Office Relocation: Facts and Figures*. London: Location of Offices Bureau.

Orrom, H. C., and Wright C. C. (1976), The spatial distribution of journey to work trips in Greater London, *Transportation*, 5, 199–222.

Roseman, C. C. (1971), Migration, the journey to work and household characteristics: an analysis based on non-areal aggregation, *Economic Geography*, 47, 467–74.

Sidwell, E. (1974), *The Problems for Employees in Office Dispersal*. London: London School of Economics, Department of Geography.

Simmons, J. W. (1968), Changing residence in the city: a review of intra-urban mobility, *Geographical Review*, 58, 622–51.

Taafe, E. J., Garner, B. J., and Yeates, M. H. (1963), *The Peripheral Journey to Work: A Geographic Consideration*. Evanston: Northwestern University Press.

Thorburn, A. (1970), A Strategy for London?, in Town and Country Planning Association, *London Under Stress*. London: Town and Country Planning Association.

Townsley, C. H. (1973), *Traffic Generation of Suburban London Offices*. London: Greater London Council, Department of Planning and Transportation Research Memorandum 398.

Wabe, J. S. (1967), Dispersal of employment and the journey to work, *J. Transport Economics and Policy*, 1, 345–61.

Wall, W. D., and Williams, H. L. (1970) *Longitudinal Studies and the Social Sciences*. London: Heinemann.

White, D. (1976), Commuters in reverse, *New Society*, 36, 341–2.

Yannopoulos, G. (1973), *The Local Impact of Decentralized Offices*, London: Location of Offices Bureau, Research Paper No. 7.

Index